CATALOGUE
OF THE
Theological Seminary
OF THE
PRESBYTERIAN CHURCH IN THE UNITED STATES,
AT
PRINCETON NEW-JERSEY,
JANUARY 1st, 1821.

Rev. ARCHIBALD ALEXANDER, D.D. Professor of Didactic and Polemic Theology.
Rev. SAMUEL MILLER, D.D. Professor of Ecclesiastical History and Church Government.
Mr. CHARLES HODGE, A.M. Assistant Teacher of the Original Languages.

[The Instruction in Biblical Literature and Pastoral Theology is conducted by Dr. Alexander;—that on the Composition and Delivery of Sermons, by Dr. Miller.]

FIRST CLASS.

NAMES.	RESIDENCE.	GRADUATED.	NAMES.	RESIDENCE.	GRADUATED.
Thomas Alexander,	Paris, Ky.		Luke Lyons,	Albany, N.Y.	
James Buber,	Caroline co. Va.		Alexander McFarlane,	Duanesburgh, N.Y.	Union Coll.
William Q. Beattie,	Shippensburgh, Pa.	Washington Coll.	James McVean,	Johnstown, N.Y.	Union Coll.
William C. Blair,	Chillicothe, Ohio,	Jefferson Coll.	Joshua Moore,	Washington,	Jefferson Coll.
Alfred Chester,	Hartford, Conn.	Yale Coll.	Benjamin Ogden,	Cumberland co. N.J.	Nassau-Hall.
Nathaniel Conkling,	Basking-Ridge, N.J.	Nassau-Hall.	Theophilus Parvin,	Fairton, N.J.	Univ. Penn.
Joseph P. Cunningham,	Lexington, Ky.	Transyl. Univ.	Horace S. Pratt,	Saybrook, Conn.	Yale Coll.
Josiah N. Danforth,	Pittsfield, Mass.	Williams Coll.	Henry L. Rice,	Corydon, Ind.	
Cyrus Douglass,	Middlebury, Vt.	Middlebury Coll.	William Scott,		
Charles Fitch,	West-Bloomfield, N.Y.	Williams Coll.	Charles Sam'l Stewart,		Nassau-Hall.
Thompson S. Harris,	Greenbrook, N.J.	Nassau-Hall.			
William Hamilton,	Lexington, Ky.		Andrew Todd,	Paris,	Jefferson Coll.
James V. Henry,	Albany, N.Y.	Nassau-Hall.	Daniel Waterbury,	Sodus, N.Y.	Union Coll.
Daniel B. Johnson,	Newark, N.J.	Nassau-Hall.	Abraham Williamson,	Flemington, N.J.	Nassau-Hall.
Robert A. Lapsley,	Lancaster, Ky.				

SECOND CLASS.

NAMES.	RESIDENCE.	GRADUATED.	NAMES.	RESIDENCE.	GRADUATED.
Robert Baird,	Fayette co. Pa.	Jefferson Coll.	Thomas Kennedy,	Easton, Pa.	Nassau-Hall.
Charles C. Beatty,	Princeton, N.J.	Nassau-Hall.	Robert R. King,	Iredell co. N.C.	Univ. of N. Car.
Artemas Bishop,	Oxford, N.Y.	Union Coll.	Thomas Lounsbury,	Elmira, N.Y.	Union Coll.
John Breckenridge,	Lexington, Ky.	Nassau-Hall.	John McLean,	Princeton, N.J.	Nassau-Hall.
Augustus L. Chapin,	W. Springfield, Mass.	Yale Coll.	James L. Marshall,	Fayette co. Ky.	
Samuel F. Darrach,	Philadelphia,	Nassau-Hall.	James M. Olmsted,	Hillis, N.Y.	Union Coll.
James Douglass,	Augusta co. Va.		Michael Osborn,	New-York.	
Edwin Dower,	Westfield, N.J.	Nassau-Hall.	George Potts,	Philadelphia,	Univ. Penn.
Moses T. Harris,	Philadelphia,		Franklin G. Smith,	Boston, Vt.	Middlebury Coll.
John Hudson,	Lexington, Ky.	Transyl. Univ.	James D. Turner,	Lexington, Ky.	
Hathaway W. Hunt,	Greenwich, N.J.	Nassau-Hall.	Alexander Williamson,	Mercersb'g, Pa.	Jefferson Coll.
Abraham B. Hatton,	Stillwater, N.Y.	Union Coll.	Hugh Wilson,	Iredell co. N.C.	Nassau-Hall.

THIRD CLASS.

NAMES.	RESIDENCE.	GRADUATED.	NAMES.	RESIDENCE.	GRADUATED.
Albert Barnes,	Rome, N.Y.	Hamilton Coll.	John H. Kennedy,	Cumberland co. Md.	Jefferson Coll.
John K. Blatchford,	Lansingburgh, N.Y.	Union Coll.	John Knox,	Landen, Va.	
George Bush,	Hanover, N.H.	Dart. Coll.	James G. McNeely,	Gettysburgh, Pa.	Dickinson Coll.
Robert B. Campbell,	Abeville, N.C.		John Peebles,	Shippensburgh, Pa.	Jefferson Coll.
Cyrenius Crosby,	Montgomery, N.Y.	Union Coll.	Nathaniel A. Pratt,	Saybrook, Conn.	Yale Coll.
Charles C. Darling,	New-Haven, Conn.	Yale Coll.	Robert Roy,	Warwick, N.Y.	
Stephen Frontis,	Raleigh, N.C.		Joseph Sanford,	Auburn, N.Y.	Union Coll.
Eldad W. Goodman,	Bolton, N.Y.	Union Coll.	George W. L. Smith,	Troy, N.Y.	Union Coll.
Baynard R. Hall,	Philadelphia,	Union Coll.	George Stebbins,	Goshen, N.Y.	Union Coll.
J. Garland Hamner,	Charlotte, Va.		Daniel Young,	Whitehall, N.Y.	Union Coll.

FIRST CLASS   29
SECOND CLASS   24
THIRD CLASS   20

TOTAL   73

THE CENTENNIAL CELEBRATION

OF THE

THEOLOGICAL SEMINARY

OF

THE PRESBYTERIAN CHURCH IN THE UNITED STATES OF AMERICA

AT PRINCETON, NEW JERSEY

THE CENTENNIAL CELEBRATION

OF THE

THEOLOGICAL SEMINARY
OF
THE PRESBYTERIAN CHURCH IN THE UNITED STATES OF AMERICA

AT PRINCETON, NEW JERSEY

MAY FIFTH—MAY SIXTH—MAY SEVENTH
NINETEEN HUNDRED AND TWELVE

Wipf and Stock Publishers
199 West 8th Avenue, Suite 3
Eugene, Oregon 97401

The Centennial Celebration of the Theological Seminary of The Presbyterian
Church in the United States of America at Princeton, NJ
By Warfield, Benjamin B., Armstrong, William P., and Robinson, Harold M.
ISBN: 1-57910-761-3
Publication date 9/17/2001
Previously published by Princeton at the Theological Seminary, 1912

TABLE OF CONTENTS

	PAGE
INTRODUCTORY NOTE	1

RESPONSES FROM THE COURTS OF THE PRESBYTERIAN CHURCH IN THE
UNITED STATES OF AMERICA 23
   From the General Assembly 25
   From the Synods (arranged alphabetically) 28
   From the Presbyteries (arranged alphabetically) 48
   From the Fifth Avenue Presbyterian Church, New York City . . 79

RESPONSES FROM THE BOARDS OF THE GENERAL ASSEMBLY OF THE PRESBYTERIAN CHURCH IN THE UNITED STATES OF AMERICA . . . 83
   The Board of Home Missions 85
   The Board of Foreign Missions 85
   The Board of Education 86
   The Board of Publication and Sabbath-School Work 86
   The Board of the Church Erection Fund 87
   The Board of Ministerial Relief 87

RESPONSES FROM OTHER ECCLESIASTICAL BODIES 89
   The General Assembly of the Church of Scotland 91
   The General Assembly of the United Free Church of Scotland . 92
   The General Assembly of the Free Church of Scotland . . . 93
   The Synod of the Free Presbyterian Church of Scotland . . . 95
   The Synod of the Presbyterian Church of England 96
   The General Assembly of the Presbyterian Church in Ireland . 97
   The Synod of Ballymena and Coleraine of the Presbyterian Church
      in Ireland 98
   The Diocese of New Jersey of the Protestant Episcopal Church . 99

RESPONSES FROM THE PRESIDING OFFICERS OF CHURCHES 101
   The Moderator of the General Assembly of the Church of Scotland 103
   The Moderator of the General Assembly of the United Free Church
      of Scotland 103
   The Moderator Designate of the General Assembly of the United
      Free Church of Scotland 104
   The Moderator of the General Assembly of the Free Church of
      Scotland 105

TABLE OF CONTENTS

	PAGE
The Moderator of the Synod of the Free Presbyterian Church of Scotland	105
The Moderator of the Synod of the Reformed Presbyterian Church of Scotland	106
The Moderator of the Synod of the United Original Seceders	107
The Moderator of the Reformed Presbyterian Synod in Ireland	107
The Moderator of the Synod of the Presbyterian Church of England	108
The Moderator for 1901 of the General Assembly of the Welsh Calvinistic Methodist Connection	109
The Moderator of the General Assembly of the Presbyterian Church in Canada	109
The Moderator of the General Assembly of the Reformed Presbyterian Church	110
The President of the General Synod of the Reformed Church in the United States	111
The President of the Northern Baptist Convention	111
The Moderator of the National Council of Congregational Churches	111
The Presiding Bishop of the Protestant Episcopal Church in the United States	112
The President of the General Council of the Reformed Episcopal Church	112
The President of the General Synod of the Evangelical Lutheran Church in the United States of America	113
The President of the General Council of the Evangelical Lutheran Church in North America	113
The President of the Evangelical Lutheran Synod of North America	114
The President of the German Evangelical Synod of North America	114
The Secretary of the Board of Bishops of the Methodist Episcopal Church	116
The Senior Bishop of the Methodist Episcopal Church, South	116
The Chairman of the Christian Union Commission of the Disciples of Christ	117
The President of the General Conference of the Mennonite Church of North America	117
RESPONSES FROM FOREIGN DIVINITY FACULTIES	119

SCOTLAND

The Faculty of Divinity of the University of Edinburgh	121
The Faculty of Divinity in the University of Aberdeen	122
New College, Edinburgh	124
The United Free Church College, Glasgow	125

[vi]

TABLE OF CONTENTS

	PAGE
The United Free Church College at Aberdeen	126
The Free Church College, Edinburgh	127

IRELAND

Assembly's College, Belfast	129
M'Crea-Magee Presbyterian College, Londonderry	130
The Theological Faculty of Dublin University	130

ENGLAND

The Faculty of Theology, University of Oxford	131
The Faculty of Divinity, University of Cambridge	131
The Theological Faculty in the University of Durham	132
The Faculty of Theology, University of London, King's College	132
The Faculty of Theology, University of London	133
Westminster College, Cambridge	133
New College and Hackney College, London	134
Mansfield College, Oxford	135
Baptist College, Regent's Park, N. W., London	136
Manchester College, Oxford	136

WALES

St. Davids College, Lampeter	137

NETHERLANDS (AND SOUTH AFRICA)

The Theological Faculty of the University of Amsterdam	137
The Theological Faculty of the University of Groningen	138
The Theological Faculty of the University of Leiden	139
The Theological Faculty of the University of Utrecht	140
The Theological Seminary of the Dutch Reformed Church, Stellenbosch, South Africa	141

DENMARK

The Theological Faculty of the University of Copenhagen	141

NORWAY

The Theological Faculty of the University of Christiania	142

FINLAND

The Theological Faculty of the University of Helsingfors	143

TABLE OF CONTENTS

GERMANY

	PAGE
The Theological Faculty of the University of Berlin	143
The Catholic Theological Faculty of the University of Bonn	145
The Royal Lyceum of Braunsberg	145
The Theological Faculty of the University of Erlangen	146
The Theological Faculty of the University of Freiburg i. B.	146
The Theological Faculty of the Royal Bavarian Lyceum, Freising	147
The Theological Faculty of the University of Giessen	148
The Theological Faculty of the University of Göttingen	148
The Theological Faculty of the University of Halle-Wittenberg	149
The Theological Faculty of the University of Heidelberg	150
The Theological Faculty of the University of Jena	151
The Theological Faculty of the University of Königsberg	151
The Theological Faculty of the University of Leipzig	152
The Theological Faculty of the University of Marburg	153
The Theological Faculty of the University of Munich	154
The Evangelical Theological Faculty of the University of Strassburg i. E.	155
The Catholic Theological Faculty of the University of Strassburg i. E.	156
The Evangelical Theological Faculty of the University of Tübingen	157
The Catholic Theological Faculty of the University of Tübingen	158

FRANCE (AND JERUSALEM)

The Catholic University of the West, Angers	158
The Catholic Faculties of Lyons	159
The Free Faculty of Protestant Theology, Montauban	159
The Faculty of Protestant Theology of the University of Paris	161
The Biblical School of Jerusalem	161

BELGIUM

The Catholic University of Louvain	162

SWITZERLAND

The Theological Faculty of the University of Basel	162
The Catholic Theological Faculty of the University of Bern	164
The Faculty of Theology of the University of Freiburg	164
The Faculty of Theology of the University of Geneva	165
The Evangelical Theological Faculty of Geneva	166

TABLE OF CONTENTS

	AG
The Faculty of Theology of the Free Church of the Canton de Vaud, Lausanne	168
The Faculty of Theology of the University of Neuchâtel	169
The Free Faculty of Theology of the Evangelical Church, Neuchâtel	170

AUSTRIA

The Theological Faculty of the University of Innsbruck	171
The Theological Faculty of Salzburg	171
The Evangelical Theological Faculty of the University of Vienna	172

HUNGARY

The Faculty of Theology of the Royal Hungarian University, Budapest	173
The Reformed Theological Academy, Budapest	174
The Theological Faculty of the Reformed College, Debreczen	175
The Unitarian Theological College, Klausenburg	178
The Reformed Theological Academy, Pápa	179
The Reformed Theological Academy, Sárospatak	179
The Evangelical Theological Academy, Sopron (Oedenbourg)	181

BOHEMIA

The Theological Faculty of the Royal Bohemian University, Prague 182

CANADA

Knox College, Toronto	183
Queen's University, Kingston	184
The Presbyterian College, Montreal	185
Manitoba College, Winnipeg	185
Westminster Hall, Vancouver	186
The Faculty of Theology of Trinity College, Toronto	186
Wycliffe College, Toronto	187

RESPONSES FROM THEOLOGICAL SCHOOLS IN THIS COUNTRY (ARRANGED ACCORDING TO DATE OF OPENING) 189

Theological Seminary of the Reformed Church in America, New Brunswick, N. J.	191
St. Mary's University and Ecclesiastical Seminary, Baltimore, Md.	191
The Xenia Theological Seminary, Xenia, Ohio	192
Hartwick Seminary, Hartwick, N. Y.	193
The Moravian College and Theological Seminary, Bethlehem, Pa.	194

TABLE OF CONTENTS

	PAGE
Andover Theological Seminary, Cambridge, Mass.	194
Union Theological Seminary, Richmond, Va.	195
Bangor Theological Seminary, Bangor, Me.	196
The General Theological Seminary of the Protestant Episcopal Church, New York City	197
Auburn Theological Seminary, Auburn, N. Y.	197
Theological Seminary, Colgate University, Hamilton, N. Y.	198
The Divinity School of Yale University, New Haven, Conn.	198
The Allegheny Theological Seminary, North Side, Pittsburgh	199
The Newton Theological Institution, Newton Centre, Mass.	200
The Theological Seminary of the Reformed Church in the United States, Lancaster, Pa.	200
Lutheran Theological Seminary, Gettysburg, Pa.	201
The Western Theological Seminary, North Side, Pittsburgh	202
Columbia Theological Seminary, Columbia, S. C.	202
Lane Theological Seminary, Cincinnati, Ohio	203
McCormick Theological Seminary, Chicago	203
Hartford Theological Seminary, Hartford, Conn.	204
Oberlin Theological Seminary, Oberlin, Ohio	204
Union Theological Seminary, New York City	205
Meadville Theological School, Meadville, Pa.	206
Wittenberg College, Hamma Divinity School, Springfield, Ohio	206
German (Eden) Evangelical Missouri College, St. Louis, Mo.	207
Rochester Theological Seminary, Rochester, N. Y.	207
Dubuque German College and Seminary, Dubuque, Ia.	208
Berkeley Divinity School, Middletown, Conn.	209
Garrett Biblical Institute, Evanston, Ill.	209
Eureka College, Department of Sacred Literature, Eureka, Ill.	210
Reformed Presbyterian Theological Seminary, Allegheny, Pa.	211
St. John's University Ecclesiastical Seminary, Collegeville, Minn.	211
St. Lawrence University, Canton Theological School, Canton, N. Y.	212
Chicago Theological Seminary, Chicago	212
Niagara University Seminary of Our Lady of Angels, Niagara Falls, N. Y.	213
Seabury Divinity School, Faribault, Minn.	213
The Mission House, Plymouth, Wis.	214
The Southern Baptist Theological Seminary, Louisville, Ky.	215
Augustana College and Theological Seminary, Rock Island, Ill.	216
Central Wesleyan College, Warrenton, Mo.	216
Lutheran Theological Seminary, Mount Airy, Philadelphia	217
De Lancey Divinity School, Geneva, N. Y.	218
The University of Chicago Divinity School, Chicago	218
Atlanta Baptist College Divinity School, Atlanta, Ga.	219
Drew Theological Seminary, Madison, N. J.	219
Episcopal Theological School, Cambridge, Mass.	220
Crozer Theological Seminary, Chester, Pa.	220

TABLE OF CONTENTS

	PAGE
Theological Department, The University of the South, Sewanee, Tenn.	220
The German Theological School of Newark, N. J., Bloomfield, N. J.	221
Pacific Theological Seminary, Berkeley, Cal.	221
Woodstock College, Woodstock, Md.	222
The Theological Seminary of the Evangelical Lutheran Church, Chicago	223
Alfred Theological Seminary, Alfred, N. Y.	223
Howard University, Theological Department, Washington, D. C.	224
The San Francisco Theological Seminary, San Anselmo, Cal.	224
Talladega College, Theological Department, Talladega, Ala.	225
Theological School and Calvin College, Grand Rapids, Mich.	225
Westminster Theological Seminary, Westminster, Md.	226
The Temple University, Department of Theology, Philadelphia	227
Western Theological Seminary, Chicago	227
University of Southern California, Maclay College of Theology, Los Angeles, Cal.	228
The Catholic University of America, School of Sacred Sciences, Washington, D. C.	228
Saint Leo Abbey, Saint Leo, Fla.	229
The Seminary of the United Norwegian Lutheran Church, Saint Anthony Park, Minn.	230
Presbyterian Theological Seminary, Omaha, Neb.	230
Houghton Wesleyan Methodist Theological Seminary, Houghton, N. Y.	231
Presbyterian Theological Seminary of Kentucky, Louisville, Ky.	231
Western Theological Seminary, Atchison, Kan.	234
Taylor University, Reade Theological Seminary, Upland, Ind.	234
Turner Theological Seminary, Morris Brown College, Atlanta, Ga.	235
Eugene Bible University, Eugene, Ore.	235
Manchester College, Biblical Department, North Manchester, Ind.	236
School of Theology, Kansas City University, Kansas City, Kan.	237
Westminster College, Theological Department, Tehuacana, Texas	238
Virginia Union University, Theological Department, Richmond, Va.	238
Atlanta Theological Seminary, Atlanta, Ga.	239
Meridian Male College, School of Theology and Evangelism, Meridian, Miss.	240
Austin Theological Seminary, Austin, Texas	240
Pacific Unitarian School for the Ministry, Berkeley, Cal.	241
The Southwestern Baptist Theological Seminary, Fort Worth, Texas	242
Central Theological Seminary of the Reformed Church in the United States, Dayton, Ohio	242
Pacific Evangelical Lutheran Seminary, Olympia, Wash.	243
St. Patrick's Seminary, Menlo Park, Cal.	244

TABLE OF CONTENTS

RESPONSES FROM MISSIONARY SEMINARIES 245

AFRICA

Albert Academy, Freetown, Sierra Leone, West Africa . . . 247
Élat Theological School, Élat, Kamerun, West Africa 247
Union Theological College, Impolweni, near Maritzburg, Natal . 248
Theological Training School, Ogbomoso, Southern Nigeria, West Africa 249

BRAZIL

Seminario Theologico da Egreja Presbyteriana no Brasil, Campinas 250

BULGARIA

The American Collegiate and Theological Institute, Samokov . . 250

BURMA

Karen Theological Seminary, Insein 251

CHINA

Fati Theological College, Canton 252
The Graves Theological School, Canton 253
Union Theological School, Foochow 253
Nanking Union Theological Seminary, Nanking 254
Theological School of Shaowu, Foochow 254
St. John's University, Shanghai 255
Ashmore Theological Seminary, Swatow 256

DENMARK

Methodist Theological Seminary, Copenhagen 257

INDIA

United Theological College, Bangalore 257
Bapatla Normal Training School, Bapatla 258
Bareilly Theological Seminary, Bareilly 259
American Baptist Telugu Mission, Theological Seminary, Ramapatnam 260
Presbyterian Theological Seminary, Saharanpur 261

ITALY

Scvola Teologica Battista, Rome 261

TABLE OF CONTENTS

JAPAN

	PAGE
The Kobe Theological School, Kobe	262
Theological School of the Kwansei Gakuin, Kobe	263
The Doshisha Theological School, Kyoto	263
North Japan College, Sendai	264
Japan Baptist Theological Seminary, Tokyo	265
Meiji Gakuin, Tokyo	265

MEXICO

Colegio Internacional, Guadalajara 266

PERSIA

Theological Department, Urumia College, Urumia 266

PHILIPPINE ISLANDS

Iloilo Bible School, Iloilo 267

PORTO RICO

The Presbyterian Theological Training School, Mayagüez . . 268

SYRIA

Presbyterian Theological Seminary, Beirut 268

TURKEY-IN-ASIA

Marash Theological Seminary, Marash 269
Western Turkey Theological Seminary, Marsovan 270

RESPONSES FROM UNIVERSITIES AND COLLEGES 271
    The Board of Trustees of Princeton University 273

CANADA

Dalhousie University, Halifax 273
The University of Toronto 274

UNITED STATES OF AMERICA (ARRANGED ACCORDING TO DATE OF OPENING)
    Harvard University 275
    Yale University 275
    University of Pennsylvania 276
    Brown University 276

TABLE OF CONTENTS

	PAGE
Rutgers College	277
Dartmouth College	277
Washington and Lee University	278
Dickinson College	278
Hampden-Sidney College	279
University of North Carolina	280
Williams College	281
Union University	281
Middlebury College	282
Washington and Jefferson College	282
Miami University	283
Columbia University	283
University of Pittsburgh	284
Amherst College	284
Franklin and Marshall College	285
Lafayette College	285
New York University	286
Pennsylvania College	287
Wabash College	288
Delaware College	288
Hanover College	289
Marietta College	289
Transylvania University	290
Davidson College	290
University of Michigan	290
Westminster College, Pa.	291
The College of the City of New York	292
Lake Forest College	292
Macalester College	293
Lincoln University	293
Park College	294
Parsons College	294
Southwestern Presbyterian University	295
Bellevue College	295
Coe College	296
The College of Emporia	296
New Windsor College	296
Alma College	297
LIST OF DELEGATES	299
PROGRAMME OF EXERCISES	319
SERMONS AND ADDRESSES	337
Princeton Seminary and the Faith, by Rev. Francis Landey Patton, D.D., LL.D.	339

TABLE OF CONTENTS

	PAGE
A Little Book of Love and Life, by Rev. Ethelbert Dudley Warfield, D.D., LL.D.	369
The Function and the Glory of the Ministry of Grace, by Rev. John Fleming Carson, D.D., LL.D.	381
The Making of a Minister, by Rev. Russell Cecil, D.D.	393
Princeton in the Work of the Pastorate, by Rev. William Leonard McEwan, D.D.	403
Princeton on the Mission Field, by Robert Elliott Speer, D.D.	418
Princeton in Theological Education and Religious Thought, by Rev. William Hallock Johnson, Ph.D.	437
Princeton in its Early Environment and Work, by Charles Beatty Alexander, LL.D.	455
On Some Church Problems, by Right Rev. Alexander Stewart, M.A., D.D.	468
A Scottish Estimate of Princeton Theology, by Right Rev. James Wells, M.A., D.D.	484
Irish and American Presbyterianism, by Right Rev. John Macmillan, B.A., D.D.	499

CONGRATULATORY ADDRESSES

From the Presbyterian Church in the United States of America, by Rev. William Henry Roberts, D.D., LL.D.	526
From the Other Presbyterian and Reformed Churches, by Rev. John Crawford Scouller, D.D.	535
From Other Churches, by Right Rev. David Hummell Greer, D.D., S.T.D., LL.D.	539
From the Seminaries of the Presbyterian Church in the United States of America, by Rev. James Gore King McClure, D.D., LL.D.	542
From the Seminaries of Other Churches, I, by Rev. Williston Walker, Ph.D., D.D., L.H.D.	549
From the Seminaries of Other Churches, II, by Rev. Edgar Young Mullins, D.D., LL.D.	553
From Princeton University, by Rev. John Grier Hibben, Ph.D., LL.D.	558

RESPONSE TO CONGRATULATORY ADDRESSES

By Rev. Francis Landey Patton, D.D., LL.D.	563

ILLUSTRATIONS

Facsimile of the catalogue of Princeton Theological Seminary for the year 1821, the earliest catalogue extant . . . . *frontispiece*

Facsimile of the Response from the Faculty of Divinity in the University of Aberdeen . . . *facing p.* 119

INTRODUCTORY NOTE

INTRODUCTORY NOTE

"The Theological Seminary of the Presbyterian Church in the United States of America," located at Princeton, New Jersey, was founded in 1812. The story of its foundation is embedded in the following extracts from the Minutes of the General Assembly.

The Committee [of Overtures] also laid before the Assembly an overture from the Presbytery of Philadelphia, for the establishment of a theological school.
The overture was read, and the Rev. Dr. Dwight, and the Rev. Messrs. Irwin, Hosack, Romeyn, Anderson, Lyle, Burch, Lacey, and Messrs. Bayard, Slaymaker, and Harrison, elders, were appointed a committee to take the overture into consideration, and report upon it.
(*Minutes of the General Assembly*, May 23rd, 1809, reprint, p. 417.)

The committee to which was referred the overture in relation to the establishment of a Theological School, brought in the following report, which being read, was adopted, viz.
The committee appointed on the subject of a Theological School overtured from the Presbytery of Philadelphia, report:
That three modes of compassing this important object have presented themselves to their consideration.
The first is, to establish one great school in some convenient place, near the centre of the bounds of our Church.
The second is, to establish two schools, in such places as may best accommodate the northern and southern divisions of the Church.
The third is, to establish such a school within the bounds of each of the Synods. . . .
Your committee therefore submit the following resolution, to wit:
Resolved, That the above plans be submitted to all the Presbyteries within the bounds of the General Assembly for their consideration,

CENTENNIAL CELEBRATION OF

and that they be careful to send up to the next Assembly, at their sessions in May 1810, their opinions on the subject.
> (*Minutes of the General Assembly*, May 27th, 1809, reprint, pp. 430, 431.)

The committee appointed to examine the reports of the several Presbyteries on the subject of Theological Schools . . . reported. . . .
On motion,
Resolved, That the same committee, with the addition of Messrs. Henry A. Rowland, and John M. Wilson, be instructed to consider the subject of Theological Schools, and report to the Assembly, whether in their opinion any thing, and if any thing, what is proper farther to be done.
> (*Minutes of the General Assembly*, May 21st, 1810, reprint, p. 439.)

The committee appointed to present to the Assembly a plan for the establishment of a Theological School, reported, and the report was laid on the table.
> (*Minutes of the General Assembly*, May 29th, 1810, reprint, p. 453.)

The committee appointed farther to consider the subject of Theological Schools, reported, and the report being read and amended, was adopted, and is as follows, viz. . . .
Resolved . . .
2. That the General Assembly will, in the name of the great Head of the Church, immediately attempt to establish a seminary for securing to candidates for the ministry, more extensive and efficient theological instruction than they have heretofore enjoyed. The local situation of this seminary is hereafter to be determined. . . .
5. That the Rev. Drs. Green, Woodhull, Romeyn, and Miller, the Rev. Messrs. Archibald Alexander, James Richards, and Amzi Armstrong be a committee to digest and prepare a plan of a Theological Seminary. . . . This plan is to be reported to the next General Assembly. . . .
> (*Minutes of the General Assembly*, May 30th, 1810, reprint, pp. 453, 454.)

PRINCETON THEOLOGICAL SEMINARY

The report of the committee appointed by the last Assembly to digest and prepare a plan of a Theological Seminary, was read; and the consideration of it was made the order of the day for tomorrow morning.

(Minutes of the General Assembly, May 17th, 1811, reprint, p. 465.)

An extract from the minutes of the Trustees of the College of New Jersey, stating the appointment of a committee of their board, to confer with a committee of this Assembly, on the establishment of a Theological School, being received, was read, and Drs. Alexander, and Nott, the Rev. John P. Campbell, Messrs. Connelly, and Bethune, were appointed a committee to confer with the committee of the Trustees.

(Minutes of the General Assembly, May 18th, 1811, reprint, p. 466.)

The order of the day, viz. the consideration of a plan of a Theological Seminary, submitted by a committee appointed by the last Assembly, was called up, and the discussion of it was postponed to hear the report of the committee appointed to confer with a committee of the Trustees of New Jersey College.

This committee reported among other things, that they deem it expedient on the part of this Assembly, to appoint a committee with ample powers to meet a committee on the part of the Trustees of the College of New Jersey, invested with similar powers to frame the plan of a constitution for the Theological Seminary, containing the fundamental principles of a union with the Trustees of that College, and the Seminary already established by them, which shall never be changed or altered without the mutual consent of both parties, provided that it should be deemed proper to locate the Assembly's Seminary at the same place with that of the College.

Resolved, That a committee for these purposes be appointed accordingly; and that said committee be further instructed, and invested with powers to receive any propositions which may be made to them for locating the said seminary in any other situation if it be found expedient; all which shall be fairly and fully reported to the next Assembly.

This report was adopted, and a resolution passed to elect said committee in the afternoon.

The subject of locating the Theological Seminary being discussed, it was determined by a vote of the Assembly that the rivers Raritan and Potomac be the limits, within which the Seminary shall be located.

(*Minutes of the General Assembly*, May 22nd, 1811, reprint, pp. 470, 471.)

Agreeably to the resolution of the forenoon, an election was held for a committee to meet with a committee of the Trustees of New Jersey College, and the ballot being taken, Drs. Alexander, Wilson and Milledoler, the Rev. Messrs. John McDowell and Janeway, and Messrs. Robert Ralston, and Divie Bethune, were declared duly elected to compose said committee of the Assembly.

Resolved, That Dr. Alexander be the chairman of this committee, and that he have power to appoint the time and place of the first meeting of the committee, and that he give notice accordingly to the members.

(*Minutes of the General Assembly*, May 22nd, 1811, reprint, p. 471.)

The order of the day was again called up; and after some progress made in reading the report of the committee appointed by last Assembly, to draw up a plan of a Theological School, the farther reading and consideration of said report was postponed till tomorrow morning.

(*Minutes of the General Assembly*, May 22nd, 1811, reprint, p. 471.)

The order for the day was again called up; and after making considerable progress in reading the report by paragraphs, and making a number of amendments and alterations in it, the Assembly adjourned until four o'clock P. M.

(*Minutes of the General Assembly*, May 23rd, 1811, reprint, p. 472.)

The order for the day was again resumed, and the reading of the report of the committee appointed by last Assembly to draw up

PRINCETON THEOLOGICAL SEMINARY

a plan for a Theological School, was finished, except articles 7th and 9th, which were referred to the consideration of next Assembly. The report being thus far corrected and amended, was adopted.

Resolved, That the committee which reported the plan for a Theological School, be continued; that they print for circulation in the churches, so much of the plan as has been adopted by the Assembly; and that they digest and prepare such farther provisions and regulations for said seminary as they may judge to be necessary, and report the same to the next Assembly.

(*Minutes of the General Assembly,* May 23rd, 1811, reprint, p. 472.)

Resolved, That the committee appointed to confer with a committee of the Trustees of the College of New Jersey, be, and they hereby are instructed to consider the several articles of the plan of a Theological Seminary, so far as the same are adopted by this Assembly, as their guide in the proposed conference, which they shall in no case contravene.

(*Minutes of the General Assembly,* May 24th, 1811, reprint, p. 479.)

It being the order of the day, the report of the committee on the subject of locating the Theological Seminary was called up.

A motion was made and seconded, that said seminary be located at Princeton. After considerable discussion on the motion, the Assembly

Adjourned till 4 o'clock P. M.

(*Minutes of the General Assembly,* May 26th, 1812, reprint, p. 496.)

The discussion of the motion made in the forenoon was resumed, and after still farther discussion of the subject, the Assembly

Adjourned till 9 o'clock tomorrow morning.

(*Minutes of the General Assembly,* May 26th, 1812, reprint, p. 496.)

The subject left unfinished yesterday afternoon was again resumed.

A motion was made and seconded, that the subject of locating the Theological School be postponed for the present year, and recommended to the attention of the next Assembly.

The question being taken was determined in the negative.

The original motion was then called up, and was amended, and with the amendment is as follows:

Resolved, That Princeton be the site of the Theological Seminary, leaving the subject open as to its permanency, agreeably to the stipulations agreed upon by the joint committee of the last Assembly and the Trustees of the College of New Jersey. After some discussion of the resolution thus amended, the Assembly adjourned till 4 o'clock, P. M.

>*(Minutes of the General Assembly,* May 27th, 1812, reprint, p. 496.)

The subject of locating the Theological Seminary was again called up, and being under discussion, the Assembly adjourned till nine o'clock, tomorrow morning.

>*(Minutes of the General Assembly,* May 27th, 1812, reprint, p. 496.)

The resolution for locating the Theological Seminary was again resumed, and after considerable discussion, and special prayer for direction on the important subject, was adopted, and is as follows, viz.

Resolved, That Princeton be the site of the Theological Seminary, leaving the subject open as to its permanency, agreeably to the stipulations agreed upon by the joint committees of the last Assembly and the Trustees of the College of New Jersey.

>*(Minutes of the General Assembly,* May 28th, 1812, reprint, p. 497.)

The following plan of an agreement between a committee appointed by the last General Assembly, and a committee of the Trustees of the College of New Jersey, for the location and establishment of a Theological Seminary, was submitted to this Assembly, and was adopted, and is as follows, viz.

1. That the Theological Seminary, about to be erected by the

PRINCETON THEOLOGICAL SEMINARY

General Assembly, shall have its location in Princeton or its immediate vicinity, in the state of New Jersey; and in such connexion with the College of New Jersey, as is implied in the following articles. . . .

9. . . . And the Trustees engage that, while the Theological Seminary shall remain at Princeton, no professorship of theology shall be established in the College. . . .

(*Minutes of the General Assembly*, May 28th, 1812, reprint, pp. 499, 500.)

Resolved, That an election for Directors of the Theological Seminary, and for a Professor of Didactic and Polemic Divinity, and other Professors, if the Assembly think proper, be held on Saturday morning next. . . .

(*Minutes of the General Assembly*, May 28th, 1812, reprint, p. 501.)

Nominations were made for Directors of the Theological Seminary.

(*Minutes of the General Assembly*, May 29th, 1812, reprint, p. 504.)

It being the order of the day, the Assembly proceeded to the election of Directors of the Theological Seminary. . . .

(*Minutes of the General Assembly*, May 30th, 1812, reprint, p. 508; for the names, see p. 509.)

The order of the day, viz. the election of professor or professors in the Theological Seminary, was postponed until Monday morning, next.

(*Minutes of the General Assembly*, May 30th, 1812, reprint, p. 509.)

The election for a Professor of Didactic and Polemic Divinity, was postponed till tomorrow morning.

(*Minutes of the General Assembly*, June 1st, 1812, reprint, p. 510.)

It being the order of the day for this morning, the Assembly proceeded to the election of a Professor of Didactic and Polemic

CENTENNIAL CELEBRATION OF

Divinity in the Theological Seminary. After special prayer for direction on the subject, the ballots were taken and read, and the Rev. Archibald Alexander, D.D., was declared duly elected. The election being closed, a special prayer was made for a divine blessing upon the Professor and the Theological Seminary.

Drs. Green and Hall were appointed a committee to wait on Dr. Alexander, and inform him of his appointment.

(*Minutes of the General Assembly*, June 2nd, 1812, reprint, p. 512.)

Resolved, That the directors of the Theological Seminary be directed to meet at Princeton, the last Tuesday in June, at 3 o'clock P. M., and afterward on their own adjournments; and Dr. Green was directed to write to those directors who were not present and give them notice of the meeting.

(*Minutes of the General Assembly*, June 2nd, 1812, reprint, pp. 512, 513.)

It being the order of the day for this morning, the directors of the Theological Seminary reported . . .

(*Minutes of the General Assembly*, May 26th, 1813, reprint, p. 526.)

The subject of locating the Theological Seminary having been postponed yesterday, was called up this morning, and after a full discussion of the subject, the following resolution was adopted, viz.

Resolved, That the permanent location of the Theological Seminary be in the borough of Princeton, New Jersey, in conformity with the agreement with the Trustees of the College, signed at Princeton, June 26th, 1811, and ratified by the General Assembly at their sessions in May, 1812.

(*Minutes of the General Assembly*, May 27th, 1813, reprint, p. 533.)

The history of the actual opening of the Seminary is recounted in the first report of the Board of Directors, made to the General Assembly of 1813. As this docu-

[8]

PRINCETON THEOLOGICAL SEMINARY

ment is not included in the reprint of the Minutes of the General Assembly, it is not generally accessible. It is, therefore, reproduced here in full:

The Board of Directors of the Theological Seminary of the Presbyterian Church in the United States of America, through the good hand of their God upon them, are enabled to present this their First Report to the General Assembly, under circumstances favourable and encouraging. According to appointment, they met on the 30th of June, 1812, in Princeton, and chose the Rev. Dr. Ashbel Green their President, the Rev. Dr. Philip Milledoler their Vice President, and the Rev. John M'Dowell, Secretary. The various and important duties committed to their trust, they have endeavoured conscientiously to fulfil, in humble, but firm confidence in that glorious Redeemer, who hath promised to be with his people to the end of the world. The account of their stewardship, they will now give with simplicity and fidelity; and then suggest such measures as they may deem worthy of the Assembly's notice.

For the sake of perspicuity they will arrange the narrative of their proceedings under distinct heads.

I. OF THE PROFESSOR AND HIS INAUGURATION

At their first meeting, the Directors received information from the Rev. Dr. Archibald Alexander of his acceptance of the office of Professor of Didactic and Polemic Theology in the Seminary. They immediately made the necessary arrangements to procure from the Presbytery of Philadelphia the dissolution of the pastoral connexion between him and his congregation, as also to inaugurate him into the office of Professor, in the event of such dissolution. On the 12th of August, the certificate of Dr. Alexander's dismission from his charge being presented to the Board, they did solemnly inaugurate him as Professor. The discourses delivered on that occasion have, by their order, been printed, under the impression that these discourses would "fully make known to the Christian public the views and designs with which the Institution under their care had been founded, and was then opened for the reception of pupils." The Assembly by noticing this publication will promote the object

CENTENNIAL CELEBRATION OF

of the Board, and the interests of the Infant Seminary, of which they are the guardians.

II. THE STUDENTS

On the day of the inauguration, William Blair, John Covert, and Henry Blatchford, were received by the Board as students in the Seminary. Subsequent to that period, Leverett I. F. Huntington, William A. M'Dowell, James H. Parmele, Henry R. Weed, Halsey Wood, and Benjamin F. Stanton, have been received. One of these, viz. William A. M'Dowell, who was far advanced in his Theological course before he entered the Seminary, has been licensed to preach the gospel by the Presbytery of New Brunswick. The remaining eight are still in the Seminary. The term of their probation being expired, the Professor, whose duty it is to report any who may be unqualified to proceed, has informed the Board that 'the capacity of every student in this Seminary, for the acquisition of knowledge, is respectable, and most of them may by care and exercise become good speakers. Their character, for piety and good conduct, he adds, is irreproachable. Their diligence in prosecuting their studies and cheerful compliance with the directions of their teacher deserve commendation.'

III. THE PLAN OF STUDIES

The Board cannot better exhibit this, than in the words of the Professor in his report to them. 'The attention of the students for that part of the first year which is past, has been directed, in the first place, to the original languages in which the Sacred Scriptures were written; and, in the next place, to the English translation of the Scriptures, which they have been reading in order. In connexion with these studies, they have paid attention to Patriarchal and Mosaical rites and institutions; to Jewish antiquities and oriental customs; to Scriptural Chronology and Geography; and to the connexion between sacred and profane history, and between the Old and New Testaments. They have been required to read compositions and speak orations of their own composing, agreeably to the plan of the Seminary adopted by the General Assembly. The Professor would observe, however, that both himself and students experi-

PRINCETON THEOLOGICAL SEMINARY

enced considerable inconvenience from the want of suitable compends on the several branches which they attempted to pursue. The knowledge sought was often contained in massy folios, and mostly in foreign languages; and such books as would have been convenient in size and suitable for our purposes, in many instances, were out of our reach; or so few copies could be obtained, that the whole class could not pursue the studies at once. Your Professor has done the best in his power to supply this deficiency by collecting scraps, and making translations and abridgments from every work which he could find suitable to his purpose. The labour which this required he does not regret to have bestowed, as he is convinced that the employment has been profitable to himself, as well as useful to the students.'

IV. ACCOMMODATION OF THE STUDENTS

The students of the Seminary have been well accommodated, both as it relates to boarding and lodging in the College: for the most part they have been room mates, and in the refectory have eaten together at a separate table. On the subject of the aid expected from the charitable funds under the controul of the Trustees of New Jersey College, the Directors deem it their duty to state the following facts. In November last, at the meeting of a number of the Trustees of the College, (a quorum of the Board not being convened,) the President was advised to afford to the students of the Seminary such assistance as they might need for the winter and spring then ensuing. In consequence of this advice, the price of board, to all who chose to receive it, has hitherto been reduced to one dollar per week; and the whole expenses of one student in the articles of board and room rent, have been defrayed from the funds of the College. At a meeting of the Board of the Trustees of the College, on the 13th of the present month, they passed the following resolutions: viz.

1. That on account of the absence of certain members of the Board who have heretofore had under their consideration some points pertaining to this subject, a final decision thereon be postponed until the next meeting.

2. That, in the mean time, the students in the Theological Seminary, with respect to pecuniary accommodation, be treated in all respects as ordinary students of College.

CENTENNIAL CELEBRATION OF

On these resolutions the Directors remark, that the Theological Seminary will be in session less than three months before the next meeting of the Board of Trustees of the College—that the deficiency in the support of the students of the Seminary, for these three months, occasioned by the resolutions recited, has been provided for by a private appropriation—that they cherish a sanguine expectation, not only from the articles of stipulation between the Assembly and the Trustees of the College, but also from the acts of the Trustees themselves, and from information received relative to the prevalent sentiments of the members of the Board of Trustees, that the Board will, at their next meeting, give considerable assistance in the support of the students of the Seminary—that the better to insure the obtaining of this assistance, the Assembly should enjoin on the Board of Directors to recommend a specific number of the Theological students as candidates for the aid, stipulated in the last article of the agreement entered into between them and the Assembly.

The Professor, in his report to the Board, states, 'that no collision, jealousy, or unpleasant feelings of any kind, have arisen between the Theological students and those of the College. As far as is known to him, they have been uniformly treated with the respect due to their station. From the President and faculty of College, every accommodation and friendly attention has been afforded which it was in their power to bestow; and from the inhabitants of the town and vicinity the students have received many civilities.'

The Board feel extremely gratified in stating to the Assembly, that experience has proved, thus far, that the two institutions have had a mutual influence in promoting each other's benefit. The students of the Theological Seminary, by their respectable personal characters, as well as their exemplary deportment, have recommended to the students of the College, with whom they live upon terms of the greatest cordiality and friendship, the religion of Jesus Christ. In return they have received many advantages, from their connexion with and residence in the College. The majority of them are members of the literary societies. Of those societies they receive the common benefits, and the use of their libraries. Besides this, they have the President's promise, that he will give them lectures and lessons on the composition and structure of sermons, and on elocution. They have, moreover, the opportunity of attending the

PRINCETON THEOLOGICAL SEMINARY

course of instruction in religion which the President gives to the students of the College.

V. OF THE FUNDS

The Board have not judged it expedient to publish an address to the Christian public, for aiding the funds of the institution as directed by the Assembly. They have, however, sent a circular letter to the Presbyterian congregations in the cities and towns of Savannah, Augusta, Charleston, Baltimore, Philadelphia, Trenton, Princeton, New Brunswick, Elizabethtown, Morristown, Orange, Newark, New York, Hudson, Albany, Schenectady, Troy, and Lansingburg; requesting them to take up a public collection in each of them, to aid in defraying the expenses of the Seminary for the present year. Nearly $1000 have been reported to the Board as thus collected: viz.

1st Congregation in Baltimore,			$107.56
2d	do.	Philadelphia,	146.18
3d	do.	do.	54.63
Elizabethtown,			103.62
Brick Church, in New York,			204.63
Wall-street,	do.	do.	180.00
Rutger's-street,	do.	do.	94.15
In addition to this the Rev. Mr. M'Dowell reported a donation from Mrs. Susan Niemceriez, of Elizabethtown, of			50.00
Total			$940.77

Of this sum, the collections made in the 2d and 3d congregations in Philadelphia are requested by the donors to be appropriated to the reduction of the board of the students; and with the consent of the Assembly will be thus used by the Directors.

The Board have directed the Treasurer of the Trustees of the Assembly to invest the funds of the Seminary uniformly in the public funded debt of the United States.

They have also adopted the following plan for a permanent and contingent fund.

CENTENNIAL CELEBRATION OF

First, Resolved, That all the subscriptions, donations, and legacies now in hand, as well as those which shall be hereafter collected, constitute a permanent fund. The principal or capital of this fund, not to be broken upon, except by very urgent circumstances; such as the building of houses for the Seminary—the purchase of a library, or other indispensable calls, incident to the infant state of the Seminary.

Second, Resolved, That the contingent fund be formed by the interest of the permanent fund; by the amount of the collections made in the congregations as heretofore recommended; by the special draughts on the permanent fund, if they shall be found indispensable; and by any donations that may be specially appropriated to this purpose: and that the contingent fund defray the expenses of the year; and that if, in any year, there be a surplusage, it be added to the capital of the permanent fund.

The Directors, finally, on this subject, with pleasure, inform the Assembly, that Richard Stockton, esq. of the borough of Princeton, has promised to convey to the Rev. John M'Dowell, Samuel Bayard, esq. and Dr. John Van Cleeve, as Trustees in behalf of this Board, or the survivors, or survivor, and their heirs respectively, a lot of four acres of land for the use of the Seminary, provided it be located in the said borough.

VI. EXAMINATION OF THE STUDENTS

The Directors have, during this month, attended to an examination of the students of the Seminary on the Hebrew language, Patriarchal and Mosaical Institutions, Jewish Antiquities, Scriptural Chronology and Geography, Biblical history, connexion between Sacred and Profane history, and between the history of the Old and New Testament. The Professor informed the Board, that the students were prepared to be examined on the original Greek of the gospels, and on a select number of Campbell's critical disputations; but their examination on these subjects was omitted for want of time.

The examination afforded the Board much satisfaction in regard to the fidelity and diligence of the Professor, and the proficiency of the students. They cannot but cherish the hope that these young men will fully realize the expectation of the friends of this institution.

PRINCETON THEOLOGICAL SEMINARY

VII. OF THE LIBRARY

An appropriation of $100 has been made for the purchase of books immediately wanted; of which sum $77.49 has been expended. For the purpose of increasing the library, the Board at an early period resolved, that every Director should solicit donations in books. The success of different applications in procuring books, has encouraged the Board to continue the resolution.

VIII. OF RESIGNATIONS

The Rev. Dr. Milledoler, having left the Presbyterian Church, and connected himself with the Reformed Dutch church, has resigned his office as Vice President. His place as Director must therefore be considered as resigned. The Rev. Dr. Samuel Miller has been elected Vice President in his place.

The Rev. Dr. Alexander has declined taking his seat as a Director, in consequence of his acceptance of the office of Professor.

The Rev. Dr. James P. Wilson has also sent in a letter to the Board, resigning his seat as a Director, in consequence of his ill health.

IX. OF EXPENDITURES

Of the $3000 appropriated by the Assembly to the order of the Board, the following sums have been expended: viz.

To removing Dr. Alexander's effects from Philadelphia to Princeton,	$22.03
To do. do. Mr. Haslet,	44.75
To blank book for Minutes,	7.00
To two do. for other uses,	4.75
To books for the use of the students of the Seminary,	77.49
To printing Discourses delivered on the occasion of Dr. Alexander's inauguration,	216.10
To rent of the Professor's house,	125.00
To stationary, &c.,	10.75
To Professor's salary, three quarters,	1350.00
To balance unexpended,	1142.13
	$3000.00

In connexion with this report, and as a part of their duty, the Directors recommend the three following subjects to the Assembly, as demanding their notice.

1. The immediate appointment of an additional professor. The necessity of this measure must be obvious to every reflecting person. One man cannot do justice to any number of students in prosecuting their theological studies. And it should be recollected, to use the language of the Professor in his report to this Board, 'that the whole of his time has been occupied in attending to those branches which do not properly belong to his department, so that he has had very little opportunity of preparing for the duties of his office in that branch of Theology which has been assigned him.' In the present state of our Seminary, it is of the last importance that we should form its character so as to procure the approbation and patronage of the Christian public. To secure this, we must place it upon a level with other institutions of a similar kind in this country, especially in the number of its Professors, and the consequent increase of advantages to the students.

2. Some provision ought to be made by the Assembly to assist in defraying the expenses of the students.

3. The Seminary ought to be permanently located.

In concluding their report, the Directors congratulate the Assembly on the present state and future prospects of their infant Seminary. Considering the difficulties attending such an institution, they have every reason to calculate, under the smiles of Divine Providence, upon final and complete success. Should they, however, fail, (which may God forbid,) they will have the satisfaction of failing in a noble cause.

Signed by order of the Board of Directors,

ASHBEL GREEN, *President*,
ZECHARIAH LEWIS, *Sec'ry pro tem.*

Extract from the *Minutes of the General Assembly of the Presbyterian Church in the United States of America*, A.D. 1813, pp. 73–81.)

As the completion of the first hundred years of the Seminary's service to the Church approached, preparations began to be made for an appropriate commemoration of its century's work. In the autumn of 1908, the Faculty presented a memorial to the Board of Directors, suggesting the appointment of a joint committee of three members each of the Board of Directors, the Board of Trustees and the Faculty, to take the matter in hand. A committee was accordingly formed, consisting, on the part of the Directors, of President E. D. Warfield, the Rev. Dr. J. Ross Stevenson, and the Hon. William M. Lanning; on the part of the Trustees, of the Rev. Drs. John Dixon and David Magie, and William P. Stevenson, Esq.; and on the part of the Faculty, of President F. L. Patton and the Rev. Drs. B. B. Warfield and William Brenton Greene, Jr. Power was given this committee to appoint a Secretary and to add to its numbers. The enlarged committee ultimately consisted of the following gentlemen: President Francis L. Patton, Chairman; Rev. Harold McA. Robinson, Secretary; Rev. Dr. George Alexander, Rev. Dr. Maitland Alexander, R. M. Anderson, Esq., Rev. Prof. William P. Armstrong, Rev. Sylvester W. Beach, Silas B. Brownell, Esq., Rev. Dr. John Dixon, Rev. J. H. Dulles, Rev. Dr. John Fox, Rev. Dr. William Brenton Greene, Jr., Rev. Dr. C. Wistar Hodge, E. Francis Hyde, Esq., Rev. C. A. R. Janvier, Rev. Dr. John B. Laird, Hon. Wm. M. Lanning, Rev. Dr. W. L. McEwan, Prof. Kerr D. Macmillan, Prof. Wm. F. Magie, Charles H. Mathews, Esq., H. S. Prentiss Nichols, Esq., E. H. Perkins, Esq., Rev. Dr. William Henry Roberts, Rev. Dr. J. Ross Stevenson, William P. Stevenson, Esq., Rev. Dr. B. B. Warfield, and President E. D. Warfield. The work of this general Centennial Committee was carried on through an Executive Committee of seven members with its sub-committee of three, and a number of specific committees, as follows:

Executive Committee: President Francis L. Patton, Chairman; Rev. Sylvester W. Beach, Silas B. Brownell, Esq., Rev. Dr. John B. Laird, Hon. Wm. M. Lanning, Rev. Dr. B. B. Warfield, President E. D. Warfield.

Sub-Committee of the Executive Committee: Rev. Dr. B. B. Warfield, Chairman; Rev. Sylvester W. Beach, President Francis L. Patton.

Committee on Entertainment: Rev. Sylvester W. Beach, Chairman; R. M. Anderson, Esq., Rev. Prof. William P. Armstrong, Prof. Kerr D. Macmillan, Prof. William F. Magie.

Committee on Invitation: Rev. J. H. Dulles, Chairman; Rev. Dr. William Brenton Greene, Jr., Rev. Dr. C. Wistar Hodge, Rev. Dr. W. L. McEwan, Rev. Dr. William Henry Roberts.

Committee on Programme: Rev. Dr. B. B. Warfield, Chairman; Rev. Dr. Maitland Alexander, Rev. Dr. John Fox, Charles H. Mathews, Esq., President Francis L. Patton.

Committee on Arrangements: Prof. Kerr D. Macmillan, Chairman; Rev. J. H. Dulles, Prof. William F. Magie.

Committee on Music: Rev. Prof. Wm. P. Armstrong, Chairman; Rev. J. H. Dulles, Prof. Kerr D. Macmillan.

Committee from the Faculty on the Volume of Biblical and Theological Studies: President Francis L. Patton, Chairman; Rev. Dr. B. B. Warfield, Rev. Dr. J. D. Davis.

Committee on Publication of the Commemoration Volume: Rev. Dr. B. B. Warfield, Chairman; Rev. Prof. William P. Armstrong, Rev. Harold McA. Robinson.

The Executive Officer of the General Committee and

PRINCETON THEOLOGICAL SEMINARY

of all its subordinate committees was the Rev. Harold McA. Robinson, its Secretary.

This is not the place to give a full account of the work undertaken or accomplished by the Centennial Committee. Let it only be said in passing that much was done to quicken in the Alumni a keener sense of the closeness of their relation to their Alma Mater; that there was given to the Alumni and the friends of the Seminary an opportunity to contribute to its endowment, which was generously embraced by many; and that a volume of Biblical and Theological Studies by the members of the Faculty was published as part of the Centennial commemoration. The object of the present volume is only to give permanent record to the details of the celebration itself, with its essential accompaniments.

Due intimation of the desire of the Seminary to celebrate its centennial was made to the General Assembly of 1911 (*Minutes of the General Assembly* for 1911, p. 186), and at the opening of the Centennial Session, in the autumn of 1911, an announcement was sent to the Synods and Presbyteries in the following form:

1812 [Seal] 1912

THE THEOLOGICAL SEMINARY OF THE PRESBYTERIAN CHURCH IN THE UNITED STATES OF AMERICA

AT PRINCETON, NEW JERSEY

ANNOUNCES THE COMPLETION, WITH ITS PRESENT SESSION,
OF THE FIRST ONE HUNDRED YEARS OF SERVICE TO
THE CHURCH AND ASKS THE GOOD WISHES
AND PRAYERS OF THE

CENTENNIAL CELEBRATION OF

Later an announcement of the proposed celebration and an invitation to appoint delegates to it was sent to the administrative Boards of the Presbyterian Church in the United States of America, and to a number of institutions of learning in the following form:

1812 [Seal] 1912

THE THEOLOGICAL SEMINARY OF THE PRESBYTERIAN CHURCH IN THE UNITED STATES OF AMERICA

AT PRINCETON, NEW JERSEY

WILL CELEBRATE THE ONE HUNDREDTH ANNIVERSARY OF ITS ESTABLISHMENT BY THE GENERAL ASSEMBLY, ON SUNDAY, MONDAY AND TUESDAY, THE FIFTH, SIXTH AND SEVENTH OF MAY, NINETEEN HUNDRED AND TWELVE.

THE DIRECTORS, TRUSTEES AND FACULTY OF THE SEMINARY HAVE THE HONOUR TO INVITE

....

TO BE REPRESENTED ON THAT OCCASION BY A DELEGATE. THE FAVOUR OF AN EARLY REPLY, ADDRESSED TO THE REVEREND HAROLD McA. ROBINSON, PRINCETON THEOLOGICAL SEMINARY, PRINCETON, NEW JERSEY, IS REQUESTED.

AT PRINCETON, NEW JERSEY,
JANUARY, 1912

PRINCETON THEOLOGICAL SEMINARY

The institutions to which this announcement and invitation was sent included all theological seminaries in the United States serving Churches "who profess and call themselves Christian," all theological schools in mission lands in connection with evangelical Churches in the United States, a large number of foreign theological faculties, and all universities and colleges, ten or more of the graduates of which have pursued theological courses in Princeton Seminary.

Still further, there was sent out a personal invitation in the following form:

1812   [Seal]   1912

THE THEOLOGICAL SEMINARY OF THE PRESBYTERIAN CHURCH IN THE UNITED STATES OF AMERICA

AT PRINCETON, NEW JERSEY

HAS THE HONOUR TO INVITE

TO BE PRESENT AT THE CELEBRATION OF THE
ONE HUNDREDTH ANNIVERSARY OF THE FOUNDING
OF THE SEMINARY
ON SUNDAY, MONDAY AND TUESDAY
THE FIFTH, SIXTH AND SEVENTH OF MAY
ONE THOUSAND, NINE HUNDRED AND TWELVE.

This invitation was sent to all the Alumni of the Seminary, to the presiding officers of all the evangelical Churches in the United States, and of the Presbyterian Churches in Great Britain, and to a number of distinguished individuals.

The response to these several announcements and invitations was very general.

The present volume contains, in the order in which they are here enumerated, the responses of the courts of the Presbyterian Church in the United States of America to the announcement of the Seminary's intention to celebrate the hundredth anniversary of its foundation, together with a number of similar congratulatory addresses from other church bodies; the responses of the presiding officers of Churches at home and abroad; the congratulatory responses to the Seminary's announcement and invitation of various institutions of learning whether theological or general; the list of delegates sent by various ecclesiastical bodies and institutions of learning to the celebration; the programme of the Centennial Exercises; and the text of some of the addresses given at the celebration.

RESPONSES FROM THE COURTS OF
THE PRESBYTERIAN CHURCH IN THE
UNITED STATES OF AMERICA

THE GENERAL ASSEMBLY OF THE PRESBYTERIAN CHURCH IN THE UNITED STATES OF AMERICA

The General Assembly, in session at Louisville, Ky., May 18th, 1912, took the following action, viz.:

The General Assembly adopted unanimously the Report of the Special Committee on the Centennial of Princeton Theological Seminary, as follows:—

The Committee to bear congratulations to Princeton Theological Seminary on its Centennial was appointed by the following action of the General Assembly of 1911:

"That the congratulations of the Church, through this General Assembly, be extended to Princeton Theological Seminary, in view of the approaching one hundredth anniversary of the founding of that institution, and that, in response to the invitation presented, the following Committee be appointed to participate in the coming Centennial: Rev. John F. Carson, D.D., Rev. William H. Roberts, D.D., the Moderator of the Synod of New Jersey, the Moderator of the Synod of New York, the Moderator of the Synod of Pennsylvania, the Hon. Woodrow Wilson, Governor of New Jersey, and the Hon. William Jennings Bryan, of Nebraska." (*Minutes*, 1911, p. 189.)

The names of the Moderators of the Synods on the Committee are as follows: the Rev. William M. Dager, A.B., Moderator of the Synod of New Jersey; the Rev. Martin D. Kneeland, D.D., Moderator of the Synod of New York; and the Rev. Samuel A. Cornelius, D.D., Moderator of the Synod of Pennsylvania.

The Committee reports the performance of its acceptable duty, and acknowledges the hearty welcome with which it was received by the authorities of "The Theological Seminary of the Presbyterian Church in the U. S. A., located at Princeton, New Jersey." The Centennial was celebrated on May 5, 6 and 7. The exercises were characterized by appropriate dignity, felicitous addresses, and by the

CENTENNIAL CELEBRATION OF

presence of more than 500 alumni, the representatives of Presbyterian and other Churches on both sides of the Atlantic, and delegates from more than one hundred institutions of learning. Specially notable was the presence of the Moderators of the General Assemblies of the Church of Scotland, the United Free Church of Scotland, the Free Church of Scotland, and the Presbyterian Church in Ireland. There were also present the Moderators or Presidents of eight American Churches. The occasion was historic and the Celebration worthy of the Seminary and the Church.

It is recommended that the following minute be approved by the Assembly:

The General Assembly hereby places upon record its congratulations to "The Theological Seminary of the Presbyterian Church in the U. S. A., located at Princeton, N. J.," upon its one hundred years of completed service to Christ and to the Church. The plan of the Institution, adopted by the General Assembly of 1811, sets forth the relation of the General Assembly to the Theological Seminary as "the patron and fountain of its power," and states the design of the Institution in definite terms. It was established—"To form men for the Gospel Ministry who shall believe and cordially love, and therefore endeavor to protect and defend in its genuineness, simplicity, and fullness, that system of religious belief and practice which is set forth in the Confession of Faith, Catechisms, and Plan of Government and Discipline of the Presbyterian Church"; also "to provide for the Church men who shall be able to defend her faith against infidels and her doctrines against heretics"; and further who shall possess "an enlightened attachment not only to the same doctrines but to the same plan of government."

The General Assembly heartily recognizes that the Boards of Directors and Trustees, and the Faculty of the Seminary, have administered with fidelity the trust committed to them, and in particular acknowledges that the educational progress made by the Institution has been for the most part due to its able and scholarly professors, who through four generations have been largely instrumental in the production of ministers competent by abilities, learning and training, for the high and holy office of ambassadors of Jesus Christ.

The General Assembly congratulates itself that forty-three of

PRINCETON THEOLOGICAL SEMINARY

its Moderators have received training within the walls of this Institution, that many of the leaders in the missionary and benevolent work of the Church have had the same privilege, and that out from it have gone hundreds of home and foreign missionaries, and above all, in the successive generations, a great number of pastors who have served faithfully in their respective spheres of labor, and have built up Christ's likeness in many human lives, and have laid the foundation of churches and organizations which have become powers in the Church Universal. The Assembly also rejoices in the catholicity of the Institution as shown by the fact that students of all evangelical churches have been freely admitted to its courses of instruction. In this breath of acknowledgment of Christian fellowship, the Seminary and the Church are one.

With grateful recognition of the loyalty of the wide-spread constituency, that from the origin of the Institution has furnished the resources and the sympathetic support which have enabled it to maintain with some degree of adequacy the purposes for which it was established, the Assembly commends the Institution to the Church at large, for a continued generous and cordial support, believing that there lies before Princeton Theological Seminary along the lines of the trust reposed in it, a most useful and great future. "Now unto Him that is able to do exceeding abundantly above all that we ask or think, according to the power that worketh in us, unto Him be glory in the Church by Christ Jesus throughout all ages, world without end. Amen."

In behalf of the Committee,

JOHN F. CARSON, *Chairman*,
WM. H. ROBERTS, *Secretary*.

Attest:
WM. H. ROBERTS, *Stated Clerk.*

CENTENNIAL CELEBRATION OF

THE SYNOD OF BALTIMORE

The following action was taken by the Synod of Baltimore in session at Wilmington, Delaware, October 23, 1911:

Whereas: The Theological Seminary at Princeton, N. J., does this year complete one hundred years of continued usefulness and service to the Church; therefore

Resolved, That the Synod of Baltimore rejoices with Princeton Seminary in the completion of so long a time of service in the cause of Christ and His Church, and would give this expression of our gratitude and appreciation.

Resolved, That the Stated Clerk be instructed to send to the President and Faculty, to the Boards of Directors and Trustees, the congratulations of this Synod, and to assure them of our prayers to Almighty God, that from generation to generation this honored servant of the Church, with increasing devotion and success, may send forth men of God, knowing the Holy Scriptures, thoroughly furnished unto all good works.

Resolved, That the Moderator appoint a Committee of four, consisting of himself and one minister from each of the three Presbyteries, to represent the Synod at the Centennial exercises of Princeton Theological Seminary.

The Committee:

> REV. JOSEPH B. TURNER, Dover, Del.
> REV. JAMES E. MOFFATT, D.D., Cumberland, Md.
> REV. GEORGE P. WILSON, D.D., Washington, D. C.
> REV. FRANCIS H. MOORE, D.D., Middletown, Del.

Attest:

N. H. MILLER, *Stated Clerk.*

McLean, Va.

PRINCETON THEOLOGICAL SEMINARY

THE SYNOD OF CALIFORNIA

The Synod authorized its Stated Clerk, in its name, to express to the Seminary its warm appreciation of the unceasing blessing the Seminary has ever been to all the great interests of the Church and the Nation. And the Synod prays the Great Head of the Church, that the Seminary may ever continue to measure up to the opportunity before it in the dear Church to which we belong, and that it may have from on high unceasingly the blessing of Him whose you are and whom you serve.
On behalf of the Synod of California,

WM. STEWART YOUNG, *Stated Clerk.*

Los Angeles, Cal., Nov. 15th, 1911.

THE SYNOD OF CANADIAN

The Synod of Canadian, being in session at Hot Springs, Ark., Oct. 5-7, set apart thirty minutes of the evening, Friday, the 6th, 8 P. M. to hold a special service of Thanksgiving, Praise and Prayer for the Seminary, for the marvelous work God has done and is doing through it. The meeting was conducted by Rev. M. L. Bethel of the Seminary Alumni.

Attest: W. H. CARROLL, *Stated Clerk.*

Valliant, Okla., Nov. 9th, 1911.

CENTENNIAL CELEBRATION OF

THE SYNOD OF COLORADO

The Rev. F. E. Smiley, D.D., reported for the Committee to which was referred the communication from Princeton Seminary. The report was received and the recommendation adopted. The report was as follows:

Whereas, the Synod of Colorado, in session at Greeley, Colo., Oct. 19th, 1911, has heard with pleasure the announcement of the completion, with its present session, of the first one hundred years of service to the Church, of the Theological Seminary of the Presbyterian Church in the United States of America, at Princeton, New Jersey,

Resolved, That we place upon our record our gratitude to God for putting into the hearts of the fathers, the laying of foundations broad and deep for this school of the prophets, where so many of the successful pastors of our beloved Church have been trained by consecrated instructors to "rightly divide the word of truth:" for the long line of trustees and teachers who during one hundred years have guarded and guided the institution from infancy to its present century strength: and for those who have stood as a bulwark against the subtle assaults of the enemy, both within and without the Church, against the Old Book, our spiritual Magna Charta, and for their unswerving devotion to the "faith once delivered to the saints."

We congratulate the trustees, faculty, students and the Church upon this auspicious occasion, and pray that all may be so endowed with the Spirit of Christ that the future, like the past, history of the Seminary may redound to the glory of God, the upbuilding of the saints and the salvation of sinners.

Resolved, That this memorial be spread upon our records and a copy be sent by the chairman of the committee of the Alumni appointed by the Moderator of Synod, to the authorities of Princeton Theological Seminary.

Respectfully submitted,

FRANCIS E. SMILEY, *Chairman.*

Attest:

GEO. R. EDMUNDSON, *Stated Clerk.*

PRINCETON THEOLOGICAL SEMINARY

THE SYNOD OF IDAHO

The Synod of Idaho has received the communication from the Princeton Theological Seminary, that it will celebrate the Centennial of its life and work, and the Synod would congratulate that venerable institution on its long career of usefulness, and assure it of our grateful appreciation of its work; of our heartfelt sympathy; and our prayers for its long continued usefulness.

JOHN GOURLEY, *Stated Clerk.*

Pocatello, Idaho, Oct. 10, 1911.

THE SYNOD OF ILLINOIS

The committee to which was referred the announcement of the completion, with the present session, of the first one hundred years of service to the Church of the Theological Seminary of the Presbyterian Church in the United States of America, at Princeton, N. J., would respectfully report, recommending that the following resolution be adopted, engrossed upon our record and a copy transmitted to the Seminary:

Resolved, That the Synod of Illinois, in session at Charleston on October 19, 1911, expresses to the Theological Seminary of the Presbyterian Church in the United States of America at Princeton, N. J., its high appreciation of the eminent services rendered by the Seminary, within the hundred years now ending, alike to the cause of Christian scholarship in the writings of its representative men, to the cause of Presbyterianism in its stedfast maintenance of our historic

CENTENNIAL CELEBRATION OF

doctrine and polity and to the practical work of the Church in the rich supply of faithful men to preach the Gospel and to minister in the name of Christ. Recognizing the great development in our system of theological institutions and the inevitable changes which have taken place in our particular relation to it, the Synod prays God's blessing upon the Seminary that it may continue through the century to come a centre of Christian learning and a source of supply for able ministers of the New Testament, men who are both faithful to the Word of God and wise to discern the signs of the times.

All of which is respectfully submitted,

W. S. PLUMER BRYAN, *Committee.*

Done in Synod at Charleston, Oct. 19th, 1911.

Attest:

JAS. FRANKLIN YOUNG, *Moderator,*
C. HARMON JOHNSON, *Stated Clerk.*

THE SYNOD OF INDIANA

At its annual meeting, held in Sullivan, Indiana, on October 10, 1911, the Synod of Indiana of the Presbyterian Church in the U. S. A. unanimously adopted the following Preamble and Resolutions, relating to the Centennial of Princeton Theological Seminary, and instructed its Stated Clerk to forward a copy of the same to the Seminary:

Whereas, The venerable Theological Seminary at Princeton, New Jersey, has announced to the Synod of Indiana the approaching completion of the first one hundred years of its service to the Church, and has asked the prayers and good wishes of our Synod, and

Whereas, The Synod of Indiana has been greatly indebted to

PRINCETON THEOLOGICAL SEMINARY

the Princeton Seminary for the theological education of many of its sons and the supply of many of its workers, having at present on our rolls some sixty alumni of the Seminary; therefore be it

Resolved, That we extend our cordial congratulations and best wishes to the Seminary upon its approaching Centennial, and that we pray the blessing of God upon its future work.

Resolved, That we recognize with gratitude its fidelity to the Bible and the standards of our Church, and the efficiency of its instruction and preparation for service.

Resolved, That we commend it as worthy of the prayers and liberality of our churches in all its efforts for the enlargement and betterment of its facilities for the training and equipment of those who shall serve the Church in the ministry of the Gospel of Christ.

Attest: LEON P. MARSHALL, *Stated Clerk.*

THE SYNOD OF IOWA

The Synod of Iowa received with great interest and sympathy the announcement of the completion of a hundred years of theological instruction at Princeton, and directed the Stated Clerk to convey to the Faculty and Directors of the Seminary its greetings and good wishes. In the name of the Synod, I congratulate both you and the Church on the noble achievements of the past. To how large a degree the Presbyterian Church has been moulded by the influence of Princeton Seminary can never be told. The contributions of the Seminary to theological learning through faculty and graduates are of inestimable value. The fidelity of its instructors to the Gospel of Jesus Christ deserves and receives the praise of the Church. We are grateful to Almighty God for this glorious history of devotion to the truth. We congratulate you upon the success of these years, and upon your present commanding position.

Our prayer is that the good work begun may be carried on and intensified in the years to come, and that Princeton may abide in strength as long as the world endures.

In the name of the Synod of Iowa,

W. O. RUSTON, *Stated Clerk.*

Dubuque, Iowa, Nov. 17, 1911.

THE SYNOD OF KENTUCKY

The Synod of Kentucky heartily unites with the whole Presbyterian Church in congratulations to Princeton Theological Seminary on the successful completion of the first one hundred years of its history. We desire to express our appreciation of the great work that the Seminary, in the Providence of God, has been enabled to do. We gratefully thank God for the men who have been trained in its halls and for the light of learning that has emanated through the century from its famous faculty.

We recognize its faithfulness in teaching the Divine Oracles and its stedfast loyalty to the Word of God.

We remember its ever-growing influence in the development of the Church, and its ever-widening power in the evangelization of the world. We invoke the Divine Blessing on the Seminary's future, and pray that the same Hand may guide in the days to come that has so wondrously prospered it in the days gone by.

It is peculiarly appropriate that such congratulatory expression should be presented formally in a meeting of the Synod of Kentucky, held in the Second Presbyterian

PRINCETON THEOLOGICAL SEMINARY

Church, Lexington, Kentucky. It was in this Church and Sunday School that the Rev. Ethelbert D. Warfield, D.D., LL.D., the present presiding officer of the Board of Directors, and the Rev. Benjamin Breckinridge Warfield, D.D., LL.D., the present Charles Hodge Professor of Didactic and Polemic Theology, were first taught the things pertaining to God.

Mingled with our feelings of debt and gratitude to Princeton Theological Seminary for its century of contribution to the Church and the whole Kingdom of God are our feelings of pride and pleasure that the Synod has had the privilege and honor to give to the Seminary two of its own sons.

CHARLES LEE REYNOLDS, *Committee.*

THE SYNOD OF MINNESOTA

This is to certify that the Synod of Minnesota, in session at Minneapolis on the 12th to 16th of October, 1911, took the following action:

Whereas, The Theological Seminary of Princeton, N. J., completes this year the first one hundred years of its history, and,

Whereas, This Synod has felt the impress and value of the Seminary's work, through the labors of Princeton's students, the past fifty years; therefore,

Resolved, That the Synod of Minnesota extend to the Board of Trustees and Faculty of the Seminary the most cordial congratulations on the splendid record of the past, and express the prayerful hope that, under the divine blessing, the Seminary will advance to a yet greater measure of service to the Church and to the Kingdom.

MAURICE D. EDWARDS, *Stated Clerk.*

St. Paul, Minn., Nov. 20, 1911.

CENTENNIAL CELEBRATION OF

THE SYNOD OF MISSOURI

The Synod of Missouri of the Presbyterian Church in the United States of America, in session at Springfield, Mo., October 12, 1911, acknowledges the receipt of the announcement of the approaching celebration of the centennial of Princeton Theological Seminary. We congratulate the Seminary upon this coming completion of one hundred years of service, and desire to express our appreciation of the great work accomplished by her.

Thirty-eight men now connected with this body, besides many others whose service has helped to make our history in the past, received all, or a part, of their theological training within her halls.

We gratefully acknowledge the large indebtedness of this Synod, and of the whole Church, to Princeton Seminary, for her thorough training of the Christian ministry, for her never ceasing championship of the truth of God's Word and for her splendid leadership of Christian thought.

We pray the blessing of the Great Head of the Church may continue with her in increasing measure through all coming years. We further commend to all our churches, and especially to individual members of means, the Centennial Fund which is being raised as a fitting memorial of her rich past and to equip her still more thoroughly to meet the responsibilities and opportunities of the future.

I certify that the above is a correct copy of the action of the Synod of Missouri.

JOHN H. MILLER, *Stated Clerk.*

Kansas City, Mo., Oct. 30, 1911.

PRINCETON THEOLOGICAL SEMINARY

THE SYNOD OF MONTANA

The Synod of Montana offers its most hearty felicitations to the Princeton Theological Seminary upon the completion of its one hundredth year—spent so loyally in the service of our beloved Church, and at this time sends its best wishes for continued prosperity, enlarged usefulness and increased influence in the special sphere marked out for her by a kind Providence.

EIKO J. GROENEVELD,
Chairman of Synod's Committee.

Butte, Mont., Oct. 26, 1911.

THE SYNOD OF NEBRASKA

The following resolution was adopted by the Synod of Nebraska:

Inasmuch as Princeton Theological Seminary has about completed a century of historic and worthy activity, having served the Church with distinguished credit,

Be it Resolved, That the Synod of Nebraska extend its heartiest congratulations to the Seminary on the completion of her first century of service and express its confident hope that the future shall be even more glorious.

Done in Synod at North Platte, Neb., on the 16th day of October, A. D. 1911.

Attest: JULIUS F. SCHWARZ, *Stated Clerk.*

CENTENNIAL CELEBRATION OF

THE SYNOD OF NEW JERSEY

Your Committee appointed to prepare resolutions of congratulation to Princeton Theological Seminary upon the fact of its approaching Centennial Celebration, would submit the following for your adoption:

This year has marked the opening of the one hundredth session of Princeton Theological Seminary. At the Commencement in May 1912 this outstanding event will be fittingly commemorated in Princeton by the Directors and Trustees and Faculty and Alumni of the Seminary. This is a great record of a great institution for a great work. It is cause for congratulation and rejoicing, not only for Princeton graduates and those who have her interests at heart because of their theological affinity, but for all who believe in the doctrines of grace, and especially for the Presbyterian Church in America.

Be it hereby Resolved, therefore, by this Synod of New Jersey, the chief recipient of blessing from this century of service in the Gospel,

FIRST, that we render profound gratitude to God for the Divine leading in the Church, looking to the higher education of the ministry, and for the action of the General Assembly of 1811 in establishing a separate institution for theological instruction, which institution was the next year opened at Princeton, with the Rev. Archibald Alexander, D.D., as Professor. It is interesting to recall that the classes were at first held in Dr. Alexander's study, and later for a time in the building of the College of New Jersey, itself the outgrowth of the Log College of Neshaminy, founded for the education of ministers. We reverently and thankfully recall to-day the words of the Assembly's "Plan of the Seminary," as follows,—"It is to form men for the Gospel ministry who shall truly believe, and cordially love, and therefore endeavor to propagate and defend in its genuineness, simplicity and fullness, that system of religious belief and practice which is set forth in the Confession of Faith, Catechisms, and Plan of Government and Discipline of the Presbyterian Church; and thus to perpetuate and extend the influence of true evangelical piety and gospel order."

We render gratitude for the Divine favor that has enabled the

PRINCETON THEOLOGICAL SEMINARY

Church to continue this school of Christian theology for a century with signal brilliancy of learning, with remarkable power of piety, and with steady and delightful growth and development, both of equipment and influence. For the glory of God and in honor of Princeton we would give praise. We would have thanksgivings rise in all our churches that the Spirit of God did thus consecrate and has continued to consecrate, as ever in the history of our blessed religion, the best scholarship to the cause of Gospel truth and Christian life, and especially for the noble men of God who first made Princeton great, and whose names are revered and loved to-day throughout our Church.

We would give praise to God for the fearless, unwavering stand Princeton Seminary has held through all these years, not only for the Calvinistic Theology as the ripest expression of the Reformed Faith, but for the defense and teaching of fundamental Christianity,—the supernatural revelation which is in Jesus Christ, the plenary inspiration and authority of the Scriptures, the precious doctrines of the free grace of God and full justification by faith, the saving power of the blood of the Lamb, the work of the Holy Spirit and the living headship of the Lord of Glory in His Church.

We thank God for the religious character of this Seminary throughout the past, the holy lives of the men who have labored for it, its choice spirit of prayer, a valuable memory to all who ever shared it, its love for the pure Word of God, its serious understanding of the vocation of the ministry, as the herald of a God-given Gospel, its simplicity of daily life, its supreme desire to exalt Jesus Christ, its cordial interest in every effort to extend the Kingdom of our Lord through His truth and Church, and especially for its consistent missionary spirit and record, a spirit that begins with the statement in the Assembly's "Plan" that one object of the Seminary is "to found a nursery for missionaries to the heathen," and is able to testify that over three hundred and eighty of the graduates have entered upon foreign missionary work. We are grateful that through these one hundred years, in this land with its marvelously enlarging territory, and in the whole world with the rapidly opening doors of its vast continents, this Seminary has been as the springs of water among the hills,—a source of supply beyond all human power to imagine. Surely God has honored His promises and led His people graciously.

CENTENNIAL CELEBRATION OF

SECOND, that Synod congratulate the Directors and Trustees and Faculty of Princeton Seminary upon the possession of a heritage that only time and the blessing of God could produce, and upon the accomplishment of a work for the Church that only eternity and the presence of God will reveal. Theirs is hallowed soil indeed. Theirs are blessed memories indeed. We congratulate them upon the fact that Princeton has continued to this day to hold her own in the front rank of American institutions of theological learning, and of note among those of the world.

We congratulate them upon the well known and unwavering and hearty stand this Seminary has maintained for the faith once delivered to the saints, and for her loyalty to the Confession of our Church, to the Covenant and to Christ. We recognize in her a leader in the fight for truth against error for the Church universal, to be honored for her work by the whole of evangelical Christendom.

We congratulate them upon the present vigor and prosperity of the Seminary. Beginning with three students, she has given instruction to five thousand, seven hundred and forty-two students, and now has sixteen instructors with one hundred and eighty-five men under their care.

We congratulate them upon having as President the Rev. Francis Landey Patton, D.D., LL.D., whose ripe and commanding powers are consecrated to the service of a conservative theology.

We congratulate them upon having a completed faculty, a soundly constructed and steadily enlarging curriculum, with splendid grounds and buildings, with the cordial confidence of the Alumni, and a secure place in the esteem of the whole Church.

We look with confidence upon her prospects for the future. We regard her as panoplied and prepared to meet the issues of the day and of the days to come. We record with pleasure that she is still sending forth men well instructed in the truth as it is in Jesus, and well fitted to be ambassadors for God and leaders of the people, that she might save society through the saving of souls. We rejoice that she is touching and tempering with a mighty influence the very life of the Church today, not only in this land but wherever the Gospel banner has been planted by the sons and daughters of God.

THIRD, that we most heartily rejoice in the proposal to signalize the completion of these one hundred years, an epoch in the history

PRINCETON THEOLOGICAL SEMINARY

of Presbyterian theological education, by securing an increased endowment for the Seminary, and commend this effort to the liberality of our pastors and churches, especially to those ministers who are Alumni of Princeton, and to those churches whose pastors are Princeton men.

FOURTH, that the Moderator of this Synod appoint a Committee of seven, four ministers and three elders, to represent the Synod at the Centennial exercises to be held in Princeton in May, 1912, the Moderator himself to be the Chairman, ex-officio, of this Committee.

FIFTH, that the Rev. Francis L. Patton, D.D., LL.D., be invited to address the Synod now upon the Seminary's plans for the celebration of this important anniversary.

Adopted by the Synod of New Jersey, in session at Atlantic City, Oct. 18, 1911.

Attest: WALTER A. BROOKS, *Stated Clerk.*

THE SYNOD OF NEW YORK

The following action was taken by the Synod of New York at its recent meeting:

In view of the approaching 100th Anniversary of the founding of the Theological Seminary of the Presbyterian Church in the U. S. A. at Princeton, the Synod of New York, in session at Auburn, October 18th, 1911, desires to place upon its minutes an expression of its sense of the noble service to our Church and to the Christian religion throughout the world rendered by this institution; its gratitude to God for the signal manifestations of His favor during the whole of the Seminary's history; and its earnest desire and devout prayer that the coming years may witness still larger prosperity and usefulness for Princeton Seminary.

A true copy.

Attest: J. WILFORD JACKS, *Stated Clerk.*

CENTENNIAL CELEBRATION OF

THE SYNOD OF NORTH DAKOTA

A Memorial was received from Princeton Theological Seminary with reference to the completion of its first one hundred years of service, asking the good wishes and prayers of the Synod of North Dakota. To this the following answer is recommended:

That this request be remembered in the closing prayer of this session, and that the Stated Clerk be instructed to notify the officials of the Seminary of that fact, assuring them of the cordial good will of the Synod.

I notice further that the closing item of that forenoon session reads:

Synod took recess until 1:30 o'clock P.M., and was closed with prayer by Rev. R. H. Myers, in behalf of Princeton Theological Seminary.

B. A. FAHL, *Stated Clerk.*

Devil's Lake, N. D., Nov. 13, 1911.

THE SYNOD OF OHIO

The Synod of Ohio held its annual meeting in Mansfield, October 10–12, 1911. In response to a request for the interest of the Synod, the following recommendations were made by the Committee on Bills and Overtures:

That the Synod of Ohio extend congratulations and good wishes to Princeton Theological Seminary upon its One Hundredth Anniversary.

That the Synod remember Princeton Theological Seminary in prayers, and that the Rev. William M. Hindman, D.D., of the Presbytery of Chillicothe, now lead us in prayer.

[42]

PRINCETON THEOLOGICAL SEMINARY

That the Stated Clerk of this Synod convey a suitable letter, covering the action of the Synod in this matter.

The foregoing recommendations were unanimously adopted, and the Rev. Dr. Hindman offered a very tender and touching prayer for the Seminary, for its present student body, and for all living students of former years.

Attest: EDWARD T. SWIGGETT, *Stated Clerk.*

THE SYNOD OF OKLAHOMA

A communication from Princeton Theological Seminary was read, announcing the one hundredth session of the Seminary, and soliciting the prayers and good wishes of the Synod.

The Moderator led the Synod in prayer for the Seminary.

The Stated Clerk was instructed to convey to the Secretary of the Seminary information of this action of the Synod.

LLOYD C. WALTER, *Stated Clerk.*

THE SYNOD OF OREGON

The Synod of Oregon, assembled in Mt. Tabor Church, Portland, adopted the following resolution Oct. 14, 1911:

That Synod sends its sincere congratulations to Princeton Seminary on the completion of 100 years of service in the Presbyterian Church and wishes for it even larger and more effective service in the future.

Extracted from minutes, Synod of Oregon, by

JOHN A. TOWNSEND, *Stated Clerk.*

CENTENNIAL CELEBRATION OF

THE SYNOD OF PENNSYLVANIA

At the meeting of the Synod of Pennsylvania, held in Warren, Pa., in the First Presbyterian Church, October 24th, 1911, after hearing an address by the Rev. Dr. Francis L. Patton, President of Princeton Theological Seminary, the Synod adopted the following Minute:

The Synod having received an intimation that the Theological Seminary of the Presbyterian Church, U. S. A., at Princeton, N. J., would celebrate the Centennial of its Foundation in May, 1912, hereby extends to the Seminary its warmest congratulations and rejoices with it in the great work which by the blessing of Almighty God it has done for Christ and His Church.

From the earliest times the ties between the Synod and the Seminary have been most close and intimate. Many of the most distinguished professors of the Seminary have been drawn from the territory, the homes and the churches now covered by this Synod. Hundreds of young men have gone from these churches to pursue their studies at the Seminary, and have returned confirmed in faith and enriched in knowledge to preach the Everlasting Gospel.

During all this period the Synod and the Seminary have been in deep and tender sympathy in reference to the great movements which have stirred the Church and advanced the Kingdom of God; and the Synod rejoices in the strength and courage with which the Seminary, upon the threshold of a new age, proclaims the faith once delivered to the saints.

May the Great Head of the Church vouchsafe to this beloved and honored institution an ever deeper sense of the glorious privilege of training men to preach the Everlasting Gospel and an ever greater power in inspiring men with the very spirit of His Grace.

At the request of the President of the Seminary that the Synod would appoint a Committee to represent it at the Centennial Celebration, the following ministers were

PRINCETON THEOLOGICAL SEMINARY
named to convey the greetings of the Synod in connection with the Centennial Celebration.

The Moderator, Rev. Samuel A. Cornelius, D.D., Oil City, Pa.
The Stated Clerk, Rev. Robert Hunter, D.D., Philadelphia.
Rev. Wm. L. McEwan, D.D., Pittsburgh, Pa.
Rev. Ebenezer Flack, D.D., Scranton, Pa.
Rev. Robert B. Beattie, Franklin, Pa.
Rev. George S. Chambers, D.D., Harrisburg, Pa.

ROBERT HUNTER, *Stated Clerk.*

THE SYNOD OF SOUTH DAKOTA

Upon receipt of a telegram from Princeton Theological Seminary in connection with their celebration of the One Hundredth Anniversary of the beginning of that Institution, Synod joined in thanksgiving for the great good that Seminary has already accomplished and in prayer for God's continued blessing upon it.

HARLAN P. CARSON, *Stated Clerk.*

Madison, S. D., Oct. 6, 1911.

THE SYNOD OF TENNESSEE

The Committee on Bills and Overtures of the Synod of Tennessee reported as follows regarding the Centennial of Princeton:

The communication from the Theological Seminary of Princeton, New Jersey, announcing the completion with its present session of the first one hundred years of service to the Church, was before us;

CENTENNIAL CELEBRATION OF

and we recommend that the Stated Clerk communicate to the Seminary the congratulations and best wishes of the Synod.

In compliance with this action of the Synod I take pleasure, as Stated Clerk, in assuring you of the hearty sympathy, good wishes, and congratulations of the Synod upon your one hundred years of great service to the Church.

The Synod of Tennessee in 1819 followed the example that Princeton had set seven years before, and organized the Southern and Western Theological Seminary, and located it at Maryville. This was the second theological seminary of our Church. Though for more than half a century, the theological seminary features have ceased, the institution, now Maryville College, is still under the care of the Synod of Tennessee.

The Synod wishes Princeton a second century of even more conspicuous service to the Church than the great century which is now closing.

SAMUEL T. WILSON, *Stated Clerk.*

Maryville, Tenn., Nov. 7, 1911.

THE SYNOD OF WASHINGTON

The Synod of Washington, in session in Spokane, Wash., October 3–5, 1911, rejoices with you in the completion of a century of good service to the churches, for our Lord and Master, and assures you of its good wishes and prayers for long-continued usefulness and success in the yet far away future.

EUGENE A. WALKER, *Stated Clerk.*

Reardan, Wash., Oct. 30th, 1911.

PRINCETON THEOLOGICAL SEMINARY

THE SYNOD OF WEST VIRGINIA

The Synod, in session at Charleston, W. Va., on Oct. 21, 1911, took the following action:

We rejoice that this Seminary has rendered to our beloved Church such faithful and efficient service of instruction and inspiration through this one hundred years. We rejoice that she has been such an able and devoted defender of the faith in all her remarkable history. We rejoice in the noble band of men whose hearts God has touched, whom she informed and trained in the things of the Kingdom. We join with the men all over the world in the best of wishes and earnest prayers that in the coming years God may graciously bless her even more abundantly both in things temporal, in increasing her needed endowment, and in things spiritual, to realize her one purpose, to raise up, train and inspire men after God's own heart to build up the people in our most holy faith.

Synod also appointed the Rev. Herman G. Stoetzer, D.D., an alumnus of the Seminary, its special representative at the commemoration services.

J. P. LEYENBERGER, *Stated Clerk.*

Wheeling, W. Va., Oct. 21, 1911.

THE SYNOD OF WISCONSIN

Synod received an invitation to attend the celebration of the one hundredth anniversary of the founding of what is commonly known as Princeton Theological Seminary. Synod stood in recognition of the courtesy and in order to give expressions of good wishes, and was led in prayer by the moderator.

Extracted from the Minutes of Synod,

C. A. ADAMS, *Stated Clerk.*

Merrill, Wis., Nov. 10, 1911.

CENTENNIAL CELEBRATION OF

THE PRESBYTERY OF BIRMINGHAM A

Whereas, The Theological Seminary of the Presbyterian Church at Princeton has announced the completion of 100 years of service to the Church, and asks the prayers and good wishes of this Presbytery; therefore,

Resolved, That the Stated Clerk be instructed to express the congratulations of this Presbytery to the Princeton Theological Seminary on the completion of 100 years of such splendid service to the Church, and give hearty assurance of the prayers and good wishes of this Presbytery.

Attest: LUTHER B. CROSS, *Stated Clerk.*

Gastonbury, Ala., May 2, 1912.

THE PRESBYTERY OF BROOKLYN

At the November meeting the members of the Presbytery of Brooklyn instructed the undersigned to convey to the Theological Seminary of the Presbyterian Church in the United States of America at Princeton, N. J., their hearty congratulations on the completion of a century of loyal and effective service for the Kingdom of our Lord and to assure the Seminary that she may be sure of the best wishes and earnest prayers of Brooklyn Presbytery for her continued success and usefulness.

JOSEPH DUNN BURRELL, *Moderator,*
JOS. G. SNYDER, *Stated Clerk.*

Nov. 28, 1911.

PRINCETON THEOLOGICAL SEMINARY

THE PRESBYTERY OF BUTLER

The Presbytery of Butler sends heartiest greetings to the Princeton Theological Seminary as it closes its first century of splendid service for the Presbyterian Church and for Protestantism on this continent and beyond the seas, and expresses the hope that the institution first established to secure a uniform, trained ministry—both scholarly and devout—shall increasingly understand the world's ills and shall count it all joy to prepare workmen who shall minister to these needs and ever seek to remove the all embracing cause.

Rejoicing with you throughout the celebration of this notable event, and invoking the divine favor and blessing upon all future efforts for the world's redemption, we subscribe in behalf of the Presbytery.

WM. R. CRAIG, *Moderator*,
WILLIS S. MCNEES, *Stated Clerk*.

Done in Presbytery, December 12, 1911.

THE PRESBYTERY OF CARLISLE

At its recent stated meeting, the Presbytery of Carlisle, having received the invitation of the Theological Seminary at Princeton to attend its approaching Centennial Anniversary Celebration, requested me to thank the Seminary for its invitation.

I desire to add my personal thanks and felicitations

CENTENNIAL CELEBRATION OF

also, having received an individual invitation and remembering with thankfulness and honor the good I received from the Institution.

Rob't F. McClean, Stated Clerk.

Mechanicsburg, Pa., April 25, 1912.

THE PRESBYTERY OF CAYUGA

The Presbytery of Cayuga desires to send its greetings to Princeton Theological Seminary on the completion of one hundred years of noble service both to our Church and to the Kingdom throughout the world.

We are grateful to God for his goodness to this institution in the past, and pray that God's richest blessing may rest abundantly on it during the coming years.

Attest: E. Lloyd Jones, *Stated Clerk.*

Cayuga, N. Y., April 26, 1912.

THE PRESBYTERY OF CENTRAL DAKOTA

The Presbytery of Central Dakota joins with others in offering to Princeton Seminary felicitations on the completion of one hundred years of service for Christ and the Church.

May the God, who has so signally blessed her with consecrated, scholarly men in her chairs for one hundred

PRINCETON THEOLOGICAL SEMINARY

THE DIOCESE OF NEW JERSEY OF THE PROTESTANT EPISCOPAL CHURCH

[TELEGRAM]

The diocese of New Jersey sends its greetings to the Princeton Seminary on the celebration of its 100th anniversary with a prayer for God's blessing upon the future life and work of the Seminary.

HOWARD E. THOMPSON, *Secretary.*

Mt. Holly, N. J., May 7, 1912.

years, richly endow her with men and money that she may render larger service to the cause.

May those who go forth from her halls be strong in the faith, well qualified and adapted to defend the position of Evangelical Christianity until the Lord come.

Wishing the Seminary larger usefulness, in behalf of the Presbytery of Central Dakota,

JOHN C. LINTON, *Stated Clerk.*

Flandreau, S. D., April 23, 1912.

THE PRESBYTERY OF CHESTER

The Presbytery of Chester, in session at Paoli, Pennsylvania, Tuesday, January 30, 1912, acknowledges with appreciation the gratifying announcement that the Theological Seminary of the Presbyterian Church in the U. S. A. at Princeton, New Jersey, completes, with its present session, one hundred years of service to the Church. The Presbytery congratulates the Seminary on this event, and assures it of its deep appreciation of the splendid work it has accomplished, and that its prayers for the future enlarged success of the Seminary shall ever ascend to the Great Head of the Church for His continued favor and blessing.

The above action, by resolution, was heartily and unanimously adopted by the Presbytery and I was directed, in my official capacity, as the Stated Clerk, to forward the same, duly attested, to the authorities of the Seminary, which duty I have great pleasure in herewith fulfilling.

WM. TENTON KRUSE, *Stated Clerk.*

Elwyn, Pa., Jan. 31, 1912.

CENTENNIAL CELEBRATION OF

THE PRESBYTERY OF CHICAGO

The Presbytery of Chicago gladly avails itself of the opportunity of extending to the Boards of Directors and Trustees, and to the Faculty and Alumni of Princeton Theological Seminary its sincerest and warmest congratulations on the occasion of its attaining the 100th anniversary of its establishment.

The strength and influence of Princeton Theological Seminary has rightly been the ground of gratification and of legitimate pride to the whole Presbyterian community of this land. Its first century of life, coinciding as it does with the most intensely active period from the intellectual point of view of the world's history, was from its nature one that required the work of such an institution as Princeton Theological Seminary. The Seminary has made its contribution to the whole current of intellectual and religious life with marked success. Presbyterianism in America, as well as throughout the whole world, has reason to rejoice and give thanks to God for the life of such an institution. In a time of intensely practical tendencies Princeton has insisted on scholarly tastes and habits of thought. In a time of questioning, with the risk of relaxing convictions, she has stood for loyalty to conviction. In a time of diminishing stress on educational qualifications for the ministry, she has lifted high the cherished ideals distinctive of Presbyterianism throughout the centuries, of a thoroughly educated ministry of the Gospel. Much of the success of the Presbyterian Church in maintaining its standards and regulating its progress is due to the fidelity with which Princeton Theological Seminary has lived and realized its ideals.

PRINCETON THEOLOGICAL SEMINARY

The Presbytery of Chicago offers the prayer, and cherishes the hope, that the first century of the life of such an institution may be followed by others of still greater and more varied usefulness.

Presented by committee, Rev. Andrew C. Zenos, Chairman. Adopted in Presbytery April 15, 1912.

Attest:

JAMES FROTHINGHAM, *Stated Clerk.*

THE PRESBYTERY OF CHILLICOTHE

The Presbytery of Chillicothe joyfully notes the One Hundredth Anniversary of the founding of our Theological Seminary at Princeton, N. J., and hereby sends sincere greeting and assurance of prayer for continued good work.

Attest: HARRY B. VAIL, *Stated Clerk.*

Washington C. H., Ohio, April 16, 1912.

THE PRESBYTERY OF COLUMBIA

The Presbytery of Columbia begs to acknowledge the receipt of the announcement of the one hundredth anniversary of the Theological Seminary at Princeton, New Jersey.

The Presbytery would express its gratification at the noble and fruitful history thus accomplished, would congratulate the faculty and officers of the Seminary upon the past, and would say that it cherishes the warmest appreciation of its present satisfactory status, and indulges the brightest hopes for its future usefulness and prosperity.

By order of Presbytery,

CHRISTOPHER G. HAZARD, *Stated Clerk.*

Catskill, N. Y., April 23rd, 1912.

THE PRESBYTERY OF COUNCIL BLUFFS

Council Bluffs Presbytery sends fraternal greetings. We are proud of Princeton Seminary; proud of her record; proud of her achievements. We praise Almighty God for such institutions as Princeton, and we pray that His richest blessing may rest upon good old Princeton.

We congratulate you on your one hundredth birthday, and it is our wish that Princeton may continue to prosper for many, many centuries. God speed your course; God bless your instructors; God bless your students.

With my whole heart I join the Presbytery in sending you these greetings.

THEO. J. ASMUS, *Stated Clerk.*

Carson, Iowa, Oct. 26, 1911.

THE PRESBYTERY OF CRAWFORDSVILLE

The Presbytery of Crawfordsville, in session at Frankfort, Ind., sends greetings and rejoices with you in the completion of your first one hundred years of service to the Church.

We assure you of our prayers for your continued success in training workers who are to go out in the great service of the Master.

GIBSON WILSON,
HUGH N. RONALD,
Committee.

Frankfort, Ind., Dec. 11, 1911.

THE PRESBYTERY OF DALLAS

The Presbytery of Dallas, Synod of Texas, sends greeting and congratulations to Princeton Theological Seminary on its 100th Anniversary.

By order of the Presbytery,

R. W. BENGE, *Stated Clerk.*

Athens, Texas, Oct. 31, 1911.

THE PRESBYTERY OF DUBUQUE

The Presbytery of Dubuque has directed me to convey to Princeton Theological Seminary its greetings and congratulations on the completion of a hundred years of distinguished service of God and of the Church, and to assure you that earnest and hearty prayers shall continually be offered for your abiding prosperity and enlarging usefulness.

W. O. RUSTON, *Stated Clerk.*

Dubuque, Iowa, April 30, 1912.

THE PRESBYTERY OF EBENEZER

The Presbytery of Ebenezer, at its stated meeting in Lexington, Ky., in October, 1911, instructed the Stated Clerk to acknowledge the receipt of the announcement of the Centennial of Princeton Theological Seminary, and to convey to you its appreciation of your long and honorable service to the Church and your loyalty to your historic conditions, as well as its earnest wish and prayer that the Seminary may have many centuries of service and a constantly increasing service to the Church.

J. N. ERVIN, *Stated Clerk.*

Dayton, Ky., Feb. 24, 1912.

THE PRESBYTERY OF IOWA CITY

The Presbytery of Iowa City joins heartily in the congratulations that are due the Theological Seminary of the Presbyterian Church in the United States of America, at Princeton, New Jersey, on the completion of One Hundred Years of service for the Church, and assures the President, Faculty and Students that they have our prayers and good wishes at this glad time, and we wish the Institution many more happy Centennial Celebrations. May all the future years be as rich in blessing as the last.

On behalf and at the direction of Iowa City Presbytery,

H. S. CONDIT, *Stated Clerk.*

Iowa City, Iowa, April 29, 1912.

PRINCETON THEOLOGICAL SEMINARY

THE PRESBYTERY OF LEHIGH

A communication having been received from the Theological Seminary of the Presbyterian Church in the United States of America at Princeton, New Jersey, announcing the completion with the present session of one hundred years of service to the Church, and asking for the good wishes and prayers of the Presbytery of Lehigh,—

Your committee recommends that the Presbytery send to the Seminary its most hearty congratulations on the completion of one hundred years of service in educating men for the Gospel Ministry, assuring it of our prayers for God's richest blessings for the years that are to come; and we further recommend that we here and now, as a Presbytery, offer united prayer for the Seminary.

In behalf of the Committee,

SAMUEL C. HODGE, *Chairman.*

Hazleton, Pa., Apr. 17, 1912.

THE PRESBYTERY OF MADISON

The Presbytery of Madison, in session at Richland Center, Wisconsin, 16 April, received your announcement of the near completion of one hundred years of service. It directs its stated clerk to send this letter of congratulation and best wishes. On taking this action the Presbytery was led in prayer by Elder H. B. Sanford, of Christ Church, Madison, on behalf of your great institution, our Seminary at Princeton.

ERNEST C. HENKE, *Stated Clerk.*

Baraboo, Wis., 22 April, 1912.

CENTENNIAL CELEBRATION OF

THE PRESBYTERY OF MATTOON

The Presbytery of Mattoon, in session at Effingham, Illinois, April 10th, 1912, took note of the completion of the first hundred years of service of the Princeton Seminary.

By formal action I was instructed to convey to you, on behalf of the Presbytery, its congratulations, good wishes and prayers.

We have a pardonable pride in your institution; we recognize its signal service in the Kingdom of our Lord; we glory in its loyalty to the faith once given to the saints.

It is in our hearts to add other centuries of like service, and pray that all in connection with Princeton may everywhere be marked as men who have been with Jesus, conspicuous for energy, effectiveness, consecration.

With the multitude who so believe, place Mattoon Presbytery.

JOHN A. TRACY, *Stated Clerk.*

Shelbyville, Ill., April 12, 1912.

THE PRESBYTERY OF MONMOUTH

Monmouth Presbytery receives with pleasure the announcement of the approaching centennial celebration of Princeton Seminary's splendid history and service.

The Presbytery is devoutly grateful to God for an institution which has stood for one hundred years a staunch defender of the faith of the fathers, as handed down in the Word of God, and for the long line of godly

PRINCETON THEOLOGICAL SEMINARY

and able ministers of the Word which has gone out from its walls to the work of the Church in all the world.

Old Monmouth Presbytery, which through all these years has been in closest touch with Princeton, and whose churches have been founded and developed so largely by Princeton graduates, would most cordially take advantage of this opportunity to express its debt to the Seminary and its joy in the Seminary's prosperity.

The Presbytery hereby sends to the Directors, Trustees and Faculty of the Seminary the assurance of its good wishes and fervent prayers for an enlarged and still grander life of usefulness through all the years to come.

Resolved, That the Presbytery recommend to the pastors of the churches within its bounds hearty co-operation in the Seminary's project to gather a centennial fund to enlarge its efficiency for the future.

Adopted in the Monmouth Presbytery Session of Jan. 23, 1912, at Atlantic Highlands, N. J.

Attest: FRANK R. SYMMES, *Stated Clerk.*

THE PRESBYTERY OF NEBRASKA CITY

The Presbytery of Nebraska City sends greetings to the Theological Seminary of Princeton, rejoicing in its century of prosperity and praying that our Heavenly Father may grant to it a long future of still richer blessings.

Done in Presbytery this fourteenth day of November, 1911.

THOMAS L. SEXTON, *Stated Clerk.*

CENTENNIAL CELEBRATION OF

THE PRESBYTERY OF NEW BRUNSWICK

At a meeting of the Presbytery of New Brunswick on January 23d, 1912, there was reported to the Presbytery the announcement of the Princeton Theological Seminary of its approaching one hundredth anniversary, together with the request of the officers of the Seminary for the interest and prayers of the Presbytery of New Brunswick.

In response to this request the Presbytery adopted the following resolutions, viz:—

First, That the members of the Presbytery will suitably remember the Seminary in private and public prayer.

Second, That in response to the request from the Seminary there shall be forwarded to its officers a paper prepared by a Committee of Presbytery and read before the Presbytery in September, 1911.

Third, That the Seminary shall be informed that the Presbytery has appointed a Committee to attend the commemorative exercises of the Seminary.

The paper referred to in these resolutions, and now forwarded to you, the officers of the Seminary, in the name of the Presbytery, is as follows:—

The need which suggested the establishment of a Theological Seminary was complex. The first need of the Church of a hundred years ago was an increased number of ministers. The nation was in the grip of a great missionary movement. William Carey had fanned the flickering flame of evangelism to a white heat, which also inflamed the Church on this continent. The Great Revival of 1800 accentuated the need for the preparation of an ample supply of ministers to safeguard the rapidly spreading cause of Christ. Another condition lay in French infidelity, which was rampant and threatened to invade the Church, as it had already invaded the Colleges and clubs of the land. This corrupt philosophy challenged the virile

PRINCETON THEOLOGICAL SEMINARY

intellect of the period and required a commanding response by an accredited scholarship. A further need for ministers consisted in the unevangelical influences of the theological seminaries and universities in the New England States. They were rapidly falling into the control of Unitarian disciples. Protestantism needed ardent believers and efficient teachers of essential Christianity rightly to direct the pulsating yearnings of the large accretions to the Church. The able and ardent ministry of the time were very busy men and were precluded from sacrificing time and energy on other than their specific work. As a matter of fact, unreliable methods of preparation existed, under instructors of less ability, and inculcated a sinister tendency. "An educated ministry" was the cry. The power and purity of the rising clergy called for true and capable experts. This was conclusively vindicated by subsequent consequences of ecclesiastical health and influence.

In recognition, then, of the imminent need of an educated ministry, the Rev. Ashbel Green, D.D., as early as 1805 sent into the General Assembly an "admirable paper" which drew the mind of the Church to this important subject. Of the particular method for raising up an efficient ministry, however, the earliest discoverable mention lies in a portion of the Moderator's sermon to the General Assembly of 1808, preached by the Rev. Archibald Alexander. "Encouraged by this," writes Dr. Green in his autobiography, "I used all my influence in favor of this measure; and in 1809 the Presbytery of Philadelphia, to which I belonged, sent into the General Assembly of that year an overture distinctly proposing the establishment of a theological school." The assembly sent down to the Presbyteries for their consideration the following alternatives: First, one great school in some convenient place near the center of the Church; second, two such schools in such places as may best accommodate the northern and southern sections of the Church; and, third, such a school within the bounds of each of the Synods. The vote of the Presbyteries strongly favored the establishment of an institution of theological learning, but left somewhat in doubt the best plan of procedure. The first and third plans commanded an equal support. The Assembly of 1810 adopted the first plan, and appointed a committee, of which Dr. Green was chairman, to draft an outline of the proposed Seminary. Dr. Green's committee laid its report in printed form before the Assembly of 1811, by whom it was adopted *in toto,* proposing that in the Seminary "when completely organized, there shall be at least three professors, who shall give a regular course of instruction in divinity, in Oriental and Biblical literature and in ecclesiastical history and church government, and such other subjects as may be deemed necessary."

The location of the theological seminary at Princeton was largely determined by two considerations, to wit, the helpful presence of the college and geographical convenience. Princeton was midway between the Synods of New York and Philadelphia. The trustees of the college proffered sufficient land for a site for the seminary, but a similar offer of Richard Stockton, noted patriot and philanthropist, was gratefully accepted.

A yet more sacred and significant necessity remained to be supplied, namely, the endowment of the embryonic institution with a living and life-giving spirit. The selection of a man to pioneer the proposed seminary through a "terra incognita" was, perhaps, the most solemn duty that ever confronted the General Assembly. In the Assembly of 1811, preceded by prayer and prosecuted in the hush of sacred awe, and "amid the tears and prayers of the Church, Dr. Alexander was elected to the office" of the first and only professor of the seminary-in-sight. On the twelfth day of August in the following year he was inducted into his high office at the age of forty years. In his characteristic modesty and faith, the newly invested professor approached the herculean difficulties of the hour. There was nothing tangible before the sight of this pathfinder, but a firm faith held him steadfast to his great Guide and Hope. The seminary began with three students and a single teacher. In the following year these were augmented to twenty-four students and two teachers, the Rev. Samuel Miller, D.D., having been added to the faculty.

This infantile institution of sacred learning begins now to develop into individuality of character. The personnel of Princeton's institutional life, from the pioneer Alexander to the present, has given it its individuality among similar institutions. Its founders and friends were men of liberal learning and searching thoughtfulness. There are in such temperaments balance and proportion, and their tendency is toward the conservation of the intellectually accredited.

PRINCETON THEOLOGICAL SEMINARY

In addition, the age and place of the early life of Princeton conduced markedly to its type of character. She was not buffeted by the restless flux that surged around other institutions. A stately equanimity and a sylvan isolation conduced to a conservative character. The location as much as the "Zeitgeist" contributed to its distinct individuality.

Princeton's character answered an existing necessity. The requirements of the age were for caution and conservatism. The natural consequences of a heated revival experience and a rapidly spreading Church were mixed accretions of impulse and fervor. The influx of French infidelity, made attractive by the charm of a sympathetic court and nation, called for a confirming conviction of faith and stedfastness. The insinuations of an insidious philosophy rapidly infested the churches and universities of New England with doubt and danger. In the midst of this instability and uncertainty Princeton sounded the clarion note of conviction and courage. The Church of to-day is not unmindful of her heroic exploits in these crises of thought and morals. She aided many a struggler in the gurgling rapids to hold fast to that which was good, and therefore enduring. The past century of our Church is secure largely because of her services in the apologetics of the Reformed faith. Her centenary memorializes her monumental achievements in sacred discipline to thousands of young men who have themselves rendered efficient work in fields at home and abroad.

What, then, of Princeton's position in the immediate present? Is her past, however glorious, the mere reflection of a closed career? That there is need in the domain of divinity for thoroughness of thought and exemplification of precept is manifest to every sober participant in the serious life of the present age. The latter half of the nineteenth century developed a spirit audacious and ominous. In every realm of thought and action radicalism holds the reins and drives the steeds. The danger of to-day is not the failure to discover new territories of truth, but the destruction of continents of conviction as a necessary trail for reaching the new treasures. Radicalism is on the road to ruin unless related to a sympathetic yet virile conservatism. The past has labored as truly as we do, and the present may enter into its labor with joy and profit. Both the radical and the conservative has his legitimate and essential place in the

CENTENNIAL CELEBRATION OF

procession and progression of the race. It is unreasonable and unfortunate to create antipathy and antagonism between correlated companions in quest of a common object.

Without stigmatizing one or despising the other, one may evaluate both. There exists at the present an imperative need for a steadying conservatism in order to retain to the Church and nation the accredited and substantial. Princeton with its characteristic type of thought and influence, is to-day an indispensable institution of sacred learning. Never did a generation need more its temperamental attitude toward fundamental questions of thought and radical problems of action. Without the slightest disparagement to others, Princeton is invaluable to the present age and for future generations for the training of young men for leadership in the Church. Her centenary is her challenge to the twentieth century of cordial interest and courageous purpose. Surrounded by a great cloud of witnesses she is buckling on her armor for continued and aggressive warfare for Christ and His Church. Every lover of the Church will acclaim her vision and commend her determination to apprehend that for which she was apprehended by her Master and founders.

In view of the proposed centennial celebration of Princeton Theological Seminary, the Presbytery adopts the following resolutions:

1. The Presbytery of New Brunswick hereby expresses its cordial appreciation of Princeton's distinguished services to the Church and nation during her century of existence. We are proud of her imperishable past. Her eminent men and her efficient achievements are illustrious in the records of the Presbyterian Church, and her devotion to the nation is the boast of every patriot.

2. The Presbytery of New Brunswick shares in the confidence of sister Presbyteries of Princeton's ability and intention to meet the present problems in the Church with sympathy and courage. We recognize her as a strong defender of our faith, delivered unto us by the great Head of the Church and transmitted to us as a sacred legacy. We know her as our chivalric contestant in the maintenance of truth and power.

3. The Presbytery of New Brunswick ardently commends Prince-

PRINCETON THEOLOGICAL SEMINARY

ton to the affectionate and liberal support of the churches within her bounds through moral and financial co-operation. We may move her to unparalleled usefulness by our fervent prayers and cordial good-will, and in view of her aspiring development of facilities and enlargement of faculty, we also earnestly commend Princeton to the liberal financial support of individuals and churches in our Presbytery. In her endeavor to increase her endowment with an additional million of dollars, greatly needed to meet the large purposes, we bespeak for Princeton the most cheerful and lavish support of our Presbyterians. We can suggest no better financial investment to men of large means than the enlargement and development of this institution of genuine culture and strategic influence.

4. The Presbytery of New Brunswick designates five commissioners as official visitors of the Presbytery to the Centennial celebration of the Seminary.

The commissioners appointed by the Presbytery are as follows: Rev. August W. Sonne, Rev. Henry Collin Minton, D.D., LL.D., Rev. Walter A. Brooks, D.D., Rev. Daniel R. Foster, Rev. Francis Palmer.

Attest: WALTER A. BROOKS, *Stated Clerk.*

THE PRESBYTERY OF NEWTON

At the stated meeting of the Presbytery of Newton, held at Newton, N. J., on April 9th, 1912, the following was adopted by a hearty and unanimous vote of the Presbytery, as the report of the Committee to which had been referred the communication from Princeton Seminary, announcing the completion, with this present session, of one hundred years of service to the Church.

Whereas, the Princeton Theological Seminary will observe its Centennial at the Commencement season in May; be it

Resolved, 1st: That the Presbytery of Newton places on record its

CENTENNIAL CELEBRATION OF

deep thankfulness to Almighty God for the great usefulness of this, the oldest Theological Seminary of the Presbyterian Church in the United States of America.

Resolved, 2nd: That we recognize, in the present Faculty, men of eminent scholarship and spiritual loyalty, fit successors to those who have gone before.

Resolved, 3rd: That we congratulate both the Faculty and the Board of Directors upon the bright prospect of future usefulness for this Institution,

Resolved, 4th: That a copy of these resolutions be forwarded to the Committee having charge of the Centennial Celebration.

J. A. ARMSTRONG,
W. C. PEABODY,
THEODORE TINSMAN,
Committee.

Attest: E. CLARKE CLINE, *Stated Clerk.*

Phillipsburg, N. J., April 11th, 1912.

THE PRESBYTERY OF NEW YORK

The Presbytery of New York acknowledges with pleasure the announcement of your 100th Anniversary at the completion of the present session of the Seminary and also your request for the good wishes and prayers of this Presbytery.

At our meeting yesterday I was instructed as stated clerk of the Presbytery to convey to you our congratulations upon this long service to the Church and the success which has crowned your efforts to extend the Kingdom of our Lord and Saviour Jesus Christ. We assure you of our good wishes and promise to remember you in our prayers.

PRINCETON THEOLOGICAL SEMINARY

May the Lord grant you His richest blessings and increase your labors and the reward which has always attended them more and more abundantly.

In behalf of the Presbytery of New York,

JESSE F. FORBES, *Stated Clerk.*

Nov. 14, 1911.

THE PRESBYTERY OF NORTH RIVER

The Presbytery of North River extends greeting to Princeton Theological Seminary upon the occasion of the celebration of her one hundredth anniversary.

We thank God for the founding of Princeton Seminary; for the great work He has enabled her to accomplish in the preparation of men for the ministry of Christ; for her noted contributions to Christian Theology; and for her consistent stand for the Faith.

With congratulations upon her past and with prayers for her future, the Presbytery of North River adds her felicitations upon this most happy occasion.

Attest: JOHN SCOTT KING, *Stated Clerk.*

Done in Presbytery, at Newburgh, N. Y., April 16, 1912.

THE PRESBYTERY OF NORTHUMBERLAND

The Presbytery of Northumberland at its two hundred and fourth stated semi-annual meeting, unanimously voted to send congratulations to Princeton Theological Seminary on completing one hundred years of splendid service for Christ and the Church. The Presbytery expresses the earnest and prayerful wish that the Seminary may ever continue her painstaking and consecrated work of loyalty to the Holy Scriptures, to the Standards of the Church and to Jesus Christ her Founder and Head.

JAMES WOLLASTON KIRK, *Moderator*,
HENRY SPERBECK, *Stated Clerk*.

April 16th, 1912.

THE PRESBYTERY OF OAKLAND

In view of the splendid record of successful service of Princeton Theological Seminary for one hundred years, the Presbytery of Oakland hereby acknowledges the announcement sent by the said institution and expresses its sincere interest and felicitations on the completion of Princeton's century; and sends her, through the Stated Clerk, hearty good wishes and prayers for God's richest blessing upon the Seminary in the coming years.

In behalf of the Presbytery,

R. S. EASTMAN, *Stated Clerk*.

Berkeley, Calif., March 1, 1912.

THE PRESBYTERY OF OMAHA

The Presbytery of Omaha has heard with much interest that the Theological Seminary of the Presbyterian Church in the United States of America, at Princeton,

PRINCETON THEOLOGICAL SEMINARY
New Jersey, is approaching the completion of one hundred years of service to the Church, and recognizes with gratitude the great work which this institution, under the blessing of God, has been able to accomplish.

Beginning at a time when the membership of the whole Church was but little larger than that of our Synod of Nebraska at the present time, it has grown with the growth of the Church; it has sent ministers of the Word, numbered by the thousand, into all parts of the world; and at the end of the century it is more adequately equipped for service than at any other period in its history.

Remembering the strong and godly men who have been connected with this institution in the past, and believing that they have been succeeded in the good work by men of like faith and spirit, we invoke God's richest blessing upon Princeton Seminary and pray that it may still be mightily used for the extension of the Kingdom of our blessed Lord.

Attest: JULIUS F. SCHWARZ, *Stated Clerk.*

Done in Presbytery in session at Fremont,
Nebraska, April 16th, A. D. 1912.

THE PRESBYTERY OF PECOS VALLEY

The Presbytery of Pecos Valley, with pleasure and sincere thanks, acknowledges the receipt of your announcement concerning the completion of the first one hundred years of service to the Church; and we desire to express our most hearty congratulations, praying God's continued blessings upon the work of this great institution.

CENTENNIAL CELEBRATION OF

By order of the Presbytery of Pecos Valley, this 5th day of April, A.D. 1912.

Attest: EBENEZER E. MATHES, *Stated Clerk.*

THE PRESBYTERY OF PHILADELPHIA

The Presbytery of Philadelphia most heartily and cordially congratulates the Seminary on its splendid achievement during all these past years, and expresses the hope that even greater things may be accomplished in the years ahead; also that a committee of three be appointed by the Moderator to attend the Anniversary services.

The Moderator appointed Rev. Robert Hunter, D.D., Stated Clerk, William P. Fulton, D.D., Permanent Clerk, and the Presbytery named Rev. C. A. R. Janvier, Moderator, as Chairman.

Attest: ROBERT HUNTER, *Stated Clerk.*

Philadelphia, Pa., April 24, 1912.

THE PRESBYTERY OF PHILADELPHIA NORTH

At a meeting of the Presbytery of Philadelphia North, held September 19, 1911, the following resolution was unanimously adopted:

Whereas this Presbytery is informed that a public meeting is to be held in Philadelphia on behalf of Princeton Seminary which is soon to celebrate its Centennial Anniversary, therefore

PRINCETON THEOLOGICAL SEMINARY

Resolved 1, That we commend this meeting to the favorable attention of our ministers and people.

2, That we desire to express our grateful sense of the benefits which have come to us as a Presbytery, and to the churches under our care, from our neighborhood to this venerable Seminary.

3, That we pray for the continued and increasing prosperity of this great School of the Prophets.

Attest: RICHARD MONTGOMERY, *Stated Clerk.*

THE PRESBYTERY OF PHOENIX

On behalf of the Presbytery of Phoenix, I beg to extend to you and to the Seminary, including all the members of the Faculty, our congratulations on the centennial occasion which the Seminary observes this year, and we pray you all possible blessing.

F. C. REID, *Stated Clerk.*

Phoenix, Ariz., April 17, 1912.

THE PRESBYTERY OF RESERVE

Reserve Presbytery met April 10th, and requested me to convey the hearty good will and appreciation of the Brethren to you for reaching the 100th Anniversary of your good work; and also the prayers of the Brethren for the success of the Institution for many centuries yet to come.

D. S. BROWN, *Stated Clerk.*

Kadoka, S. D., April 17th, 1912.

THE PRESBYTERY OF ROCHESTER

Gathered in regular Spring Meeting, the Presbytery of Rochester takes great pleasure in extending a unanimous vote of congratulation to the Theological Seminary of the Presbyterian Church in the United States of America at Princeton, New Jersey, on the occasion of the celebration of the One Hundredth Anniversary of the Founding of the Seminary.

Our vote is not alone one of congratulation, but also of appreciation. We feel that we honor ourselves in honoring an Institution that has done such great and notable work in advancing the Kingdom of our Lord and Saviour Jesus Christ in America and throughout the world in all these years.

The Presbytery hereby appoint Reverend George Herman Fickes and Reverend Gerard B. F. Hallock, Stated Clerk, to convey our greetings and, if possible, to attend the Anniversary Exercises.

We take pleasure in forwarding the above action, and will attend your celebration if possible.

For the Presbytery of Rochester.

GEO. HERMAN FICKES,
G. B. F. HALLOCK,
Committee.

Rochester, N. Y., April 22nd, 1912.

THE PRESBYTERY OF SAINT LAWRENCE

We, the Presbytery of Saint Lawrence, now in session, send greetings to Princeton Theological Seminary and hearty congratulations on its completion of one hundred years of efficient service to the Church.

The long roll of noble and distinguished men that this Seminary has sent forth to the Church and the world is well known to all. Princeton has, for these hundred years, stood for a strong and conservative Church, with a policy that has been a great source of strength to its communion in preventing much loose and unorthodox thought from being brought into our Church by the ministry it has sent forth.

We therefore, with a hope of long continued prosperity, send our prayers and greetings.

DANIEL A. FERGUSON, *Stated Clerk.*

Canton, St. Lawrence Co., N. Y., April 16th, 1912.

THE PRESBYTERY OF SAINT LOUIS

The Presbytery of Saint Louis has received the announcement from the Seminary of the approaching Centennial of its organization.

It has requested me to reply to this, and to say that the Presbytery holds your venerable institution in the highest esteem, and that it is grateful to God for the abundant service it has rendered to the Church in preparing an able, faithful and orthodox ministry during the hundred years of its existence.

It cordially responds to your request and prays for the continued peace and prosperity of your great institution.

Yours in behalf of the Presbytery,

SAM'L G. NICCOLLS.

St. Louis, Mo., Oct. 24, 1911.

THE PRESBYTERY OF SAINT PAUL

The Presbytery of Saint Paul extends cordial greetings and expresses its appreciation of the splendid record in work and influence of this the Mother Seminary of American Presbyterianism.

The attainments of the past have made Princeton a household word in the religious world.

The Presbytery of Saint Paul, while thus rejoicing with the whole Church over the past one hundred years, is confident that God has great blessings still to diffuse through the agency of this, our representative institution, in whose ideals and spirit are found devotion and loyalty to the great principles and magnificent theology of the Reformed Church.

Attest: J. C. ROBINSON, *Stated Clerk.*

THE PRESBYTERY OF SAN FRANCISCO

The Presbytery of San Francisco, in session this day, receives with pleasure from the Theological Seminary of the Presbyterian Church in the United States of

PRINCETON THEOLOGICAL SEMINARY

America, at Princeton, New Jersey, the announcement of its completion, with the present session, of one hundred years of service to the Church, expresses to the Seminary profound appreciation of its noble work, tenders to it hearty congratulations, and pledges prayers for its ever increasing prosperity and power.

REV. E. K. STRONG,
REV. J. H. LAUGHLIN,
Committee.

Oct. 10th, 1911.

THE PRESBYTERY OF SEDALIA

Resolved, That the Presbytery of Sedalia extends its heartiest congratulations to the Princeton Theological Seminary on the completion of its one hundred years of faithful and efficient service of the Church, and that we pray for continued usefulness, and that our Stated Clerk extend our congratulations and good wishes to said Seminary.

Attest: J. W. MITCHELL, *Stated Clerk.*

THE PRESBYTERY OF SYRACUSE

The Presbytery of Syracuse acknowledges the graceful announcement of the completion of the first one hundred years of the Seminary's service, and with profound gratitude to God desires to assure the Seminary of its best wishes and continued prayers for increased prosperity and enlarged service in the work of the Kingdom of God to the glory of our Lord Jesus Christ.

By order of the Presbytery,

JOHN G. TRUAIR, *Stated Clerk.*

Dec. 21, 1911.

THE PRESBYTERY OF TOPEKA

The Presbytery of Topeka, in session at Lawrence, Kansas, on April 10, 1912, recognizes with gratitude to the great Head of the Church the century of service completed and to be celebrated in May. It acknowledges the value of the Seminary in contributing to the equipment of ministers of the Gospel, sound in faith and consecrated to the work of the Kingdom. It congratulates the management on the hopeful outlook for the future. It joins in the petitions to the Sovereign Disposer of all events for the continuance of His favor as the years and even centuries go.

Attest: A. H. HARSHAW, *Stated Clerk.*

THE PRESBYTERY OF UTICA

The Presbytery of Utica recognizes with profound gratitude the completion by Princeton Theological Seminary of its first one hundred years of magnificent service to the Church of our Lord and Redeemer, Jesus Christ.

PRINCETON THEOLOGICAL SEMINARY

We extend to the Seminary, in its Centennial celebration, our good wishes for continued prosperity and our earnest prayer for ever enlarging usefulness.

LOUIS G. COLSON, *Committee.*

Attest:
OLIVER A. KINGSBURY, *Stated Clerk.*

Clinton, N. Y., April 9th, 1912.

THE PRESBYTERY OF WESTCHESTER

At a meeting of the Presbytery of Westchester, held in New York, January 16, 1912, the following minute was adopted:

The Presbytery of Westchester notes with gratitude to God the completion of one hundred years of service rendered by the Theological Seminary of Princeton, N. J., to the cause of Christ in America, and throughout the world.

We add to the prayers of the unnumbered friends of Princeton our prayers that an ever increasing sphere of usefulness, filled with the power of God, may be granted to this venerable institution of learning.

Attest: W. J. CUMMING, *Stated Clerk.*

THE PRESBYTERY OF WESTERN AFRICA

The Presbytery of Western Africa acknowledges with great pleasure the announcement received from Princeton Theological Seminary of the completion of its one

CENTENNIAL CELEBRATION OF

hundredth anniversary of service to the Church; and hereby conveys the expressions of its great appreciation for the eminent services rendered by this grand Institution, as well as the assurances of its best wishes and fervent prayers for many more years of usefulness and prosperity.

By the Presbytery,

WILLIAM H. BLAINE, *Stated Clerk.*

Monrovia, Dec. 14, 1911.

THE PRESBYTERY OF WEST JERSEY

The Presbytery of West Jersey extends to the Seminary at Princeton on the occasion of its celebration of its first century of service to the Church, its heartiest congratulations, with gratitude to God for the distinguished service to the cause of Christ and to the purity of the faith once committed to the Fathers, which has been rendered by this institution of our Church, and with acknowledgment of the incalculable value of the work accomplished in providing for the Church and the mission-field a mighty band of ministers and missionaries grounded in the truth.

We express the hope for the continued favor and blessing of God, and our prayer that the Seminary in the coming years may gain larger opportunities and accomplishments for the Kingdom of our Lord.

Attest: A. P. BOTSFORD, *Stated Clerk.*

Salem, N. J., April 16, 1912.

PRINCETON THEOLOGICAL SEMINARY

THE PRESBYTERY OF WHITEWATER

The Presbytery of Whitewater gratefully acknowledges the receipt of the announcement of the completion of the first 100 years of service of the grand, sturdy and loyal Seminary at Princeton, and officially assures the Trustees and Faculty of the good wishes and prayers of this Presbytery.

THOMAS JACKSON GRAHAM, *Stated Clerk.*

Ordered by motion at meeting of Presbytery
April 9, 1912, at Cambridge City, Indiana.

THE FIFTH AVENUE PRESBYTERIAN CHURCH OF THE CITY OF NEW YORK

To the Theological Seminary of Princeton.

In view of the celebration by the Theological Seminary at Princeton of its Centennial Anniversary, the Session of the Fifth Avenue Presbyterian Church of the City of New York desires to send its salutations and greetings to the Seminary.

We recall the intimate relations between this Church and the Theological Seminary of Princeton in its establishment, and during the whole century of its existence.

As early as 1809 the first pastor of this Church, the Rev. Dr. John Brodhead Romeyn, was one of a committee appointed by the General Assembly, to which was referred an overture for the establishment of a Theological School, and which reported three plans, which were referred to the Presbyteries for their opinion and report at the next General Assembly.

On the replies from the Presbyteries the General Assembly of 1810, of which Dr. Romeyn was Moderator, resolved to proceed with the establishment of a Seminary, and appointed a committee, of which he was one, to prepare a plan to be reported to the next General Assembly. He was also appointed to solicit donations for the establishment and support of such Theological Seminary.

The Committee reported a plan which was adopted by the General Assembly of 1811, providing for the choice by the General Assembly of a Board of Directors consisting of twenty-one ministers and nine ruling elders, and Divie Bethune, one of the Elders of the Church, was appointed upon a Committee to confer with the Trustees of the College of New Jersey upon the establishment of the Seminary at Princeton.

When the General Assembly organized the Seminary in 1812, it chose Dr. Romeyn and two of our Elders, Divie Bethune and Zechariah Lewis, among its first Directors.

Eight of the nine Pastors of this Church have been among the Seminary Directors, and two of our Pastors have come to our Church from successful Professorships in the Seminary. During the whole century one or more of our Elders have been Directors of the Seminary, and ever since 1822, when its Trustees were incorporated, one or more of the members of our Session have been among its Trustees.

Members of our Church have provided large endowments for the Seminary, and as early as 1810 a Society was formed in our Church to provide aid and comfort for its students.

PRINCETON THEOLOGICAL SEMINARY

Descendants of the Rev. Dr. Archibald Alexander to the third and fourth generation have been members of our Church and congregation; of whom two became students of the Seminary and honored and useful ministers of the Presbyterian Church.

These things move us to felicitate the officers and Faculty of Princeton Theological Seminary upon the first century of its existence and fruitful experience, and to hope for it the continuance and increase of the favor and blessing of Almighty God, which has always crowned its days and made it a faithful minister to the Church of Christ in its onward march both at home and abroad.

By order of Session,

S. B. BROWNELL, *Clerk of Session.*
J. H. JOWETT, *Moderator.*

New York, May 9, 1912.

RESPONSES FROM THE BOARDS OF THE
GENERAL ASSEMBLY OF THE
PRESBYTERIAN CHURCH IN THE UNITED
STATES OF AMERICA

THE BOARD OF HOME MISSIONS

It gives me pleasure to inform you that the Board of Home Missions cordially accepts the invitation of Princeton Seminary to be represented at the approaching Centennial, and has appointed its Secretary, Rev. Charles L. Thompson, D.D., to that duty.

JOHN DIXON, *Clerk of the Board.*

March 15, 1912.

THE BOARD OF FOREIGN MISSIONS

I acknowledge herewith the receipt of the invitation of the Directors, Trustees and Faculty of the Seminary, to the Board of Foreign Missions of the Presbyterian Church in the U. S. A., to be represented on the occasion of the one hundredth anniversary of the establishment of the Seminary by the General Assembly, on May 5–7, 1912.

Our Board has duly appointed its President, the Rev. George Alexander, D.D., 47 University Place, N. Y. City, to represent them on that occasion.

STANLEY WHITE, *Secretary.*

March 7, 1912.

CENTENNIAL CELEBRATION OF

THE BOARD OF EDUCATION

The invitation of the Theological Seminary of the Presbyterian Church in the United States of America, Princeton, N. J., to the Presbyterian Board of Education to be represented by a delegate upon the celebration of the one hundredth anniversary of the establishment of the Seminary is accepted, and the Board has elected the Reverend Charles Wadsworth, Jr., D.D., as such representative.

I write this for the Board, in the absence of the Corresponding Secretary, Dr. Cochran.

RICHARD C. HUGHES, *Sec'y for University Work.*

February 20, 1912.

THE BOARD OF PUBLICATION AND SABBATH-SCHOOL WORK

At the meeting of the Board of Publication and Sabbath-School Work, held yesterday afternoon, I presented the invitation of the Theological Seminary at Princeton requesting the Board to appoint a delegate who would represent it at the celebration of the one hundredth anniversary of the Seminary.

The Board accepted the invitation, and elected the Hon. Robert N. Willson, 2226 Spruce Street, President of our Board, as its delegate. At the same time, it elected the Rev. Louis F. Benson, D.D., 2014 Delancey Street, to be the alternative, in case Judge Willson should be unable to attend.

With best wishes for the success of the coming celebration,
ALEXANDER HENRY, *Secretary.*

February 28th, 1912.

PRINCETON THEOLOGICAL SEMINARY

THE BOARD OF THE CHURCH ERECTION FUND

The communication of the Directors, Trustees and Faculty of the Seminary, inviting the Board of Church Erection to be represented on the occasion of the Seminary's One Hundredth Anniversary, was received by the Board at its monthly meeting yesterday.

I am instructed to return the thanks of the Board for this invitation, and to inform you that the Hon. Frederick Gordon Burnham, President of our Board, whose address is Morristown, N. J., was elected as the Board's representative.

D. J. McMILLAN, *Cor. Sec'y.*

Feb. 21, 1912.

THE BOARD OF RELIEF FOR DISABLED MINISTERS AND THE WIDOWS AND ORPHANS OF DECEASED MINISTERS

The Presbyterian Board of Relief for Disabled Ministers at its regular meeting May 2nd, 1912, appointed the following members of the Board as its representatives at the Centennial Celebration of Princeton Theological Seminary:

Rev. S. T. Lowrie, D.D., H. S. P. Nichols, Esq., Rev. Marcus A. Brownson, D.D., and Rev. William W. Heberton, D.D.

W. W. HEBERTON, *Rec. Secy.*

May 3rd, 1912.

RESPONSES FROM OTHER
ECCLESIASTICAL BODIES

THE GENERAL ASSEMBLY OF THE CHURCH OF SCOTLAND

To the President, Board of Trustees and Faculty of the Theological Seminary, Princeton, N. J., U. S. A.

The General Assembly of the Church of Scotland, having been informed by Principal Stewart of the communication which he had received from the Seminary intimating that the Seminary was to celebrate the first hundredth anniversary of its foundation in the beginning of the present month, and inviting this Church to be represented on the occasion, desires to acknowledge the kind intimation and invitation extended to it. Unfortunately no meeting of the Assembly, or of its Commission, took place between the receipt of the intimation, and the present meeting of Assembly. The Assembly has heard with pleasure the Report of Principal Stewart as to his visit to the Celebration at Princeton, and cordially endorses the kindly greetings which he gave in the name of the Church to the Members of the Seminary. The Assembly recalls with deep interest the remarkable history of Princeton Theological Seminary, and desires to express its earnest hope that the work of the Seminary may be long continued, that it may have much prosperity and that the blessing of God may rest upon it.

In the name of the General Assembly of the Church of Scotland,

S. MARCUS DILL, D.D., *Moderator.*

Edinburgh, May 29th, 1912.

CENTENNIAL CELEBRATION OF

THE GENERAL ASSEMBLY OF THE UNITED FREE CHURCH OF SCOTLAND

To the Members of the Faculty and Governing Board of Princeton Theological Seminary.

We, the Members of the Commission of the General Assembly of the United Free Church of Scotland, offer you our cordial congratulations upon the centenary of your Seminary.

Your School of Divinity has been greatly esteemed in our land, especially in the churches which now form the United Free Church of Scotland. In former days, you were in fraternal alliance with those who formed the United Presbyterian Church, and in 1843 those who severed their connection with the State to form the Free Church of Scotland found in Princeton generous and helpful friends. We are united today in gratefully acknowledging our indebtedness to the eminent Princeton Theologians of last century, and gladly embrace the opportunity of joining with you in honouring the men who, by their piety and their learning, have made Princeton famous throughout Christendom.

Your Church and ours have the same parentage, they have been nourished by the same doctrine, they equally prize the Spiritual Independence of Christ's Church, they have the same evangelical traditions, and the same conceptions of their mission at home and abroad.

Recognising that you are richly endowed with inspiring associations, we pray God that your School of the Prophets may continue to be the Alma Mater to an increasing band of consecrated and well instructed students, who will prove the devoted heralds of Jesus Christ in their native land and throughout the world.

Signed in name of the Commission of Assembly of the United Free Church of Scotland,

JAMES WELLS, D.D., *Moderator.*

THE GENERAL ASSEMBLY OF THE FREE CHURCH OF SCOTLAND

[SEAL]

The Moderator of the Free Church of Scotland most cordially thanks the Faculty of the Princeton Theological Seminary for the honour done to the Free Church in sending their kind invitation to take part in the celebration of the One Hundredth Anniversary of the Founding of their Seminary; herewith most gratefully recalling the help and encouragement so generously rendered by the Princeton Seminary to our Church in her arduous contendings for her spiritual independence during the Ten Years' Conflict.

The Free Church of Scotland most warmly congratulates the Presbyterian Church of the United States on the possession of its noble Theological Seminary at Princeton; venerable even in the earlier stadia of its career by association with the memory and achievement of such great men as Jonathan Dickinson, Jonathan Edwards, Samuel Davies, Gilbert Tennent, John Witherspoon, and Ashbel Green; whilst in these latter days it has attained world-wide renown by the massive learning of such illustrious divines as Archibald Alexander,

CENTENNIAL CELEBRATION OF

Samuel Miller, Charles Hodge, Addison Alexander, William Henry Green, and Archibald Alexander Hodge. The preservation of this glorious heritage from the past, in combination with a singular capacity to meet the exacting requirements of the present, evokes our liveliest admiration.

The Free Church of Scotland also offers its heartiest felicitations to the Princeton Seminary on its most efficient defence of the Scriptures of the Old and New Testament against the attacks of Modern Rationalism; meeting rash assertion by reasoned argument, crude speculation by exact scholarship, bold sophistry by calm demonstration; thus exhibiting the Higher Criticism as essentially a pretentious dogmatism of negation and omniscience. The great success which has ever attended the Princeton Seminary in the rearing of a learned and godly Ministry, renowned at home, revered abroad, likewise wins our sincerest regard. We earnestly pray that the Divine blessing may still rest upon the manifold labours of its eminent Professors and the varied studies of its numerous Alumni, so that in ever-increasing degree, it may be as "a fountain of gardens, a well of living waters, and streams from Lebanon."

Signed in the name of the General Assembly of the Free Church of Scotland,

WM. MENZIES ALEXANDER, *Moderator,*
M.A., B.Sc., M.D., B.D. (Glasgow University).

Assembly Hall, Edinburgh,
11th March, 1912.

PRINCETON THEOLOGICAL SEMINARY

THE SYNOD OF THE FREE PRESBYTERIAN CHURCH OF SCOTLAND

The Synod of the Free Presbyterian Church of Scotland beg to thank the Theological Seminary of the Presbyterian Church in the United States of America, at Princeton, New Jersey, for their courtesy in inviting the Rev. Duncan Mackenzie, Moderator of this Synod, to be present at the celebration of the One Hundredth Anniversary of the Founding of the Seminary, on the fifth, sixth, and seventh days of May of this year.

The Synod would take this opportunity of congratulating your Seminary on the completion of one hundred years of useful work. They rejoice to think that although the beginnings of your Institution were small in point of numbers, there is, at the present date, scarcely a better equipped Theological Faculty in the world than Princeton. The Synod bless the name of Christ, the adorable Head, that, for the edification of His Church at large, He has bestowed upon your Seminary during the whole course of its history such remarkable and gracious gifts. Your leading men have been examples of profound piety as well as indefatigable labours. From your Seminary has issued the noblest defence of the Calvinistic System of Theology which the world has seen within the period of your existence as a Faculty. The ablest vindication of the Oracles of God, as against the adverse criticism of the so-called Higher Critics, has been rendered by Princeton Professors. What noble memories cluster around the names of Dr. Archibald Alexander, Dr. Joseph Addison Alexander, Dr. Charles Hodge, Dr. William Henry Green in the several respects which have been named of gracious character and faithful work for Christ! The Synod rejoice to think that the existing Faculty of Theological Professors at Princeton is true to Princeton's past history, and that, without dissimulation, it may be said in gifts and graces you fall little short of your distinguished predecessors.

The Synod pray that the adorable Head of the Church may pour the benign influences of His Spirit more and more abundantly upon you, that in the future, as in the past, you may witness a good confession for God and His Word, and that when, God willing, Princeton shall hold its bi-centenary, the men of that future period may think as kindly of the men of 1912 as you now think of Dr. Archibald Alexander.

As the Moderator is unavoidably prevented from attending your celebrations, the Synod send these greetings by the hand of the Rev. John R. Mackay, M.A., one of their members, and a Teacher in Theology.

Signed in name and on behalf of the Synod of the Free Presbyterian Church of Scotland,

DUNCAN MACKENZIE, *Moderator,*
JAMES STEVEN SINCLAIR, *Clerk.*

April, 1912.

THE SYNOD OF THE PRESBYTERIAN CHURCH OF ENGLAND

[TELEGRAM]

On motion of Rev. Dr. Thornton, retiring Moderator, "The Synod of the Presbyterian Church of England, assembled in London, sends hearty greetings and con-

PRINCETON THEOLOGICAL SEMINARY

gratulations to Princeton Seminary, on attaining its 100th Anniversary, and prays that God may make the Institution a continued blessing to the Church of Christ in America, and throughout the world."

DAVID FOTHERINGHAM, J. P., *Moderator,*
WM. LEWIS ROBERTSON, M. A., *Clerk.*

May 7th, 1912.

THE GENERAL ASSEMBLY OF THE PRESBYTERIAN CHURCH IN IRELAND

[SEAL]

The Presbyterian Church in Ireland to the Rev. Francis L. Patton, D.D., LL.D., President of the Theological Seminary, Princeton, N. J., U. S. A.

Reverend and Dear Sir,

On the evening of 3rd June, at the inaugural meeting of the General Assembly of 1912, in the Assembly Hall, Belfast, the Moderator reported that in accordance with an invitation very kindly extended to him by the Faculty and Trustees of the Princeton Theological Seminary, he had attended and taken part in the Centennial Celebrations held at Princeton on 5th, 6th, and 7th May.

"It was unanimously agreed that a message—signed by the Moderator and Clerk—be sent to the President of the Princeton Theological Seminary, conveying the felicitations of the General Assembly in connection with the Centenary of the famous seat of sacred learning over which he presided, and its extreme gratification that the

CENTENNIAL CELEBRATION OF

Moderator had been able to attend and take part in the most impressive and successful Centennial Celebrations of last month."

We have therefore unusual pleasure in forwarding to you the foregoing minute from the records of the General Assembly; and in re-echoing the sentiments already expressed in person by the Moderator.

With best wishes for the continued and growing success of the Theological Seminary, which is so dear to our Church; and for the prosperity of the Church you chiefly and so conspicuously serve,

We remain, Reverend and Dear Sir,
faithfully and fraternally,
JOHN MACMILLAN, *Moderator,*
WM. JAMES LOWE, *Clerk.*

3rd June, 1912.

THE SYNOD OF BALLYMENA AND COLERAINE

At the annual meeting of the Synod of Ballymena and Coleraine, held on the 23rd of April, 1912, it was moved, seconded and unanimously agreed to, "That the Rev. David Russell Mitchell, of Broughshane, be appointed a deputy from this Synod, to attend the hundredth anniversary of the Princeton Theological Seminary, and to convey the cordial good wishes of the members of this Synod for the future prosperity of the Institution."

Extracted from the Minutes of the Synod this 23rd day of April, 1912, and signed,

CHARLES W. HUNTER, M.A., *Moderator,*
JAMES B. ARMOUR, M.A., *Clerk.*

PRINCETON THEOLOGICAL SEMINARY

THE DIOCESE OF NEW JERSEY OF THE PROTESTANT EPISCOPAL CHURCH

[TELEGRAM]

The diocese of New Jersey sends its greetings to the Princeton Seminary on the celebration of its 100th anniversary with a prayer for God's blessing upon the future life and work of the Seminary.

HOWARD E. THOMPSON, *Secretary.*

Mt. Holly, N. J., May 7, 1912.

RESPONSES FROM THE PRESIDING OFFICERS OF CHURCHES

MODERATOR OF THE GENERAL ASSEMBLY OF THE CHURCH OF SCOTLAND

Principal Stewart has much pleasure in accepting the invitation of the Theological Seminary of the Presbyterian Church in the United States of America at Princeton, New Jersey, to be present at the Celebration of the Hundredth Anniversary of the Foundation of the Seminary on 5th to 7th May next.

St. Mary's College, St. Andrews, Scotland.
28th February, 1912.

MODERATOR OF THE GENERAL ASSEMBLY OF THE UNITED FREE CHURCH OF SCOTLAND

Dr. Wells has special pleasure in accepting the kind invitation to the celebration of the One Hundredth Anniversary of the founding of the Princeton Seminary on the 5th, 6th and 7th of May 1912.

42 Aytoun Road, Pollokshields, Glasgow,
February, 26, 1912.

CENTENNIAL CELEBRATION OF

MODERATOR DESIGNATE OF THE GENERAL ASSEMBLY OF THE UNITED FREE CHURCH OF SCOTLAND

Will you please to convey to the Senatus of the Theological Seminary of Princeton my sincere thanks for their kind invitation to the Hundredth Anniversary of the Founding of their distinguished Seminary?

It would have afforded me the greatest pleasure had I been able to accept the invitation so generously extended to me, as I have for more than half a century been acquainted with the fame of Princeton; but my prospective election in May to the Moderatorship of the United Free Church of Scotland renders it undesirable that I should undertake a trip to America so near the day of opening the Assembly.

I recently attended the 50th Anniversary of the Founding of St. Andrews University, my Alma Mater, which was a splendid success; and I hope a like success will wait on your celebrations.

During the past century, Princeton has rendered invaluable service to Evangelical Theology; may her future be even more glorious than her past, and may she never want gifted sons who will publish and uphold the cause of Truth—the Gospel of the Glory of the Blessed God.

With every good wish and earnest prayer for the prosperity of Princeton,

I am,

Yours sincerely,

THOMAS WHITELAW.

Kilmarnock, 1 March, 1912.

PRINCETON THEOLOGICAL SEMINARY

MODERATOR OF THE GENERAL ASSEMBLY OF THE FREE CHURCH OF SCOTLAND

Your kind invitation has just reached me this afternoon and for it I thank you most warmly. I regret exceedingly that duties here in connection with the opening of our General Assembly on 21st May deprive me of the great honour and pleasure of being among your guests on this historic occasion. The Address from our Church will be presented by Principal M'Culloch who represents our College. We pray that every felicity and blessing may attend this august Centennial Celebration of your world-renowned Seminary.

I have the honour to be
    Yours most sincerely,

      WM. MENZIES ALEXANDER.

Free Church College, The Mound, Edinburgh, 27 April, 1912.

MODERATOR OF THE SYNOD OF THE FREE PRESBYTERIAN CHURCH OF SCOTLAND

I regret that, on account of the state of my health, I shall not be able to attend, on the 5th, 6th and 7th May next, the 100th anniversary of the Founding of Princeton Theological Seminary.

I trust you will be favoured with much blessing from on high in connection with the services, and that Princeton Theological Seminary will always remain faithful in all things to the glorious Head of the Church, and that, at all times, it will be wealthy in sending forth able men endued with power from on high to declare the whole counsel of God.

I shall ask the Canadian or Colonial Committee if they will send a representative.

Again wishing you the blessing of the Most High, I remain,

Revd. Dear Sir,
Yours sincerely,
DUNCAN MACKENZIE.

Strathearn House, Crieff, N. B.
13 March, 1912.

MODERATOR OF THE SYNOD OF THE REFORMED PRESBYTERIAN CHURCH OF SCOTLAND

I have to acknowledge with much heartiness and appreciation the most kind invitation I have received at your hands to the Centennial of the Princeton Seminary.

It would have been to me an unqualified pleasure had I been able to accept and be present on such an auspicious occasion.

The Princeton Theological Seminary has a name of rich savor and high honor in the Church of which I am a humble minister, and it would have been not only a great pleasure to myself, but an expression of our united veneration and esteem, had I been able to be present. I am sorry indeed, that I am not able to cross the Atlantic at this time.

PRINCETON THEOLOGICAL SEMINARY

Speaking for myself and my brethren I send you our cordial greetings and earnest wishes for abounding usefulness and prosperity.

Yours very sincerely,

JOHN MCDONALD.

R. P. Manse, Airdrie, 4 March, 1912.

MODERATOR OF THE SYNOD OF THE UNITED ORIGINAL SECEDERS

As I have just returned to India after furlough, I regret that I cannot accept your kind invitation to be present at the celebration of the One Hundredth Anniversary of the founding of the Princeton Theological Seminary.

Though unable to be present you may be assured of my best wishes for the occasion.

Very sincerely yours,

JOHN MCNEEL.

Seoni Chhapara, C. P., India,
21 March, 1912.

MODERATOR OF THE REFORMED PRESBYTERIAN SYNOD IN IRELAND

I regret it will not be possible for me to be present at the celebration of the 100th Anniversary of the founding of the Princeton Theological Seminary.

It has never been my privilege, either as a student of

Theology or as a Minister of the Gospel, to visit the College. But for a long time, I have known some of the Theological Professors by their writings, which I greatly admire, and from the study of which I have, I think, derived much profit.

My prayer is that God may use the Princeton Theological Seminary even more in the future than in the past, for the maintenance and defence of His truth, and for the extension of His Kingdom in the world.

I am,   Sincerely yours,

S. R. McNEILLY.

Bailiesmills Manse, Lisburn,
  30 April, 1912.

MODERATOR OF THE SYNOD OF THE PRESBYTERIAN CHURCH OF ENGLAND

I greatly appreciate the honor done me in giving me an invitation to attend your Centennial Celebration on 5th, 6th and 7th of May next.

As our English Presbyterian Synod will be in session in London at that time, I cannot, as its retiring Moderator, be absent. But I would like to propose that the Synod send you a cablegram of congratulation.

I am proud to think that my late father (Rev. R. Hill Thornton), of Oshawa, Ont., Canada, had the honorary degree of D.D. from your distinguished seat of learning. I also rejoice to think that my old fellow student, Francis L. Patton, D.D., is still with you.

R. M. THORNTON.

18, Hilldrop Road, Camden Road, N., London,
  3 March, 1912.

PRINCETON THEOLOGICAL SEMINARY

MODERATOR FOR 1901 OF THE GENERAL ASSEMBLY OF THE WELSH CALVINISTIC METHODIST CONNECTION

I thank you very much for your kind invitation to be present in the Centenary Celebration of the Princeton Seminary. But my departure from Liverpool is fixed for May 7th, and therefore too late for me to attend any of the Centenary meetings. I regret it very much, for nothing would afford me more genuine pleasure than to see and hear your eminent men on so important an occasion. The names of your professors, past and present, are well known to me, and the Princeton Review comes regularly to my home. All this makes me sincerely regret my inability to accept your kind invitation.

With fraternal regards,

Yours faithfully,

J. CYNDDYLAN JONES.

Whitechurch, Cardiff, March 21st, 1912.

MODERATOR OF THE GENERAL ASSEMBLY OF THE PRESBYTERIAN CHURCH IN CANADA

Your kind invitation to be present at the celebration of the One Hundredth Anniversary of the Theological Seminary has been received. It is an invitation of peculiar interest and I am hoping to make it possible to be with you. The Presbyterian Church in Canada owes much to Princeton. Many of our ministers received their theological training there, and we are now reaping the benefits of the type of theology and spiritual inspiration received there. I trust that all things will conspire to make it an occasion not only of much interest, but of special helpfulness as you enter upon a new century of your history.

I am, Yours sincerely,

R. P. MACKAY.

Toronto, February 27th, 1912.

MODERATOR OF THE GENERAL ASSEMBLY OF THE REFORMED PRESBYTERIAN CHURCH

An invitation to attend the One Hundredth Anniversary of the Founding of the Theological Seminary of the Presbyterian Church at Princeton, New Jersey, on May fifth to the seventh, reached me some time ago.

I have delayed replying in the hope of arranging my work so that I could attend; but in this my efforts have failed.

I must therefore deny myself a very enjoyable and profitable event, and thankfully decline your honoring invitation.

Congratulating you on what the Seminary has done during the first century of its existence, and praying that it may continue the good work until schools of the prophets are needed no more,

I am, Yours in sincerity,

SAMUEL G. SHAW.

West Hebron, N. Y., March 29, 1912.

PRINCETON THEOLOGICAL SEMINARY

PRESIDENT OF THE GENERAL SYNOD OF THE REFORMED CHURCH IN THE UNITED STATES

Many thanks for your kind invitation to the Centennial of Princeton Theological Seminary. I hope to be present on Monday and Tuesday.

Yours,

JAMES I. GOOD.

Philadelphia, March 9th, 1912.

PRESIDENT OF THE NORTHERN BAPTIST CONVENTION

I was very much interested in receiving the announcement of the Centennial Anniversary of the Princeton Seminary. I regret it will not be possible for me to attend.

Yours very truly,

EMORY W. HUNT.

April 13, 1912, Granville, Ohio.

MODERATOR OF THE NATIONAL COUNCIL OF CONGREGATIONAL CHURCHES

It will be a great pleasure to accept the appreciated honor of the invitation to the Centennial Celebration of Princeton Seminary, May 5–7th.

Yours very sincerely,

NEHEMIAH BOYNTON.

Brooklyn, N. Y., March 28, 1912.

CENTENNIAL CELEBRATION OF

PRESIDING BISHOP OF THE PROTESTANT EPISCOPAL CHURCH IN THE UNITED STATES

I beg to return my warm thanks for your courteous kindness in sending me an invitation to be present at the Centennial Anniversary of the founding of your Seminary.

I heartily wish I could come, but engagements of official duty will keep me here.

May I send to your Seminary my cordial congratulations upon reaching so great an age of dignity, and my earnest good wishes for years yet to come of prosperity and usefulness in your great work?

Faithfully and gratefully,
Your brother,
DANIEL G. TUTTLE,
Bishop of Missouri.

The Bishop's House, St. Louis, Mo.
March 1, 1912.

PRESIDENT OF THE GENERAL COUNCIL OF THE REFORMED EPISCOPAL CHURCH

I greatly appreciate the honor of the invitation to be present at the celebration of the One Hundredth Anniversary of the founding of the Seminary at Princeton, on Sunday, Monday and Tuesday, May 5th, 6th and 7th. It would give me very great pleasure indeed, to accept the invitation, but unfortunately the pressure of my many duties will prevent my attendance.

[112]

PRINCETON THEOLOGICAL SEMINARY

We all honor Princeton Seminary, and the noble men who have been identified with it.

Very sincerely yours,

SAMUEL FALLOWS.

Baltimore, Md., March 4, 1912.

PRESIDENT OF THE GENERAL SYNOD OF THE EVANGELICAL LUTHERAN CHURCH IN THE UNITED STATES OF AMERICA

I will, if possible, be present at the Centenary of the Theological Seminary at Princeton, May 5–7, to which you so kindly invite me.

Sincerely yours,

JUNIUS B. REMENSNYDER.

New York, N. Y., March 8, 1912.

PRESIDENT OF THE GENERAL COUNCIL OF THE EVANGELICAL LUTHERAN CHURCH IN NORTH AMERICA

To my regret, it will not be possible for me to attend the One Hundredth Anniversary of the Founding of the Theological Seminary of the Presbyterian Church in the United States at Princeton.

With hearty congratulations on the attainment of your centennial,

Believe me to be,

Very sincerely yours,

THEODORE E. SCHMAUCK.

Lebanon, Pennsylvania, March 5, 1912.

CENTENNIAL CELEBRATION OF

PRESIDENT OF THE EVANGELICAL LUTHERAN SYNOD OF NORTH AMERICA

Habe die freundliche Einladung, an der hundertjährigen Feier des theologischen Seminars Ihrer Kirche im Mai d. J. teilnehmen zu wollen, erhalten. Indem ich Ihnen für diese Einladung meinen herzlichen Dank ausspreche, muss ich Ihnen mitteilen, dass ich dieser Einladung nicht Folge leisten kann. Ich stehe jetzt im 88ten Lebensjahr und kann eine so weite Reise nach New Jersey nicht mehr unternehmen.

Ich wünsche Ihnen aber zu Ihrer Jubelfeier des Herrn reichsten Segen. Möge er sich auch in Zukunft zu dieser Ihrer Anstalt mit seiner Gnade bekennen, wie er es bisher gethan hat.

Mit freundlichem Gruss

Ihr

JOHANNES BADING.

Milwaukee, Wis., March 11, 1912.

PRESIDENT OF THE GERMAN EVANGELICAL SYNOD OF NORTH AMERICA

It is with profound gratitude that I acknowledge your kind and considerate invitation, to attend the Centennial of Theological Seminary, Princeton, N. J. The occasion truly is one at which representatives of all the branches of Christ's Church should gather to enunciate their warmest felicitations, to join in the praise of our God and Father, who, by His Blessings and Grace, has made Princeton historic, and to unite all prayers for that one great purpose, that the Kingdom of our Lord may be still more intensely furthered as Princeton enters upon the threshold of a new era, and that the future results of Princeton may be even greater than the past.

Indeed I am sorry that, when the gates of Princeton shall be opened to the festive throngs, I will be at my annual tours, visiting the nineteen District Conferences of the German Evangelical Synod of North America. The attendance upon these Conferences is simply obligatory.

But for the reason above stated, I desire the presence of a Representative of our Synod at your celebration. Therefore, I beg to be permitted to send an able substitute, namely, Rev. T. F. Bode, of St. Peter's Evangelical Church, Buffalo, N. Y., wishing to be shown to him all courtesies you would show me.

May the Triune God enrich you, and the celebrated Institution of Spiritual Science, by the manifold manifestation of His Holy Spirit.

With fraternal greetings in the love of Christ,

I am,

Yours,

JACOB PISTER.

Cincinnati, O., April 6th, 1912.

CENTENNIAL CELEBRATION OF

SECRETARY OF THE BOARD OF BISHOPS OF THE METHODIST EPISCOPAL CHURCH

I am in receipt of your very kind invitation to the celebration of the One Hundredth Anniversary of the Founding of the Seminary on May fifth, sixth and seventh, and greatly appreciate your courtesy. It would give me great pleasure to be present, but for the fact that the General Conference of our Church will, at that time, be in session in the City of Minneapolis, and it is expected that all our Bishops be in attendance.

I rejoice in the work which your Theological Seminary has accomplished during the past century, and pray that during the years to come, it may continue to send forth into all the fields, at home and abroad, those who shall defend the faith and publish to the world the Gospel of our Lord and Master.

Regretting that I cannot be with you, but trusting that the occasion may be one of pleasure and inspiration, I am, Very truly yours,

Philadelphia, Pa., April 10th, 1912. L. B. WILSON.

SENIOR BISHOP OF THE METHODIST EPISCOPAL CHURCH, SOUTH

The Reverend Bishop Alpheus W. Wilson regrets that his May engagements prevent his presence at the One Hundredth Anniversary of the Founding of Princeton. It would have given him pleasure to attend, if it had been possible.

Baltimore, Md.

PRINCETON THEOLOGICAL SEMINARY

CHAIRMAN OF THE CHRISTIAN UNION COMMISSION OF THE DISCIPLES OF CHRIST

I am honored with an invitation to the one hundredth anniversary of the Theological Seminary, at Princeton, and if possible, I shall be glad to accept the courtesy of your invitation. I have an important engagement at the University of Illinois the last of April, and at this writing, the exact date has not been settled. I hope if my April engagements run over into May, it will not be more than a day or two, so that I can be with you certainly on Monday or Tuesday, or may be both days.

I await your further advice.

Your servant in Jesus Christ,

Baltimore, Md., March 1, 1912. PETER AINSLIE.

PRESIDENT OF THE GENERAL CONFERENCE OF THE MENNONITE CHURCH OF NORTH AMERICA

I gratefully acknowledge the receipt of your kind invitation to the One Hundredth Anniversary of the Founding of the Theological Seminary of your Church, and it would, indeed, be a great pleasure to me to share with you and many others the blessings of this important occasion if circumstances did not prevent me from it. With my thoughts and prayers, I shall be one of your guests though, and I hope that the school will, under God's guidance and protection, prosper in the future as in the past.

With congratulations and best wishes,

Yours fraternally,

Hillsboro, Kan., March 25, 1912. H. D. PENNER.

RESPONSES FROM
FOREIGN DIVINITY FACULTIES

THE FACULTY OF DIVINITY OF THE UNIVERSITY OF EDINBURGH, SCOTLAND

To the Directors, Trustees and Faculty of the Princeton Theological Seminary.

The members of the Faculty of Divinity in the University of Edinburgh desire to send their most cordial greetings to the Princeton Theological Seminary on the celebration of the Hundredth Anniversary of its establishment by the General Assembly. They rejoice at the brilliant services which all during its history it has rendered in defence of the faith "once for all delivered to the saints," at the eminent names with which that history has been associated, at the lofty academic ideals which it has maintained, at the splendid equipment which it possesses for the training of candidates for the ministry in every branch of theological science and every department of ministerial work.

They pray that the blessing of God which has attended its work so richly in the past may abide upon it not less richly in the years to come, so that, in the new century of work on which it is entering, it may contribute in ever-increasing measure to the advance of truth and the promotion of the Kingdom of God.

In name and by authority of the Faculty of Divinity,

JOHN PATRICK, D.D., *Dean of the Faculty.*

March 1912.

CENTENNIAL CELEBRATION OF

THE FACULTY OF DIVINITY IN THE UNIVERSITY OF ABERDEEN, SCOTLAND

[SEAL]

To the Directors, Trustees and Faculty of the Theological Seminary at Princeton, New Jersey.

We the Dean, Secretary and Members of the Faculty of Divinity in the University of Aberdeen, gratefully acknowledge your courtesy in inviting us to send a representative of our Faculty to be present at the celebration of the Centenary of your far-famed Seminary. We deeply regret that no member of the Faculty finds it in his power to attend, but we have delegated the Reverend Professor John Macnaughton, B.A., of M'Gill University, Montreal, a distinguished Graduate of the University of Aberdeen, to represent us and to be the bearer of this Address.

Holding the same Reformed Faith as yourselves, adhering to the same Theological Standards and maintaining the same form of Church Government, we avail ourselves gladly of this opportunity to congratulate you on the noble service you have rendered to the cause of Christian Truth during the last hundred years. Whilst the distinctive type of theological scholarship which has come to be associated with Princeton has been conservative both in criticism and doctrine, we gratefully recognize that your Scholars have been ready to follow the guidance of the Spirit of Truth into new fields of Christian thought and service.

We are proud to recall that an illustrious President of Princeton College was a Scotsman descended from John

Knox, Dr. John Witherspoon; that Dr. James M'Cosh, a Scotsman with special ties to our University, was largely instrumental in giving expansion to the old Princeton College a generation ago; and that on the honoured roll of your past Teachers our Graduates have not been unrepresented.

On this auspicious occasion we are glad to acknowledge our deep indebtedness to the great Divines and Scholars who have rendered your Seminary eminent throughout the whole Christian world. The names of the Alexanders, the Hodges, of William Henry Green, and of Benjamin Breckinridge Warfield (still happily among you in intellectual vigour), are held in honour among us and in all the Churches of our country. Nor are we insensible of the impulse which has been given by Princeton to the noble cause of world-evangelization, and of the splendid labours of such men as Dr. Robert Elliott Speer who have carried the influence of Princeton over the seas to the older lands.

It is our heartfelt prayer that the usefulness and honour which have fallen to you in the century that has gone may be increased many fold in the century to which you look forward.

In name of the Faculty and by authority of the Senatus Academicus.

(Signed)   THOMAS NICOL, M.A., D.D., *Dean,*
   WILLIAM A. CURTIS, B.D., D.Litt.,
   Secretary.

At Aberdeen April, 1912.

CENTENNIAL CELEBRATION OF

NEW COLLEGE, EDINBURGH, SCOTLAND

To the Principal and Professors of Princeton Theological Faculty.

We greatly regret that it is impossible for us to accept your friendly invitation, and to commission one of our number to present our congratulations personally at your Celebrations. It would have been a privilege to visit scenes associated, as the Burgh and College of New Jersey are, with the names of George Washington and Jonathan Edwards and with the early political and religious history of your great Republic, and, especially, to join in your devout thanksgivings for the blessings which God has vouchsafed to you since the foundation of your Seminary in 1812. Both of the Churches which constitute the United Free Church of Scotland, while profiting from their fraternal relation with the Presbyterian Churches of America, have learned to hold in special honour theologians, pastors, and missionaries trained within your walls. At New College we gladly recall the fact that when in 1844, after the Disruption, Principal William Cunningham was dispatched by our General Assembly to investigate the working of the chief theological institutions in America, he spent many days as the guest of your eminent President, Dr. Charles Hodge, and formed intimate relations greatly valued by our College. Since that date a sense of brotherhood has been maintained by frequent intercourse and occasional interchange of students, which will, we venture to hope, not only continue but increase.

We recognise respectfully the contributions which have been made to the cause of sacred learning by the

PRINCETON THEOLOGICAL SEMINARY

members of your staff, and the value of the training which you give to students not only for the home ministry, but for the service of Christ in the mission field.

We trust that in the approaching celebrations you will be cheered and led forward by the assurance of the goodwill of other Seminaries, by the increased loyalty of your alumni, and by manifest tokens of the favouring presence of Almighty God.

With renewed fraternal greetings and congratulations, and with high regard,
We are,
Yours very faithfully,
ALEXANDER WHYTE, D.D., LL.D., *Principal,*
ALEXANDER MARTIN, D.D., *Secretary.*

2nd April, 1912.

THE UNITED FREE CHURCH COLLEGE, GLASGOW, SCOTLAND

I am instructed by the Secretary of this College to acknowledge gratefully the invitation of the Directors, Trustees and Faculty of Princeton Theological Seminary to send a delegate to their Centenary Celebration in May.

The Senatus, though unable to accept this honourable invitation, desire to join with the friends of the Christian faith and of Christian learning everywhere in offering to the representatives of Princeton Seminary their cordial and respectful congratulations on so interesting

an occasion. They are well aware of the distinguished service Princeton has rendered to the Church in the past, and wish for it a no less honourable future.
I am,
Ever yours sincerely,
JAMES DENNEY, *Clerk to Senatus.*
March 6, 1912.

THE UNITED FREE CHURCH COLLEGE AT ABERDEEN, SCOTLAND

To the Directors, Trustees and Faculty of Princeton Theological Seminary.

We, the members of the Senatus Academicus in the United Free College at Aberdeen, send hearty congratulations and brotherly greetings on the occasion of the one hundredth anniversary of the Institution.

In no place outside of America itself is Princeton more esteemed and loved than in Scotland. The names of her great teachers are household words amongst us, and their works are on the shelves of our manses.

We recall with pride the copious and priceless influences contributed for a hundred years to the growing life of a great nation by the Seminary, as well as the constant stream of men sent forth into the Foreign Mission field.

The perfection of the Seminary's equipment, while a monument to the Christian liberality of the Presbyterian Church, is a model for the schools of the prophets in the whole world.

Finally, it is our hope and prayer, that the benediction

of Heaven may rest on the Seminary in the future as it has done in the past, and that there may be constant expansion, to meet the necessities of the country and the opportunities afforded by Providence, while the ideal, expressed in the Plan of Foundation, is ever held fast— to unite with solid learning the piety of the heart.

JAMES IVERACH, D.D., *Principal,*
GEO. G. CAMERON, D.D., *Secretary,*
JAMES STALKER, D.D.,
DAVID S. CAIRNS, D.D.

28 March, 1912.

THE FREE CHURCH COLLEGE, EDINBURGH, SCOTLAND

[SEAL]

We, the Principal and Professors of the Free Church College, Edinburgh, desire very warmly to thank the Faculty of the Princeton Theological Seminary for their kind invitation to send a delegate to take part in the forthcoming celebration of the Centenary of the Founding of their Seminary.

In glad compliance with that invitation, the Senatus of this College have appointed the Rev. Principal M'Culloch as their representative, and herewith recall with pleasure and gratitude the fraternal relations existing of old between the Princeton Seminary and our Church. We recall more specially the congratulations sent by the New College, Edinburgh, to Dr. Hodge on the completion of his Systematic Theology, and to Dr. Green on the attainment of his professorial jubilee.

We also tender to the Princeton Seminary our heartiest felicitations on its long and prosperous career, so richly adorned at every stage by the ripe scholarship and exalted piety of its renowned divines; whilst the Princeton School of today, continuing the early tradition of unswerving fidelity to the Word of God and the Standards of the Reformed Church, has attained foremost rank by its valiant and victorious defence of the Scriptures of the Old and New Testaments against the assaults of the Higher Critics, as well as by its profound and refreshing exposition of the Calvinistic type of Theology in relation to modern thought, aspiration and necessity.

We likewise offer to the Princeton Seminary our sincerest congratulations on its splendid academic equipment, its brilliant staff of Professors, the number and excellence of its Students, and the sound evangelical spirit which pervades all its activities. We earnestly pray that the Divine blessing may rest yet more and more upon its Professors and Students, so that in ever-growing measure it may continue to be a centre of light and a tower of strength to all who love the Kingdom of our Lord.

  JAMES D. M'CULLOCH, *Principal,*
  WM. MENZIES ALEXANDER, M.A., B.Sc., M.D.,
            B.D., *Professor,*
  COLIN A. BANNATYNE, *Professor,*
  ROBERT MOORE, B.A., B.D., *Professor,*
  J. KENNEDY CAMERON, *Professor,*
  JOHN MACLEOD, M.A., *Professor.*

Free Church College, The Mound,
 Edinburgh, 12th March, 1912.

PRINCETON THEOLOGICAL SEMINARY

ASSEMBLY'S COLLEGE, BELFAST, IRELAND
[SEAL]

The Faculty of the Assembly's College, Belfast, Ireland, thanks the Directors, Trustees and Faculty of Princeton Theological Seminary for the honour of their invitation to send a delegate to the celebration of the one hundredth anniversary of the establishment of their Seminary.

The Faculty congratulates Princeton Seminary on its continued and increasing prosperity, and rejoices in the great work which it has done during the last hundred years in teaching, maintaining and defending the authority and inspiration of the Holy Scriptures and the pure doctrines of Evangelical Theology, and prays that God will continue to bless the Seminary by making it still more and more in the centuries yet to come a great spiritual and intellectual force in the promotion of the truth and righteousness of His everlasting Kingdom.

The Faculty regret that none of its members is able to go to Princeton, but they appoint as their delegate an alumnus of their College as well as of Princeton Seminary, the Rev. John MacMillan, D.D., the Moderator of the General Assembly of the Presbyterian Church in Ireland.

MATTHEW LEITCH, *President of Faculty.*

22d March, 1912.

CENTENNIAL CELEBRATION OF

M'CREA-MAGEE PRESBYTERIAN COLLEGE, LONDONDERRY, IRELAND

[SEAL]

The Trustees and Faculty of the Magee Presbyterian College, Londonderry, beg to thank the Directors, Trustees and Faculty of the Princeton Theological Seminary for their kind invitation to send a delegate to the Centenary Celebration of the Seminary on May fifth, sixth and seventh next, and to express their regret that they are unable to have the pleasure of accepting this invitation.

J. R. LEEBODY, D.Sc., *President of Faculty.*

March 16, 1912.

THE THEOLOGICAL FACULTY OF DUBLIN UNIVERSITY, IRELAND

I am requested by the Theological Faculty of Dublin University to thank cordially the Princeton Theological Seminary for their request to send a delegate to represent Dublin at the Princeton Centenary Celebration in May.

As that, however, is the busiest time of the year in our Divinity School, it will be quite impossible for us to send a delegate to Princeton.

We send fraternal greetings and hope that God's blessing may rest upon your proceedings, and prosper your subsequent Seminary life.

I am, Yours very truly,

NEWPORT J. D. WHITE,
Deputy Regius Professor of Divinity.

19 February, 1912.

PRINCETON THEOLOGICAL SEMINARY

THE FACULTY OF THEOLOGY, UNIVERSITY OF OXFORD, ENGLAND

I have received your kind invitation addressed to the Theological Faculty of the University of Oxford, and inviting them to be represented by a Delegate at your Meeting in May. I laid it before the Board of the Faculty, and they begged me to thank you for the honour of the invitation, but unluckily your Meeting comes in the middle of our Term, when it is quite impossible for anybody really representative of the Cause in Oxford to be absent from work. It seemed to them unreal to send anybody who did not come out of the heart of the life here, and therefore they find themselves forced to decline.

With many thanks, Believe me, Yours very truly,

R. S. HOLLAND,
March 15th, 1912.   *Regius Professor of Divinity.*

THE FACULTY OF DIVINITY, UNIVERSITY OF CAMBRIDGE, ENGLAND

The Professors of Divinity in the University of Cambridge beg leave to thank the Theological Seminary at Princeton, New Jersey, for the invitation to send a delegate to be present at the 100th anniversary of the establishment of this Seminary. They regret that as the anniversary falls in May, when full term is being kept at Cambridge, they are unable to avail themselves of this kind offer.

H. B. SWETE, *Regius Professor of Divinity.*
17 February, 1912.

CENTENNIAL CELEBRATION OF

THE THEOLOGICAL FACULTY IN THE UNIVERSITY OF DURHAM, ENGLAND

On behalf of the Theological Faculty in the University of Durham, I am desired to express our best wishes to the Theological Seminary of the Presbyterian Church, Princeton, New Jersey, on the occasion of their one hundredth anniversary. We had appointed a delegate to represent us, the Right Reverend, the Bishop of Massachusetts, but he was unfortunately unable to act for us, and we had no time out of term to appoint anyone in his place.

With our renewed good wishes for the continuous success of a Seminary to which we owe so much, believe us,

Yours very truly,

R. J. KNOWLING, D.D., *Dean of the Faculty, Professor of Divinity and Canon of Durham.*

May 2, 1912.

THE FACULTY OF THEOLOGY, UNIVERSITY OF LONDON, KING'S COLLEGE

I beg to inform you that the Council at their meeting this week resolved to appoint the Rt. Rev. Bishop Courtney, Rector of St. James, New York, as their representative at the one hundredth anniversary of the establishment of the Theological Seminary of the Presbyterian Church in the United States of America at Princeton, New Jersey.

We are writing to the Bishop asking him if he would be able to represent the College on the occasion.

Yours faithfully,

March 7th, 1912. WALTER SMITH, *Secretary.*

PRINCETON THEOLOGICAL SEMINARY

THE FACULTY OF THEOLOGY, UNIVERSITY OF LONDON

I have to inform you that the Establishment and General Purposes Committee of the Senate, at their last meeting, had under consideration the invitation of the Directors, Trustees and Faculty of the Princeton Theological Seminary to appoint a delegate to represent the Faculty of Theology of this University on the occasion of the celebration of the one hundredth anniversary of the establishment of the Seminary, to be held in Princeton, New Jersey, on May 5th, 6th and 7th, 1912.

With reference thereto, the Committee have directed me to thank you for the invitation and to express their regret that it has not been possible to find a delegate able to leave this country at the time mentioned.

I am further to convey to you the warmest wishes of the Committee for the continued prosperity of your Seminary. I have the honour to be, Sir,

Your most obedient Servant,

March 22nd, 1912. HENRY A. MIERS, *Principal*.

WESTMINSTER COLLEGE, CAMBRIDGE, ENGLAND

The Senatus of Westminster College, being prevented by the exigencies of the present term and the breadth of the Atlantic from accepting the invitation to appear by delegate at the celebration of the centenary of Princeton Theological Seminary, can but send their greetings and good wishes by the imperfect medium of writing. Only one of our number has ever had the honour of being within your precincts, but we all know that you are the most frequented of Presbyterian Colleges among the English-speaking race, that you have had teachers famous on both sides the Atlantic, that your alumni have taken a large and honourable part in shaping the religious life of America, and that your present is worthy of your past. We offer you our heartiest congratulations on your achievement, and express our hopes of still greater things that God may have in store for you in the time to come.

Would that we, the sole Presbyterian Theological College in all England, could anticipate for ourselves a like position and influence; but we trust at least that God has still larger truth in store for us both, that our service will not fail to meet the perplexities of our time and the vast social and religious problems which are much alike in the New World and the Old, and that, as God measures our real influence for truth and godliness, we shall, through His blessing, have good success.

JOHN SKINNER, D.D., *Principal,*
JOHN GIBB, D.D., *Professor,*
[Seal] JOHN OMAN, D.PHIL., D.D., *Professor,*
April, 1912 C. ANDERSON SCOTT, D.D., *Professor.*

NEW COLLEGE AND HACKNEY COLLEGE, LONDON

The Joint Theological Faculty of New and Hackney Colleges, Hampstead, London, desire to thank the Theological Seminary of Princeton, New Jersey, for the honour of an invitation to its Centenary festival in May. It is a matter of great regret to us that circumstances

PRINCETON THEOLOGICAL SEMINARY

do not allow us to send a personal representative to an occasion so happy and distinguished.

But we beg that we may not be denied the privilege of being heard among the many congratulations from the realms both of sound learning and true piety.

We remember the high tradition and the famous men that have made the name of Princeton familiar to the world and precious to the Church as a seat of sacred letters and Godly discipline.

We welcome the opportunity of rejoicing in the joy of a sister Communion; and of recognising that the Churches of the Gospel are members one of another.

We, further, hail an occasion of expressing the unity of two nations which are one in blood and speech, one in a long common history, and one in the culture that makes the nations members of Humanity.

And we pray that, as Princeton is beautiful for situation, so also it may continue to be rich in Christ's Wisdom and Knowledge, and powerful for the world purposes of the Eternal Spirit.

ALFRED E. GARVIE, M.A., D.D.,
Principal of New College.
P. T. FORSYTH, M.A., D.D.,
Principal of Hackney College.
WM. H. BENNETT, D.D., Litt.D.
HERBERT T. ANDREWS, B.A.
HERBERT HAYES SCULLARD, M.A., D.D.

MANSFIELD COLLEGE, OXFORD, ENGLAND

I write on behalf of the Professors and Tutors of Mansfield College to thank you for the invitation you have conveyed to us to be represented at the Centenary

Celebrations of Princeton Seminary. It is a matter of great regret to us that as the date falls in our working term we are unable to send a delegate. At the same time I am instructed to convey to you our warmest congratulations on the occasion and our good wishes for the future.
I am,
Yours faithfully,
March 19, 1912.   W. B. SELBIE, *Principal.*

BAPTIST COLLEGE, REGENT'S PARK, N. W., LONDON

The members of the Theological Faculty of the Baptist College, at Regent's Park, London, send cordial congratulations to the Theological Seminary of the Presbyterian Church at Princeton, New Jersey, and express their regret that they cannot avail themselves of its invitation to send a representative to attend the Centenary Celebration to be held in May next.

February 20, 1912.

MANCHESTER COLLEGE, OXFORD, ENGLAND

We are much honoured by the invitation of the Directors, Trustees and Faculty of your Seminary to take part in the Centenary Celebration of its foundation next May. I greatly regret that we can none of us avail ourselves of the opportunity to meet the many distinguished scholars who will be then assembled, and enjoy the hospitality of your famous School. Our philosophical lecturer, the Rev. L. P. Jacks, M.A., is to visit your country this spring; but he informs me to-day that he cannot

PRINCETON THEOLOGICAL SEMINARY

leave here till May 7th, and we must consequently forego the pleasure of being represented at your gathering.

With best wishes for the success of your gathering, and the future prosperity of your Seminary, believe me,

Very faithfully yours,

J. ESTLIN CARPENTER, *Principal.*

February 28th, 1912.

ST. DAVIDS COLLEGE, LAMPETER, WALES

I am sorry it is impossible at the date you mention for us to send a representative of this College to join in the celebration of the one hundredth anniversary of your establishment.

But I am requested to convey to you our congratulations, and to express the hope that your gathering may be in every way successful and that your work may go on successfully in the future.

Yours faithfully,

March 1, 1912. LL. J. M. BEBB, *Principal.*

THE THEOLOGICAL FACULTY OF THE UNIVERSITY OF AMSTERDAM, NETHERLANDS

De Theologische faculteit der gemeentelijke Universiteit te Amsterdam ontving met groote belangstelling Uwe mededeeling betreffende de viering van het honderdjarig bestaan van het Theologisch Seminarie te Princeton, New Jersey, en is zeer erkentelijk voor de vriendelijke uitnoodiging aan haar gericht om zich daarbij te doen vertegenwoordigen. Deze uitnoodiging op hoogen prijs stellende, ziet de Theologische faculteit der stede-

CENTENNIAL CELEBRATION OF

lijke Universiteit van Amsterdam zich tot haar leedwezen verplicht U mede te deelen dat zij zich niet zal kunne doen vertegenwoordigen bij gelegenheid der feestviering van Uw Seminarie. Zij volgt evenwel met levendige en begrijpelijke belangstelling deze Uwe feestviering en wenscht U toe dat de tweede nu aanbrekende eeuw van het bestaan van Uw Seminarie van niet minder activiteit en vruchtbaarheid op het terrein der theologische studie moge getuigen dan dit in de eerste eeuw van het bestaan van Uw Seminarie het geval heeft mogen zijn. Moge Uw Seminarie zich voortdurend verheugen in toenemenden bloei en Gods zegen rijkelijk rusten op den arbeid van allen die er aan werkzaam zijn.

De theologische faculteit van de gemeentelijke Universiteit van Amsterdam.

Maart 1912.   D. E. J. VÖLTER, *voorz. Her.*

THE THEOLOGICAL FACULTY OF THE UNIVERSITY OF GRONINGEN, NETHERLANDS

The Theological Faculty of the University of Groningen, greatly honoured by your invitation for the hundredth Anniversary of your establishment, feels obliged to answer that it did not succeed in finding a delegate for the occasion. Nevertheless the Faculty expresses its best wishes for the success of the festival and the future welfare of the Seminary.

The Theological Faculty of Groningen,

C. D. VAN RHIJN, *President.*
H. U. MEYBOOM, *Secretary.*

February 27th, 1912.

PRINCETON THEOLOGICAL SEMINARY

THE THEOLOGICAL FACULTY OF THE UNIVERSITY OF LEIDEN, NETHERLANDS

To the Theological Seminary of the Presbyterian Church in the United States of America, at Princeton, New Jersey.

The theological Faculty of the University of Leiden regrets that it is impossible for it to accept the invitation of the Directors, Trustees and Faculty to send a representative to the celebration of the one hundredth anniversary of the foundation of the Theological Seminary at Princeton by the General Assembly of the Presbyterian Church in the United States of America.

The members of the Faculty and the Ecclesiastical Professors associated with them desire to express their sincere congratulations on the long and valuable services which the Theological Seminary has been enabled to render to the education of ministers in the Presbyterian Church, to the deepening and broadening of the spiritual life of the citizens of the United States, and to the cause of learning in all countries of the world. They hope that the second century of life on which the Seminary is now entering may be as distinguished in enterprise and as brilliant in achievement as the hundred years which have now been brought to so honourable a close.

B. D. EERDMANS, *President*.
KIRSOPP LAKE, *Secretary*.

Leiden, 27 February, 1912.

[SEAL]

CENTENNIAL CELEBRATION OF

THE THEOLOGICAL FACULTY OF THE UNIVERSITY OF UTRECHT, NETHERLANDS

Seminarii Theologici, quod Ecclesiae Presbyterianae in oppido Princetone est, Curatoribus Professoribus Doctoribus S. P. D. Facultas Theologica Universitatis Ultraiectinae.

Propter Seminarii Vestri dignitatem et doctrinae celebritatem eximiam cum magnopere optaremur ut nobis contingeret, Viri Amplissimi Clarissimi Doctissimi, Vos praesentes compellare, hanc nobis felicitatem negavit adversitas temporis, quoniam causae multae ac variae impediebant ne quis nostrum mense Maio legatus ad Vos proficisceretur.

Ergo quod praesentibus non licet, per hasce litteras facimus ut Vobis, Viri Amplissimi Clarissimi Doctissimi, centesimum natalem Vestri Seminarii ex animi sententia gratulemur. Ut saeculum alterum quod iam instat Deus O. M. Vobis fortunet toto pectore nos precari scitote.

Quod nos amicos hospitesque gaudiis Vestris caeremoniisque interesse voluistis, Vobis debitas agimus gratias.

Denique ita Deus O. M. Vos omni bonorum fortunarumque genere cumulet, ut Vos ipsi, quos propter insignem humanitatem, doctrinam, virtutem magni facimus, eximia Vestra benevolentia nos dignari voluistis.

H. VISSCHER, *Dr. Theol.*
ord. h. t. pr.
J. A. C. VAN LEEUWEN, *Dr. Theol.*
ord. h. t. ab-actis.

Dabamus Traiecti ad Rhenum
Id. April. a. MCMXII.

THE THEOLOGICAL SEMINARY OF THE DUTCH REFORMED CHURCH, STELLENBOSCH, SOUTH AFRICA

The Professors of the Theological Seminary of the D. R. Church, at Stellenbosch, wish to express their appreciation of your kind invitation to be represented by a delegate at the celebration of the one hundredth anniversary of the establishment of your Seminary.

They regret that it will not be possible for them to participate in the celebration of an event, which has proved such a rich blessing to the Presbyterian Church in America and such a power for good in the development of religion and theological thought, and they earnestly pray that your Seminary may ever by divine grace be enabled to uphold the glorious traditions of the past.

I have the honor to be,

Yours in our common Lord and Saviour,

A. MOORREES,
Scriba of the Faculty.

March 20, 1912.

THE THEOLOGICAL FACULTY OF THE UNIVERSITY OF COPENHAGEN, DENMARK

The Theological Faculty of the University of Copenhagen sends its cordial thanks to the Theological Seminary of the Presbyterian Church in the United States of America at Princeton, New Jersey, for the invitation

CENTENNIAL CELEBRATION OF

to be represented by a delegate at the centennial anniversary but regrets being unable to accept the invitation. We express our best wishes for the future of the Seminary.

J. P. BANG, *Decanus.*

April 4, 1912.

THE THEOLOGICAL FACULTY OF THE UNIVERSITY OF CHRISTIANIA, NORWAY

[SEAL]

The Theological Faculty of the University of Norway acknowledges with thanks the invitation to name a delegate to represent her at the Celebration of the one hundredth Anniversary of the Theological Seminary of the Presbyterian Church, Princeton, New Jersey, on the 5th, 6th and 7th of May, this year.

Our Faculty heartily congratulates the Theological Seminary upon one hundred years of glorious history, but regrets being unable to send a delegate to this important Celebration.

ANDREAS BRANTRUD, *Dean.*
S. SVERDRUP, *Secretary.*

April 4, 1912.

THE THEOLOGICAL FACULTY OF THE UNIVERSITY OF HELSINGFORS, FINLAND

On behalf of the Theological Faculty of the University of Helsingfors, I beg to acknowledge your kind invitation to the celebration of the one hundredth anniversary of the Theological Seminary at Princeton, New Jersey, and to thank you most cordially for it.

It is with very great regret that we are compelled to refuse the invitation, as we have no opportunity of sending a delegate to represent us on that occasion.

Believe me,
            Yours faithfully,

                    G. G. ROSENQVIST, *Dean.*

March 13th, 1912.

THE THEOLOGICAL FACULTY OF THE UNIVERSITY OF BERLIN, GERMANY

Dem theologischen Seminar zu Princeton, New Jersey, entbietet die Theologische Fakultät zu Berlin ihre wärmsten Grüsse. Indem wir für die so freundliche Einladung zu Ihrem Jubelfest unseren ehrerbietigen Dank aussprechen, bedauern wir zugleich lebhaft keinen Delegirten senden zu können, da wir ja Ende April unsere Semesterarbeit wieder aufnehmen müssen. Aber es ist uns ein aufrichtigsters Bedürfnis mit unseren aus warmen Herzen kommenden Segenswünschen bei Ihrem Fest vertreten zu sein.

Von Anfang an hat Ihre Kirchengemeinschaft Gewicht gelegt auf die umfassende wissenschaftliche Ausrüstung der Geistlichkeit. Aus dieser Tendenz ist auch das Theologische Seminar zu Princeton hervorgegangen und es hat ihr gedient nun ein Jahrhundert über in ernster und hingebender Arbeit. Hundert Jahre sind es auch her, dass unsere Berliner Theologische Fakultät zu demselben Zweck tätig gewesen ist und schon in unseren Anfängen ist einer der Ihrigen Charles Hodge, der für Ihre Sache dann so grosse Bedeutung gewonnen hat, unser Gast gewesen. Aber an einem hohen Fest, wie Sie es begehen, denkt man nicht nur der Beziehungen der einzelnen Personen, sondern vor allem empfängt man das starke Bewusstsein der Zusammengehörigkeit im Rückblick auf die gemeinsamen Aufgaben, die uns zu lösen übertragen waren. Es galt Ihnen wie uns um die Wahrheit ringen und mit ihr die junge Mannschaft auszurüsten, die in die heiligen Kriege des himmlischen Herrn ausziehen sollten. Aus solcher Gemeinschaft der höchsten Aufgaben hervor rufen wir Ihnen von Herzen den Wunsch zu, dass Sie das Banner unseres himmlischen Herrn Jesus Christus auch weiterhin in ungeschwächter Freudigkeit festhalten mögen und dass Gott in Gnaden die Kirche und ihre künftigen Diener auch in Ihrer Gemeinschaft um dies Banner sammeln möge!

Mit dem nochmaligen Ausdruck der wärmsten Segenswünsche zu Ihrem Jubiläum,

Die theologische Fakultät zu Berlin

DR. REINHOLD SEEBERG,
Dekan.

15. April 1912.

THE CATHOLIC THEOLOGICAL FACULTY OF THE UNIVERSITY OF BONN, GERMANY

Dem hochgeehrten Theologischen Seminar zu Princeton beehrt sich der Dekan der katholisch-theologischen Fakultät zu Bonn für die Einladung zum hundertjährigen Jubilaeum am 5. bis 7. Mai 1912 den geziemenden Dank auszusprechen. Damit verbinde ich meine herzlichste Gratulation zur ehrwürdigen Gedenkfeier und den innigen Wunsch, dass das Theologische Seminar auch im zweiten Saeculum seines Bestehens für Gott, Vaterland und Wissenschaft arbeiten und herrliche Erfolge erzielen möge.

In ausgezeichneter Hochschätzung
          ergebenst

                    FELDMANN, *Dekan.*

28. April 1912.

THE ROYAL LYCEUM OF BRAUNSBERG, GERMANY

[TELEGRAM]

Herzlichen Glückwunsch.

          THEOLOGISCHE FAKULTÄT BRAUNSBERG.

May 5, 1912.

CENTENNIAL CELEBRATION OF

THE THEOLOGICAL FACULTY OF THE UNIVERSITY OF ERLANGEN, GERMANY

Für Ihre gütige Einladung zur Jubelfeier sagen wir herzlichen Dank. Da diese Feier in den Anfang unserer Semesterarbeit fällt, so mussten wir aus Rücksicht auf unsre Berufspflichten es uns versagen, einen Abgeordneten zu diesem Feste zu entsenden. Gerne aber und von Herzen bringen wir Ihnen warme Glückwünsche dar. Mit Befriedigung blicken Sie auf ein Jahrhundert treuer und erspriesslicher Arbeit zurück. Möchte es Ihnen gegönnt sein, im Dienst Ihrer Kirche und des gemeinsamen Herrn der Kirche fruchtbar weiterzuwirken für den christlichen Glauben und seine Geltung innerhalb der weiten Menschheit!

Hochachtungsvollst u. ergebenst
Theologische Fakultät der Universität Erlangen

D. BACHMANN,
z. Z. Dekan.

1. April 1912.

THE THEOLOGICAL FACULTY OF THE UNIVERSITY OF FREIBURG i. B., GERMANY

Die theologische Fakultät der Universität zu Freiburg i. B., Deutsches Reich, ist durch die berufliche Tätigkeit verhindert, die Hundertjahrfeier Ihres theologischen Seminars durch einen Vertreter aus ihrer Mitte zu beschicken.

PRINCETON THEOLOGICAL SEMINARY

Sie dankt verbindlichst für die ehrenvolle Einladung und wünscht, dass die Feier der Wissenschaft zum Segen gereichen möge.

Im Geiste, der Zeugnis gibt, dass Christus die Wahrheit ist, [1 Joh. 5, 6]

Hochachtend

Dr. Simon Weber,
d. zt. Dekan.

8. März 1912.

THE THEOLOGICAL FACULTY OF THE ROYAL BAVARIAN LYCEUM, FREISING, GERMANY

Wir danken den Rev. Herren Kollegen für die gütige Einladung zur Säkularfeier Ihres Bestehens und Wirkens und indem wir bedauern, dass es uns nicht möglich war, einen Vertreter zu delegieren, wünschen wir den Rev. Herren Kollegen noch viele Jahrhunderte erspriesslichen segensreichen Wirkens.

Im Auftrag der theologischen Abteilung des Kgl. Bayr. Lyzeums Freising:

D. Dr. Joseph Schlecht,
p. t. Rektor.

7. Mai 1912.

[SEAL]

CENTENNIAL CELEBRATION OF

THE THEOLOGICAL FACULTY OF THE UNIVERSITY OF GIESSEN, GERMANY

Im Namen und Auftrag meiner Herren Kollegen danke ich verbindlichst für die uns freundlich zugesandte Einladung zur Jubelfeier des Seminars. Wir sind leider verhindert, einen Vertreter zu dieser Feier zu senden, gedenken aber des Seminars, dem wir uns auch auf dem Gebiet der wissenschaftlichen Arbeit verbunden und verpflichtet fühlen, mit treuen Segenswünschen.

DR. GUSTAV KRÜGER,
derzeit. Dekan.

24. 2. 12.

THE THEOLOGICAL FACULTY OF THE UNIVERSITY OF GÖTTINGEN, GERMANY

Sagen wir für die liebenswürdige Einladung zur Jahrhundertfeier Ihres theologischen Seminars unsern verbindlichen Dank. Es ist uns leider nicht möglich, einen Abgeordneten zu Ihrem Feste zu senden, aber wir geben dem Wunsche Ausdruck, dass das Seminar auch im kommenden Jahrhundert sich als Pflanzstätte charaktervoller Frömmigkeit, als theologische Bildungsstätte und als Bollwerk theologischer wissenschaftlicher Arbeit bewähren möge.

Die theologische Fakultät

TITIUS.

15. März 1912.

PRINCETON THEOLOGICAL SEMINARY

THE THEOLOGICAL FACULTY OF THE UNIVERSITY OF HALLE-WITTENBERG, GERMANY

Dem Theological Seminary in Princeton N. J. sende ich zu seiner Hundertjahrfeier den herzlichen Glückwunsch unserer Fakultät leider zu spät. Eine schwere Erkrankung unseres gegenwärtigen Dekans bitte ich als Entschuldigung dieser Versäumnis gelten zu lassen.

Das Princeton-Theological-Seminary kann mit dankbarer Freude zurückblicken auf die 100 Jahre seit 1812. Nicht mehr als neun Studenten sammelten sich 1812 um den ersten und einzigen Professor, Dr. Archibald Alexander. Hunderte von Studenten sind seitdem durch das Seminar gegangen; und die jetzige Zahl der Studenten wird das Zwanzigfache der Anfangzeit sein. Das Seminar hat in den hundert Jahren, auf die es jetzt zurücksieht, der presbyterianischen Kirche wertvolle Dienste geleistet. Und manche Professoren haben in dem Jahrhundert an dem Seminar gewirkt, deren Gedächtnis noch heute in Ehren steht.

Möge das neue Jahrhundert, das dem Seminar begonnen hat, seine gesegnete Wirksamkeit ihm erhalten und sie steigern—zum Besten der presbyterianischen Kirche und zur Ehre dessen, dem alle theologische Arbeit dienen soll!

In hochachtungsvoller Begrüssung
ergebenst

D. FRIEDRICH LOOFS,
Prodekan.

29. April 1912.

CENTENNIAL CELEBRATION OF

THE THEOLOGICAL FACULTY OF THE UNIVERSITY OF HEIDELBERG, GERMANY

Die Theologische Fakultät der Universität Heidelberg spricht ihren ganz ergebenen Dank aus für die freundliche und ehrenvolle Einladung zum Jubiläum Ihres Seminars. Wir bedauern lebhaft, dass die Arbeit des Semesters keinem unsrer Professoren gestatten wird, an Ihrem Feste teilzunehmen. Um so mehr haben wir den Wunsch, Ihnen auszusprechen, dass wir an der Freude und dem Ernste, mit denen Sie Ihre Feier begehen werden, von Herzen teilnehmen.

Wir wissen uns mit Ihnen einig in der Ueberzeugung, dass das Evangelium der Gegenwart ebenso unentbehrlich ist wie der Vergangenheit, dass es aber seine Aufgabe an der heutigen Welt nur erfüllen kann, wenn es mit allen edlen Bestrebungen der Wahrheitserkenntnis mit verbindet.

Wir sind mit Ihnen überzeugt, dass theologische Arbeit lauterstes Wahrheitsstreben aber auch tiefsten sittlichen und religiösen Ernst zur Voraussetzung hat.

Wir glauben und hoffen mit Ihnen, dass es der Theologie gelingen möge, immer mehr zu solchen Ergebnissen zu gelangen, die ein Gemeingut aller Theologen und, wenn Gott will, auch aller Christen werden können.

In diesem Sinne reichen wir Ihnen die Hand mit den wärmsten Segenswünschen für Ihre Arbeit.

Im Auftrage der Theologischen Fakultät

D. JOHANNES WEISS
h. t. decanus

13. April 1912.

PRINCETON THEOLOGICAL SEMINARY

THE THEOLOGICAL FACULTY OF THE UNIVERSITY OF JENA, GERMANY

Dem hochwürdigen Vorstande und Professorencollegium des Theologischen Seminars zu Princeton, New Jersey, spricht die Theologische Fakultät zu Jena verbindlichsten Dank aus für die Mitteilung über die am 5.–7. Mai 1912 stattfindende Saecularfeier des Seminars und für die freundliche Einladung, einen Vertreter zur Teilnahme an dieser Feier zu senden. Leider ist es wegen der weiten Entfernung nicht möglich, dieser Einladung zu entsprechen. Aber die Theologische Fakultät zu Jena sendet dem Theologischen Seminare zu Princeton ihre herzlichsten Glück- und Segenswünsche zu der bevorstehenden Saecularfeier. Mögen dem Seminare noch viele Jahrhunderte erfolgreichen Wirkens im Dienste der christlichen Theologie und Kirche beschieden sein!

Die Theologische Fakultät der Universität Jena.

D. H. H. WENDT,

5. März 1912. *z. Z. Dekan.*

THE THEOLOGICAL FACULTY OF THE UNIVERSITY OF KÖNIGSBERG, GERMANY

Dem Theologischen Seminar von Princeton sendet die theologische Facultät von Königsberg zu dem glücklich vollendeten ersten Jahrhundert ihre herzlichen Glückwünsche.

Wie von Königsberg durch den kategorischen Imperativ Kants eine Erneuerung des sittlichen Bewusstseins in Deutschland erging, so hat der ernste und tapfere Geist des Presbyterianismus in Ihrer Facultät eine hervorragende Stätte seiner Betätigung gefunden. Männer von weithin bekannten Namen haben dem College von Princeton angehört und zu der Blüte desselben beigetragen.

Möge auch in dem neuen Jahrhundert das theologische Seminar von Princeton ein weithin leuchtendes Licht auf dem Berge sein, möge es den echten Geist theologischer Wissenschaft fort und fort pflegen, möge die enge Beziehung zwischen deutscher und amerikanischer Wissenschaft zum Segen beider Länder auch in dem neuen Saeculum, in das Ihr Seminar eintritt, ihre heilsamen Früchte zeitigen und der geistige Austausch diesseits und jenseits des Oceans eine stete gegenseitige Bereicherung hervorbringen.

Die theologische Facultät
der Albertus-Universität Königsberg

D. Dr. Dorner,
z. Z. Dekan.

März 1912.

[SEAL]

THE THEOLOGICAL FACULTY OF THE UNIVERSITY OF LEIPZIG, GERMANY

Für die uns zugekommene Einladung zur Feier Ihres hundertjährigen Jubiläums sagen wir Ihnen unsern verbindlichen Dank.

Ist es auch bei der grossen Entfernung zu unserem Bedauern nicht möglich, dass eines unserer Mitglieder

PRINCETON THEOLOGICAL SEMINARY

Ihnen persönlich unsere herzlichen Segenswünsche ausspricht, so nehmen wir doch nicht minder warmen Anteil an Ihrer Feier. Möge des Allmächtigen Gnade und Segen Sie und Ihre Arbeit ferner begleiten und möge es Ihnen auch in der Zukunft wie bisher vergönnt sein, der Kirche Christi und der Wissenschaft Männer heranzubilden, die beiden in gleichem Masse zur Ehre gereichen.
 In amtsbrüderlicher Verbundenheit
  Die theologische Fakultät Leipzig
   D. Rud. Kittel, z. Z. *Dekan.*
3. März 1912.

[SEAL]

THE THEOLOGICAL FACULTY OF THE UNIVERSITY OF MARBURG, GERMANY

Dem Theologischen Seminar in Princeton danken wir herzlich für die Einladung zu der Jahrhundertfeier am 5. 6. und 7. Mai. Zu unserm Bedauern ist es uns aus aüssern Gründen nicht möglich gewesen, uns durch einen Delegierten vertreten zu lassen. Aber wir nehmen auch in der Ferne aufrichtigen und herzlichen Anteil an der schönen Feier der nächsten Tage. Wir beglückwünschen das Seminar, dass es ihm durch Gottes Gnade vergönnt ist, auf diese lange Zeit reicher Arbeit zurückzublicken, und freuen uns des grossen Segens, dessen Quelle es für die Presbyterian Church gewesen ist. Herzlich wünschen wir, dass Gottes Gnade ferner über dem Seminar walte, es für die heimatliche Kirche zu einer unversieglichen Quelle des Segens mache und zu einer blühenden

CENTENNIAL CELEBRATION OF

Pflegstätte theologischer Wissenschaft, welcher der gesamte Protestantismus sich zu Dank verpflichtet weiss. Wir grüssen das Seminar im Namen und Geist Jesu Christi.

Die Theologische Fakultät der ältesten protestantischen Universität.

Der Dekan:

DR. THEOL. W. HEITMÜLLER.

27. April 1912.

THE THEOLOGICAL FACULTY OF THE UNIVERSITY OF MUNICH, GERMANY

Das theologische Seminar der Presbyterian Church in den Vereinigten Staaten von America zu Princeton New Jersey hat die theologische Fakultät der Universität München zur Teilnahme an der hundertjährigen Gedächtniss-Feier ihres Bestehens in edler collegialer Gesinnung eingeladen. Wir danken aufrichtig und herzlich für diese Aufmerksamkeit. Leider ist es uns nicht möglich, einen Delegierten dahin abzuordnen. Wir beglückwünschen das Seminar von ganzem Herzen zu der so schönen und erfreulichen und erhabenen Feier und wünschen zugleich, dass dasselbe für alle Zukunft wachse, blühe und gedeihe.

In aller Verehrung

PROF. DR. L. ATZBERGER,
z. Z. Dekan der theol. Fakultät.

26. April 1912.

PRINCETON THEOLOGICAL SEMINARY

THE EVANGELICAL THEOLOGICAL FACULTY OF THE UNIVERSITY OF STRASSBURG I. E., GERMANY

Der freundliche Einladung zu Ihrer Jahrhundertfeier vermag kein Mitglied unsrer Fakultät zu folgen. Auch abgesehen von der Grosse der Entfernung macht der Umstand, dass Ihr Fest in die Zeit des begonnenen Sommer-Semesters fällt, die persönliche Teilnahme eines der Unsere zu einer Unmöglichkeit. Aber wir dürfen versichern, dass wir in den Festtagen Ihrer nicht nur in Gemeinschaft des Geistes und des Glaubens gedenken werden, sondern auch Ihrer hohen Schule, Lehrenden wie Lernenden, zum Heile der theologischen Wissenschaft und zum Segen der evangelischen Kirche in der neuen Welt ein ferneres fröhliches Gedeihen von Herzen wünschen.

Persönlich begrüsst der Unterzeichnete noch mit besonderer Freude eine Arbeitsgenossenschaft, welche, wie er der Kirche Calvins zugehörig, auch für die Zukunft der Sache des Evangeliums die Güter zu erhalten strebt, die der Christenheit und insbesondere der Theologie, ja der allgemeinen Wohlfahrt und Weltkultur durch den Wahrheitsernst und die sittliche Zucht, durch die Standhaftigkeit und die Opfermut unsrer reformierten Glaubensväter erworben wurden.

Möge die gesegnete Stätte Ihrer Wirksamkeit bis in die fernsten Zeiten ein Licht bedeuten und weithin das stolze und kühne apostolische Bekenntnis verkündigen: "Unser Glaube ist der Sieg, der die Welt überwunden hat" [1 Joh. 5, 4].

CENTENNIAL CELEBRATION OF

Im Auftrage der evangelisch-theologischen Fakultät
der Kaiser-Wilhelms-Universität Strassburg:

DR. JULIUS SMEND, D.D.,
ordentlicher Professor der Theologie,
z. Zt. Dekan.

Am Tage des Edikts von Nantes,
den 13. April 1912.

[SEAL]

THE CATHOLIC THEOLOGICAL FACULTY OF THE UNIVERSITY OF STRASSBURG I. E., GERMANY

Der hohen Fakultät des theologischen Seminars der presbyterianischen Kirche d. V. St. spricht die katholisch-theologische Fakultät der Kaiser-Wilhelms-Universität zu Strassburg ihren ergebensten Dank aus für die gütige Einladung zur hundertjährigen Gedenkfeier. Leider haben die Verhältnisse unserer Fakultät es uns unmöglich gemacht, einen Abgesandten an der Feier teilnehmen zu lassen. So bitten wir, auf diesem Wege unsere Glückwünsche darbringen zu dürfen.

Die katholisch-theologische Fakultät

BÖCKENHOFF,
z. Z. Dekan.

25. April 1912.

[SEAL]

PRINCETON THEOLOGICAL SEMINARY

THE EVANGELICAL THEOLOGICAL FACULTY OF THE UNIVERSITY OF TÜBINGEN, GERMANY

Unsere Fakultät spricht für die Einladung zu der Hundertjahrfeier Ihres Seminars den verbindlichsten Dank aus. Da es keinem unserer Mitglieder möglich ist bei der Feier persönlich zu erscheinen, senden wir Ihnen die herzlichsten Glückwünsche aus der Gemeinschaft des evangelischen Glaubens und der Arbeit an der theologischen Jugend heraus.

Unsere Arbeit muss mit jedem Jahrgang Studierender neu anfangen, und jedes Geschlecht stellt unserer Wissenschaft neue Aufgaben der Abwehr, Neubegründung und neuer Begriffsbildung. Was uns die Sicherheit und die gewisse Hoffnung gibt bei dieser stets wechselnden Aufgabe, das ist die Zuversicht, dass unser Glaube in ewigem Grunde wurzelt, ein Gut über der Zeit, darum auch gemeinsames Band von Glaubensgenossen verschiedener Continente und Völker. In dieser Zuversicht grüssen wir und wünschen für das zweite Jahrhundert die Gnade des ewigen Gottes.

D. WURSTER,
Dekan der evang. theolog.
Fakultät Tübingen.

12. März 1912.

CENTENNIAL CELEBRATION OF

THE CATHOLIC THEOLOGICAL FACULTY OF THE UNIVERSITY OF TÜBINGEN, GERMANY

Die katholisch-theologische Fakultät wünscht dem Theologischen Seminar zu Princeton alles Gute zum hundertjährigen Jubiläum, vor allem einen glänzenden Verlauf der Festesfeier. Ihre Mitglieder sind leider verhindert, daran teilzunehmen.
                Mit vorzüglicher Hochachtung

RIESSLER,
Derzeit. Dekan.

26. Februar 1912.

[SEAL]

THE CATHOLIC UNIVERSITY OF THE WEST, ANGERS, FRANCE

Le Doyen et les Professeurs de la Faculté de Théologie de l'Université catholique de l'Ouest remercient les Directeurs, Administrateurs et Faculté du Séminaire théologique de l'Eglise presbytérienne de Princeton de la gracieuse invitation qu'ils leur ont adressée. Ils regrettent de ne pouvoir y répondre par l'envoi d'un délégué, vu la distance qui les sépare de l'Amérique. Mais ils s'unissent à eux de cœur pour fêter le centième anniversaire de leur fondation. Ils sont heureux d'offrir, sur le terrain scientifique, un fraternel hommage à des professeurs dont les travaux ont porté au loin la réputation.

PRINCETON THEOLOGICAL SEMINARY

Ils souhaitent au Séminaire de Princeton, un des plus anciens et des plus illustres foyers de la science américaine, des succès toujours nouveaux, dignes de son glorieux passé.

Le Doyen,
A. LEGENDRE.

le 25 mars 1912. [SEAL]

[SEAL]

THE CATHOLIC FACULTIES OF LYONS, FRANCE

Le Recteur des Facultés catholiques; le Doyen et les Professeurs de la Faculté de Théologie ont l'honneur d'exprimer à Messieurs les Directeurs et Administrateurs du Séminaire de Princeton leurs remerciements pour leur aimable invitation. La Faculté ne pourra pas se faire représenter par un délégué; mais elle fait les meilleurs vœux pour le succès de la fête du centenaire.

F. LAVALLÉE,
recteur.

le 19 février 1912.

THE FREE FACULTY OF PROTESTANT THEOLOGY, MONTAUBAN, FRANCE

La Faculté de Montauban s'est sentie très honorée par l'invitation que vous lui avez adressée—en même temps que par les invitations spéciales faites à deux de ses membres, qui ont eu le très grand regret de ne pouvoir y répondre.

Elle vous remercie. Elle sait qu'il y a entre le Séminaire théologique de Princeton et la Faculté de Montauban un lieu tout spécial. Ici et là, on cultive avec un soin particulier la mémoire du Réformateur Calvin. Nous n'ignorons pas tout ce que vous avez fait par vos ouvrages et par votre Revue pour faire connaître et apprécier l'œuvre et la pensée de celui qui fut un des plus grands Français de France et un des plus grands chrétiens de la chrétienté.

Et précisément ces jours-ci, un disciple du Séminaire théologique de Princeton, le missionnaire et secrétaire général du mouvement des étudiants volontaires, Monsieur Wilder, nous a raconté comment ce fut à Princeton que naquit la Fédération universelle des étudiants chrétiens, cette Fédération dont le caractère est œcuménique et dont la devise est: "faire Christ Roi":—un caractère et une devise spécialement calvinistes.

C'est dans ces sentiments que nous vous envoyons nos vœux les plus sincères pour votre Séminaire,—et que nous demandons à Dieu de faire reposer sa bénédiction sur son activité ultérieure.

Recevez, Monsieur, l'assurance de nos sentiments confraternels et chrétiens.

                Pour la Faculté
                  Le Doyen
                      E. DOUMERGUE.

le 1er mars 1912.

PRINCETON THEOLOGICAL SEMINARY

THE FACULTY OF PROTESTANT THEOLOGY OF THE UNIVERSITY OF PARIS

La Faculté libre de théologie protestante de Paris a été très honorée et touchée de l'invitation que le Theological Seminary of the Presbyterian Church de Princeton lui a adressée de se faire représenter aux fêtes du jubilé centenaire de cet' établissement.

La Faculté eût été heureuse de charger un de ses membres de vous porter en personne ses salutations et ses vœux. Malheureusement les circonstances ne le lui permettent pas. Aussi doit-elle se contenter de vous envoyer par écrit l'expression de sa gratitude en même temps que ses vœux pour que votre maison continue d'être bénie.

Dans le siècle d'activité que vous terminez, il vous a été donné de rendre d'importants services à la science chrétienne et à l'Église pour laquelle vous travaillez. Nous demandons à Dieu de féconder votre activité dans la période nouvelle de vie qui s'ouvre pour vous.

Le Doyen

le 17 mars 1912.   ED. VAUCHER.

THE BIBLICAL SCHOOL OF JERUSALEM

[SEAL]

Les Professeurs de l'École biblique de Jérusalem sont, comme moi, très honorés de votre invitation d'assister au centenaire de la fondation de votre séminaire théologique. Nous regrettons que la distance ne nous permette pas d'envoyer du moins un délégué à cette imposante cérémonie.

CENTENNIAL CELEBRATION OF

Veuillez agréer, très Révérend Monsieur, l'expression de mes sentiments les plus distingués,

M. J. LAGRANGE.
Correspondant de l'Institut,
Directeur de l'École biblique.

[SEAL]

Couvent des Dominicains
de St. Étienne
Jérusalem le 8 mars 1912.

THE CATHOLIC UNIVERSITY OF LOUVAIN, BELGIUM

La Faculté de Théologie de l'Université catholique de Louvain remercie le Séminaire Théologique de Princeton de son invitation aux fêtes de son centenaire, et lui adresse à cette occasion ses sincères félicitations.

Elle regrette vivement que ces fêtes étant fixées à l'époque où les professeurs de l'Université ne peuvent interrompre leurs cours, il lui est impossible de s'y faire représenter par un délegué.

Au nom de la Faculté
Le Secrétaire de l'Université

le 23 mars 1912.   J. VAN BIERVLIET.

THE THEOLOGICAL FACULTY OF THE UNIVERSITY OF BASEL, SWITZERLAND

[ARMS]

Empfangen Sie zu Handen der Directors, Trustees und Facultät des Theologischen Seminars zu Princeton den ergebensten Dank der theologischen Facultät Basel, die

PRINCETON THEOLOGICAL SEMINARY

es zur Ehre anrechnet, von Ihnen zur Jahrhundertfeier Ihres theologischen Seminars eingeladen zu werden. Leider ist kein Mitglied unsrer Facultät in der Lage, Ihrer ehrenvollen Einladung Folge leisten zu können. Die theologische Facultät Basel hat mir aber als ihrem derzeitigen Dekan den Auftrag gegeben, Ihnen mit dem Dank und der Entschuldigung für unser Nichterscheinen zugleich den herzlichsten Glückwunsch der Facultät zu Ihrer Feier auszurichten. Sie dürfen auf ein Jahrhundert reicher geistiger Arbeit zurückblicken, auch auf ein Jahrhundert mannigfacher theologischer Kämpfe und vielfacher Schwierigkeiten, die jedoch ihr theologisches Seminar tapfer und siegreich überwunden hat. Wir wissen uns mit Ihnen einig im strengen wahrhaftigen Erforschen der Wahrheit wie im Dienst des Evangeliums und im Vertrauen, dass gerade in der freien Wahrheitsforschung ein besonders wichtiger und unentbehrlicher Dienst am Evangelium bestehe und wir wünschen Ihnen dasselbe, was wir uns wünschen, dass das kommende Jahrhundert ein Jahrhundert reicher geistiger Arbeit und immer tieferen Verständnisses des Evangeliums werden möge.

Mit den besten Wünschen zu dem Gedeihen Ihres Festes grüsst Sie zugleich im Namen meiner Collegen in grösster Hochachtung

16. März 1912.

PROFESSOR D. PAUL WERNLE,
Dekan d. theol. Facultät Basel.

CENTENNIAL CELEBRATION OF

THE CATHOLIC THEOLOGICAL FACULTY OF THE UNIVERSITY OF BERN, SWITZERLAND

Im Auftrag der kath. theol. Fakultät der Universität Bern übermittelt ihr derzeitiger, unterzeichneter Dekan dem Venerable Theological Seminary of the Presbyterian Church in the United States of America at Princeton die herzlichsten Glückwünsche zu seinem hundertjährigen Bestehen, wünscht ihm fernere gleichsegensreiche Wirksamkeit und bedauert durch die weite Entfernung gehindert zu sein, der gütigen Einladung zur Festfeier zu folgen.

DR. PH. WOKER,
Professor der allgemeinen Geschichte und der Kirchengeschichte an der Universität Bern.

12. März 1912.

THE FACULTY OF THEOLOGY OF THE UNIVERSITY OF FREIBURG, SWITZERLAND

Für die freundliche Einladung zu der Jahrhundertfeier des Theological Seminary of the Presbyterian Church at Princeton New Jersey danken wir verbindlichst, bedauern aber dieser gütigen Einladung nicht folgen zu können.

DR. PRÜMMER,
Dekan d. theol. Facultät.

Friburgi Helvetiorum, die 26 mensis Martii 1912.

PRINCETON THEOLOGICAL SEMINARY

THE FACULTY OF THEOLOGY OF THE UNIVERSITY OF GENEVA, SWITZERLAND

La Faculté de Théologie de l'Université de Genève témoigne au Séminaire Théologique de l'Église Presbytérienne à Princeton sa bien cordiale sympathie à l'occasion du Centenaire qu'il va célébrer.

Elle regrette que les circonstances ne permettent pas des relations personnelles entre professeurs et étudiants des deux pays.

Elle félicite le Séminaire théologique de Princeton de sa prospérité et elle souhaite que les fêtes prochaines soient pour lui le signal de nouveau progrès.

Nous trouvant dans l'impossibilité de déléguer un de nos professeurs aux Fêtes du Centenaire à Princeton nous avons appris que M. le Professeur Schaff, Doctor honoris causa de notre Faculté, se proposait de se rendre à Princeton, et nous l'avons prié de représenter notre Faculté.

Veuillez avoir la bonté de le recevoir à vos fêtes comme le témoin de nos sentiments bien cordiaux à votre égard.

Veuillez agréer l'assurance de nos sentiments bien dévoués.

G. FULLIQUET,
Doyen.

le 20 avril 1912.

CENTENNIAL CELEBRATION OF

THE EVANGELICAL THEOLOGICAL FACULTY OF GENEVA, SWITZERLAND

À Messieurs les membres du Board of Directors et à Messieurs les Professeurs du Theological Seminary de Princeton:

La Faculté de Théologie évangelique de Genève est heureuse, à l'occasion du centenaire de la fondation du Theological Seminary de Princeton, de vous offrir l'hommage de sa respectueuse sympathie et ses félicitations les plus chaleureuses.

Nous le faisons avec une joie d'autant plus grande que nos deux facultés sont unies, depuis de longues années, par les liens d'une profonde estime et d'une parfaite confraternité théologique. En 1838, l'un de nos plus éminents fondateurs, Merle d'Aubigné, l'historien de la Réformation, eut l'honneur de voir ses premiers travaux récompensés par la haute distinction que vous lui avez accordée alors, en lui conférant le doctorat en théologie; et son successeur dans la chaire d'Histoire de l'Église, notre collègue M. le professeur Louis Ruffet, eut le privilege d'être en 1874, l'objet de la même distinction de votre part. Il nous est particulièrement agréable de rappeler ces souvenirs, à l'heure où vous célébrez, avec le protestantisme presbytérien tout entier, la date mémorable de la fondation de votre Faculté.

Vos devanciers et vous, Messieurs, leurs dignes et distingués successeurs, vous avez accompli une œuvre grande et bénie, à la gloire de Jésus-Christ notre commun Seigneur et Sauveur. Vous avez envoyé, au service des Églises de votre patrie et dans le vaste champ des Missions, des légions de ministres vaillants et solidement préparés pour l'œuvre de l'avancement du règne de Dieu dans le monde. Vous avez poursuivi votre noble tâche dans un esprit de fidélité aux précieuses Vérités de l'Évangile que nos bienheureux réformateurs ont remises en lumière et proclamées avec l'énergie d'une foi puissante et d'une inébranlable conviction. Nous nous réjouissons, avec l'Église entière, de l'activité si étendue, et si féconde que, au cours du siècle qui vient de s'écouler il vous a été donné de déployer par le moyen de vos professeurs et des pasteurs et missionnaires qui ont été instruits dans votre faculté.

Vos fils spirituels sont devenus, au près et au loin, les témoins vivants de l'Évangile de vérité et de salut. En ce jour de solennelle commémoration, ils pensent, en tous lieux, à leur Alma Mater, et, comme les fils de la Femme vaillante du livre des Proverbes, "ils se lèvent et la disent bienheureuse"; ils lui adressent le témoignage de leur respectueux attachement et de leur profonde reconnaissance.

Et nous, enfants comme vous de la Réforme calvinienne, vos frères d'armes dans le pays de langue française, c'est avec joie que nous nous associons à ces hommages et que nous y joignons nos vœux les plus sincères et les plus fraternels, en demandant au Souverain Chef de l'Église de demeurer avec vous dans l'avenir, comme Il l'a été dans le passé.

Veuillez, Messieurs et très honorés Collègues, agréer l'assurance de notre haute considération et de notre dévouement en Jésus-Christ.

Au nom du Comité Directeur de la Faculté de Théologie évangélique:

Le président: W. N. DE ST. GEORGE,
ALEX. CLAPARÈDE.   *Vice-prés^t B: Sc:*

Au nom de la Commission des Études:
Le président:
    CH. DURAND-PALLOT,   ANTONY KRAFFT,
      B. D. pasteur.   *B. D. pasteur.*

Le Collège des Professeurs:
    LOUIS RUFFET, D.D., *Président.*
    JULES BREITENSTEIN, *Secrétaire.*
    ANT. BAUMGARTNER, Ph.D.
    FRANK THOMAS, M.A.,
        pasteur et professeur.
    A. BERTHOUD, *professeur.*

[SEAL]

THE FACULTY OF THEOLOGY OF THE FREE CHURCH OF THE CANTON DE VAUD, LAUSANNE, SWITZERLAND

Veuillez recevoir, au nom de la Faculté que j'ai l'honneur de représenter, nos remerciements les plus sincères pour votre si cordiale et fraternelle invitation à célébrer avec vous le Centenaire de la Faculté de théologie de l'Église Presbytérienne des États-Unis d'Amérique. C'est avec le plus grand plaisir que nous aurions répondu à l'honneur que vous nous faites en déléguant un de nos membres à ces belles Fêtes. Malheureusement les circonstances présentes de notre Faculté, dont deux professeurs sont malades, nous rend la chose impossible. C'est avec un très sincère regret que nous le constatons. Nous nous réservons de prendre part, au moment voulu, par un message officiel, aux Fêtes de votre Centenaire; pour l'instant nous n'avons voulu que vous exprimer nos vifs remerciements et notre profonde estime.

Veuillez agréer, Monsieur et très honoré Frère, mes respectueux compliments et me croire votre dévoué

CHARLES O. MERCIER,
professeur.

le 26 février 1912.

THE FACULTY OF THEOLOGY OF THE UNIVERSITY OF NEUCHÂTEL, SWITZERLAND

[SEAL]

À la Direction du Séminaire théologique des Églises presbytériennes des États-Unis d'Amérique, Princeton.

Vous avez bien voulu inviter notre Faculté de théologie de l'Université de Neuchâtel à se faire représenter au centième anniversaire de la fondation du Séminaire théologique des Églises presbytériennes des États-Unis d'Amérique. Vu la distance qui nous sépare de votre pays, nous avons le regret de ne pouvoir répondre à votre aimable invitation. Mais nous ne sommes pas moins très sensibles à l'honneur que vous nous avez fait en nous conviant à votre Jubilé, et nous vous en exprimons toute notre reconnaissance.

Nous sommes heureux de pouvoir saisir cette occasion pour vous présenter, avec nos félicitations, tous nos vœux pour la prospérité croissante de votre Séminaire théologique. Que Dieu bénisse de plus en plus votre travail, de telle sorte que vous puissiez donner à vos Églises, en nombre toujours plus considérable, des serviteurs éclairés, fidèles et devoués ! Qu'il bénisse en même temps vos Églises; qu'il fasse fructifier les semences divines de vérité, de liberté, de justice et de paix qu'elles répandent dans le monde !

Veuillez agréer, Monsieur le Directeur et très honorés Messieurs, l'assurance de notre respectueux dévouement.

Au nom de la Faculté de théologie

Le Doyen
E. Dumont.

le 19 avril 1912.

THE FREE FACULTY OF THEOLOGY OF THE EVANGELICAL CHURCH, NEUCHÂTEL, SWITZERLAND

En réponse à l'aimable invitation que vous avez bien voulu nous adresser et qui nous a vivement touchés, nous avons le regret de vous informer qu'il ne nous sera pas possible de nous faire représenter au centenaire que vous vous préparez à célébrer.

Mais nous nous associerons à votre Jubilé par notre fraternel intérêt et notre sympathie chrétienne, et nous vous prions d'agréer les vœux très sincères que nous formons pour la prospérité de votre Faculté de théologie et de votre Église.

PRINCETON THEOLOGICAL SEMINARY

Veuillez agréer, très honoré Monsieur, avec nos remerciements, l'expression de notre respectueux dévouement.

Au nom de la Faculté de théologie de l'Église évangélique neuchâteloise indépendante de l'État,
le président du conseil des professeurs,

PAUL COMTESSE, FILS.

le 26 février 1912.

THE THEOLOGICAL FACULTY OF THE UNIVERSITY OF INNSBRUCK, AUSTRIA

Das Professorenkollegium der theologischen Fakultät in Innsbruck hat in seiner Sitzung vom 7. März d. J. den unterzeichneten Dekan beauftragt, dem theologischen Seminar der presbyterianischen Kirche in den Vereinigten Staaten von Nord-Amerika für die freundliche Einladung zur Teilnahme an der hundertjährigen Jubelfeier bestens zu danken und zugleich mitzuteilen, dass die Entsendung eines Delegaten unmöglich ist.

In ausgezeichneter Hochachtung

DR. JOHANN STUFLER,
d. Z. Dekan der theol. Fakultät.

8. März 1912.

THE THEOLOGICAL FACULTY OF SALZBURG, AUSTRIA

Facultas theologica Salisburgensis maxime gaudet de celebritate centeniaria Seminarii theologici Princeton

erecti. Quae gratias agit optimas pro attentione facultati amice oblata. Dolore afficitur, quod ratio studiorum hicce vigens non permittat, delegatum ad festivitatem hanc magnam dimittere. Omnes actus festivos eosque perficientes votis bonis presequens salutem dicit.
C. R. Facultas Salisburgensis:

DR. A. EBERHARTER,
h. t. Decanus.

Salisburgi, die XXI. Febr. 1912.

THE EVANGELICAL THEOLOGICAL FACULTY OF THE UNIVERSITY OF VIENNA, AUSTRIA

Die k. k. evangelisch-theologische Facultät in Wien beehrt sich, mit dem besten Dank für die uns freundlichst übermittelte Einladung, Ihnen die ergebensten Glückwünsche zu dem hundertjährigen Jubiläum der theologischen Hochschule in Princeton auszusprechen. Möge der Segen des Allmächtigen, der bisher so sichtbar über der Anstalt gewaltet, auch in Zukunft auf ihr ruhen zum Heil für die Kirche.

In grösster Hochachtung
ergebenst
die k. k. evang.-theol. Facultät in Wien.

PROF. D. WILKE,
d. z. Dekan.

15. April 1912.

PRINCETON THEOLOGICAL SEMINARY

THE FACULTY OF THEOLOGY OF THE ROYAL HUNGARIAN UNIVERSITY, BUDAPEST, HUNGARY

Inclyto Seminario Presbyterianorum in Princeton, Rectori simulque omnibus Membris Collegii nobis Honorandis!

Nuntium Seminarii Vestri in primo centenario feliciter transacto exsultantis simulque nos ad concelebrandum invitantis grato animo accepimus et familiarem Vestram benevolentiam honorantes congratulamur beneficia a D. O. M. in Vos collata. Licet non parem in omnibus habeamus fidei professionem, tamen in plurimis contra eosdem armemur necesse est inimicos Dei Christique ejus. Optamus Vos valere et bonum certamen abhinc quoque certare, ut repositam habeatis Vobis coronam justitiae. Distantia nimia, mare interjectum et cura studiorum quotidiana nos a commeatu prohibent. Rogamus ergo, habeatis nos excusatos. De cetero gratia Domini Nostri Jesu Christi, et charitas Dei et communicatio sancti Spiritus sit cum omnibus Vobis.

Nomine Facultatis Theologicae Universitatis Budapestinensis omnia felicia faustaque Vobis adprecatur.

Budapestini die 29. Martii anni 1912.

Dr. Aladarus Zubriczky,
*Decanus h. a. Facultatis Theologicae
Univ. Budapest.*

[SEAL]

CENTENNIAL CELEBRATION OF

THE REFORMED THEOLOGICAL ACADEMY, BUDAPEST, HUNGARY

We beg to acknowledge with hearty thanks the receipt of the invitation to the centenary celebrations of our Sister Institution. With deep regret, however, we must intimate that we are unable to send a special delegate from our College to represent us on the occasion—not only because of the great distance, but more because the work and arrangements of our institution oblige all of us to be in Budapest in the month of May.

The occasion, however, affords us opportunity of expressing our warm brotherly interest in and love toward our American brethren.

We know the great service rendered by the Presbyterian Church in the United States in the extension of Gospel Light, in bearing faithful and unshaken witness to Christ, and in the expansion of the life of the great American nation.

But we know and acknowledge with deep gratitude that service also, which the ministers of the American Presbyterian Church have, from the very first, rendered so unweariedly and with such noble disinterestedness on behalf of the evangelisation of our emigrant brethren. That Church was the first to interest itself in them.

And now, when one of the most important and most cherished of the institutions of that Church is able, by the grace of God, to look back on a past of one hundred years, we, the Budapest Theological Academy of the Hungarian Reformed Church, pray in the spirit of true Christian fellowship and brotherhood, that the blessing of God may rest abundantly on our Sister Seminary on the occa-

PRINCETON THEOLOGICAL SEMINARY

sion of its celebrations; may it, as it has heretofore, still stand for many generations as the pillar and ground of the faith and of true Christian doctrine and truth, a mighty instrument of all such good work as has its source in the command of our Lord Jesus Christ.

On behalf of the Professoriate of the Budapest Reformed Church Theological College,

PROF. S. B. PAP,
Principal.

[SEAL]

4th March 1912.

THE THEOLOGICAL FACULTY OF THE REFORMED COLLEGE, DEBRECZEN, HUNGARY

A debreceni református kollégium Akadémiájának theológiai tanárikara örömmel fogadta a princetoni theológiai seminárium részéről a meghivást létezésének századik évfordulója ünnepélyére.

Az a tény, hogy a theológiai tudományok hatalmas vára él 1812—től fogva az Egyesült államok szabad földjén,—igaz örömmel tölti el szivünket, hiszen ezen mindig erősödő intézmény az ut, igazság és élet fejedelmének áldása.

A keresztyénség első századaiban virult régi főiskolák Azsiában és Afrikában megszüntek létezni,—és imé! az Ujvilágban támadnak uj főiskolák azokat helyettesíteni és pótolni a veszteségeket. Az önök semináriuma hasonló

CENTENNIAL CELEBRATION OF

testvérintézetek közt képviseli a presbyterián világ egyik világitó tornyát.

A princetoni seminárium irodalmi munkái és tanárainak érdemei ismeretesek Európában a tudósok előtt s mindenütt köztiszteletet vivtak ki.

Köszönjük a megtiszteltetést, hogy meghivtak százados ünnepelyökre, de részínt a nagy távolság, részint iskola évűnkben épen azon időszakra eső legsürgősebb elfoglaltságunk miatt nem lehetséges képviselőt küldeni körünkből, hanem meg kell elégednünk ott lélekben, elménkkel jelen lenni csak.

Fogadják azért keresztyéni és testvéri üdvözletünket azon forró kivánságunkkal, hogy a nagy Isten virágoztassa önök semináriumát és gazdagitsa anyagi és szellemi segitségével a megváltó Jézus Krisztus szolgálatában a jövendő nehéz időkben is szilárdan megállani.

Theológiai akadémiánk tanárainak nevében s megbizásából

Debrecenben, a régi kollégium épületében, 1912, márc. 26.

tiszteletteljesen

DR. GÉZA LENCZ,
theológiai dékán.

[SEAL]

[TRANSLATION]

The Theological Academy of the Reformed College of Debreczen in Hungary has had the pleasure of receiving the invitation of Princeton Theological Seminary to the celebration of the centennial of its existence.

PRINCETON THEOLOGICAL SEMINARY

The fact that a powerful seat of theological learning has existed since 1812 on the free soil of the United States fills our hearts with true joy because this ever-growing Institute is a visible blessing granted by the Prince of "the Way, the Truth and the Life".

The ancient schools of the first centuries in Asia and Africa ceased to live, but, behold! in the new world—never dreamed of by the Apostle Paul—rose new ones to replace the losses. Your Seminary among its sister establishments represents one lighthouse in the Presbyterian world.

Princeton Seminary's literary works and her professors' merits are known in Europe among scholars, and have acquired common esteem everywhere.

We are thankful for the honour of being invited to your jubilee festival, but on account of the great distance and chiefly because of the busy occupations of our scholastic year, we cannot send a delegate: we must be satisfied with being present in heart and mind.

Accept therefore our brotherly salutation and our warm wish that the great God may extend and enrich your Seminary with both material and spiritual blessings for the service of the Saviour Jesus Christ in the important period to come.

In the name of the Theological Professors, in the College buildings, Debreczen, Hungary, 26 March 1912.

Respectfully yours,

DR. GÉZA LENCZ,
Dean of the theol. Academy.

CENTENNIAL CELEBRATION OF

THE UNITARIAN THEOLOGICAL COLLEGE, KLAUSENBURG, HUNGARY

We received with great pleasure your kind invitation to the celebration which your Theological Seminary holds on the 5th, 6th, and 7th of May on the occasion of the hundredth anniversary of its establishment. Up to this day we hoped to be able to send a representative of ours to you. But to our great regret we have been prevented from doing so; therefore, we express our heartiest greetings to you in this way, wishing from the bottom of our hearts that your College may prosper with God's help for hundreds and hundreds of years and may do the best of work in the interest of the moral and religious advance of mankind.

May God's blessings be and remain upon your College, your works and you all.

From the meeting of the directory of the Unitarian Theological College at Kolozsvár (Klausenburg) held on the 27th of March, with kindest regards,

               We remain,
                  Yours faithfully,

                     EUGEN GÓL,
                          President.

SOLOMON CSIFÓ,   LAWRENCE GÁLFI,
  Dean of the College.   *Notary.*

THE REFORMED THEOLOGICAL ACADEMY, PÁPA, HUNGARY

Having received the kind invitation of the Directors, Trustees and Faculty of your Seminary to take part in the celebration of the one hundredth anniversary of the establishment of it, we are very sorry that we cannot be represented on that occasion. Nevertheless the professors and trustees of our Theological Academy celebrate with you in spirit. We wish most heartily that your Theological Seminary vivat, crescat, floreat ad multos annos! May God grant to it a most glorious future, that it may bring up many faithful pupils as in the past, who will contend bravely for the cause of the Gospel and count not their life dear unto themselves, so that they may finish their course with joy, that is, may propagate the Kingdom of God!

Believe me, Honoured Sir, in the name of the Senatus of the Reformed Theological Academy.

LEWIS CZIZMADIA,
[SEAL] *h. t. rector professor.*

THE REFORMED THEOLOGICAL ACADEMY, SÁROSPATAK, HUNGARY

Theologiai intézetök jubileumi ünnepségeire szóló szives meghivásukat megkaptuk. Fogadják érte legszivesebb köszönetünket.

Nagyon óhajtanánk mi abban személyesen is részt venni mindannyian, vagy legalább is küldöttség útján; de nagyon sajnáljuk, hogy nem tehetjük, részint a távolság miatt, részint és különösebben azért, mert már vége felé járunk iskolai félévünknek. De ha személyesen nem lehetünk is ott jelen, lélekben Önökkel leszünk. Mi ugy érezzük, hogy a nagy földrajzi távolság mellett is közel vagyunk egymáshoz. A köztünk levő szellemi rokonság, a közös protestáns érdekek, közös törekvéseink az evangeliomi világosság terjesztésében, kiváltképen az a benső viszony, a melyben Önök ama magyar református honfitársainkkal vannak, akik szülőföldjüktől távol az Önök és az Önök presbyterianus ama mi honfitársainkról való szives gondoskodása— mindez a legszorosabb kapcsolatot képezi Önök között és mi közöttünk.

Fogadják hát testvéri szivünkből származó legszivesebb üdvözletünket, Princetoni theologiai intézetök jubileuma alkalmából.

Öszinte tisztelettel
  a sárospataki ref. theologiai akademia, annak
    tanárai sazok nevében

      Nágy Béla,
       dékán.

[TRANSLATION]

Your kind invitation to the jubilee-solemnities of your theological Seminary reached us duly and we express our heartiest thanks for it.

We all should like to participate in it personally or by deputation at least, but we are very sorry that we are not able to do so, partly because of the great distance, partly and especially because we are nearly at the end of our second semester.

Though we cannot be present there personally, we will be with all our soul with you. In spite of the great geographical distance we feel we are near to each other. The spiritual relationship, the common interests of Protestantism, our common efforts in spreading the evangelical light and especially that intimate relation existing between you and our Hungarian Reformed fellow-countrymen living in your state, far from their native land, and the kindness of your Presbyterian Church in taking care of them—these all make the closest connection between you and ourselves.

Receive therefore our kindest greetings coming out of our brotherly hearts on the occasion of the jubilee of your Theological Seminary of Princeton. Vivat, crescat, floreat—ad maiorem Dei gloriam!

Yours very sincerely,
  The Reformed Theological Academy of Sárospatak, its professors, and in their name.

        Béla Nágy,
          Dean.

20th April, 1912.

[SEAL]

THE EVANGELICAL THEOLOGICAL ACADEMY, SOPRON (OEDENBOURG), HUNGARY

As it is not in our power to be represented on the solemn one hundredth anniversary of the establishment of your Faculty, we send, with many thanks for your kind

CENTENNIAL CELEBRATION OF

invitation, our heartiest congratulations and our best wishes for the new century of your Seminary.

For the Evangelical Theological Academy: Sopron (Oedenbourg), March 30, 1912.

ANT. BANCSÓ,
Director.

CH. PROEHLE,
Prof. and Secretary.

[SEAL]

THE THEOLOGICAL FACULTY OF THE ROYAL BOHEMIAN UNIVERSITY, PRAGUE, BOHEMIA

Bohoslovecká fakulta c. k. české Karlo-Ferdinandovy university v Praze, jsouc si dobře vědoma zásluh jichž "The Theological Seminary of the Presbyterian Church in the United States of America at Princeton, New Jersey" za sto let svého trvání o povznesení křestánství si získal, vzkazuje témuž slovutnému Semináři ke dnům 5.–7. května t. r., kdy sto let svého trvání oslavovati bude, srdečné blahopřaní, žádajíc mu na Bohu, aby i v příštích dobách kvetl a se vzmáhal ku blahu vlasti a k prospěchu křestánstva a jsa vždy věren idealům slavných zakladatelů svých, šířil ideu křestánskou, kulturu a humanitu.

Děkujíce srdečně za Vaše milé a cestné pozvání, prosíme, aby slovutný bohoslovecký seminář blahopřání naše přívětivě přijati rácil.

V Praze dne 22. budna léta Páně 1912.

PROF. DV. AL. SOLDAT,
S. c. děkan.

[SEAL]

PRINCETON THEOLOGICAL SEMINARY

[TRANSLATION]

Theologica Facultas c. r. bohemicae Carolo-Ferdinandea Universitatis Pragae, haud immemor meritorum, quae "The Theological Seminary of the Presbyterian Church in the United States of America at Princeton, New Jersey" per hos centum annos ad rem christianam augendam et amplificandam sibi paravit, eidem celeberrimo Seminario ad dies 5.–7. Maji a. c., quibus centenaria sua celebrabit, gratulatur optimisque ominibus prosequitur, exoptans, ut etiam in posterum floreat et augeatur ad salutem patriae, rei christianae incrementum semperque clarissimorum Fundatorum suorum rationes secutum ideam christianam, cultum atque humanitatem propaget.

Pro benevola et honorifica invitatione sinceras gratias agentes, rogamus, ut celeberrimum theologicum Seminarium gratulationem nostram humanissime accipiat.
Pragae Bohemorum a. d. VIII. Kalendas Maji a. D. 1912.

KNOX COLLEGE,
TORONTO

I have presented the gracious invitation from Princeton Theological Seminary to the Faculty of Knox College.

Our Faculty is not an official body with power to appoint a representative, but we have decided to ask the Board of Management of Knox College to appoint Professor James Ballantyne, D.D., as our representative at the celebration of the One Hundredth Anniversary of the Establishment of Princeton Theological Seminary. Our Board does not meet until the first week in April, but you may be assured that this appointment will be made and may place Professor Ballantyne's name upon your list as the one who will represent Knox College.

With congratulations on the great history and the great work of Princeton during the past hundred years,

I am,

Yours faithfully,

ALFRED GANDIER,
Principal.

29th February, 1912.

QUEEN'S UNIVERSITY, KINGSTON, ONTARIO

I beg to advise that at a meeting of the Senate of Queen's University held yesterday, the 13th instant, the Reverend W. G. Jordan, B.A., D.D., Professor of Hebrew and Old Testament Criticism, was appointed to represent the University at the celebration of the One Hundredth Anniversary of the Theological Seminary of the Presbyterian Church in the United States of America, at Princeton, New Jersey.

Yours sincerely,

GEORGE Y. CHOWN,
Registrar.

March 14, 1912.

PRINCETON THEOLOGICAL SEMINARY

THE PRESBYTERIAN COLLEGE, MONTREAL

The Faculty of the Presbyterian College, Montreal, have much pleasure in accepting the courteous invitation of the Princeton Theological Seminary to be represented at the celebration of the hundredth anniversary of its establishment, and have named the Principal as their delegate with the Rev. Prof. R. E. Welsh, D.D., as alternate.

I have the honor to be,
        Yours very sincerely,

JOHN SCRIMGER,
Principal.

February 16th, 1912.

MANITOBA COLLEGE, WINNIPEG

The Senate of Manitoba College, Winnipeg, congratulate the Theological Seminary of Princeton on the attainment of its centenary, and have appointed the Rev. Dr. Baird, Acting-Principal of Manitoba College, as delegate to represent it at the coming celebration in May.

J. DICK FLEMING,
Secretary of Senate.

15th March, 1912.

CENTENNIAL CELEBRATION OF

WESTMINSTER HALL, VANCOUVER, BRITISH COLUMBIA

Please excuse delay in replying to your very kind invitation to Westminster Hall to be represented at the one hundredth anniversary of Princeton Theological Seminary. I had hoped to be in the East about that time, but now I find that to be impossible. We have appointed as our representative, Rev. A. J. MacGillivray, M.A., D.D., Merton, Ont., one of your own graduates and one of the first two D.D.'s of our College.

Thanking you for the invitation and with best wishes for the success of your celebration,

Sincerely yours,

JOHN MACKAY,
Principal.

April 20th, 1912.

FACULTY OF THEOLOGY OF TRINITY COLLEGE, TORONTO

A few days ago I received from you the very kind invitation given by the Theological Seminary of the Presbyterian Church of the United States of America at Princeton, New Jersey, to the Faculty of Theology of the University of Trinity College, Toronto, to be represented by a delegate on the occasion of the Celebration of the One Hundredth Anniversary of the establishment of the said Seminary, such celebration to be held on 5th, 6th, and 7th May, 1912.

PRINCETON THEOLOGICAL SEMINARY

In response to this invitation we have very much pleasure in nominating as our delegate the Reverend E. Vicars Stevenson, M.A., graduate of this University, whose present address is 130 East Sixth Street, Plainfield, N. J.

With sincere thanks for the courtesy of your invitation, and with all best wishes for the success of the Celebration, and for the continued prosperity of your Theological Seminary,

I have the honour to remain,
Faithfully yours,

T. C. P. MACKLEM,
Provost.

April 22, 1912.

WYCLIFFE COLLEGE,
TORONTO

The President, Principal and Council of Wycliffe College, Toronto, regret that it will not be possible for them to accept the kind invitation of the Directors, Trustees and Faculty of the Princeton Theological Seminary to be represented at the one hundredth anniversary of the establishment of that noble institution, owing to the absence of the Principal in Europe, and the fact that the other officers of the Council and Faculty will be otherwise engaged. They desire to express their deep sense of appreciation of the kind act of the Authorities of the Princeton Seminary in inviting them to take part on this most auspicious occasion. They hope and pray that the proceedings may be greatly owned and blessed of

PRINCETON THEOLOGICAL SEMINARY

God, and that the noble institution which is celebrating its one hundredth birthday may be long favored by God with the continuance of ever deepening and most useful service in these days of golden opportunity on our North American Continent.

11th April, 1912.

RESPONSES FROM THEOLOGICAL SCHOOLS IN THIS COUNTRY

THEOLOGICAL SEMINARY OF THE REFORMED CHURCH IN AMERICA, NEW BRUNSWICK, NEW JERSEY

The Faculty of the Theological Seminary of the Reformed Church in America directs me to acknowledge with thanks the receipt of an invitation to be represented at the one hundredth anniversary of the founding of the Theological Seminary of the Presbyterian Church in the United States at Princeton, N. J., on the fifth, sixth, and seventh of May next. I am also instructed by the Faculty to inform you that the undersigned has been chosen as their delegate. It will give me great pleasure to be present.

Yours very sincerely,

J. PRESTON SEARLE,
President of the Faculty.

ST. MARY'S UNIVERSITY AND ECCLESIASTICAL SEMINARY, BALTIMORE, MARYLAND

The President and Faculty of St. Mary's University and Ecclesiastical Seminary greatly appreciate the honor of the invitation to participate in the celebration of the one hundredth anniversary of the establishment of

CENTENNIAL CELEBRATION OF

the Theological Seminary of the Presbyterian Church in the United States of America at Princeton, New Jersey.

While for reasons which will be doubtless properly appreciated they cannot send a representative on that occasion, they wish to extend their hearty congratulations to the Princeton Theological Seminary on its eminent services to religion by its high and conservative scholarship and particularly by its able and unswerving support of the Divinity of Our Lord, and they heartily wish it continued and increased influence in this noble cause.

E. R. DYER, D.D.,
President.

February 29th, 1912.

THE XENIA THEOLOGICAL SEMINARY, XENIA, OHIO

I am directed by the Faculty of the Xenia Theological Seminary to say that Prof. W. G. Moorehead, D.D., LL.D., has been appointed to represent this Seminary at the celebration of the One Hundredth Anniversary of the Princeton Theological Seminary, May 5–7, 1912.

Thanking you for the honor extended by your invitation, I am,

Very truly yours,

JOSEPH KYLE,
Secretary of Faculty.

April 8, 1912.

HARTWICK SEMINARY, HARTWICK, NEW YORK

Thanks for your kind invitation to have Hartwick Seminary represented at the coming Centennial of Princeton Theological Seminary in May, 1912. It would afford us as a Faculty great pleasure to be represented personally by one of our number at that interesting anniversary, but inasmuch as that will be impracticable, I, as the dean of the Theological Faculty and as the representative of the oldest Lutheran Theological School in America, hereby extend to the Princeton Theological Seminary our cordial greetings and good wishes. We celebrated our Centennial in 1897, and like Princeton, we represent the old theology of sin and salvation. May your Institution, which has already attained such distinguished prominence as a center of Theological learning, continue to send forth into the great harvest field an increasing number of men richly endowed and fully equipped for extending the kingdom of our common Lord and Saviour.

Yours fraternally,

ALFRED HILLER,
Dean.

February 23, 1912.

CENTENNIAL CELEBRATION OF

THE MORAVIAN COLLEGE AND THEOLOGICAL SEMINARY, BETHLEHEM, PENNSYLVANIA

The announcement of the celebration of the one hundredth anniversary of the establishment of your institution and the courteous invitation extended the above named institution to be represented on that auspicious occasion came to hand in due time. For various reasons a reply could not be sent ere this. At a meeting held this morning, the faculty directed that thankful acknowledgment be made of the courtesy extended and elected the undersigned to be its delegate during the festal days.

With heartiest greetings and hoping that the celebration may mean all for Princeton that is expected of so interesting an occasion,

Yours very sincerely,

W. N. SCHWARZE,
The Resident Professor.

May 1, 1912.

ANDOVER THEOLOGICAL SEMINARY, CAMBRIDGE, MASSACHUSETTS

The Faculty of Andover Theological Seminary have the honor to acknowledge the invitation of the Directors, Trustees, and Faculty of the Theological Seminary of the Presbyterian Church in the United States of America, at Princeton, New Jersey, to be represented by a

PRINCETON THEOLOGICAL SEMINARY

delegate at the celebration of the one-hundredth anniversary of the establishment of the Seminary by the General Assembly, on the fifth, sixth, and seventh of May, nineteen hundred and twelve, and to state that the Reverend President Albert Parker Fitch, D.D., has been appointed as the Andover representative on that occasion.

On behalf of the Faculty,

JOHN WINTHROP PLATNER,
Secretary.

UNION THEOLOGICAL SEMINARY, RICHMOND, VIRGINIA

I write in the name of the faculty of Union Theological Seminary in Virginia to express to the directors, trustees and faculty of the Theological Seminary of the Presbyterian Church in the United States of America at Princeton, New Jersey, the thanks of our faculty for the invitation to have this institution represented by a delegate at the celebration of the one hundredth anniversary of the establishment of your venerable school on Sunday, Monday and Tuesday, the fifth, sixth and seventh of May, nineteen hundred and twelve, and to say that the faculty has appointed the Rev. Thos. R. English, D.D., Henry Young Professor of Biblical Literature and the Interpretation of the New Testament, to represent us on this interesting occasion and has appointed the Rev. Chas. C. Hersman, D.D., LL.D., Professor Emeritus of

Biblical Literature and the Interpretation of the New Testament, as his alternate.
Sincerely yours,
W. W. MOORE,
March 8, 1912.   *President.*

BANGOR THEOLOGICAL SEMINARY, BANGOR, MAINE

Will the venerated institution at Princeton pardon the President of a sister institution, herself in her ninety-sixth year, for this—almost unpardonable—negligence?

Our Faculty accepted with appreciation the invitation for the Exercises of May 5, 6, 7, and named me to be their representative, and, alas! in extreme pressure of many matters, acknowledgment and notification got neglected and overlooked. I beg a thousand pardons.

If I may be forgiven, and my presence after such a lapse will be acceptable, please send me, on receipt of this, a collect telegram, and I shall plan to be with you. I may have to arrive on Monday, but will do my best.

This Seminary has much in common with Princeton; we are trying to do a reasonably conservative and a distinctly constructive work. Also, I grew up in New Jersey, in one of the Oranges, and in that neighborhood my ancestry, from 1685 had its life.

With sincere contrition, I remain,
Respectfully and truly yours,
DAVID N. BEACH,
April 30, 1912.   *President.*

PRINCETON THEOLOGICAL SEMINARY

THE GENERAL THEOLOGICAL SEMINARY OF THE PROTESTANT EPISCOPAL CHURCH, NEW YORK CITY

The Faculty of the General Theological Seminary congratulate the Theological Seminary of the Presbyterian Church at Princeton, New Jersey, upon the approach of its Centennial Celebration and, in response to its gracious invitation to be represented on that occasion, have appointed as delegates the Reverend Arthur Prime Hunt, M.A., B.D., Professor of Christian Ethics, and the Reverend Dickinson S. Miller, Ph.D., Professor of Christian Apologetics, in the General Theological Seminary.

CHARLES N. SHEPARD,
Secretary.

February 16, 1912.

AUBURN THEOLOGICAL SEMINARY, AUBURN, NEW YORK

Auburn Theological Seminary salutes the Theological Seminary of the Presbyterian Church in the United States of America located at Princeton, New Jersey; and presents congratulations upon the completion of one hundred years of noble service in the cause of sacred learning and of the Christian Religion; and offers best wishes for ever-enlarging usefulness.

CENTENNIAL CELEBRATION OF

THEOLOGICAL SEMINARY, COLGATE UNIVERSITY, HAMILTON, NEW YORK

The Faculty of Colgate Theological Seminary accept with pleasure the invitation of the Directors, Trustees, and Faculty of Princeton Theological Seminary to be represented by a delegate at the One-hundredth Anniversary of the establishment of the Seminary on the fifth, sixth, and seventh of May. We have appointed Prof. David F. Estes, Hamilton, N. Y., as such representative.

Sincerely yours,

GEORGE R. BERRY,
Secretary of the Seminary Faculty.

February 21, 1912.

THE DIVINITY SCHOOL OF YALE UNIVERSITY, NEW HAVEN, CONNECTICUT

The Yale University Divinity School has received with satisfaction the invitation to be present at the celebration of the one hundredth anniversary of the establishment of the Theological Seminary of the Presbyterian Church in the United States of America to be held on the 5th, 6th and 7th of May next. At a meeting of its Faculty held on February 15th it voted that Professor Williston Walker be the delegate of the Divinity School on this occasion.

Wishing you all success and congratulating you on the

PRINCETON THEOLOGICAL SEMINARY approaching completion of one hundred years of distinguished service in the advancement of the Kingdom of God, I am, on behalf of the Faculty,
Yours very truly,

WILLISTON WALKER,
Secretary of the Faculty.

February 16, 1912.

THE ALLEGHENY THEOLOGICAL SEMINARY, NORTH SIDE, PITTSBURGH, PENNSYLVANIA

On behalf of the Faculty of the Allegheny Theological Seminary (United Presbyterian) I express appreciation of the invitation to have our Seminary represented at the one hundredth anniversary of the establishment of Princeton Theological Seminary. Owing to our commencement week being fixed for the same date, it will not be practicable for any member of the Faculty to be present at Princeton on this interesting occasion, this very much to our regret. With the many friends of Princeton Theological Seminary we share heartily in devout thanksgiving over the eminently fruitful history of the institution and in earnest prayer that the favor of the Great Head of the Church may attend its work from year to year and give it an increasingly prosperous future.

Fraternally yours,

JOHN MCNAUGHER,
President of the Faculty.

20th March, 1912.

CENTENNIAL CELEBRATION OF

THE NEWTON THEOLOGICAL INSTITUTION, NEWTON CENTRE, MASSACHUSETTS

The Faculty of the Newton Theological Institution have received with pleasure the invitation to be represented at the celebration of the one hundredth anniversary of the establishment of Princeton Theological Seminary on the fifth, sixth and seventh of May, nineteen hundred and twelve.

They have requested their President, the Reverend Professor George Edwin Horr, D.D., to represent them on this occasion and bear their congratulations to the Seminary.

THEOLOGICAL SEMINARY OF THE REFORMED CHURCH IN THE UNITED STATES, LANCASTER, PENNSYLVANIA

In behalf of the Faculty of our Theological Seminary, I am pleased to acknowledge the receipt of the invitation extended to us to attend the One Hundredth Anniversary of your institution. As President of our Theological Seminary, I have been chosen by my colleagues to represent our Faculty on that occasion.

I regret very much that the dates which are fixed for your Anniversary services are the same as those covered by our Seminary Commencement dates. Notwithstanding the claims of our own Seminary upon my time, I hope to be able to arrange to be present at least part of

PRINCETON THEOLOGICAL SEMINARY

the time set apart for your One Hundredth Anniversary services.

Yours very truly,

JOHN C. BOWMAN,
President.

March 8th, 1912.

LUTHERAN THEOLOGICAL SEMINARY, GETTYSBURG, PENNSYLVANIA

The Faculty of the Evangelical Lutheran Theological Seminary at Gettysburg, Pa., beg leave to acknowledge the honor of the invitation to be represented on the occasion of the celebration of the one hundredth anniversary of the founding of Princeton Seminary.

They have appointed me as their delegate, and it will give me great pleasure to be present.

Our Seminary (founded in 1826) is under obligations to your more venerable institution in that our first President, Dr. S. S. Schmucker, was educated in Theology at Princeton.

Fraternally yours,

J. A. SINGMASTER,
President.

March 14, 1912.

CENTENNIAL CELEBRATION OF

THE WESTERN THEOLOGICAL SEMINARY, NORTH SIDE, PITTSBURGH, PENNSYLVANIA

The Western Theological Seminary accepts with pleasure the invitation of Princeton Theological Seminary to be represented at the celebration of the One Hundredth Anniversary of the establishment of Princeton Seminary. The Faculty of Western Seminary has chosen as its representative on that occasion the President, Rev. James Anderson Kelso, Ph.D., D.D.

WILLIAM R. FARMER,
Secretary of the Faculty.

March 7, 1912.

COLUMBIA THEOLOGICAL SEMINARY, COLUMBIA, SOUTH CAROLINA

I am directed by the Faculty of the Theological Seminary of the Synods of South Carolina, Georgia, Alabama and Florida, usually known as Columbia Theological Seminary, to express the Faculty's appreciation of your kindness in tendering an invitation to attend the exercises connected with the one hundredth anniversary of the establishment of Princeton Seminary. The Faculty of Columbia Seminary accepts the invitation and appoints as delegate to represent this Seminary on the occasion named, Henry Alexander White, A.M., Ph.D., D.D., LL.D., Professor of New Testament Literature

PRINCETON THEOLOGICAL SEMINARY

and Exegesis in Columbia Theological Seminary, and a member of the Class of 1889 of Princeton Seminary.

Sincerely,

HENRY A. WHITE,
Secretary of Faculty.

February 28, 1912.

LANE THEOLOGICAL SEMINARY, CINCINNATI, OHIO

The Lane Theological Seminary acknowledges the invitation to be represented by a delegate at the celebration of the one hundredth anniversary of the establishment of the Theological Seminary of the Presbyterian Church in the United States of America at Princeton, New Jersey, May fifth, sixth and seventh, nineteen hundred and twelve, and has appointed the Reverend Professor Edward Mack, D.D., as its delegate.

McCORMICK THEOLOGICAL SEMINARY, CHICAGO, ILLINOIS

The Faculty of McCormick Theological Seminary is in receipt of the invitation to be present at the celebration of the one hundredth anniversary of the establishment of Princeton Theological Seminary.

We take pleasure in accepting the invitation and shall

be represented by the Reverend Professor Andrew C. Zenos, D.D.

Yours very truly,

A. S. CARRIER,
February 21, 1912. *Secretary of the Faculty.*

HARTFORD THEOLOGICAL SEMINARY, HARTFORD, CONNECTICUT

The Faculty of the Hartford Theological Seminary have received the invitation of the Directors, Trustees and Faculty of the Princeton Theological Seminary, that they be represented at the celebration of the One Hundredth Anniversary of the establishment of Princeton Theological Seminary by the General Assembly.

The Faculty have appointed one who is highly honored by both Seminaries, to represent them on this occasion, namely, the Rev. M. W. Jacobus, D.D., Dean of the Hartford Theological Seminary, and an alumnus of Princeton Seminary.

Yours sincerely,

W. DOUGLAS MACKENZIE,
March 1st, 1912. *President.*

OBERLIN THEOLOGICAL SEMINARY, OBERLIN COLLEGE, OBERLIN, OHIO

Oberlin Theological Seminary, the Theological Department of Oberlin College, accepts with pleasure the

PRINCETON THEOLOGICAL SEMINARY
invitation of the Theological Seminary of the Presbyterian Church in the United States of America, at Princeton, New Jersey, to be represented at its One Hundredth Anniversary, the 5th, 6th and 7th of May, 1912. The delegate representing Oberlin Seminary will be Professor Kemper Fullerton, A.M. (Princeton), Professor of Old Testament Language and Literature.
For the Faculty,
G. W. FISKE,
March 16, 1912. *Junior Dean.*

UNION THEOLOGICAL SEMINARY, NEW YORK CITY

I have the honor to acknowledge the receipt by the Faculty of this Seminary, of the invitation to be represented on the occasion of the celebration of the one hundredth anniversary of the establishment of the Theological Seminary of the Presbyterian Church in the United States of America at Princeton, New Jersey, on the fifth, sixth and seventh of May, nineteen hundred and twelve, and to signify the acceptance of the invitation.

The Faculty directs me to inform you that they have appointed the Reverend Professor Francis Brown, Ph.D., D.D., LL.D., D.Litt., President of the Faculty, as their representative on this occasion.

Yours very truly,
CHARLES R. GILLETT,
Secretary of the Faculty.
February 22, 1912.

CENTENNIAL CELEBRATION OF

MEADVILLE THEOLOGICAL SCHOOL, MEADVILLE, PENNSYLVANIA

At a meeting of the Faculty of the Meadville Theological School held on Tuesday, March 5, 1912, it was voted that the President, Franklin C. Southworth, D.D., be requested to represent the school as a Delegate at the celebration of the one hundredth anniversary of the establishment of the Theological Seminary of the Presbyterian Church in the United States of America at Princeton, New Jersey, by the General Assembly, on Sunday, Monday and Tuesday, the fifth, sixth and seventh of May, nineteen hundred and twelve. With congratulations upon the approaching event and wishes for a pleasant celebration,
I remain sincerely yours,

WALTER C. GREEN,
Secretary of the Faculty.

March 6, 1912.

WITTENBERG COLLEGE, HAMMA DIVINITY SCHOOL, SPRINGFIELD, OHIO

I am authorized by the Faculty of our Seminary to express to you our thanks for the invitation to send a representative from our school to attend the celebration of the One Hundredth Anniversary of Princeton Seminary. I would say that I have been appointed to repre-

PRINCETON THEOLOGICAL SEMINARY

sent our Seminary at the Princeton Centennial. If I am unable to be present, as I now hope to be in attendance, I shall endeavor to have some one take my place.

Sincerely yours,

D. H. BAUSLIN,
Dean.

March 28, 1912.

GERMAN (EDEN) EVANGELICAL MISSOURI COLLEGE, ST. LOUIS, MISSOURI

Will you, please, excuse me for not answering sooner? The members of our faculty have been deliberating on the invitation of Princeton Seminary, but as no conclusion was reached then, the matter was laid aside for some time.

We cannot, however, make arrangements to make it possible for any member of our faculty to be absent just at that time, and so we are sorry that we cannot send a delegate.

Yours truly,

W. W. BECKER,
President.

April 6, 1912.

ROCHESTER THEOLOGICAL SEMINARY, ROCHESTER, NEW YORK

On behalf of the Faculty of this Seminary I beg to acknowledge your invitation extended to us to send a dele-

gate to the celebration of the one hundredth anniversary of Princeton Theological Seminary. We congratulate you upon this event. We regret, however, very much that we cannot send a delegate. Our anniversaries come on the exact dates of your celebration.
I am,
      Sincerely yours,
        J. W. A. STEWART,
        Dean of the Faculty.
March 7, 1912.

DUBUQUE GERMAN COLLEGE AND SEMINARY, DUBUQUE, IOWA

Dubuque German College and Seminary acknowledges the kind invitation of Princeton Theological Seminary to participate in the celebration of its One Hundredth Anniversary. At the annual meeting of the Board of Directors, Dr. William Hiram Foulkes, D.D., of the Rutgers Presbyterian Church, New York City, was appointed a delegate for this occasion. Dr. Foulkes is the President of our Board and, as such, is qualified to represent our Institution.

With warm felicitations and sincere good wishes for the continued prosperity of Princeton Seminary,
    Respectfully yours,
       WILLIAM GRAHAM,
       Secretary of the Board.
April 25th, 1912.

PRINCETON THEOLOGICAL SEMINARY

BERKELEY DIVINITY SCHOOL, MIDDLETOWN, CONNECTICUT

We have received the courteous invitation of the Theological Seminary of the Presbyterian Church at Princeton to be represented at the celebration of the one hundredth anniversary of its establishment; and we desire to express our thanks for the same. And I have the honor to say that our President, the Bishop of Connecticut, and our Faculty desire me, as the Dean of the School, to represent this institution on that occasion, and that I accept the invitation as desired.

Very truly yours,
22 February, 1912.   SAMUEL HART,
Dean.

GARRETT BIBLICAL INSTITUTE, EVANSTON, ILLINOIS

It is my privilege and honor to bring from the Trustees and the Faculty of the Garrett Biblical Institute, at Evanston, Illinois, our fraternal greeting and most cordial congratulations to the Theological Seminary of the Presbyterian Church in the United States of America, at Princeton, New Jersey.

We share the pride of all the Churches in the noble record of your hundred years. We acknowledge with keen appreciation the great work and worth of your Faculty whose names are in high esteem in all our theological schools, and whose contributions to theological literature are prized by all ministers and teachers. The goodly influences of this Seminary have gone out into all the earth and have been a noteworthy power in advancing the interests of the Kingdom of God. You have kindly welcomed to your halls students from all religious denominations, and your genuine courtesy has ever commanded a warm reciprocal affection. Your ample endowments, your extensive libraries, your learned, able and devoted teachers, and the inspirations to high scholarship which suffuse the very air of Princeton have brought unspeakable blessing to three generations of the American people. Your gospel-trumpet has sent forth no uncertain voice. With other Christian schools and Churches, we gladly join in devout thanksgiving to the Father of mercies for the manifold blessings of the past, and in earnest supplication that your prosperity and usefulness may increase through all the years to come.

MILTON S. TERRY,
Delegate representing Garrett Biblical Institute.

EUREKA COLLEGE, DEPARTMENT OF SACRED LITERATURE, EUREKA, ILLINOIS

It is with great regret that we find ourselves unable to send a representative to carry personal greetings to Princeton Theological Seminary on the occasion of its One Hundredth Anniversary. We must, therefore, be content to wish for the Theological Seminary the greatest prosperity and usefulness.

Sincerely,

CHARLES E. UNDERWOOD,
April 3, 1912. *President.*

REFORMED PRESBYTERIAN THEOLOGICAL SEMINARY, ALLEGHENY, PENNSYLVANIA

The invitation to this Seminary to be represented at the Centennial of Princeton Theological Seminary has been received. Possibly Prof. Richard Cameron Wylie, D.D., LL.D., of this Seminary may be present. Any further communication you may address to him, West McIntyre Avenue, North Side, Pittsburgh, Pa.
                    Yours truly,
                              D. B. WILLSON,
                                   Senior professor.

February 24, 1912.

ST. JOHN'S UNIVERSITY ECCLESIASTICAL SEMINARY, COLLEGEVILLE, MINNESOTA

We have received your kind invitation to attend the hundredth anniversary of the establishment of your esteemed Seminary, but regret that it will be impossible for us to send a delegate at the time.

Wishing you continued success in your field of labor, I beg to remain,
                    Yours truly,
                              ALCUIN DEUTSCH,
                                   Rector.

February 21, 1912.

CENTENNIAL CELEBRATION OF

ST. LAWRENCE UNIVERSITY, CANTON THEOLOGICAL SCHOOL, CANTON, NEW YORK

The courteous invitation of Princeton Theological Seminary has been received. It gives me pleasure to reply that I hope and intend to be present on that occasion as a representative of the Theological Seminary of St. Lawrence University.

Respectfully yours,

HENRY P. FORBES,
Dean of Seminary.

February 27th, 1912.

CHICAGO THEOLOGICAL SEMINARY, CHICAGO, ILLINOIS

The Faculty of Chicago Theological Seminary accept with pleasure the invitation of the Directors, Trustees and Faculty of the Princeton Theological Seminary to be represented at the Centennial of the Seminary May fifth–seventh, nineteen hundred and twelve, and have requested the Rev. George S. Rollins, D.D., Pastor of the Hope Congregational Church, Springfield, Mass., to represent us on that auspicious occasion.

On behalf of the Faculty,

Very sincerely yours,

CLARENCE A. BECKWITH,
Secretary of the Faculty.

PRINCETON THEOLOGICAL SEMINARY

NIAGARA UNIVERSITY SEMINARY OF OUR LADY OF ANGELS, NIAGARA FALLS, NEW YORK

President Edward J. Walsh, of Niagara University Seminary of Our Lady of Angels, begs to acknowledge the favor of the invitation to attend the Centenary Exercises of the Princeton Theological Seminary, and to render sincere thanks for the courtesy. He will not be able to accept, but he wishes a very successful celebration on this significant occasion.

February 29, 1912.

SEABURY DIVINITY SCHOOL, FARIBAULT, MINNESOTA

At a meeting of the Faculty of Seabury Divinity School, March 15, 1912, the Reverend William Austin Smith of the class of 1898, now Rector of Christ Church, Springfield, Massachusetts, was duly appointed as a delegate to represent Seabury Divinity School at the Centennial Celebration of the Princeton Theological Seminary on Sunday, Monday and Tuesday, May fifth, sixth and seventh, nineteen hundred and twelve. He has been notified of his appointment and we hope that he will be able to be present.

Sincerely yours,

ELMER E. LOFSTROM,
Secretary of the Faculty.

March 19, 1912.

CENTENNIAL CELEBRATION OF

THE MISSION HOUSE, PLYMOUTH, WISCONSIN

To the Directors, Trustees and Faculty of the Theological Seminary of the Presbyterian Church in the United States of America, at Princeton, New Jersey:—In Christ Jesus dearly beloved Fathers and Brethren:

We hereby acknowledge the receipt of your invitation to the Theological Seminary of the Mission House to be represented at the celebration of the One Hundredth Anniversary of the establishment of the Theological Seminary of the Presbyterian Church in the United States of America, at Princeton, New Jersey.

We regret that causes beyond our control render it almost or quite impossible for us to send a delegate to take part in the celebration in the first week in May.

We regret this the more, as we cherish the most kindly feelings toward your Seminary, and owe a debt of gratitude to the great teachers of our Reformed faith, the Alexanders, the Hodges, Miller, Green and others, whose writings have been a source of instruction and encouragement both to our teachers and to our students.

We, therefore, most gratefully acknowledge these benefits derived from your Seminary; and, in so doing, we bespeak for you in the new century, upon which, in the providence of God, you are now entering, the blessing, protection and guidance of the triune God; and we trust and pray, that, in this age of apostasy, your Seminary may continue to be a bulwark against the onslaughts of the enemy that is so violently attacking the Church and the Gospel of our blessed Lord and Saviour

PRINCETON THEOLOGICAL SEMINARY

Jesus Christ; and that your professors may still, as in the past, and even more, if that be possible, prove champions of the faith which was once delivered to the saints.

In the years to come, our eyes shall still be turned toward Princeton, and our ears shall hearken for the public expression of the sage Christian instructions and counsels delivered in your halls.

That the "Lord may bless you out of Zion, and may do to you exceeding abundantly above all that you ask or think" is the sincere wish of the Faculty of the Theological Seminary of the Mission House of the Reformed Church in the United States.

E. A. HOFER, *President*,
FRANK GRETHER, *Secretary*.

February 23rd, 1912.

[SEAL]

THE SOUTHERN BAPTIST THEOLOGICAL SEMINARY, LOUISVILLE, KENTUCKY

I am due you an apology for a serious oversight. In some way the invitation to our Faculty to send a representative to the celebration of the One Hundredth Anniversary of Princeton Seminary was overlooked. At our last Faculty meeting, however, action was taken, appointing me as our official representative to the celebration. Asking your pardon for the delay, I am

Yours sincerely,

E. Y. MULLINS,
President.

April 5, 1912.

CENTENNIAL CELEBRATION OF

AUGUSTANA COLLEGE AND THEOLOGICAL SEMINARY, ROCK ISLAND, ILLINOIS

I desire to acknowledge the receipt of an invitation from the Directors, Trustees and Faculty of the Princeton Theological Seminary to Augustana College and Theological Seminary, to be represented by a delegate at the Hundredth Anniversary of the establishment of the Seminary by the General Assembly, on Sunday, Monday, and Tuesday, the 5th, 6th, and 7th of May next. I would say that our General Faculty has appointed President Gustav Andreen, Ph.D., to represent our institution on that occasion.

Thanking you for this invitation, and assuring you that we highly appreciate the honor you have conferred upon us, I am,

Sincerely yours,

E. F. BARTHOLOMEW,
Acting President.

April 1, 1912.

CENTRAL WESLEYAN COLLEGE, WARRENTON, MISSOURI

In reply to your cordial invitation to send a representative of our Theological Seminary to be present at the celebration of the one hundredth anniversary of the establishment of the Princeton Theological Seminary, I desire herewith to express our sincere thanks. At the

PRINCETON THEOLOGICAL SEMINARY

same time I would express our regrets that it will be impossible for any one of our professors or officers to be present. However if it is desired, we shall be glad to be represented by Rev. F. J. Hubach, Phillipsburg, New Jersey. He is an alumnus of our school and has both the A.B. and the B.D.

Thanking you again most sincerely,
Very truly yours,

HENRY VOSHOLL,
Secretary of the Faculty.

February 26, 1912.

LUTHERAN THEOLOGICAL SEMINARY, MOUNT AIRY, PHILADELPHIA

The Faculty of the Lutheran Theological Seminary at Philadelphia hereby acknowledges the receipt of an invitation to be represented at the One Hundredth Anniversary of the establishment of the Theological Seminary of the Presbyterian Church in the United States at Princeton, N. J., to be celebrated on the fifth, sixth and seventh of May, and has instructed me to inform you that Rev. Henry Eyster Jacobs, D.D., S.T.D., LL.D., Dean of our Seminary and Chairman of its Faculty, will be our representative on that interesting occasion.

Yours truly,

JACOB FRY,
Secretary of Faculty.

February 22, 1912.

CENTENNIAL CELEBRATION OF

DE LANCEY DIVINITY SCHOOL, GENEVA, NEW YORK

The Trustees of the De Lancey Divinity School beg to acknowledge the courtesy of the most kind invitation of the Directors, Trustees and Faculty of the Theological Seminary of the Presbyterian Church in the United States at Princeton, N. J., to send a delegate on the occasion of the One Hundredth Anniversary of the establishment of the Seminary at Princeton, May 5-7, 1912, and hope to be able to send such a delegate, to be appointed at a later meeting of the Trustees.

I am, faithfully yours,

THOMAS B. BERRY,

March 1, 1912. *Warden.*

THE UNIVERSITY OF CHICAGO DIVINITY SCHOOL, CHICAGO, ILLINOIS

The Faculty of the Divinity School of the University of Chicago regrets the impossibility of sending a delegate to participate in the celebration of the One Hundredth Anniversary of the founding of Princeton Theological Seminary. The Faculty wishes, however, to express its hearty felicitations on this occasion, and to share in the universal appreciation of the services rendered by Princeton Theological Seminary to its denomination and to the cause of learning.

HARRY PRATT JUDSON, *President,*
April 5, 1912. SHAILER MATHEWS, *Dean.*

PRINCETON THEOLOGICAL SEMINARY

ATLANTA BAPTIST COLLEGE DIVINITY SCHOOL, ATLANTA, GEORGIA

The invitation of the Theological Seminary to attend the Celebration of its One Hundredth Anniversary has been received and is deeply appreciated by Atlanta Baptist College Divinity School. I cannot say just yet whether it will be practicable for me to attend and shall have to write you later more definitely.

Sincerely yours,

JOHN HOPE,
President.

February 17, 1912.

DREW THEOLOGICAL SEMINARY, MADISON, NEW JERSEY

The Faculty of Drew Theological Seminary, recognizing the honor of invitation to share in the celebration of the One Hundredth Anniversary of the Establishment of Princeton Theological Seminary on Sunday, Monday and Tuesday, the fifth, sixth and seventh of May, nineteen hundred and twelve, have designated the Reverend President Henry A. Buttz, D.D., LL.D.; to represent them and to extend their most cordial greetings and felicitations.

By order of the Faculty,

CHAS. F. SITTERLY,
Secretary.

March 1, 1912.

CENTENNIAL CELEBRATION OF

EPISCOPAL THEOLOGICAL SCHOOL, CAMBRIDGE, MASSACHUSETTS

The Faculty of the Episcopal Theological School in Cambridge acknowledge with thanks the kind invitation of the Princeton Theological Seminary, and will send as their delegate to the celebration of the one hundredth anniversary the Rev. Prof. Henry Sylvester Nash, D.D.

February 17, 1912.

CROZER THEOLOGICAL SEMINARY, CHESTER, PENNSYLVANIA

I have the honor to reply to the invitation to send a delegate to the One Hundredth Anniversary that our Faculty voted to send the President, M. G. Evans, D.D., thanking you for the invitation, and directing me to communicate to you their action.

ALVAH S. HOBART,
Secretary.

February 22, 1912.

THEOLOGICAL DEPARTMENT, THE UNIVERSITY OF THE SOUTH, SEWANEE, TENNESSEE

It is with keen regret that I find that it will be impossible for our Theological Department to be represented at your anniversary celebration. I had hoped that some of us might be able to arrange it.

With best wishes and heartiest congratulations, I am very faithfully yours,

C. K. BENEDICT,
Dean Theological Department.

March 20th, 1912.

THE GERMAN THEOLOGICAL SCHOOL OF NEWARK, NEW JERSEY, BLOOMFIELD, NEW JERSEY

Your kind invitation extended to "The German Theological School of Newark, N. J." to attend the one hundredth anniversary celebration of the Princeton Theological Seminary has been received and was duly submitted to the Faculty at their regular meeting on March 4th, 1912. The Faculty have appointed the Rev. Henry J. Weber, Ph.D., D.D., Chairman of the Faculty, to represent our School.

Respectfully yours,
CHARLES T. HOCK,
Secretary.

March 7th, 1912.

PACIFIC THEOLOGICAL SEMINARY, BERKELEY, CALIFORNIA

Pacific Theological Seminary gratefully acknowledges the invitation of Princeton Theological Seminary and appreciates the honor. It regrets that by reason of distance it cannot be represented by a delegate on the occasion of the one-hundredth anniversary, the fifth, sixth and seventh of May, and sends its earnest wishes for the success of that event and the long prosperity of Princeton Theological Seminary.

March 1st, 1912.

WOODSTOCK COLLEGE, WOODSTOCK, MARYLAND

The President and Faculty of Woodstock College are sincerely grateful to the Directors, Trustees and Faculty of Princeton Theological Seminary for the honor of their kind invitation to be present at the celebration of the one hundredth anniversary of Princeton's establishment, and regret that a partial coincidence with Georgetown's celebration and examination duties at home will prevent them from being present.

Wishing the Princeton Seminary all the blessings of heaven needed for a second century of success, I remain,

Yours sincerely,

A. J. MAAS, S. J.,
President.

April 15, 1912.

PRINCETON THEOLOGICAL SEMINARY

THE THEOLOGICAL SEMINARY OF THE EVANGELICAL LUTHERAN CHURCH, CHICAGO, ILLINOIS

The Faculty of the Theological Seminary of the Evangelical Lutheran Church, at Chicago, Ill., acknowledges with pleasure the announcement of the One Hundredth Anniversary of the Establishment of The Theological Seminary of the Presbyterian Church in the United States of America at Princeton, New Jersey, on May Fifth, Sixth and Seventh, Nineteen Hundred Twelve.

The Faculty has designated to represent it on that occasion The Reverend Revere Franklin Weidner, D.D., LL.D., President.

By the Faculty,

ALFRED RAMSEY,

March 19, 1912. *Secretary.*

ALFRED THEOLOGICAL SEMINARY, ALFRED, NEW YORK

Your invitation to our Seminary to be represented at the one hundredth anniversary of Princeton's establishment is gratefully acknowledged.

Nothing unforeseen preventing, either President B. C. Davis of our University, or myself, will be present.

Meanwhile accept our congratulations upon Princeton's great history, and believe us to be,

Fraternally yours,

ARTHUR E. MAIN,

February 18th, 1912. *Dean.*

CENTENNIAL CELEBRATION OF

HOWARD UNIVERSITY, THEOLOGICAL DEPARTMENT, WASHINGTON, DISTRICT OF COLUMBIA

I beg to inform you that the Rev. Dr. Isaac Clark, for many years the Dean of the School of Theology of Howard University, has been appointed to represent the Board of Trustees and Faculty at the coming Centenary of the Theological Seminary of Princeton.
Very sincerely yours,

W. P. THIRKIELD,
President.

April 13, 1912.

THE SAN FRANCISCO THEOLOGICAL SEMINARY, SAN ANSELMO, CALIFORNIA

The San Francisco Theological Seminary has received with appreciation the invitation to be present at the one hundredth anniversary of the founding of Princeton Theological Seminary. It will be represented on that occasion by its President, the Rev. Warren Hall Landon, D.D.
By order of the Faculty,

WARREN H. LANDON,
President.

February 23, 1912.

TALLADEGA COLLEGE, THEOLOGICAL DEPARTMENT, TALLADEGA, ALABAMA

The Theological Department of Talladega College received with pleasure the announcement that the Theological Seminary of the Presbyterian Church in the United States of America at Princeton, New Jersey, will celebrate the one hundredth anniversary of its establishment by the General Assembly, on May fifth, sixth and seventh, nineteen hundred and twelve, and the invitation of the Directors, Trustees and Faculty of the Seminary to be represented on that occasion by a delegate.

We regret that it will not be practicable for us to send a representative to the celebration of this notable anniversary, but extend our congratulations to the Theological Seminary at Princeton upon its long and honored service to the Christian Churches of America, and pray that for centuries to come it may continue its splendid career of training men for the Christian ministry.

April 1912.

THEOLOGICAL SCHOOL AND CALVIN COLLEGE, GRAND RAPIDS, MICHIGAN

Your kind invitation extended to our Faculty to participate in the Centennial Celebration of Princeton Theological Seminary was gratefully received and brought before our faculty meeting.

As the secretary of our Faculty, I am instructed to

thank you for the honor bestowed by your invitation upon our young and still small institution; and to inform you that we have appointed as a delegate from our school Prof. L. Berkhof.

He will convey to the Princeton Theological Seminary our friendly greetings and heartfelt congratulations.

May our God bless your honored and worthy Institution abundantly in the future for the promotion and advancement of His Eternal Kingdom.

From the Faculty of the Theological School and Calvin College of the Christian Reformed Church at Grand Rapids, Mich.

K. SCHOOLLAND,
Secretary.

March 20, 1912.

WESTMINSTER THEOLOGICAL SEMINARY, WESTMINSTER, MARYLAND

In reply to the invitation of the Princeton Theological Seminary to send a representative to the one hundredth anniversary of that institution, I beg leave to notify you that we highly appreciate the honor and have expressed it by electing the Secretary of our Faculty, Rev. Claude Cicero Douglas, A.M., B.D., to be our representative upon that notable occasion.

Sincerely,

H. L. ELDERDICE,
President.

February 22nd, 1912.

THE TEMPLE UNIVERSITY, DEPARTMENT OF THEOLOGY, PHILADELPHIA

On behalf of the Faculty of Temple University, Department of Theology, I extend to you its felicitations upon the celebration of the one hundredth anniversary of the establishment of the Theological Seminary of the Presbyterian Church at Princeton, New Jersey.

The Faculty also desires me to thank you for inviting it to be represented at this centennial by a delegate, and has appointed Professor, the Reverend George Handy Wailes to be present at the exercises.

Yours sincerely,
WALTER B. SHUMWAY,
Dean.

April 22, 1912.

WESTERN THEOLOGICAL SEMINARY, CHICAGO, ILLINOIS

The Western Theological Seminary, at Chicago, Illinois, regrets its inability to accept the kind invitation of the Directors, Trustees and Faculty of the Princeton Theological Seminary of the Presbyterian Church, to be represented on the occasion of its one hundredth anniversary on Sunday, Monday and Tuesday, the fifth, sixth and seventh of May, 1912.

Very sincerely yours,
WM. C. DE WITT,
Dean.

February 23rd, 1912.

CENTENNIAL CELEBRATION OF

UNIVERSITY OF SOUTHERN CALIFORNIA, MACLAY COLLEGE OF THEOLOGY, LOS ANGELES, CALIFORNIA

I acknowledge with cordial thanks, on behalf of the Maclay College of Theology, the invitation to be represented by a delegate at the celebration of the one hundredth anniversary of the establishment of the Theological Seminary at Princeton, New Jersey. Please convey to the directors, trustees and faculty of the Seminary our friendly greeting with the earnest wish that your fine old Seminary may fill a second century with even more good work than has characterized its first.

We are unable to be represented by a delegate but are happy to send this greeting.

Very sincerely yours,

E. A. HEALY,
Dean.

May 3, 1912.

THE CATHOLIC UNIVERSITY OF AMERICA, SCHOOL OF SACRED SCIENCES, WASHINGTON, DISTRICT OF COLUMBIA

Our School of Sacred Sciences acknowledges the receipt of the invitation of Princeton Theological Seminary to the celebration of the Hundredth Anniversary of its foundation. While it will not be possible for us to participate in that event, we extend to all the members of

PRINCETON THEOLOGICAL SEMINARY

Princeton Theological Seminary our best wishes for their personal welfare and we trust that the celebration itself will be all that they could desire.
I remain,
Very sincerely yours,
PATRICK J. HEALY,
Dean of the Faculty of Theology.

March 21st, 1912.

SAINT LEO ABBEY,
SAINT LEO, FLORIDA

My dear Mr. Robinson:

Your Church has done much good in America. Dr. Smith, for many years an intimate friend of mine during my missionary experience in Greensboro, N. C., was goodness itself. His death was a great loss to Christendom.

Will you please act as our delegate during the Centenary Celebration? Distance is too great and I have not the time to spare.

I wish you every success.
Cordially yours,
RT. REV. ABBOT CHARLES.

17 February, 1912.

CENTENNIAL CELEBRATION OF

THE SEMINARY OF THE UNITED NORWEGIAN LUTHERAN CHURCH, SAINT ANTHONY PARK, MINNESOTA

The Faculty of the Seminary of the United Norwegian Lutheran Church acknowledge the receipt of an invitation to be represented at the celebration of the one hundredth anniversary of the Theological Seminary at Princeton, N. J.

We thank you for the invitation and regret that it will be impossible for us to send a representative.

We congratulate the Seminary upon its achievements for the Kingdom of Christ and wish it God's richest blessings.

On behalf of the Faculty,

CARL M. WESWIG,
Secretary.

April 8, 1912.

PRESBYTERIAN THEOLOGICAL SEMINARY, OMAHA, NEBRASKA

I am writing to acknowledge the receipt of an invitation from Princeton Seminary to be present, May 5–7, 1912, at the celebration of the One Hundredth Anniversary of the founding of the Seminary, and to say that if I am unable to be in Princeton at the time it will be a great disappointment to me. There are, however, at the present time serious obstacles in the way, principally the closing exercises of our Seminary which extend so far into the preceding week that it may not be possible to reach Princeton in time after their conclusion. We hope our Seminary may be represented by one of our Professors at the Celebration. Four of the members of our Faculty are graduates of Princeton Seminary and we are very much interested in this great event in the history of our Alma Mater.

Yours cordially,
A. B. MARSHALL,
President.

February 29, 1912.

HOUGHTON WESLEYAN METHODIST THEOLOGICAL SEMINARY, HOUGHTON, NEW YORK

The Faculty of the Houghton Wesleyan Methodist Seminary accept with pleasure the invitation of the Theological Seminary of the Presbyterian Church in the United States of America at Princeton, N. J., to be represented by a delegate at the one hundredth anniversary of its establishment by the General Assembly. Prof. H. R. Smith has been elected as this delegate.

March 12, 1912.

PRESBYTERIAN THEOLOGICAL SEMINARY OF KENTUCKY, LOUISVILLE, KENTUCKY

In response to the invitation extended our Faculty to be represented by a Delegate at the celebration of the one hundredth anniversary of the founding of Princeton Theological Seminary, the Faculty appointed some weeks ago the Rev. Professor Jesse Lee Cotton, D.D., its representative and the bearer of its greetings, of which appointment you have, I believe, received information.

The Faculty desire me, on their behalf, to convey also by letter their felicitations on this notable occasion.

We congratulate your venerable institution on being in a sense "the mother of us all," and on your having set high standards for all similar institutions that have been established within the past hundred years.

We congratulate you on the illustrious names that adorn the roll of your Professors, whose piety, scholarship, teaching power, and writings have carried the name and fame of Princeton throughout the world.

We congratulate you on the unwavering fidelity of the Seminary to the Holy Scriptures, the Reformed Faith, and the Presbyterian Church, with which has been united a large-hearted devotion to a truly Catholic Christianity and the Church Universal, so that the Princeton theology and spirit are known and honored in every part of Christendom.

We congratulate you on the hundreds of young men who have been trained for the ministry within your walls, who have enriched the Church and the world by their labors, who have served the Church at home in every department of her manifold work, and who have preached the Gospel in every continent and in the islands of the sea.

We congratulate you on the present prosperity of the Seminary with its splendid equipment and able Faculty, and especially on the service it is rendering the whole

Church of God in the confirmation and defence of the truth.

For the years to come, we do not know that we can offer any better prayer for you than to supplicate the grace of God upon your great institution in such measure as to make its future worthy of its past. In company with a multitude of others in this and every land, we pray there may be granted to all connected with the Seminary the unfailing presence and power of the Holy Spirit.

On behalf of the Faculty,

Faithfully yours,

CHARLES R. HEMPHILL,
President.

May 2, 1912.

[TELEGRAM]

The Board of Directors of the Presbyterian Theological Seminary of Kentucky, in session to-day at Louisville, send greetings and congratulations on Princeton's Centennial Anniversary. "Peace be within thy walls and prosperity within thy palaces."

PEYTON H. HOGE,
President.

May 7, 1912.

CENTENNIAL CELEBRATION OF

WESTERN THEOLOGICAL SEMINARY, ATCHISON, KANSAS

I have the honor to inform you that at a meeting of the Faculty of the Western Theological Seminary, held in Atchison, Kansas, April 21, 1912, the Rev. Frederick G. Gotwald, D.D., was chosen to represent the Institution at the one hundredth anniversary of the establishment of the Princeton Theological Seminary, to be held at Princeton, New Jersey, May 5th, 6th, and 7th, 1912.
Sincerely yours,

HOLMES DYSINGER,
Dean.

April 22, 1912.

TAYLOR UNIVERSITY, READE THEOLOGICAL SEMINARY, UPLAND, INDIANA

We have your kind invitation to be represented at your Anniversary exercises. Thank you indeed for the invitation, but my engagements are such just at this time that it will be impossible for me to attend. Trust your next hundred years may be greatly blessed of the Lord.
Most sincerely yours,

M. VAYHINGER,
President.

February 26, 1912.

PRINCETON THEOLOGICAL SEMINARY

TURNER THEOLOGICAL SEMINARY, MORRIS BROWN COLLEGE, ATLANTA, GEORGIA

Having been selected by Turner Theological Seminary, Morris Brown College, to represent them at the One Hundredth Anniversary of the establishment of your Seminary, I had high hopes of the full enjoyment of all of the pleasures represented by your very kind invitation, but at the last moment I find myself unavoidably detained and prevented from being present in person.

Permit me to say that we most sincerely rejoice in your remarkable prosperity and successful round out of One Hundred Years.

We view with delight your long and illustrious line of representative men as Clergymen, Authors, Statesmen and Scholars, justly the pride of any institution or denomination.

While we pray for all of the anticipated pleasures of this, your One Hundredth Anniversary occasion, we also trust the coming century may hold in store for you larger blessings and greater triumphs.

Again regretting my inability to be present, I am,
Very faithfully yours,
W. G. ALEXANDER,
May 4, 1912.   *Dean.*

EUGENE BIBLE UNIVERSITY, EUGENE, OREGON

The announcement of the hundredth anniversary of the Princeton Theological Seminary, to be observed

CENTENNIAL CELEBRATION OF

from the fifth to the seventh of May, and your kind invitation to attend the celebration, received. I am authorized to say for the Trustees and Faculty of the Eugene Bible University that we appreciate this invitation and kindly notice. We also honor the institution of learning from which this invitation comes for its faithfulness to the Holy Scriptures and to the Saviour, and for its world-wide influence in behalf of evangelical Christianity.

We regret that we can not have a representative from our school to be with you at the time you suggest.

Most cordially and faithfully yours,

EUGENE BIBLE UNIVERSITY,

By E. C. SANDERSON,
President.

February 21, 1912.

MANCHESTER COLLEGE, BIBLICAL DEPARTMENT, NORTH MANCHESTER, INDIANA

The Biblical Department of Manchester College, North Manchester, Indiana, desires to acknowledge the receipt of your invitation to be represented at your one hundredth anniversary on the 5th–7th of May next. We wish to express our thanks for your kind invitation, but do not see our way clear to be represented by a delegate on that important occasion.

May Princeton Theological Seminary have many

more years in the training of men for the most important work in the world.

> Yours very sincerely,
>
> S. S. BLOUGH,
> *Dean.*

March 4, 1912.

SCHOOL OF THEOLOGY, KANSAS CITY UNIVERSITY, KANSAS CITY, KANSAS

The Kansas City University School of Theology acknowledges with pleasure the receipt of the invitation from the Directors, Trustees and Faculty of the Princeton Theological Seminary to be represented at the One Hundredth Anniversary Celebration of the Seminary on the fifth, sixth and seventh of May, nineteen hundred and twelve.

We most heartily congratulate you and the Seminary on the happy completion of one hundred years of noble service to the intellectual and spiritual welfare of mankind. The name and influence of "Princeton" are vitally and inspiringly connected with the early history of our beloved country and have done a vast deal to shape and conserve American ideals, and to give character and effectiveness to missionary endeavor in many lands, and thus largely to enter into the world's life for its lasting betterment.

If possible, we shall be represented and will ask the Reverend D. Baines-Griffith, of Spuyten Duyvil, New York City, a former instructor in Kansas City University, to be present as our representative.

CENTENNIAL CELEBRATION OF

We join in the prayers for multiplied blessing and usefulness for your splendid Institution in the years to come.

Very sincerely yours,

HERBERT TAYLOR STEPHENS,
Dean.

March 23, 1912.

WESTMINSTER COLLEGE, THEOLOGICAL DEPARTMENT, TEHUACANA, TEXAS

The faculty of Westminster College regrets that it will not be able to send a representative to the celebration in honor of the one-hundredth anniversary of the Theological Seminary of the Presbyterian Church in the United States of America. We extend to the Seminary our heartiest congratulations, and hope that the noble work it has done will be increased and multiplied in the coming years.

Very truly yours,

H. H. PRICE,
President.

March 18, 1912.

VIRGINIA UNION UNIVERSITY, THEOLOGICAL DEPARTMENT, RICHMOND, VIRGINIA

Permit me to acknowledge the courtesy of an invitation from you to attend the one hundredth anniversary

PRINCETON THEOLOGICAL SEMINARY

of the establishment of the Theological Seminary at Princeton. I regret that it does not seem possible for any official representative of the Theological Departmen of Virginia Union University to be present on that occasion.

We, however, send most cordial congratulations on your distinguished work for a century, and the best wishes for its continuance and enlargement in the years to come.

Very respectfully yours,

GEORGE RICE HOVEY,
President.

14 March, 1912.

ATLANTA THEOLOGICAL SEMINARY, ATLANTA, GEORGIA

In the absence of the President, I write to acknowledge the receipt of your kind favor of March twenty-fifth. And I am instructed to report that the Delegate appointed to represent the Atlanta Theological Seminary at the Princeton Centennial in May is the Reverend James Wilson Bixler, D.D., Professor Elect, Natural Theology, of New London, Connecticut, who plans to be with you, bearing the greetings of our Institution on that happy occasion.

Very truly yours,

MRS. E. LYMAN HOOD.

April 4, 1912.

[SEAL]

CENTENNIAL CELEBRATION OF

MERIDIAN MALE COLLEGE, SCHOOL OF THEOLOGY AND EVANGELISM, MERIDIAN, MISSISSIPPI

In behalf of the President and Faculty of Meridian Male College, and as Dean of the School of Theology and Evangelism, I take pleasure in acknowledging receipt of your invitation to be represented at the "Centennial" of good, grand old "Princeton".

While distance and date will preclude the probability of our being then represented in person, our prayers are with you and our love.

Fraternally yours,

JOSEPH H. SMITH.

February 21, 1912.

AUSTIN THEOLOGICAL SEMINARY, AUSTIN, TEXAS

Please permit me to convey to you and to the Faculty and Directors of Princeton Seminary the thanks of the Faculty of the Austin Presbyterian Theological Seminary for your kind invitation to attend the exercises celebrating the one hundredth anniversary of the founding of your great institution.

It would give us a great deal of pleasure to be able to be represented by a delegate on that occasion, but unfortunately it comes just at the time of the closing of our own session and the annual meeting of the Board of

Trustees of this Seminary, at which time, owing to peculiar circumstances, it is important that every member of our Faculty shall be present here. Personally I wish that it were otherwise, for I should count it not only an honor but a great privilege to be with you in May and nothing short of necessity would prevent my so doing.

Princeton is known and loved all over the South and nowhere more than in Texas, and we wish for her many centuries of loyal service to our Lord and of steadfast adherence to the principles of our common faith. May the great Head of the Church crown her efforts with His presence and blessing and make her increasingly fruitful in the work of the Kingdom.

Most cordially and sincerely yours,

ROBERT E. VINSON,
President.

March 8, 1912.

PACIFIC UNITARIAN SCHOOL FOR THE MINISTRY, BERKELEY, CALIFORNIA

Pacific Unitarian School for the Ministry accepts the invitation of the Directors, Trustees and Faculty of the Theological Seminary of the Presbyterian Church in the United States of America at Princeton, New Jersey, to be represented by a delegate on the occasion of the celebration of the one hundredth anniversary of the Seminary's establishment, on Sunday, Monday and Tuesday, the fifth, sixth and seventh of May, nineteen hundred and twelve, and has appointed as its delegate the Reverend William Sacheus Morgan, B.D., Ph.D., Professor of Systematic Theology.

February 20th, 1912.

THE SOUTHWESTERN BAPTIST THEOLOGICAL SEMINARY, FORT WORTH, TEXAS

The Faculty of the Southwestern Baptist Theological Seminary appreciate very highly the invitation of Princeton Theological Seminary to send a representative to the celebration of the Hundredth Anniversary of that honored institution, and I have been honored with appointment to represent our Seminary on that occasion. I hope to be present to join with many others in recognizing the great service that Princeton has rendered to the cause of evangelical religion.

Sincerely yours,

ALBERT HENRY NEWMAN,
Dean and Professor of Church History.

February 23, 1912.

CENTRAL THEOLOGICAL SEMINARY OF THE REFORMED CHURCH IN THE UNITED STATES, DAYTON, OHIO

The invitation to send a delegate to the celebration of the Centennial of Princeton Seminary was received and laid before the faculty of this institution.

I have been instructed to notify you that we greatly

appreciate the honor of this invitation, and that Rev. Prof. J. I. Good, D.D., LL.D., at present residing at 3262 Chestnut Street, Philadelphia, Pa., has been appointed to represent our Seminary on the occasion of your celebration.

Fraternally yours,

PHILIP VOLLMER,
Secretary of the Faculty.

February 21, 1912.

PACIFIC EVANGELICAL LUTHERAN SEMINARY, OLYMPIA, WASHINGTON

The Pacific Lutheran Seminary wishes to announce the receipt of the invitation extended by your Honorable Body to attend the celebration, on the 5th, 6th and 7th of May, of the one hundredth anniversary of the establishment by the General Assembly of the Theological Seminary at Princeton, New Jersey.

The Faculty, in the name of the Institution, desires to extend cordial felicitations and hearty well-wishes, and hopes that the future will be as prosperous for the Seminary as has been the past.

The Board, however, regrets exceedingly that adverse circumstances will not make it possible to send a representative to attend the festivities.

Yours fraternally,

ARMIN PAUL MEYER,
President.

April 1, 1912.

PRINCETON THEOLOGICAL SEMINARY

SAINT PATRICK'S SEMINARY, MENLO PARK, CALIFORNIA

The Faculty of the St. Patrick's Seminary are very thankful for the honor of your invitation to be represented by a Delegate at the celebration of the one hundredth anniversary of Princeton Theological Seminary, but regret to be unable to send any one to be present on the occasion.

RESPONSES FROM
MISSIONARY SEMINARIES

ALBERT ACADEMY, FREETOWN, SIERRA LEONE, WEST AFRICA

I wish to acknowledge with many thanks the invitation sent to Albert Academy to send a delegate to the one hundredth anniversary celebrations of the Theological Seminary of the Presbyterian Church at Princeton, New Jersey.

We have elected as our delegate the Vice-Principal of Albert Academy, the Rev. Edwin M. Hursh, A.B., who is at present taking special work in Chicago University. His address is 332 East 55th Street, Chicago, Ill. I have written to inform him of his election as delegate and trust he will be able to attend.

Very sincerely yours,

RAYMOND P. DOUGHERTY,
Principal.

March 9, 1912.

ÉLAT THEOLOGICAL SCHOOL, ÉLAT, KAMERUN, WEST AFRICA

In reply to the kind invitation from Princeton Theological Seminary to the Theological School at Élat, asking representation at the celebration of Princeton's one hundredth anniversary, we hasten to say that our Theological Seminary is a very modest affair. The building cost about fifteen dollars; the class now embraces six Bulu young men and one Ñgumba; the faculty consists of the writer of these lines; and the subjects being taught at present are Church History, Acts of the Apostles, Life of Christ, and Theology of the Shorter Catechism. But embryonic as we are out here in the bush, we believe that our work counts in the redemption of Africa, and we are not without aspirations to be useful, if not large.

We much appreciate the invitation, and would gladly accept if distance and limitation of time did not forbid. Speaking as a little child to a mighty giant, we beg to wish grand old Princeton another hundred years of fruit-bearing. And we take this opportunity to raise again the Macedonian call for some more of her students to come over and help us.

With fraternal and prayerful thoughts for Princeton in anticipation of those glad May days of celebration,

On behalf of the Theological work at Élat,

Yours sincerely,

MELVIN FRASER.

March 25, 1912.

UNION THEOLOGICAL COLLEGE, IMPOLWENI, NEAR MARITZBURG, NATAL

The Faculty of this Union Theological College feels highly honoured by the invitation of the Directors, Trustees and Faculty of your world-famed Theological Seminary to be represented at the coming celebration of the

PRINCETON THEOLOGICAL SEMINARY one hundredth anniversary of its establishment. Not having any one in your country at present to represent us, we must be satisfied with the expression of our best wishes and prayers for the success of your celebration.
Believe me,
Yours very sincerely,

JAS. LUKE,
Principal.

30th May, 1912.

THEOLOGICAL TRAINING SCHOOL, OGBOMOSO, SOUTHERN NIGERIA, WEST AFRICA

[SEAL]

Your kind invitation for the Training School of Ogbomoso to be represented at the celebration of your One Hundredth Anniversary was duly received. In the absence of any representative from our Theological School, I send to you our hearty congratulations and greetings, and trust that the years of the second century of your noble Institution may be crowned with even greater usefulness and blessing than the first.

I thank you personally for the thoughtfulness and missionary interest that lie behind the invitation, that the great and noble Princeton Theological Seminary could find a place on its list of invitations for the Theological Training School of Ogbomoso, West Africa.

Yours fraternally,

(REV.) GEORGE GREEN, M.D.

April 27th, 1912.

CENTENNIAL CELEBRATION OF

SEMINARIO THEOLOGICO DA EGREJA PRESBYTERIANA NO BRASIL, CAMPINAS, BRAZIL

Coming back to the Seminary, I found the beautiful invitation which the Theological Seminary at Princeton has sent to ours.

The Faculty of this Seminary has elected the Rev. Dr. J. M. Kyle, who for many years has been the Chairman of our Board of Trustees and who had given valuable help to this institution when he was here in Brazil, to be our delegate at the celebration of the Centenary of the Princeton Seminary.

I remain, dear sir,
    Your obedient servant,

ERASMO BRAGA,
Dean.

March 8th, 1912.

THE AMERICAN COLLEGIATE AND THEOLOGICAL INSTITUTE, SAMOKOV, BULGARIA

The invitation of the Directors, Trustees and Faculty of Princeton Seminary to the Collegiate and Theological Institute of Samokov, Bulgaria, to be represented by a delegate at the approaching celebration of the centenary of the Seminary, has been received. The Trustees of the Institute deeply appreciate the courtesy and honor thus extended, and at a recent meeting voted a hearty expression of thanks for the invitation. They also desire to congratulate the Seminary on the completion of one hundred years of splendid work for the kingdom of Christ at home and abroad, and to extend sincerest wishes for its future growth, prosperity and usefulness. It may be interesting to state that one of the present Trustees is himself a graduate of Princeton Seminary, Rev. D. N. Furnajieff, of the class of 1898.

The Trustees also selected as the representative of the Collegiate and Theological Institute at the centennial celebration, Rev. Lewis Bond, for many years a missionary of the American Board in European Turkey. Mr. Bond's present address is No. 720 Kensington Ave., Plainfield, N. J. It is hoped that he will be able to accept this appointment, and he will be requested to inform you as to his decision.

With cordial and fraternal greetings, I remain,
Very sincerely yours,

ROBT. THOMSON,
13 March, 1912.   *President of the Trustees.*

[SEAL]

KAREN THEOLOGICAL SEMINARY, INSEIN, BURMA

To the Directors, Trustees and Faculty of the Theological Seminary of the Presbyterian Church in the United States of America at Princeton, New Jersey, Greeting:

The Karen Theological Seminary regrets that it cannot be represented by a delegate on the occasion of the

CENTENNIAL CELEBRATION OF

Hundredth Anniversary of the Princeton Theological Seminary, as no member of its Staff will be in America at that time.

March, 1912.

FATI THEOLOGICAL COLLEGE, CANTON, CHINA

On behalf of the Fati Theological College, I write, at this too late date, to express our cordial appreciation of your kind invitation sent to us to send a delegate to the celebration of the one hundredth anniversary of the establishment of Princeton Theological Seminary.

At this distance we were of course unable to send a delegate, but we do not forget that our Presbyterian Mission in Canton has had worthy representatives from Princeton: in the earlier years, Rev. Charles F. Preston, easily among the first in ability to speak the Chinese language; Rev. B. C. Henry, well known at Princeton as elsewhere; later Rev. C. E. Patton, still with us; then our martyred Peale whose short life here left its blessing; and last Rev. J. W. Creighton.

We shall be glad to have more of your men.

Yours very sincerely,

HENRY V. NOYES.

June 21st, 1912.

THE GRAVES THEOLOGICAL SCHOOL, CANTON, CHINA

We send you our sincere and hearty congratulations on the 100th celebration of your work for the Master. We appreciate very much your kindness in asking us to send a representative of our institution on the happy occasion, but regret that we cannot be present.

We pray that God's richest blessing may rest upon your efforts to promote the cause of our common Lord and Master, Jesus Christ.

In behalf of the Faculty,

R. S. GRAVES.

UNION THEOLOGICAL SCHOOL, FOOCHOW, SOUTH CHINA

The Baldwin School of Theology and the School of the A. B. C. F. M. in Foochow, together with that of the English Church Missionary Society, have just established a Union Theological School. At the last meeting of the Board of Managers the invitations from the Princeton Theological Seminary to the Baldwin School and the A. B. C. F. M. School were presented, and I was asked to write on behalf of the Board of Managers to convey our best thanks to the Directors, Trustees and Faculty of the Princeton Theological Seminary and to say that we are asking Dr. W. W. White, of New York, to represent this Union Theological School at the celebration of the Centenary of the Princeton Theological Seminary in May next.

CENTENNIAL CELEBRATION OF

With our best wishes for a very successful celebration, on behalf of the Board of Managers, Union Theological School, Foochow,
> Yours very faithfully,
>
> H. M. W. PRICE,
> *Bishop of the Church of England in Fuhkien.*

March 25, 1912.

NANKING UNION THEOLOGICAL SEMINARY, NANKING, CHINA

In response to your kind invitation just received, the Faculty of the Nanking Union Theological Seminary is asking the Rev. J. E. Williams, of our Board of Directors, to act as our delegate on the occasion of the one hundredth anniversary of Princeton Theological Seminary. We shall greatly appreciate the opportunity of being represented on this auspicious occasion, and join in heartiest wishes for the future.

Believe me,
> Sincerely yours,
>
> J. C. GARRITT,

March 22, 1912. *President.*

THEOLOGICAL SCHOOL OF SHAOWU, FOOCHOW, CHINA

Your kind invitation to the one hundredth anniversary of the Princeton Theological Seminary has come to

PRINCETON THEOLOGICAL SEMINARY

hand, and I wish to express our appreciation of the high honor conferred upon us.

It has long been the day of beginnings in China, but some of our teachings are finding congenial soil. China is not like any other non-Christian country. Only one-tenth can read, but the reading tenth is so distributed that a very large majority of the people have near relatives who can read; and the future of China is to a peculiar degree in the hands of the reading tenth. There is opening up a commanding position for an educated ministry.

Rev. C. L. Storrs, of our Station, is now on his way home for a well-earned furlough, and I am forwarding your invitation to him. He is worthy of double honor for thorough work, both educational and evangelistic.

As Shaowu is out of reach of telegraphic communication, we are not permitted to reside there just now, but hope to be back there soon.

Very heartily yours,

J. E. WALKER.

March 18, 1912.

ST. JOHN'S UNIVERSITY, SHANGHAI, CHINA

I am in receipt of your invitation, inviting St. John's University to send a representative to attend the celebration of the one hundredth anniversary of your Theological Seminary, and appreciate the courtesy you have extended to us. I have asked Dr. William H. Jefferys, who is now in the United States, to act as our representative and hope he may be able to attend.

Yours sincerely,

F. L. HAWKS POTT,
President.

March 15th, 1912.

ASHMORE THEOLOGICAL SEMINARY, SWATOW, CHINA

The Faculty of Ashmore Theological Seminary beg to acknowledge your invitation to send a delegate to the celebration of the one hundredth anniversary of the Princeton Theological Seminary. We appreciate the honor you do us, and are asking Rev. A. F. Groesbeck, a trustee of our Seminary when on the mission field, and just returned to the United States on furlough, to represent us, if possible, on that occasion.

May God continue to richly bless Princeton Theological Seminary in its work of building up and extending His Kingdom in all the earth.

The Secretary of our Faculty, a Chinese teacher, sends acknowledgment in the usual Chinese form.

In behalf of the Faculty of Ashmore Theological Seminary,

WM. ASHMORE,
President.

March 21, 1912.

METHODIST THEOLOGICAL SEMINARY, COPENHAGEN, DENMARK

Though I would have reckoned it a great honor to have been present at your anniversary May 5–7, I must deplore not being able, though I hope to be in the United States at that time. The duties of a General Conference Delegate constrain me to stay in Minneapolis. And any other representation our small school cannot afford to send.

I congratulate your Church on its great school, and you on your long and honorable record.

Yours truly,

L. C. LARSEN,
President.

February 20th, 1912.

UNITED THEOLOGICAL COLLEGE, BANGALORE, SOUTH INDIA

On behalf of the United Theological College of South India and Ceylon, I wish to express our appreciation of the kind invitation, just received, to be represented at the celebration of the one hundredth anniversary of the establishment of the Princeton Theological Seminary, on the 5th, 6th and 7th of May.

Our College regrets its inability to send a representative to Princeton. But, rejoicing at the long record of fruitful service to Christ's Church upon which the Princeton Theological Seminary is able to look back, we join with its many friends in all good wishes for its future.

I am,

Yours truly,

L. P. LARSEN,
Principal.

March 14th, 1912.

BAPATLA NORMAL TRAINING SCHOOL, BAPATLA, SOUTH INDIA

In the name of the Bapatla Normal Training School, I thank you for your courtesy in asking us to send a delegate on the occasion of your celebration of the 100th anniversary of your great institution.

It gives me pleasure to inform you that Rev. John Newcomb is returning to America and he has kindly consented to represent us as our delegate. Please receive him as a brother beloved.

We praise God that your noble Seminary has been permitted to do such a great work for the Master during the past one hundred years. May our Master make you more and more to abound in His work, since that work has not been, is not and never can be in vain, as your history so clearly proves.

Our work is the same as yours, for we are preparing in our humble school, workers for the Master's vineyard.

PRINCETON THEOLOGICAL SEMINARY

So we gladly join hands with you on this glorious occasion, for

"Ob nah, ob fern,
Unsere Arbeit macht uns eins in dem Herrn!"

Your co-worker in the Master's vineyard,

GEO. N. THOMSSEN,
President.

March 18, 1912.

BAREILLY THEOLOGICAL SEMINARY,
BAREILLY, INDIA

I have the pleasure to acknowledge your invitation for the Bareilly Theological Seminary to be represented by a delegate on the occasion of the one hundredth anniversary of your Seminary, and to reply that the Trustees and Faculty of the Bareilly Theological Seminary have asked the Rev. Thomas Jefferson Scott, D.D., of Ocean Grove, New Jersey, who was for thirty years the Principal of the Seminary, to represent us on that occasion. Will you kindly address any necessary correspondence to him directly?

Wishing you abundant success in the honorable and important function for which you are preparing, I am,

Yours sincerely,

W. A. MANSELL,
Principal.

March 14, 1912.

CENTENNIAL CELEBRATION OF

AMERICAN BAPTIST TELUGU MISSION, THEOLOGICAL SEMINARY, RAMAPATNAM, NELLORE DISTRICT, INDIA

The communication from the Princeton Theological Seminary inviting our Seminary to be represented by a delegate on the occasion of the celebration of the one hundredth anniversary of its establishment by the General Assembly, on the 5th, 6th and 7th of May, was duly received and appreciated.

At a meeting of the faculty and students of our Seminary, held yesterday, it was

Resolved: (1) To cordially thank the Directors, Trustees and Faculty of the Princeton Theological Seminary for their remembrance and recognition of our institution as well as for the honor of the invitation to be present on this great occasion; (2) To convey our united congratulations to your institution on this occasion, coupled with the prayer that God, who has so signally blessed the Princeton Seminary in the past, may continue to do so in the future for His honor and glory and the extension of His kingdom in every land; and (3) To elect the Rev. W. L. Ferguson, D.D., a former member of our faculty, who happens to be home on furlough, to represent us on this occasion.

Yours sincerely,

J. HEINRICHS,
President.

PRESBYTERIAN THEOLOGICAL SEMINARY, SAHARANPUR, NORTHWEST PROVINCES, INDIA

In reply to your invitation to the Presbyterian Theological Seminary at Saharanpur, to send a delegate to be present at the 100th Anniversary of the establishment of Princeton Theological Seminary, to be held on May 5th, 6th and 7th, 1912, I write to inform you that we have requested Rev. Fred J. Newton, an alumnus of Princeton Seminary, and a member of the Punjab Mission, which maintains the Saharanpur Seminary, to represent us on that occasion.

Regretting very much that I am unable to be present, I remain,

Yours very truly,

H. C. VELTÉ.

March 14, 1912.

SCVOLA TEOLOGICA BATTISTA, ROME, ITALY

Owing to a mistake at the post-office the invitation to have our school represented at the great anniversary of Princeton only reached me a few days ago, hence the delay in replying to an honour so appreciated. It is with real regret that I must decline the invitation to be present on an occasion so interesting. I have always had an ardent admiration for the Princeton School, and a peculiar sympathy for the noble Church it represents; if I

were not a Baptist I should have to become a Presbyterian on the spot. Fortunately, however, no Church can confine our brotherly love which goes out in warm congratulations from our baby Seminary to your full-grown and stalwart one. May God grant Princeton another hundred years as fruitful as her last, is the wish of
Yours fraternally,

April 25, 1912.   D. G. WHITTINGHILL.

THE KOBE THEOLOGICAL SCHOOL, KOBE, JAPAN

The Kobe Theological School desires to thank you for the kind invitation to be represented at the celebration of the one hundredth anniversary of the establishment of Princeton Seminary. We regret that it will be impossible for us to send a delegate on that occasion. But we wish to congratulate you on the splendid history of your institution, and to rejoice with you in view of all that has been accomplished by her for the advance of Christ's Kingdom during the past hundred years. Also we pray that under the blessing of God you may have an even more successful future—a future in which you may continue, as during the past century, to witness with power for the "faith once delivered to the saints."

Praying God's richest blessing upon your Seminary, we are,

Yours very sincerely,
KOBE THEOLOGICAL SCHOOL,
S. P. FULTON,
Principal.

April 4th, 1912.

PRINCETON THEOLOGICAL SEMINARY

THEOLOGICAL SCHOOL OF THE KWANSEI GAKUIN, KOBE, JAPAN

In response to the kind invitation to the Theological School of the Kwansei Gakuin to be represented by a delegate at your centennial celebration in May, this year, I have the honor to inform you that we have requested the Rev. S. E. Hager, formerly a professor in our Theological School and now in America on furlough, to represent us on that occasion.

Thanking you for the invitation and hoping that our delegate will attend, I am,
Sincerely yours,

THOS. H. HADEN,
Dean.

March 25, 1912.

THE DOSHISHA THEOLOGICAL SCHOOL, KYOTO, JAPAN

The Doshisha Theological School at Kyoto, Japan, acknowledges with appreciation the invitation to attend by delegate the One Hundredth Anniversary of the establishment of the Theological Seminary of the Presbyterian Church in the United States of America at Princeton, New Jersey, on Sunday, Monday and Tuesday, the fifth, sixth and seventh of May, nineteen hundred and twelve; and hereby introduces the Reverend George M. Rowland, D.D., of Sapporo, Japan, now in

CENTENNIAL CELEBRATION OF

the United States, as its delegate by vote of the Faculty, March fifteenth, nineteen hundred and twelve.

TASUKU HARADA,
President.

March 16, 1912.

NORTH JAPAN COLLEGE, SENDAI, JAPAN

The Board of Directors of North Japan College appreciates greatly the honor of being invited to be represented by a delegate at the celebration of the one hundredth anniversary of the establishment of the Theological Seminary of the Presbyterian Church in the United States of America at Princeton, New Jersey, and instructs me in its name to accept with thanks the invitation and to say that Professor Teizaburo Demura, A.M., Dean of the Higher Department of North Japan College, has been authorized to represent our institution at the celebration. His address is No. 12 Divinity Hall, Cambridge, Mass.

With heartfelt wishes for the success of the celebration, and for the continued prosperity and usefulness of Princeton Theological Seminary, I have the honor to subscribe myself,

Very respectfully yours,

DAVID B. SCHNEDER,
President.

March 21st, 1912.

JAPAN BAPTIST THEOLOGICAL SEMINARY, TOKYO, JAPAN

In accordance with your very kind invitation, at a faculty meeting held this morning, we elected Prof. Chas. B. Tenney, of the New Testament Department, to be our representative at the celebration of the 100th anniversary of the founding of Princeton Theological Seminary.

On behalf of the faculty of the Japan Baptist Theological Seminary,

W. B. PARSHLEY,
March 6th, 1912. *President.*

MEIJI GAKUIN, TOKYO, JAPAN

The Theological Faculty of Meiji Gakuin has appointed us to reply to the courteous invitation to Meiji Gakuin to appoint a delegate to represent it on the occasion of the one hundredth anniversary of the establishment of Princeton Theological Seminary. Were it not for the great distance, it would be a great pleasure to accept the invitation.

We congratulate Princeton on the great work which it has done for the Kingdom of God in the past, and pray that its future may give even greater cause for thanksgiving. In particular we desire to express our gratitude for what it has contributed through so many of its graduates to the Church of Christ in Japan.

Sincerely yours,

KAJINOSUKE IBUKA,
March 6th, 1912. WILLIAM IMBRIE.

CENTENNIAL CELEBRATION OF

COLEGIO INTERNACIONAL, GUADALAJARA, MEXICO

We feel highly honored by the unexpected invitation to send a delegate to the centennial of Princeton Seminary. Although there has been no personal or official connection between this school and the Seminary, educators in all parts of the world must have an interest and pride in the splendid achievement and priceless service rendered to the church and the world by your institution. So we gladly accept your gracious invitation and name as delegate to represent our humble establishment on the memorable occasion the Rev. A. C. Wright, formerly associate principal of the "Colegio Internacional" of Guadalajara. He is now pursuing especial studies in Hartford Theological Seminary. Should he be able to attend the celebration he will notify you opportunely.

Thanking you for the unmerited consideration, I remain,

Yours very truly,

JOHN HOWLAND.

February 21, 1912.

THEOLOGICAL DEPARTMENT, URUMIA COLLEGE, URUMIA, PERSIA

I had the pleasure recently to receive your kind invitation to be present at the one hundredth Anniversary of the founding of Princeton Seminary, next May.

PRINCETON THEOLOGICAL SEMINARY

I regret exceedingly my inability to be present with you all on such a memorable occasion, and confess it is a deep disappointment, especially as my furlough comes this year. But our own Theological Department does not close until a date too late to admit of any possibility of being there.

I take pleasure, however, in appointing the Rev. R. M. Labaree as delegate from the Theological Department of Urumia College, and have advised him of the same. He left for the United States nearly a month ago and is to be congratulated on the opportunity of being there with you at this time.

I shall think of you all those days and hope they may be fraught with great good for the dear old Seminary.

Sincerely yours,

FRED'K G. COAN.

March 29th, 1912.

ILOILO BIBLE SCHOOL, ILOILO, PHILIPPINE ISLANDS

The invitation to attend the one hundredth anniversary of the establishment of the Princeton Theological Seminary is at hand today. The Iloilo Bible School appreciates the honor of being invited, and regrets that circumstances make it impossible to accept the invitation.

Yours very truly,

HENRY WESTON MUNGER,
Assistant Principal.

March 25, 1912.

CENTENNIAL CELEBRATION OF

THE PRESBYTERIAN THEOLOGICAL TRAINING SCHOOL, MAYAGÜEZ, PORTO RICO

The Presbyterian Theological Training School, the youngest daughter of Princeton Theological Seminary, sends greetings on the occasion of the One Hundredth Anniversary of the Founding of the Seminary, and regrets that no one can be present at that joyous time to represent this school.

JAMES ALEXANDER MCALLISTER,
President.

April, 1912.

PRESBYTERIAN THEOLOGICAL SEMINARY, BEIRUT, SYRIA

We have recently received the invitation to the 100th anniversary of the establishment of the Princeton Theological Seminary, and I have the great pleasure of writing of the same to all the members of our Mission. Seeing that there are two members of our Theological Faculty in the United States, we shall have great pleasure in requesting one of them to represent us at this great gathering, and just as soon as I can secure answers to a circular vote which I am sending round the Mission, I will give you the name and address of our delegate.

It will interest you to know that we are about taking a good step forward in the matter of theological training here in Syria. We are erecting a new building at a cost of $12,000 and, nothing preventing, hope to assemble a good class this coming fall. Our present Faculty will consist of Rev. O. J. Hardin, Rev. F. W. March, Rev. George Ford, D.D., and myself, together with some native instructors and lecturers from the Faculty of the Syrian Protestant College and neighboring Missions. While under the care of the Presbyterian Mission, we hope to make the enterprise inter-denominational and as far as possible supply the needs of a number of missionary enterprises at work in the Levant.

Very cordially and sincerely yours,

FRANKLIN E. HOSKINS,
Stated Clerk to the Syria Mission.

March 14, 1912.

MARASH THEOLOGICAL SEMINARY, MARASH, TURKEY-IN-ASIA

Let me acknowledge with gratitude, on behalf of Marash Theological Seminary, the invitation of the Directors, Trustees and Faculty of Princeton Theological Seminary with reference to the one hundredth anniversary of the latter. It is our hope that Rev. W. N. Chambers, D.D., of Adana, recently honored with the degree of D.D. by Princeton University, will be able to be present as our delegate.

Yours sincerely,

FRED FIELD GOODSELL.

March 11th, 1912.

WESTERN TURKEY THEOLOGICAL SEMINARY, MARSOVAN, TURKEY-IN-ASIA

Your invitation to the Western Turkey Theological Seminary to be represented at the one hundredth anniversary of the establishment of the Theological Seminary has duly come to hand. We have taken action requesting our former associate, Rev. George F. Herrick, D.D., for many years a member of this Mission Station, and one of the faculty of the Theological Seminary, but now in America on furlough, to act as our representative on your centennial occasion. I am writing him direct and we hope very much that he may be able to be present. He certainly will be an able representative of our Seminary if he can attend your exercises.

We congratulate you on the great work done by the Seminary. Rev. T. A. Elmer, one of our present teachers, is a graduate of Princeton College and Seminary, and Rev. Edward Riggs, D.D., for many years one of our leading instructors in the Seminary, was a graduate of Princeton College.

Sincerely yours,

G. E. WHITE.

March 2, 1912.

RESPONSES FROM
UNIVERSITIES AND COLLEGES

THE BOARD OF TRUSTEES OF PRINCETON UNIVERSITY

Resolved, That the Board of Trustees of the University tender to the Board of Trustees of the Theological Seminary their cordial appreciation of the invitation extended to them so courteously through the President of the Board of Trustees of the Seminary in person, to attend the Centennial Exercises of the Seminary, to be held on the fifth, sixth and seventh days of May, next, and hereby accept the invitation so extended; and be it further

Resolved, That this Board hereby tender to the Theological Seminary for the Centennial Exercises the use of Alexander Hall for the Celebration, and be it further

Resolved, That a delegation be appointed from the Trustees to represent this Board at the Celebration.

In accordance with the third resolution, the President of the University, *pro tempore,* appointed as a delegation to represent the Board at the Centennial Exercises of the Theological Seminary, Hon. William J. Magie, Rev. Dr. Simon J. McPherson, Hon. Bayard Henry, Mr. James W. Alexander, Mr. Robert Garrett.

CHAS. W. MCALPIN,
Secretary.

DALHOUSIE UNIVERSITY, HALIFAX, NOVA SCOTIA

The Senate of Dalhousie University wish to acknowledge with many thanks the favour of the invitation

CENTENNIAL CELEBRATION OF

from the Directors, Trustees and Faculty of the Theological Seminary of the Presbyterian Church in the United States of America at Princeton, New Jersey, to take part in the celebration of the one hundredth anniversary of the establishment of the Seminary.

We regret very much that we have not been able at an earlier date to name our delegate for that occasion. I now have the honour to inform you that the Reverend M. J. MacLeod, of the Collegiate Church, New York, has found it possible to represent us, and he will convey to you the felicitations of this University on this occasion of rejoicing.

I have the honour to be,
                Very faithfully yours,
                        A. STANLEY MACKENZIE,
May 1, 1912.   *President.*

THE UNIVERSITY OF TORONTO, TORONTO, CANADA

I have asked the Rev. Professor Kerr D. Macmillan, B.A., who is on your staff, to represent the University of Toronto at the celebration of the one hundredth anniversary of the establishment of the Theological Seminary of Princeton. Mr. Macmillan is a graduate of the University of Toronto and is thus fully competent to represent us.

                Yours sincerely,
                        ROBT. A. FALCONER,
                                President.
March 6th, 1912.

PRINCETON THEOLOGICAL SEMINARY

HARVARD UNIVERSITY, CAMBRIDGE, MASSACHUSETTS

Harvard University accepts with pleasure the invitation of the Directors, Trustees and Faculty of the Theological Seminary of the Presbyterian Church at Princeton, New Jersey, to the celebration of the one-hundredth anniversary of its establishment, to be held on the fifth, sixth and seventh of May, 1912, and has appointed William Wallace Fenn, Bussey Professor of Theology, and Dean of the Faculty of Divinity, as its delegate on that occasion.

[SEAL]

YALE UNIVERSITY, NEW HAVEN, CONNECTICUT

I have the honor to inform you that Professor Williston Walker has been appointed the delegate of Yale University at the one hundredth anniversary of the establishment of the Princeton Theological Seminary, which is to be celebrated on Sunday, Monday and Tuesday, the fifth, sixth and seventh of May, nineteen hundred and twelve.

Very truly yours,

EDWIN ROGERS IMBRIE,
Acting for the Absent Secretary.

March 4, 1912.

CENTENNIAL CELEBRATION OF

UNIVERSITY OF PENNSYLVANIA, PHILADELPHIA, PENNSYLVANIA

It gives me pleasure to advise you that the official representative of the University of Pennsylvania at the one hundredth anniversary of the establishment of the Theological Seminary to be held on the fifth, sixth and seventh of May, nineteen hundred and twelve, will be Professor James Alan Montgomery, Ph.D., S.T.D.

With best wishes for a happy reunion on the part of the friends of the Seminary, I am,

Yours sincerely,

EDGAR F. SMITH,
Provost.

February 26th, 1912.

BROWN UNIVERSITY, PROVIDENCE, RHODE ISLAND

In accordance with your invitation I have appointed Professor Henry T. Fowler, Ph.D., Professor of Biblical Literature in Brown University, to represent us at the One Hundredth Anniversary of Princeton Theological Seminary on the fifth, sixth and seventh of May. I know that he cannot be present all three days, but he will endeavor to be present as long as possible, selecting the most favorable time after the full program is sent him.

Brown University joins with all other institutions of

PRINCETON THEOLOGICAL SEMINARY

learning in congratulating the Seminary on its notable anniversary.

Sincerely yours,

W. H. P. FAUNCE,
President.

February 29th, 1912.

RUTGERS COLLEGE,
NEW BRUNSWICK, NEW JERSEY

The Trustees and Faculty of Rutgers College accept with appreciation the invitation of the Theological Seminary at Princeton, New Jersey, to be represented by a delegate at the celebrating of the one hundredth anniversary of the establishment of the Seminary on the fifth, sixth and seventh of May, nineteen hundred and twelve.

February 19th, 1912.

DARTMOUTH COLLEGE,
HANOVER, NEW HAMPSHIRE

Pray allow me, in behalf of Dartmouth College, to acknowledge with appreciation the receipt of an invitation from Princeton Theological Seminary to the College, to send a delegate to the celebration of the one hundredth anniversary of the Seminary.

The College has appointed the Reverend Benjamin

CENTENNIAL CELEBRATION OF

Tenney Marshall, pastor of the First Presbyterian Church of New Rochelle, New York, to represent it on this occasion.

Yours with sincere respect,

ERNEST FOX NICHOLS,
President.

3rd April, 1912.

WASHINGTON AND LEE UNIVERSITY, LEXINGTON, VIRGINIA

In reply to the invitation of the Directors, Trustees, and Faculty of the Theological Seminary of the Presbyterian Church in the United States of America, Princeton, N. J., to take part in the celebration of the one hundredth anniversary of its establishment by the General Assembly, the Faculty of Washington and Lee University has appointed as its delegate Rev. Dr. James Robert Howerton, Professor of Philosophy, to represent Washington and Lee University on that occasion.

Yours very truly,

H. D. CAMPBELL,
Dean.

February 20, 1912.

DICKINSON COLLEGE, CARLISLE, PENNSYLVANIA

The President and Faculty of Dickinson College acknowledge with appreciation the invitation of the Theo-

PRINCETON THEOLOGICAL SEMINARY

logical Seminary of the Presbyterian Church in the United States of America at Princeton, New Jersey, to attend the one hundredth anniversary of its establishment on the fifth, sixth and seventh of May, nineteen hundred and twelve, and have designated the president of the College, Eugene Allen Noble, L.H.D., as its accredited representative on this occasion, which calls for congratulation and thanksgiving.

February 29th, 1912.

HAMPDEN-SIDNEY COLLEGE, HAMPDEN-SIDNEY, VIRGINIA

I beg to acknowledge the receipt of your very courteous invitation to Hampden-Sidney College to be represented at the Centennial Celebration of your venerable Seminary. It would afford me personally very especial gratification to be present on that happy occasion, inasmuch as the honored founder of your Seminary, Dr. Archibald Alexander, had filled with distinction the presidency of this College. I am satisfied that it was the ability demonstrated and the reputation achieved as President of Hampden-Sidney College that pointed him out as the logical man to take charge of the proposed Theological School at Princeton, New Jersey. At any rate, our institutions are certainly very closely linked in this way.

We have appointed the Rev. W. Creighton Campbell, D.D., pastor of the First Presbyterian Church, Roanoke, Virginia, as the representative of Hampden-Sidney College at your approaching Centennial. Dr. Campbell is an alumnus of the College, a member of our Board of Trustees, and one of the prominent ministers of our Virginia Synod. He will probably be present throughout the entire Centennial Exercises. I regret that I cannot be present in person and have a share in these impressive exercises.

With very kind regards, I am,
Cordially yours,

H. TUCKER GRAHAM,
President.

February 23, 1912.

UNIVERSITY OF NORTH CAROLINA, CHAPEL HILL, NORTH CAROLINA

The faculty of the University of North Carolina appreciate the invitation to send a delegate to the celebration of the One Hundredth Anniversary of the establishment of the Princeton Theological Seminary.

We regret that it will be impracticable to send a delegate on that occasion, but wish to tender our congratulations on the completion of these hundred years of useful service and to give expression to our best wishes for the future welfare and prosperity of the institution.

Very truly yours,

FRANCIS P. VENABLE,
President.

February 27, 1912.

PRINCETON THEOLOGICAL SEMINARY

WILLIAMS COLLEGE, WILLIAMSTOWN, MASSACHUSETTS

On behalf of Williams College, I beg to acknowledge receipt of the very courteous invitation of the Directors, Trustees and Faculty of the Seminary to send a delegate to attend the One Hundredth Anniversary of the establishment of Princeton Theological Seminary. I have communicated with Dr. William Rankin, our oldest living graduate, now a resident of Princeton, and am in receipt of a letter from his son stating that it will give his father pleasure to serve as a delegate on that occasion.
Very sincerely yours,

H. A. GARFIELD.
President.

April 11, 1912.

UNION UNIVERSITY, SCHENECTADY, NEW YORK

Union University takes pleasure in appointing the Rev. Charles Alexander Richmond, D.D., LL.D., President of Union College and Chancellor of Union University, as the official delegate at the celebration of the one hundredth anniversary of the Princeton Theological Seminary on the fifth, sixth and seventh of May, nineteen hundred and twelve.

April 4th, 1912.

CENTENNIAL CELEBRATION OF

MIDDLEBURY COLLEGE, MIDDLEBURY, VERMONT

I beg to acknowledge the kind invitation of Princeton Theological Seminary to the one hundredth anniversary of its establishment on May 5th, 6th, and 7th. We appreciate the courtesy of your invitation and shall wish to be represented at the anniversary exercises.

I am asking Rev. Charles E. Hesselgrave, Ph.D., pastor of the Stanley Congregational Church, Chatham, New Jersey, and a graduate of Middlebury College in the class of 1893, to represent Middlebury College at your centennial. Faithfully yours,

JOHN M. THOMAS,
President.

March 8, 1912.

WASHINGTON AND JEFFERSON COLLEGE, WASHINGTON, PENNSYLVANIA

I have been appointed by the Faculty of Washington and Jefferson College to attend the Centennial Celebration of Princeton Theological Seminary, May fifth, sixth and seventh, and it is my intention to be present.

Yours truly,

J. D. MOFFAT,
President.

April 24, 1912.

PRINCETON THEOLOGICAL SEMINARY

MIAMI UNIVERSITY, OXFORD, OHIO

Miami University regrets that it will be impossible to accept the invitation of the Directors, Trustees and Faculty of the Princeton Theological Seminary to be represented at the one hundredth anniversary of its establishment by the General Assembly, on Sunday, Monday and Tuesday, the fifth, sixth and seventh of May, nineteen hundred and twelve.

COLUMBIA UNIVERSITY, IN THE CITY OF NEW YORK

I am directed by the Board of Trustees to say in reply to your courteous invitation for Columbia University to be represented at the one hundredth anniversary of the establishment of the Theological Seminary of the Presbyterian Church in the United States of America, that the invitation is accepted with thanks, and that the University will be represented by Dickinson S. Miller, Ph.D., Professor of Philosophy, and Raymond C. Knox, B.D., Chaplain of the University.
     Very truly yours,

       FRANK D. FACKENTHAL,
         Secretary.

March 21, 1912.

CENTENNIAL CELEBRATION OF

UNIVERSITY OF PITTSBURGH, PITTSBURGH, PENNSYLVANIA

On behalf of the University of Pittsburgh, I wish to acknowledge receipt of the invitation to attend the celebration of the one hundredth anniversary of the establishment of the Theological Seminary of the Presbyterian Church in the United States of America at Princeton, New Jersey. The University of Pittsburgh extends its hearty congratulations to the Seminary on its long and useful career of noble service, and wishes for it many more years of enlarged influence and power.

The representative of the University of Pittsburgh will be S. B. Linhart, A.M., D.D., Secretary of the University.

Cordially yours,

S. B. LINHART,

April 29th, 1912. *Secretary.*

AMHERST COLLEGE, AMHERST, MASSACHUSETTS

Amherst College accepts with pleasure the very kind invitation of the Directors, Trustees and Faculty of the Princeton Theological Seminary to be represented at the one hundredth anniversary of its establishment, May 5th, 6th, and 7th, 1912.

President George Harris will represent Amherst College.

March 12th, 1912.

PRINCETON THEOLOGICAL SEMINARY

FRANKLIN AND MARSHALL COLLEGE, LANCASTER, PENNSYLVANIA

President Henry Harbaugh Apple regrets very much that he is unable to accept the kind invitation to attend the One Hundredth Anniversary of the establishment of the Theological Seminary of the Presbyterian Church in the United States of America on May fifth, sixth and seventh.

He sends most cordial greetings and best wishes from Franklin and Marshall College and ardent prayer for the work of the Princeton Theological Seminary.

April 12th, 1912.

LAFAYETTE COLLEGE, EASTON, PENNSYLVANIA

To the Directors, Trustees and Faculty of the Theological Seminary of the Presbyterian Church in the United States of America at Princeton, N. J.—Greeting:

Lafayette College offers its congratulations to the Theological Seminary of the Presbyterian Church at Princeton, N. J., upon the completion of one hundred years of service in the education of men to preach the glorious gospel of the blessed God, and rejoices with it in its record as a seminary of learning and as a nursing mother of those who, through so long a period, with unfaltering loyalty to the truth, have prosecuted their ministry. Lafayette College has sent many of its sons to be trained in the Seminary, foremost among them William Henry Green whose memory is dear alike to College and Seminary, and marks with satisfaction that at the present time no college has so many students on the roll of the Seminary. It also acknowledges with gratitude its debt to the Seminary for teachers and trustees who have brought from the Seminary knowledge and zeal for the truth. May this celebration redound to the glory of God, and introduce with fitting dignity a new century of yet more faithful service.

Lafayette College designates its President, Ethelbert D. Warfield, D.D., LL.D., President of the Board of Directors of the Seminary, and John Moffat Mecklin, Ph.D., Professor of Philosophy, a graduate of the Seminary, to represent it at the Celebration May 5th, 6th and 7th, 1912.

WM. S. HALL,
Clerk of the Faculty.

April 29, 1912.

[SEAL]

NEW YORK UNIVERSITY, NEW YORK CITY

I beg to acknowledge on behalf of New York University the invitation of the Theological Seminary of the Presbyterian Church at Princeton, N. J., to be represented by a delegate at the one hundredth anniversary.

The University has appointed Prof. Herman H.

PRINCETON THEOLOGICAL SEMINARY

Horne, Ph.D., Professor of the History of Education and of the History of Philosophy, as its delegate to represent the University at the Centennial, May 5th–7th.
Very truly yours,
JOHN H. MACCRACKEN,
Syndic.
February 26, 1912.

PENNSYLVANIA COLLEGE,
GETTYSBURG, PENNSYLVANIA

On behalf of the Faculty of Pennsylvania College, Gettysburg, I have the honor to acknowledge the invitation of Princeton Theological Seminary, through its Directors, Trustees and Faculty, to be represented by a delegate at the celebration of the one-hundredth anniversary of its establishment, and to reply that we accept and have appointed Professor Philip M. Biklé, Ph.D., Dean of the College, as our delegate. Should Dean Bicklé not be able to attend, he is authorized to appoint a substitute, of which due notice will be given.
With best wishes for the Seminary,
Very truly yours,
H. A. RINARD,
Secretary of the Faculty.
February 22, 1912.

CENTENNIAL CELEBRATION OF

WABASH COLLEGE, CRAWFORDSVILLE, INDIANA

Rev. Arthur J. Brown, D.D., 156 Fifth Avenue, New York, will represent Wabash College at the forthcoming anniversary of Princeton Theological Seminary.

Trusting that your anticipation of the event may be fully realized, I am,
      Very sincerely yours,
         G. L. MACKINTOSH,
           President.
March 1, 1912.

DELAWARE COLLEGE, NEWARK, DELAWARE

The Faculty of Delaware College accept with thanks the invitation of the Directors, Trustees, and Faculty of the Seminary to send a delegate to the One Hundredth Anniversary of its establishment by the General Assembly, on Sunday, Monday and Tuesday, the 5th, 6th and 7th of May, 1912. The Rev. Dr. W. J. Rowan of the College Faculty has been designated as our delegate to the Anniversary and will be in attendance at that time.
    Very truly yours,
        EDW. LAURENCE SMITS,
          Secretary pro tem.
February 27, 1912.

PRINCETON THEOLOGICAL SEMINARY

HANOVER COLLEGE,
HANOVER, INDIANA

In response to the invitation received from Princeton Theological Seminary requesting Hanover College to be represented by a delegate on the occasion of the celebration of the 100th anniversary of its establishment, I have the honor and pleasure of certifying to the appointment of the Reverend John Simonson Howk, D.D., Secretary of Hanover College, as her delegate for the occasion, and extending to the Seminary the greetings of Hanover College.

Very sincerely yours,

W. A. MILLIS,
February 21, 1912. *President.*

MARIETTA COLLEGE,
MARIETTA, OHIO

Marietta College desires to be represented at the One Hundredth Anniversary of the Seminary and in the inability of the President or member of the Faculty to attend has designated Rev. William T. Wilcox, D.D., a graduate of the College in 1891, of Bloomfield, N. J., to represent us on that occasion.

Very truly yours,

ALFRED T. PERRY,
President.

April 13, 1912.

CENTENNIAL CELEBRATION OF

TRANSYLVANIA UNIVERSITY, LEXINGTON, KENTUCKY

The President of Transylvania University acknowledges with pleasure the invitation to attend the Hundredth Anniversary of the Theological Seminary of the Presbyterian Church in the United States of America, at Princeton, New Jersey, and regrets exceedingly that a delegate cannot be sent to represent us on this occasion.

DAVIDSON COLLEGE
DAVIDSON, NORTH CAROLINA

I have received the invitation of Princeton Seminary, and take great pleasure in appointing as the delegate from Davidson College on that occasion our Professor of Modern Languages, Rev. Thos. W. Lingle, Ph.D., who is himself an alumnus of Princeton Seminary.

Cordially yours,

HENRY LOUIS SMITH,
President.

February 23, 1912.

UNIVERSITY OF MICHIGAN, ANN ARBOR, MICHIGAN

I beg to acknowledge the receipt of the invitation of the Princeton Theological Seminary to the University of

PRINCETON THEOLOGICAL SEMINARY

Michigan to be represented by delegate upon the occasion of the exercises in celebration of the one hundredth anniversary of the establishment of the Seminary, to be held Sunday, Monday, and Tuesday, the 5th, 6th, and 7th of May, 1912. This is to notify you that the Reverend Walter A. Brooks, of Trenton, New Jersey, a graduate of the University of Michigan, has been appointed to act as our delegate. Mr. Brooks has accepted the appointment.

Very sincerely yours,
H. B. HUTCHINS,
President.

March 21, 1912.

WESTMINSTER COLLEGE, NEW WILMINGTON, PENNSYLVANIA

In response to the kind invitation of Princeton Theological Seminary that Westminster College shall be represented by a delegate at the 100th anniversary celebration May 5, 6, 7, 1912, would say, that it will be my pleasure as President of Westminster College to represent the institution on that occasion.

With much appreciation of the courtesy extended by the Theological Seminary of Princeton, I remain,

Sincerely yours,
R. M. RUSSELL,
President.

February 19, 1912.

CENTENNIAL CELEBRATION OF

THE COLLEGE OF THE CITY OF NEW YORK, NEW YORK CITY

In response to the invitation of the Theological Seminary of the Presbyterian Church at Princeton, New Jersey, I am instructed to inform you that the College of the City of New York will be represented by President John H. Finley at the celebration of the one hundredth anniversary of the establishment of the Seminary on Sunday, Monday and Tuesday, the fifth, sixth and seventh of May, nineteen hundred and twelve.

Yours very truly,

H. L. McCartie,
Secretary to the President.

March 14th, 1912.

LAKE FOREST COLLEGE, LAKE FOREST, ILLINOIS

I wish to acknowledge receipt of the invitation of the Directors, Trustees, and Faculty of the Seminary to Lake Forest College to be represented at the one hundredth anniversary of the establishment of the Seminary, on the 5th, 6th and 7th of May. I shall hope to be present myself to represent Lake Forest on that occasion.

Sincerely yours,

John S. Nollen,
President.

February 21, 1912.

PRINCETON THEOLOGICAL SEMINARY

MACALESTER COLLEGE, SAINT PAUL, MINNESOTA

The faculty and trustees of Macalester College request me to convey to you and through you to the officers and faculty of Princeton Theological Seminary their pleasure over the invitation so kindly extended to send a delegate to the Hundredth Anniversary of your honorable institution.

They have elected an alumnus of Macalester College and an alumnus of Princeton Seminary in the person of Rev. W. P. Lee, D.D., of Germantown, Pa. He has been notified of this action by the faculty and if he is able to be present will doubtless register as the official delegate of Macalester College.

Respectfully,
T. MOREY HODGMAN,
President.

February 29, 1912.

LINCOLN UNIVERSITY, CHESTER COUNTY, PENNSYLVANIA

Lincoln University appreciates the honor of an invitation to the One Hundredth Anniversary of Princeton Seminary.

J. B. Rendall, principal, or Rev. Robert L. Stewart, D.D., alternate, either the one or the other, will have the pleasure of being present as a delegate.

Very sincerely,
J. B. RENDALL,
President.

March 5th, 1912.

CENTENNIAL CELEBRATION OF

PARK COLLEGE, PARKVILLE, MISSOURI

The Faculty of Park College begs to make appreciative acknowledgment of the invitation of Princeton Theological Seminary to appoint a representative upon the occasion of the celebration of the one hundredth anniversary of the establishment of the Seminary. We have requested Rev. C. B. McAfee, D.D., Park 1884, of Brooklyn, N. Y., to serve as our representative.

With sincere good wishes for the continued prosperity and work of the Seminary, I am,
Very truly,
ROY V. MAGERS,
February 20, 1912.   *Secretary of the Faculty.*

PARSONS COLLEGE, FAIRFIELD, IOWA

President Parsons wishes me to acknowledge the receipt of the invitation to Parsons College to be represented on the occasion of the One Hundredth Anniversary of Princeton.

He wishes me also to state that he plans to be present himself and will represent Parsons College. If President Parsons finds that he is unable to attend later on, you will be duly notified.

With best wishes for the occasion, I am,
Very truly yours,
C. E. DOWNARD,
February 21st, 1912.   *Secretary to the President.*

PRINCETON THEOLOGICAL SEMINARY

SOUTHWESTERN PRESBYTERIAN UNIVERSITY, CLARKSVILLE, TENNESSEE

In behalf of this University and its Theological Department, I am instructed by our faculty to thank you for the invitation to be represented at your centennial in May. We regret that we shall be unable to accept.
With best wishes,

WILLIAM DINWIDDIE,
Chancellor.

February 20, 1912.

BELLEVUE COLLEGE, BELLEVUE, NEBRASKA

The invitation of Princeton Theological Seminary to Bellevue College to be represented on the occasion of the one hundredth anniversary of its establishment by the General Assembly has been received and is deeply appreciated.

We have the honor to appoint Rev. A. J. Dressler to represent Bellevue College on that occasion.

I am sorry that the invitation did not come into my hands until recently and, therefore, that notification of this appointment has been so much delayed.

Very sincerely yours,

S. W. STOOKEY,
President.

April 1, 1912.

CENTENNIAL CELEBRATION OF

COE COLLEGE,
CEDAR RAPIDS, IOWA

Coe College accepts with pleasure the invitation to attend the celebration of the One Hundredth Anniversary of Princeton Theological Seminary, May 5, 6 and 7, 1912. The College will be represented by the President of its Board of Trustees, Rev. Edward R. Burkhalter, D.D., LL.D.

JOHN A. MARQUIS,
President.

February 20, 1912.

THE COLLEGE OF EMPORIA,
EMPORIA, KANSAS

I regret that it is impossible for the College of Emporia to be represented at the one hundredth anniversary of Princeton Seminary. Let me convey to you our congratulations and good wishes upon that occasion.

Sincerely yours,

H. C. CULBERTSON,
February 22, 1912. *President.*

NEW WINDSOR COLLEGE,
NEW WINDSOR, MARYLAND

I have the honor to inform you that the invitation to attend the Hundredth Anniversary of Princeton Seminary was received; and it gives me pleasure to state (D.V.) that I hope to attend personally, and enjoy the great occasion.

Trusting that your efforts may prove a success,
I am most respectfully yours,

JAMES FRASER,
President.

February 20, 1912.

ALMA COLLEGE,
ALMA,
MICHIGAN

The Faculty of Alma College acknowledge the receipt of your invitation in behalf of the Directors, Trustees and Faculty of Princeton Theological Seminary to be present at the Celebration of the one hundredth anniversary of the establishment of the institution; and send greetings, and compliment you upon the work your institution has been able to accomplish in the one hundred years just closing, but regret to say that Alma College will be unable to be represented by a delegate.

Very truly yours,

F. E. WEST,
Secretary of the Faculty.

February 26, 1912.

To
The Directors, Trustees and Faculty of
The Theological Seminary at Princeton New Jersey.

We the Dean, Secretary and Members of the Faculty of Divinity in the University of Aberdeen gratefully acknowledge your courtesy in inviting us to send a representative of our Faculty to be present at the celebration of the Centenary of your far-famed Seminary. We deeply regret that no member of the Faculty finds it in his power to attend, but we have delegated The Reverend Professor John Macnaughton, M.A., of M'Gill University, Montreal, a distinguished Graduate of the University of Aberdeen, to represent us and to be the bearer of this Address.

Holding the same Reformed Faith as yourselves, adhering to the same Theological Standards and maintaining the same form of Church Government, we avail ourselves gladly of this opportunity to congratulate you on the noble service you have rendered to the cause of Christian Truth during the last hundred years. Whilst the distinctive type of theological scholarship which has come to be associated with Princeton has been conservative both in criticism and doctrine, we gratefully recognize that your Scholars have been ready to follow the guidance of the Spirit of Truth into new fields of Christian thought and service.

We are proud to recall that an illustrious President of Princeton College was a Scotsman descended from John Knox; Dr. John Witherspoon; that Dr. James M'Cosh, a Scotsman with special ties to our University, was largely instrumental in giving expansion to the old Princeton College a generation ago; and that on the honoured roll of your past Teachers our Graduates have not been unrepresented.

On this auspicious occasion we are glad to acknowledge our deep indebtedness to the great Divines and Scholars who have rendered your Seminary eminent throughout the whole Christian world. The names of the Alexanders, the Hodges, of William Henry Green, and of Benjamin Breckenridge Warfield (still happily among you in intellectual vigour), are held in honour among us and in all the Churches of our country. Nor are we insensible of the impulse which has been given by Princeton to the noble cause of world-evangelization, and of the splendid labours of such men as Dr. Robert Elliott Speer who have carried the influence of Princeton over the seas to the older lands.

It is our heartfelt prayer that the usefulness and honour which have fallen to you in the century that has gone may be increased many fold in the century to which you look forward.

In name of the Faculty and by authority of the Senatus Academicus.

Thomas Nicol, M.A., D.D.
Dean.

William A. Curtis, B.D., D.Litt.
Secretary.

At Aberdeen
April, 1912.

LIST OF DELEGATES

THE GENERAL ASSEMBLY OF THE PRESBYTERIAN CHURCH IN THE UNITED STATES OF AMERICA

John F. Carson, D.D., LL.D., Moderator
William H. Roberts, D.D., LL.D., Stated Clerk
Rev. William M. Dager, A.B., Moderator of the Synod of New Jersey
Martin D. Kneeland, D.D., Moderator of the Synod of New York
Samuel A. Cornelius, D.D., Moderator of the Synod of Pennsylvania
His Excellency Woodrow Wilson, Ph.D., Litt.D., LL.D.
Hon. William Jennings Bryan, LL.D.

THE TRUSTEES OF PRINCETON UNIVERSITY

Hon. William J. Magie, LL.D.
Simon J. McPherson, D.D.
Hon. Bayard Henry, A.M.
James W. Alexander, A.M.
Robert Garrett, B.S.

COURTS OF SCOTCH, IRISH AND CANADIAN CHURCHES

Alexander Stewart, M.A., D.D., Moderator of the General Assembly
of the Church of Scotland
James Wells, M.A., D.D., Moderator of the General Assembly of the
United Free Church of Scotland
James D. McCulloch, D.D., representing William Menzies Alexander,
M.A., B.Sc., M.D., B.D., Moderator of the General Assembly
of the Free Church of Scotland

CENTENNIAL CELEBRATION OF

John R. Mackay, M.A., representing Duncan Mackenzie, D.D., Moderator of the Synod of the Free Presbyterian Church of Scotland
John Macmillan, B.A., D.D., Moderator of the General Assembly of the Presbyterian Church in Ireland
Robert P. Mackay, D.D., Moderator of the General Assembly of the Presbyterian Church in Canada
Rev. David Russell Mitchell, Delegate of the Synod of Ballymena and Coleraine of the Presbyterian Church in Ireland

THE PRESIDING OFFICERS OF AMERICAN CHURCHES

John F. Carson, D.D., LL.D., Moderator of the General Assembly of the Presbyterian Church in the United States of America
Russell Cecil, D.D., Moderator of the General Assembly of the Presbyterian Church in the United States
John C. Scouller, D.D., Moderator of the General Assembly of the United Presbyterian Church of North America
James I. Good, D.D., LL.D., President of the General Synod of the Reformed Church in the United States
Nehemiah Boynton, D.D., Moderator of the National Council of Congregational Churches
Junius B. Remensnyder, D.D., LL.D., President of the General Synod of the Evangelical Lutheran Church in the
United States of America
Peter Ainslee, D.D., Chairman of the Christian Union Commission of the Disciples of Christ
T. F. Bode, D.D., representing J. Pister, D.D., President of the German Evangelical Synod of North America
Robert F. Rudolph, A.M., D.D., representing Samuel Fallows, D.D., LL.D., President of the General Council of the Reformed Episcopal Church

PRINCETON THEOLOGICAL SEMINARY

SUBORDINATE COURTS OF THE PRESBYTERIAN CHURCH IN THE UNITED STATES OF AMERICA

Synod of New Jersey
Eben B. Cobb, D.D., Vice-Moderator
Rev. Frank Lukens, A.M.
John T. Kerr, D.D.
Rev. Clarence E. Macartney, A.B.
Hon. Woodrow Wilson, Ph.D., Litt.D., LL.D.
Robert E. Speer, D.D.
Edward P. Holden, Esq.
William H. Vail, Esq.

Synod of Pennsylvania
Samuel A. Cornelius, D.D., Moderator
Robert Hunter, D.D.
William L. McEwan, D.D.
Ebenezer Flack, D.D.
Rev. Samuel Semple, A.M.
J. Vernon Bell, D.D.

Synod of Baltimore
Rev. Joseph Turner, A.B., Moderator
James E. Moffatt, D.D.
George P. Wilson, D.D.
Francis H. Moore, D.D.

Synod of West Virginia
Herman G. Stoetzer, D.D.

Presbytery of New Brunswick
Rev. August W. Sonne, A.M., Moderator
Henry C. Minton, D.D., LL.D.
Walter A. Brooks, D.D.
Rev. Daniel R. Foster, A.M.
Rev. Francis Palmer, A.M.

CENTENNIAL CELEBRATION OF

Presbytery of Philadelphia
Rev. C. A. R. Janvier, A.M., Moderator
Robert Hunter, D.D.
William P. Fulton, D.D.

Presbytery of Newton
Rev. Oscar J. Hardin, A.B., Moderator
Rev. E. Clarke Cline, A.B.
Rev. J. Newton Armstrong, A.B.
Rev. Ward C. Peabody, A.M.
Theodore Tinsman, Esq.

Presbytery of Rochester
G. B. F. Hallock, D.D.
Rev. George H. Fickes, A.M.

Presbytery of New Albany
John Simonson Howk, D.D.

Alumni in the Synod of California
James S. McDonald, D.D.

THE BOARDS OF THE GENERAL ASSEMBLY OF THE PRESBYTERIAN CHURCH IN THE UNITED STATES OF AMERICA

The Board of Home Missions
John Dixon, D.D., an Associate Secretary

The Board of Foreign Missions
George Alexander, D.D., President

PRINCETON THEOLOGICAL SEMINARY

The Board of Education
Charles Wadsworth, Jr., D.D., President

The Board of Publication and Sabbath School Work
Hon. Robert N. Willson, President

The Board of the Church Erection Fund
Hon. Frederick G. Burnham, President

The Board of Relief
Samuel T. Lowrie, D.D.
H. S. P. Nichols, Esq.
William W. Heberton, D.D.
Marcus A. Brownson, D.D.
Members of the Board

The College Board
John H. MacCracken, Ph.D., President
John R. Mackay, Ph.D., Member of the Board

FOREIGN THEOLOGICAL FACULTIES

The Faculty of Divinity of the University of Edinburgh
Alexander Stewart, M.A., D.D., St. Mary's, St. Andrews, Scotland

The Theological Faculty of the University of Glasgow
Norman Kemp Smith, D.Phil., Stuart Professor of Psychology,
Princeton University

The Faculty of Divinity of the University of Aberdeen
John Macnaughton, M.A., Professor of Latin in
McGill University, Montreal

Free Church College, Edinburgh
James D. McCulloch, D.D., Principal

CENTENNIAL CELEBRATION OF

Assembly's College, Belfast
John Macmillan, B.A., D.D., Belfast

The Theological Faculty of King's College, London
Frederic Courtney, D.D., D.C.L., New York City

The Theological Faculty of the University of Geneva
David S. Schaff, D.D., Professor of Ecclesiastical History and History of Doctrine, Western Theological Seminary, Pittsburgh

The Faculty of Evangelical Theology of Geneva
Alexander Couper Proudfit, A.M., Princeton, N. J.

The Presbyterian College, Halifax
J. W. Falconer, D.D., Professor

Knox College, Toronto
James Ballantyne, D.D., Professor of Church History

Queen's University, Kingston, Ontario
W. G. Jordan, D.D., Professor of Hebrew and
Old Testament Criticism

The Presbyterian College, Montreal
John Scrimger, D.D., Principal

Manitoba College, Winnipeg
A. B. Baird, D.D., Acting Principal and Professor of
Church History

Westminster Hall, Vancouver, B. C.
A. J. MacGillivray, D.D., Merton, Ontario

The Faculty of Theology of Trinity College, Toronto
Rev. E. Vicars Stevenson, M.A., Plainfield, N. J.

PRINCETON THEOLOGICAL SEMINARY

THEOLOGICAL SEMINARIES OF THE PRESBYTERIAN CHURCH IN THE UNITED STATES OF AMERICA

Auburn Theological Seminary
George B. Stewart, D.D., LL.D., President

The Board of Directors of Auburn Theological Seminary
Wilton Merle-Smith, D.D., Member of the Board

Western Theological Seminary
James Anderson Kelso, Ph.D., D.D., President

Lane Theological Seminary
Edward Mack, D.D., Professor of Hebrew and Old Testament Literature

The Theological Seminary of Kentucky
Jesse Lee Cotton, D.D., Professor in the School of Old Testament Exegesis

McCormick Theological Seminary
Andrew C. Zenos, D.D., Professor of Ecclesiastical History

San Francisco Theological Seminary
Warren Hall Landon, D.D., President

The German Presbyterian Theological School of the Northwest
William H. Foulkes, D.D., President of the Board of Directors

The German Theological School of Newark, N. J.
Arnold W. Fismer, Ph.D., Professor of New Testament Exegesis and Ethics

The Theological Seminary of Lincoln University
Robert L. Stewart, D.D., Professor of Pastoral Theology, Evidences of Christianity and Biblical Archæology

Omaha Theological Seminary
Albert B. Marshall, D.D., LL.D., President

CENTENNIAL CELEBRATION OF

OTHER THEOLOGICAL SEMINARIES IN THIS COUNTRY

Theological Seminary of the Reformed Church in America, New Brunswick, N. J.
J. Preston Searle, D.D., President

Xenia Theological Seminary, Xenia, Ohio
Joseph Kyle, D.D., LL.D., Professor of Systematic Theology and Homiletics

The Moravian College and Theological Seminary, Bethlehem, Pa.
W. N. Schwarze, Ph.D., the Resident Professor

Andover Theological Seminary, Cambridge, Mass.
John W. Platner, D.D., Professor of Church History

Union Theological Seminary, Richmond, Va.
Thomas R. English, D.D., Henry Young Professor of Biblical Literature and the Interpretation of the New Testament

Bangor Theological Seminary, Bangor, Me.
David N. Beach, D.D., President

General Theological Seminary of the Protestant Episcopal Church, New York City
Arthur Prime Hunt, M.A., B.D., Professor of Christian Ethics
Dickinson S. Miller, Ph.D., Professor of Christian Apologetics

Colgate Theological Seminary, Hamilton, N. Y.
David F. Estes, D.D., Professor of New Testament Interpretation and Librarian

Yale University Divinity School, New Haven, Conn.
Williston Walker, Ph.D., D.D., L.H.D., Titus Street Professor of Ecclesiastical History

PRINCETON THEOLOGICAL SEMINARY

Protestant Episcopal Theological Seminary in Virginia, Alexandria, Va.
Angus Crawford, D.D., Dean

Theological Seminary of the Reformed Church in the United States, Lancaster, Pa.
John C. Bowman, D.D., President

Newton Theological Institution, Newton Centre, Mass.
George Edwin Horr, D.D., President

Evangelical Lutheran Theological Seminary, Gettysburg, Pa.
J. A. Singmaster, D.D., President

Columbia Theological Seminary, Columbia, S. C.
Henry Alexander White, Ph.D., D.D., LL.D., Professor of New Testament Literature and Exegesis

Hartford Theological Seminary, Hartford, Conn.
Lewis Bayles Paton, Ph.D., D.D., Nettleton Professor of Old Testament Exegesis and Criticism

Oberlin Theological Seminary, Oberlin, Ohio
Rev. Kemper Fullerton, A.M., Professor of Old Testament Language and Literature

Union Theological Seminary, New York City
Francis Brown, Ph.D., D.D., LL.D., Litt. D., President

Boston University School of Theology, Boston, Mass.
William I. Haven, D.D., a Corresponding Secretary of the American Bible Society

Meadville Theological School, Meadville, Pa.
Franklin C. Southworth, D.D., President

CENTENNIAL CELEBRATION OF

The Hamma Divinity School, Springfield, Ohio
David H. Bauslin, D.D., Dean

Garrett Biblical Institute, Evanston, Ill.
Milton S. Terry, D.D., LL.D., Professor of Christian Doctrine

Berkeley Divinity School, Middletown, Conn.
Samuel Hart, D.D., D.C.L., LL.D., Dean

Reformed Presbyterian Theological Seminary, Allegheny, Pa.
Richard Cameron Wylie, D.D., LL.D., Professor of Church History, Homiletics, Systematic and Pastoral Theology

St. Lawrence University, Canton Theological School, Canton, N. Y.
Henry P. Forbes, D.D., Professor of Biblical Literature

Chicago Theological Seminary, Chicago, Ill.
G. S. Rollins, D.D., Pastor of the Hope Congregational Church, Springfield, Mass.

Seabury Divinity School, Faribault, Minn.
Rev. William Austin Smith, Rector of Christ's Church, Springfield, Mass.

Susquehanna University School of Theology, Selinsgrove, Pa.
Charles T. Aikens, D.D., President
Frank P. Manhart, D.D., Dean

Southern Baptist Theological Seminary, Louisville, Ky.
Edgar Y. Mullins, D.D., LL.D., President.

Augustana College and Theological Seminary, Rock Island, Ill.
Carl A. Blomgren, Ph.D., Professor of Hebrew

The Theological Seminary of the Evangelical Lutheran Church at Philadelphia
Henry E. Jacobs, D.D., S.T.D., LL.D., Dean.

PRINCETON THEOLOGICAL SEMINARY

Central Wesleyan College, Warrenton, Mo.
F. J. Hubach, B.D., Plainfield, N. J.

Atlanta Baptist College Divinity School, Atlanta, Ga.
Rev. John Hope, President

Episcopal Theological School, Cambridge, Mass.
Henry Sylvester Nash, D.D., Professor of New Testament

Drew Theological Seminary, Madison, N. J.
Charles F. Sitterly, Ph.D., S.T.D., Professor of Biblical Literature and English Bible

Crozer Theological Seminary, Chester, Pa.
Milton G. Evans, D.D., President

The Theological Seminary of the Evangelical Lutheran Church at Chicago, Ill.
Revere Franklin Weidner, D.D., LL.D., President

Alfred Theological Seminary, Alfred, N. Y.
B. C. Davis, D.D., President

School of Theology, Howard University, Washington, D. C.
Isaac Clark, D.D., Dean

Vanderbilt University, Biblical Department, Nashville, Tenn.
Wilbur F. Tillett, D.D., LL.D., Dean

The Theological School and Calvin College of the Christian Reformed Church at Grand Rapids, Mich.
Louis Berkhof, B.D., Professor of Exegetical Theology

Westminster Theological Seminary, Westminster, Md.
Claude Cicero Douglas, A.M., B.D., Secretary

CENTENNIAL CELEBRATION OF

Temple University, Department of Theology, Philadelphia, Pa.
Rev. George H. Wailes, Professor

St. Leo Abbey, St. Leo, Fla.
Harold McA. Robinson, B.D., Princeton, N. J.

Houghton Wesleyan Methodist Seminary, Houghton, N. Y.
Rev. H. R. Smith, Professor of English

Western Theological Seminary, Atchison, Kansas
Frederick G. Gotwald, D.D., York, Pa.

Turner Theological Seminary, Morris Brown College,
Atlanta, Ga.
W. G. Alexander, D.D., Dean

School of Theology, Kansas City University, Kansas City, Kansas
Rev. D. Baines-Griffith, A.M., Spuyten Duyvil, N. Y.

Atlanta Theological Seminary, Atlanta, Ga.
John Wilson Bixler, D.D., Professor elect of Natural Theology

Pacific Unitarian School for the Ministry, Berkeley, Cal.
William Sacheus Morgan, B.D., Ph.D., Professor of
Systematic Theology

Southwestern Baptist Theological Seminary, Fort Worth, Texas
Albert Henry Newman, D.D., LL.D., Dean and Professor of
Church History

Central Theological Seminary of the Reformed Church
in the United States, Dayton, Ohio
James I. Good, D.D., LL.D., Professor of Reformed Church History

Theological Seminary of the Reformed Episcopal Church,
Philadelphia, Pa.
Robert L. Rudolph, A.M., D.D., Professor of Systematic Theology,
Biblical Theology and Ethics

PRINCETON THEOLOGICAL SEMINARY

MISSIONARY SEMINARIES

Albert Academy, Freetown, Sierra Leone, West Africa
Rev. Edwin M. Hursh, A.B., Vice-Principal

*Seminario Theologico da Edgreja Presbyteriana no Brasil,
Campinas, Brazil*
John Merrill Kyle, D.D., Lowell, Mass.

American Collegiate and Theological Institute, Samokov, Bulgaria
Rev. Lewis Bond, Plainfield, N. J.

Union Theological School, Foochow, China
Wilbert W. White, Ph.D., D.D., New York City.

Nanking Union Theological Seminary, Nanking, China
Rev. J. E. Williams, Member of the Board of Directors

Theological School of Shaowu, China
Rev. C. L. Storrs, Shaowu

St. John's University, Shanghai, China
William H. Jefferys, D.D., Shanghai

Ashmore Theological Seminary, Swatow, China
Rev. A. F. Groesbeck, Member of the Board of Trustees

Bapatla Normal Training School, Bapatla, South India
Rev. John Newcomb, Bapatla

Bareilly Theological Seminary, Bareilly, India
Thomas Jefferson Scott, D.D., Ocean Grove, N.J.

CENTENNIAL CELEBRATION OF

American Baptist Theological Seminary, Ramapatnam, India
W. L. Ferguson, D.D., Newton Centre, Mass.

Presbyterian Theological Seminary, Saharanpur, India
Rev. Fred. J. Newton, A.M., Professor

The Theological School of the Kwansei Gakuin, Kobe, Japan
Rev. S. E. Hager

Doshisha Theological School, Kyoto, Japan
George M. Rowland, D.D., Sapporo

North Japan College, Sendai, Japan
Teizaburo Demura, A.M., Dean of the Higher Department

Japan Baptist Theological Seminary, Tokyo, Japan
Rev. Charles B. Tenney, Professor of Greek Language and Exegesis

Colegio Internacional, Guadalajara, Mexico
Rev. A. C. Wright, Auburndale, Mass.

Theological Department of Urumia College, Urumia, Persia
Rev. Robert M. Labaree, Urumia

Presbyterian Theological Seminary, Beirut, Syria
Rev. Oscar J. Hardin, Professor

Marash Theological Seminary, Marash, Turkey-in-Asia
W. N. Chambers, D.D., Adana

Western Turkey Theological Seminary, Marsovan, Turkey-in-Asia
George F. Herrick, D.D., New York City

PRINCETON THEOLOGICAL SEMINARY

UNIVERSITIES AND COLLEGES

Faculty of Princeton University
Theodore Whitefield Hunt, Ph.D., L.H.D., Professor of English

Robert College, Constantinople
George Washburn, D.D., Boston, Mass.

Dalhousie University, Halifax
Malcolm James MacLeod, D.D., Minister of the Collegiate Church, New York City

University of Toronto
Kerr Duncan Macmillan, B.D., Instructor in Church History, Princeton Theological Seminary

Harvard University
William Wallace Fenn, D.D., Bussey Professor of Theology and Dean of the Faculty of Divinity

Yale University
Williston Walker, Ph.D., D.D., L.H.D., Titus Street Professor of Ecclesiastical History

University of Pennsylvania
James Alan Montgomery, Ph.D., S.T.D., Assistant Professor of Hebrew

Brown University
Henry T. Fowler, Ph.D., Professor of Biblical Literature

Rutgers College
W. H. S. Demarest, D.D., LL.D., President

CENTENNIAL CELEBRATION OF

Dartmouth College
Rev. Benjamin Tenney Marshall, Pastor First Presbyterian Church, New Rochelle, N. Y.

Washington and Lee University
James Robert Howerton, D.D., Professor of Philosophy

Dickinson College
Eugene Allen Noble, L.H.D., President

Hampden-Sidney College
W. Creighton Campbell, D.D., Member of the Board of Trustees

Williams College
William Rankin, LL.D., Princeton, N. J.

Washington College
James Sylvester Armentrout, B.D., Lancaster, Pa.

Union University
Charles Alexander Richmond, D.D., LL.D., President of Union College and Chancellor of Union University

Middlebury College
Charles E. Hesselgrave, Ph.D., Pastor of the Stanley Congregational Church, Chatham, N. J.

Washington and Jefferson College
James D. Moffat, D.D., LL.D., President

Columbia University
Raymond C. Knox, B.D., Chaplain
Dickinson S. Miller, Ph.D., Professor of Philosophy

University of Pittsburgh
S. B. Linhart, D.D., Secretary

PRINCETON THEOLOGICAL SEMINARY

Amherst College
George Harris, D.D., LL.D., President

Lafayette College
Ethelbert D. Warfield, D.D., LL.D., President
John M. Mecklin, Ph.D., Professor of Philosophy

New York University
Herman H. Horne, Ph.D., Professor of the History of Education and the History of Philosophy

Pennsylvania College
Philip M. Biklé, Ph.D., Dean

Wabash College
Arthur J. Brown, D.D., New York City

Delaware College
William James Rowan, Ph.D., Professor of Rhetoric and Oratory

Marietta College
William T. Wilcox, D.D., Bloomfield, N. J.

Hanover College
John Simonson Howk, D.D., Secretary

Davidson College
Thomas W. Lingle, Ph.D., Professor of Modern Languages

University of Michigan
Walter A. Brooks, D.D., Trenton, N. J.

Westminster College, Pennsylvania
Robert McWatty Russell, D.D., LL.D., President

The College of the City of New York
John H. Finley, Ph.D., LL.D., President

PRINCETON THEOLOGICAL SEMINARY

Lake Forest College
John S. Nollen, Ph.D., President

Macalester College
William Porter Lee, D.D., Pastor of the Westside Presbyterian Church, Germantown, Pa.

University of Wooster
Louis Edward Holden, D.D., LL.D., President

Park College
Cleland Boyd McAfee, Ph.D., D.D., Pastor of the Lafayette Avenue Presbyterian Church, Brooklyn, N. Y.

Parsons College
Willis E. Parsons, D.D., President

Bellevue College
Rev. A. J. Dressler, A.B., Princeton, N. J.

Coe College
Edward R. Burkhalter, D.D., LL.D., President of the Board of Trustees

New Windsor College
James Fraser, Ph.D., D.D., President

THE PROGRAMME OF EXERCISES

THE FIRST DAY

SUNDAY, MAY FIFTH
ELEVEN A. M.
THE FIRST PRESBYTERIAN CHURCH

Doxology

Invocation

THE REVEREND SYLVESTER WOODBRIDGE BEACH, A.M.
The Pastor of the Church

Hymn

"All people that on earth do dwell"

Reading of the Scriptures

Ephesians iv: 1–16

THE REVEREND SYLVESTER WOODBRIDGE BEACH, A.M.

Prayer

THE RIGHT REVEREND ROBERT P. MACKAY, D.D.
Moderator of the General Assembly of the Presbyterian Church
in Canada

Hymn

"The Lord 's my Shepherd, I 'll not want"

Anthem

"Teach me, O Lord" (Thomas Attwood)

CENTENNIAL CELEBRATION OF

Sermon

THE REVEREND FRANCIS LANDEY PATTON, D.D., LL.D.
Stuart Professor of Ethics, Princeton University
President of the Seminary

Hymn

"How sweet and awful is the place"

The Administration of the Lord's Supper

THE REVEREND FRANCIS LANDEY PATTON, D.D., LL.D.
and
THE REVEREND SYLVESTER WOODBRIDGE BEACH, A.M.

Hymn

"Rock of Ages, cleft for me"

Benediction

THE REVEREND FRANCIS LANDEY PATTON, D.D., LL.D.

FOUR P. M.

THE MILLER CHAPEL

Conference for Prayer

LED BY THE REVEREND JOHN DIXON, D.D.
An Associate Secretary of the Board of Home Missions
of the Presbyterian Church in the United States of America
Secretary of the Board of Trustees

Hymn

"I love Thy kingdom, Lord"

[322]

PRINCETON THEOLOGICAL SEMINARY

Prayer
THE REVEREND EIKO J. GROENEVELD, D.D.
Pastor of the First Presbyterian Church
Butte, Montana

Announcement
With reference to the tablet
in memory of
The Reverend Professor Charles Augustus Aiken, Ph.D., D.D.
by
THE REVEREND FRANCIS LANDEY PATTON, D.D., LL.D.
President of the Seminary

Hymn
"For all the saints who from their labors rest"

Reading of the Scriptures
Matthew ix: 35–38
Acts xiii: 1–3
THE REVEREND JOHN DIXON, D.D.

Address
THE REVEREND JOHN DIXON, D.D.

Hymn
"The Son of God goes forth to war"

Prayer
THE REVEREND MAITLAND ALEXANDER, D.D.
Pastor of the First Presbyterian Church
Pittsburgh, Pennsylvania

Hymn
"Who is on the Lord's side?"

CENTENNIAL CELEBRATION OF

Prayer

THE REVEREND JAMES D. MOFFAT, D.D., LL.D.
President of Washington and Jefferson College
and
THE REVEREND SAMUEL MCLANAHAN, A.M.
Princeton

Hymn

"Blest be the tie that binds"

Benediction

THE REVEREND FRANCIS LANDEY PATTON, D.D., LL.D.

SEVEN-FORTY-FIVE P. M.

THE FIRST PRESBYTERIAN CHURCH

Hymn

"Sun of my soul, Thou Saviour dear"

Invocation

THE REVEREND SYLVESTER WOODBRIDGE BEACH, A.M.
The Pastor of the Church

Hymn

"Crown Him with many crowns"

Reading of the Scriptures

John i: 1–5; 15–20; 29–51

THE REVEREND ETHELBERT DUDLEY WARFIELD, D.D., LL.D.
President of Lafayette College
President of the Board of Directors

PRINCETON THEOLOGICAL SEMINARY

Prayer
THE REVEREND ETHELBERT DUDLEY WARFIELD, D.D., LL.D.

Anthem
"What are these that are arrayed in white robes" (J. Stainer)

Hymn
"My faith looks up to Thee"

Sermon
THE REVEREND ETHELBERT DUDLEY WARFIELD, D.D., LL.D.

Hymn
"Jesus, the very thought of Thee"

Prayer
THE REVEREND ROBERT McWATTY RUSSELL, D.D., LL.D.
President of Westminster College, Pennsylvania

Anthem
"Nunc Dimittis" (B. Tours)

Benediction
THE REVEREND ROBERT McWATTY RUSSELL, D.D., LL.D.

CENTENNIAL CELEBRATION OF

THE SECOND DAY

MONDAY, MAY SIXTH

NINE-FIFTEEN A. M.

The Academic Procession formed in the Faculty Room of Princeton University, Nassau Hall

KERR DUNCAN MACMILLAN, B.D., Marshal

TEN A. M.

ALEXANDER HALL

THE REVEREND ETHELBERT DUDLEY WARFIELD, D.D., LL.D.
President of Lafayette College
President of the Board of Directors
Presiding

Address of Welcome

THE REVEREND JOHN GRIER HIBBEN, PH.D., LL.D.
President of Princeton University

Response

THE REVEREND ETHELBERT DUDLEY WARFIELD, D.D., LL.D.
President of the Board of Directors

Hymn

"O heavenly Fount of light and love"

Reading of the Scriptures

II Timothy ii: 1–26

THE REVEREND ETHELBERT DUDLEY WARFIELD, D.D., LL.D.
President of the Board of Directors

PRINCETON THEOLOGICAL SEMINARY

Prayer

THE REVEREND HENRY EYSTER JACOBS, D.D., S.T.D., LL.D.
Dean and Chairman of the Faculty
The Theological Seminary of the Evangelical Lutheran Church
at Philadelphia

Address to the Graduating Class
and
Distribution of Diplomas

THE REVEREND ETHELBERT DUDLEY WARFIELD, D.D., LL.D.
President of the Board of Directors

Announcements
Fellowships and Prizes

THE REVEREND SYLVESTER WOODBRIDGE BEACH, A.M.
Secretary of the Board of Directors

Conferring the Degree of Bachelor of Divinity
Address to the Graduating Class

THE REVEREND FRANCIS LANDEY PATTON, D.D., LL.D.
President of the Seminary

Singing of the Class Hymn

"Onward, Christian Soldiers"

THE GRADUATING CLASS

Address

THE FUNCTION AND THE GLORY OF THE MINISTRY OF GRACE

THE REVEREND JOHN FLEMING CARSON, D.D., LL.D.
Pastor of the Central Presbyterian Church, Brooklyn
Moderator of the General Assembly of the Presbyterian Church
in the United States of America

CENTENNIAL CELEBRATION OF

Address

THE MAKING OF A MINISTER

THE REVEREND RUSSELL CECIL, D.D.
Pastor of the Second Presbyterian Church, Richmond
Moderator of the General Assembly of the Presbyterian Church
in the United States

Prayer

THE REVEREND JOHN PRESTON SEARLE, D.D.
President of the Faculty of the Theological Seminary of the
Reformed Church in America at New Brunswick, N. J.

Hymn

"O Spirit of the living God"

Benediction

THE REVEREND ETHELBERT DUDLEY WARFIELD, D.D., LL.D.
President of the Board of Directors

THREE P. M.

ALEXANDER HALL

THOMAS WHITNEY SYNNOTT, ESQUIRE
Vice-President of the Board of Trustees
Presiding

Hymn

"Our God, our Help in ages past"

Reading of the Scriptures

I Corinthians i: 4–31

THE REVEREND PROFESSOR CASPAR WISTAR HODGE, PH.D.
Princeton Theological Seminary

PRINCETON THEOLOGICAL SEMINARY

Prayer

THE REVEREND DICKINSON SERGEANT MILLER, PH.D.
Professor of Christian Apologetics
The General Theological Seminary of the Protestant
Episcopal Church, New York City

Address

PRINCETON IN THE WORK OF THE PASTORATE

THE REVEREND WILLIAM LEONARD McEWAN, D.D.
Pastor of the Third Presbyterian Church, Pittsburgh

Address

PRINCETON ON THE MISSION FIELD

ROBERT ELLIOTT SPEER, D.D.
A Corresponding Secretary of the Board of Foreign Missions
of the Presbyterian Church in the United States of America

Hymn

"Lift up your heads, ye gates of brass"

Address

PRINCETON IN THEOLOGICAL EDUCATION AND
RELIGIOUS THOUGHT

THE REVEREND WILLIAM HALLOCK JOHNSON, PH.D.
Professor of Greek and New Testament Literature and Exegesis
Lincoln University, Pennsylvania

Address

PRINCETON IN ITS EARLY ENVIRONMENT AND WORK

CHARLES BEATTY ALEXANDER, LL.D.
New York City

Prayer

THE REVEREND JAMES DUNLOP PAXTON, D.D.
Pastor of the First Presbyterian Church, Lynchburg, Virginia

CENTENNIAL CELEBRATION OF

Hymn

"Glory to Thee, Lord of Glory, for Thy saints at rest above"

Benediction

THE REVEREND PROFESSOR CASPAR WISTAR HODGE, PH.D.
Princeton Theological Seminary

FIVE-THIRTY TO SIX-THIRTY P. M.

Informal Reception at Springdale by the President of the Seminary and Mrs. Patton

SEVEN P. M.

THE CASINO

Alumni Dinner

THE REVEREND JOSEPH HEATLY DULLES, A.M.
President of the Alumni Association
Presiding

Grace

THE REVEREND DANIEL NILES FREELAND, A.M.
New York City
Of the Class of 1847

After-Dinner Speakers

THE REVEREND FRANCIS LANDEY PATTON, D.D., LL.D.
President of the Seminary

For the Class of 1862
THE REVEREND JAMES SMITH MCDONALD, D.D.
Corcoran, California

PRINCETON THEOLOGICAL SEMINARY

For the Class of 1872
THE REVEREND WILLIAM COOPER ROMMEL, A.M.
Elizabeth, New Jersey

For the Class of 1882
THE REVEREND CHARLES LEE, D.D.
Carbondale, Pennsylvania

For the Class of 1892
THE REVEREND MAITLAND ALEXANDER, D.D.
Pittsburgh, Pennsylvania

For the Class of 1902
THE REVEREND WILSON THOMAS MOORE BEALE, A.M.
Salisbury, Maryland

THE THIRD DAY

TUESDAY, MAY SEVENTH

NINE-FORTY-FIVE A. M.

The Academic Procession formed in the Faculty Room of Princeton University, Nassau Hall

KERR DUNCAN MACMILLAN, B.D., Marshal

TEN-THIRTY A. M.

ALEXANDER HALL

THE REVEREND FRANCIS LANDEY PATTON, D.D., LL.D.
President of the Seminary
Presiding

CENTENNIAL CELEBRATION OF

Hymn
"A mighty Fortress is our God"

Reading of the Scriptures
Ephesians i: 3–23

THE REVEREND HENRY ALEXANDER WHITE, PH.D., D.D., LL.D.
Professor of New Testament Literature and Exegesis
Columbia Theological Seminary
Columbia, South Carolina

Prayer

THE REVEREND WILLIAM DOUGLAS MACKENZIE, D.D., LL.D.
President of Hartford Theological Seminary
Hartford, Connecticut

Address
ON SOME CHURCH PROBLEMS

THE RIGHT REVEREND ALEXANDER STEWART, M.A., D.D.
Principal of St. Mary's College and
Primarius Professor of Divinity in the University of St. Andrews
Moderator of the General Assembly of the Church of Scotland

Address
A SCOTTISH ESTIMATE OF PRINCETON THEOLOGY

THE RIGHT REVEREND JAMES WELLS, M.A., D.D.
Minister of the West Church, Pollokshields, Glasgow
Moderator of the General Assembly of the
United Free Church of Scotland

Hymn
"O God of Bethel, by whose hand"

PRINCETON THEOLOGICAL SEMINARY

Address

IRISH AND AMERICAN PRESBYTERIANISM

THE RIGHT REVEREND JOHN MACMILLAN, B.A., D.D.
Minister of the Cooke Centenary Church, Belfast
Moderator of the General Assembly of the Presbyterian
Church in Ireland

Prayer

THE REVEREND CHARLES FREMONT SITTERLY, PH.D., S.T.D.
Professor of Biblical Literature and Exegesis of the English Bible
Drew Theological Seminary, Madison, New Jersey

Hymn

"Now thank we all our God"

Benediction

THE REVEREND JAMES D. MCCULLOCH, D.D.
Principal of the Free Church College
Edinburgh

ONE-THIRTY P. M.

THE CASINO

Commemorative Luncheon

THE REVEREND ETHELBERT DUDLEY WARFIELD, D.D., LL.D.
President of the Board of Directors
Presiding

Grace

THE REVEREND THOMAS REESE ENGLISH, D.D.
Henry Young Professor of Biblical Literature and the
Interpretation of the New Testament
Union Theological Seminary, Richmond, Virginia

CENTENNIAL CELEBRATION OF
Congratulatory Speeches
From the Presbyterian Church in the United States of America
THE REVEREND WILLIAM HENRY ROBERTS, D.D., LL.D.
Stated Clerk of the General Assembly
American Secretary of the World Presbyterian Alliance

From the Other Presbyterian and Reformed Churches
THE REVEREND JOHN CRAWFORD SCOULLER, D.D.
Pastor of the Fourth United Presbyterian Church, Philadelphia
Moderator of the General Assembly of the United
Presbyterian Church of North America

From Other Churches
THE RIGHT REVEREND DAVID HUMMELL GREER, D.D., S.T.D., LL.D.
Bishop of the Protestant Episcopal Church in the
Diocese of New York

*From the Seminaries of the Presbyterian Church
in the United States of America*
THE REVEREND JAMES GORE KING MCCLURE, D.D., LL.D.
President of McCormick Theological Seminary
Chicago, Illinois

From the Seminaries of Other Churches
THE REVEREND WILLISTON WALKER, PH.D., D.D., L.H.D.
Titus Street Professor of Ecclesiastical History
Yale University Divinity School
New Haven, Connecticut
and
THE REVEREND EDGAR YOUNG MULLINS, D.D., LL.D.
President of the Southern Baptist Theological Seminary
Louisville, Kentucky

From Princeton University
THE REVEREND JOHN GRIER HIBBEN, PH.D., LL.D.
President of Princeton University

PRINCETON THEOLOGICAL SEMINARY
Response
THE REVEREND FRANCIS LANDEY PATTON, D.D., LL.D.
President of the Seminary

Benediction
THE REVEREND JAMES ISAAC GOOD, D.D., LL.D.
Professor of Reformed Church History in the
Central Theological Seminary, Dayton, Ohio
President of the General Synod of the Reformed Church
in the United States

SERMONS AND ADDRESSES

PRINCETON SEMINARY AND THE FAITH

SERMON

BY THE REVEREND FRANCIS LANDEY PATTON, D.D., LL.D.
Stuart Professor of Ethics, Princeton University
President of the Seminary

"Beloved, when I gave all diligence to write unto you of the common salvation, it was needful for me to write unto you, and exhort you that ye should earnestly contend for the faith which was once delivered unto the saints." Jude 3.

PRINCETON Theological Seminary opened its doors a hundred years ago with one professor and three students—a ratio of instructor to pupils which ought to satisfy the most exacting demands of modern pedagogy. Dr. Miller was associated with Dr. Alexander a little later, and soon after that Dr. Hodge, then a very young man, began his long career as a member of the teaching staff. These three men, as Mr. Dulles has well said, determined the character of Princeton Seminary. We like to think that the institution has not lost the spirit of fervent piety into which it was baptized in its infancy, and that the stamp of religious character which was impressed upon it at the beginning has not been altogether effaced.

Dr. Alexander was an acute thinker on theological and philosophical subjects, a man of great sagacity, keen in his analysis of religious states, and very spiritually minded. Dr. Miller was a courtly gentleman of elegant scholarship and wide reading. He was an industrious writer and a stalwart defender of the great principles of Presbyterian doctrine and polity. Dr. Hodge came to his position with special equipment for his work. He had enjoyed the advantage of study in Germany, and was fully abreast of the theological controversies of his day. He won enduring fame as exegete, controversialist, ecclesiastic and dogmatician; lived in the service of the Seminary to a ripe old age, and garnered the wisdom and experience of his life in his "Systematic Theology". With these men there was associated later on Dr. Joseph Addison Alexander, a man of rare literary genius and great linguistic attainments, who served the Seminary with remarkable power and efficiency until the time of his death. Dr. John Breckinridge was also a professor in the Seminary for a short time during the early years of its history, but he left it to enter upon another form of ministerial labor; and the same is to be said of Dr. James W. Alexander, whose distinguished career as pastor of what is now known as the Fifth Avenue Presbyterian Church is one of the brightest pages in the annals of the American pulpit.

Dr. William Henry Green, whom many of us still remember, entered upon the work of instruction in the Seminary when he was quite young, and like Dr. Charles Hodge filled the full tale of fifty years in the Seminary's service. He did conspicuous work in the department of Old Testament Literature, achieved a world-wide reputation as an able supporter of conservative views in regard to Old Testament criticism, and rendered a lasting service to the church by his defence of the Mosaic authorship of the Pentateuch. Dr. Hodge had as his successors two sons who, during the later years of his life, acted as his colleagues. Dr. Archibald Alexander Hodge, a man of less learning than his father, but, as I think, of more genius, took the chair of Systematic Theology. He was distinguished by keen metaphysical insight and a marvelous power of extemporaneous expression. Dr. Caspar Wistar Hodge, the distinguished successor of Dr. Addison Alexander, added the work of exegetical theology to his previous duties as professor of New Testament Literature. He was a man of refined scholarship, of sane and penetrating judgment, and commanding influence. He was an inspiring teacher, and was singularly reverent in his attitude toward the Scriptures. Following Dr. Hodge in the chair of New Testament Literature came Dr. Purves, the pupil succeeding his teacher as Dr. Hodge had succeeded his. Dr. Purves, after several years of service in the Seminary, resigned his position to take the same pulpit in New York which Dr. James W. Alexander had taken years before. Dr. Purves was one of those rare men who combine in equal degree the qualities of an exact scholar and a popular preacher.

Dr. Moffat, a man of fine classical scholarship, succeeded Dr. Miller in the department of Church History. Coming to his position from the chair of Greek in the College of New Jersey, it was not to be expected that he would feel a deep interest in the discussion of theological subtleties. He preferred to look at church history on its literary side; and he accordingly presented the story of the church's life in the form of flowing and interesting narrative. Dr. Aiken served the Seminary with unfailing ability and fidelity during the twenty years of his life among us, bringing to the work of his chair the resources of a broad and exact scholarship and, though laboring under the great disadvantage of growing enfeeblement during the later years of his life, is still remembered as one who with great patience and self-sacrifice devoted himself to the defence of the gospel.

Dr. McGill was a professor in the Seminary as far back as when I was a student here: a man of great subtlety of thought, mighty in the Scriptures, singularly copious and felicitous in prayer, an exceptionally fine teacher of homiletics and an able defender of the Presbyterian form of church government, though I confess that in his zeal for a *jure divino* polity he sometimes seemed to me to put a burden upon certain proof texts greater than they were able to bear. Dr. Paxton succeeded Dr. McGill, bringing with him the ripe experiences of large pastorates in Pittsburgh and New York, particularly in that historic church in the latter city whose members—I refer especially to the Lenox family—have done so much for this Seminary and for our Church at large. He was no novice in the department of Homiletics, for he had lectured on this subject before, both in Pittsburgh and New York; and the art of preaching had enlisted his deepest interest during his entire ministry.

These men of course were not all alike; but they all spoke the same thing and there were no divisions among them. There may be some advantage in giving students object lessons in independent thinking by allowing them to hear the opinions of one professor flatly contradicted by the teaching of another professor in an adjoining classroom. But this advantage, whatever it be, is in my humble judgment more than counterbalanced by the advantage of institutional solidarity which has been so conspicuously manifested in the history of Princeton

Theological Seminary. Some of the men to whom I have referred brought with them the ripe results of a long experience in the pastorate. This is a matter for which we should be profoundly grateful. There should always be in the Seminary—as there are today, and never in larger proportion than today—a number of men who when they speak to students in regard to the work upon which they are about to enter can speak out of an affluent ministerial experience. But of course it would hardly do to say that every professor in a theological seminary should first of all go through the apprenticeship of pastoral experience. We should at least find it difficult to adjust such a view to the attitude we have taken toward some of the most distinguished men who have adorned the chairs of this Seminary. Dr. Charles Hodge never had a pastorate so far as my knowledge goes. Dr. Addison Alexander was never a pastor. Dr. Green I believe was a pastor for a short time, but I do not suppose that his experience in that capacity was of much help to him as a student of Old Testament criticism. Dr. Caspar Wistar Hodge was a pastor for a few years, but I imagine that this can be regarded as a negligible element in his equipment for the chair of New Testament Literature. It is safe to say that a man can no longer enter upon a professorship that calls for exact scholarship and wide reading after long service in the pastorate and hope to render the kind and degree of service that is expected of a professor in these days. The reason is obvious. The functions of the pastor and of the professor have been so differentiated in these latter years that the minister of a modern church has no time for the acquisition of highly specialized learning, and the work of a professorship, at least in some of the departments of the theological curriculum, involves such exact knowledge and wide reading that the best results can be hoped for only in one who enters early in life upon the duties of his chair and gives his undivided interest to them.

The theological attitude of Princeton Theological Seminary is, I think, pretty well understood: but lest there should be any misapprehension as to what that attitude is, I wish to say a word, even at the risk of taxing your patience somewhat, in regard to our theological position. I do not for a moment deny that there may be a place in the world for an institution the professors of which work in the unhampered exercise of their judgment in the search for theological truth; but in the nature of the case the seminary which is ecclesiastical in its origin and relationships and which does its work under the rubric of confessional obligations cannot have that sort of freedom. Princeton Theological Seminary, as you all know, is the creature of the Presbyterian General Assembly, and is committed by the terms of its constitution to the propagation and defence of the Reformed Theology. Therefore you need not be surprised when told that during the hundred years of its history it has been a conservative institution. Now, I am not ashamed of being conservative on any subject, and least of all have I any misgivings in regard to conservatism in theology; but then there are several kinds of conservatism, and if you will bear with me I will say a word or two in regard to some of these forms of conservatism.

There is, for example, what I may call the conservatism of ignorance. I do not use the expression in any disparaging sense; and, what is more, I have great respect for conservatism of the kind I have mentioned. We cannot well begin our work in any department without some assumptions. Just what these assumptions shall be will depend upon circumstances. You do not expect a political economist, for example, to preface his lectures with a theory of the universe, though some theory of the universe must underlie what he has to say. It may therefore very easily happen that a man who starts with the assumption that the Bible is the word of God may do very valuable work as an expounder of the Bible though he know but little of the arguments wherewith his assumption is discredited. If in our chairs of historical criticism our object is so to discuss the questions regarding the authorship of the books of the New Testament that our students may thereby be the more confident of their position as to the divine authority of the New Testament, who shall say that those who without any minute acquaintance with contrary positions already believe in that authority may not do a most important work in the presentation of the truths of Scripture to their congregations? If a man should say to me, "I take the Bible as the word of God. This is my great assumption; and with such fluency of speech and power of exposition as have been given to me, I preach it to the world", I for my part am ready to say that he is fulfilling a most important function. If our object in our chairs of historical criticism is to lead men to a sure knowledge that the Bible is God's word, and there are men who have already got there without being led there, and they with this supreme unchallenged assumption are ready to go out and preach the word, then in God's name let them go and may God bless them! I have nothing to say against this sort of conservatism, but I ought to say at the same time that this is not the type of conservatism which we are seeking to illustrate here.

Then again there is the conservatism of the advocate. A man, that is to say, may feel that he holds a brief for a certain opinion or set of opinions and that he is called upon to defend these opinions with a certain amount of enthusiasm. The objection will immediately be made that he is not free in his search for truth, that he is handicapped by having his conclusions made for him in advance, and that he knows when he begins his inquiry just what is to be looked for at the end of the road. There is a certain amount of force in this criticism which I do not overlook, though I think that far too much is made of it. But we must be careful, in acknowledging the element of justice in the criticism, not to fall into the very common mistake of supposing that a man's position as an advocate operates to the prejudice of his full knowledge of the facts. Biassed he may be, but ignorant he need not be. When the muniments of title are assailed, it is likely that the defendant's counsel knows the strength of his opponent's case quite as well as he does himself. He is none the less possessed of legal knowledge and forensic skill because he has espoused a cause and advocates it with the warmth of a partisan. He may not be as dispassionate as the judge, but he ought to know quite as well as the judge the full value of the facts. It is quite possible, however, that an apologete may come to feel that he has espoused a cause that he cannot honestly defend; and under these circumstances, if he is an honest man, he will throw down his brief and retire from the case. I am not ashamed to admit that our Princeton theologians have to a great extent been advocates. They have felt that their function was forensic as well as didactic. They have spoken and written in the warm glow of enthusiasm. They have used well the weapons of controversy, and they have given expression to their thoughts through the copious vocabulary of invective, ridicule and sarcasm, and in the use of the hot rhetoric of telling phrase and pungent argument. I confess that I miss this in the theological discussions of today, and I sometimes think that we lose in force what we gain in politeness.

There is, however, a third type of conservatism; and that is the conservatism of calm scientific conviction. Now this scientific attitude toward open questions in theology is more suited to the psychological climate in which we live today. Men feel that epithets are not arguments, and that you can get better and more permanent results through a calm statement of the facts than you can through fine writing and florid rhetoric. I sympathize with this view very heartily. And still I miss the enthusiasm of the old controversies too; and I would like to remind the younger theologians of the fact that they are defenders as well as investigators. Princeton Seminary, it is true, has taken a leading place in theological controversy; but she has shown herself capable also of placid scientific inquiry, and we have a good illustration of both the polemic and the scientific conservatism of the Seminary in the controversial articles of Dr. Charles Hodge on the one hand and in his "Systematic Theology" on the other.

Let us remember, then, that Princeton Seminary by its constitution is committed to that body of divinity known as the Augustinian or Calvinistic Theology. This theology presupposes of course the great truths of Natural Theology and the divine authority of the Bible. The whole area of controversial theology was therefore properly within the purview of the Princeton theologians.

Still the great debates were on grounds which presupposed the theological prolegomena to which I have just referred. In the early days of the Seminary's life philosophy did not enter largely into the reading of a minister. In fact philosophy was very little read by anybody. Mr. Riley, in his book on American Philosophy, brings together the evidence of philosophical activity in this country during the eighteenth and early part of the nineteenth century, but it makes a poor showing. There was some idealism in New Haven; Priestley had a few followers in Pennsylvania; and there was some literary and a somewhat amateurish pantheism in New England: but philosophy was not a large factor in our theology; and in our colleges the Scottish philosophy of common sense was what was generally taught. It is likewise true that acute interest in the questions of the Higher Criticism came at a later date. We were slow to recognize the immigration of German thought as having any important bearing upon our theological life. Accordingly theological controversy was largely of an interdenominational sort. We discussed Presbyterianism *versus* Prelacy; and infant baptism in opposition to those who denied its Scriptural warrant. We had debates on the Trinity and the Divinity of Christ. We fought over again the battle between Calvinism and Arminianism; and against the sects that rose up to contradict it, we defended the traditional doctrine of future retribution. These discussions for the most part proceeded upon exegetical grounds, each side maintaining that its position was the doctrine of the Bible, and neither disputing that the Bible was authoritative. In all these discussions Princeton Seminary bore an honorable part and rendered important service.

There was also in the family of Churches holding the Reformed Theology an intra-Calvinistic development. Under the influence of the New England theologians, such as Emmons, Hopkins, Edwards, Taylor and Park, there grew up certain modifications of the Calvinistic system which constitute a very important chapter in the history of opinion in America. I always had great respect for the New England theologians. I used to read them, and have never ceased to admire them, and by that I mean that I still cherish the admiring recollection I have of them. They were original, they were independent. These discussions were largely ethico-metaphysical. They dwelt on the problem of God's relation to the world, and of the human will. They entered with great minuteness of discrimination into anthropological inquiries respecting original sin and the distinction between natural and moral inability. Our friends in New England did a great work, and as I have already intimated opened a splendid chapter in the history of opinion. They built their tabernacle with strict regard to the plans and specifications of their architects. We have nothing but admiration for the fine lines of the structure, but we somehow feel that they departed somewhat from the pattern shown us in the mount.

Now Princeton Seminary, it should be said, never contributed anything to these modifications of the Calvinistic system. She went on defending the traditions of the Reformed Theology. You may say she was not original: perhaps so, but then, neither was she provincial. She had no oddities of manner, no shibboleths, no pet phrases, no theological labels, no trademark. She simply taught the old Calvinistic Theology without modification: and she made obstinate resistance to the modifications proposed elsewhere, as being in their logical results subversive of the Reformed faith. There has been a New Haven theology and an Andover theology; but there never was a distinctively Princeton theology. Princeton's boast, if she have reason to boast at all, is her unswerving fidelity to the theology of the Reformation. *Semper eadem* is a motto that would well befit her.

The theological position of Princeton Seminary is exactly the same today that it was a hundred years ago. This may seem like a strange statement to make about a living institution in this very progressive age. We have of course put a new interpretation on the "days" of Genesis; and in other particulars have used the results of science to help us in the interpretation of the Scriptures. I am speaking now, however, of the distinctive dogmatic content of the Reformed Theology. We are in possession of new material for studying the historical problems connected with the origin and growth of Biblical Literature. We have a better text of the New Testament and a better understanding of the meaning of the New Testament than were possessed by those to whom this Seminary owes the beginnings of its life. But have any of these improvements made necessary any modification of our belief as to the authority of Scripture or as to the dogmatic content of the Scripture? I am not aware of any such necessity. Why then should our doctrinal position undergo a change? I can think of several things that might be said in reply to this question, but I do not feel that any of them should influence us very materially. "Do you mean to tell us"—I can imagine some one saying—"that you still adhere to that old theology of the Reformers which men in these days have so generally abandoned?" I am not aware, to begin with, that it is so generally abandoned. But if it were, that would not prove it to be untrue. It would only prove that it is not fashionable. Professor James remarks somewhere in one of his later books that "souls are not fashionable". Some of us nevertheless go on believing in "souls", hoping that by and by there will be a reaction, and that some of our philosophical friends will reconsider their hasty attitude toward the spiritual side of our nature. This is the way we feel toward the old theology. It may come into fashion again.

"Has not modern philosophy made it difficult, if not impossible, to maintain the positions of the old theology?" some one else may ask. I am not aware of that state of things. I know that certain forms of philosophical opinion are incompatible with dogmatic Christianity, but I do not know of any necessity for adopting those forms of philosophical opinion. "Can you continue to hold", one may ask, "the numerical distinction between God and the world in view of the teaching of contemporary metaphysic?" Quite as well, I answer, as we could when Spinoza identified *natura naturans* and *natura naturata*. Not all philosophers are pantheists, and if they were, I should not feel under obligation to accept their teaching. I know that psychology is invading the field of theology, and some of its representatives are trying to explain "conversion" by expressing the change involved in it in the terms of a natural process. My judgment is that they have met with very indifferent success in their endeavor to desupernaturalize conversion: but it interests me to notice that just now when the ministers seem disposed to stop talking about conversion the psychologists are turning their attention to it.

Still again it may be said that the Christian consciousness, if it has not changed the meaning of the great doctrines of Christianity, has given us a new scale of values in regard to them. But that is only on the assumption that the so-called Christian consciousness has a right to supplement the Scriptures or contradict their obvious meaning. If there is any value at all in the argument based on the Christian consciousness, it is to the effect that the New Testament is itself only an expression of the religious consciousness of the period in which it was written and may therefore be set aside by the Christian consciousness of today whenever the religious experiences of the two periods do not coincide. I should like to know, however, by what process we could secure a consensus of opinion that might be taken as an expression of the religious consciousness of today, and I should like to know, moreover, what authority it would possess if we had it. What basis should we have for religious certitude, once we conceded that our only reason for faith is found in the religious consciousness, and that as the religious consciousness of yesterday is set aside by the religious consciousness of today, so also the religious consciousness of today may be contradicted by the religious consciousness of tomorrow?

Once more our objector may say that it is not a difference in the interpretation of the Scripture but a difference of attitude toward the Scripture which makes the old theology unpalatable to the modern mind. "Our change of belief", he would say, "is not due to exegesis or historical criticism. Grammar and logic have had little to do with our changed theological position. We reverence the writings—say those of Paul—but we do not read them literally; we see in their concrete statements the embodiment of great transcendental ideas."

This is an implied admission that if we do read Paul literally it is hard to escape the conclusion that Paul believed what the Christian world has always supposed that he believed. And the issue I am convinced is really whether we shall go on believing in what Paul teaches or give him up altogether. I cannot attach much value to what I have just referred to as a new attitude toward Paul and the other writers of the New Testament. And yet I would not be wilfully blind to a certain element of truth that may underlie this view of the matter. For I am not prepared to say that the language of the New Testament, with its imagery borrowed from the world of sense, adequately expresses all that it was intended to convey. I am not prepared to say that there are not some great ideas pertaining to the world of spiritual values which Paul's language borrowed from the world of fact but imperfectly adumbrated. Be that as it may, however, it is still true that when we impute to Paul a meaning which in all probability had never entered his mind, and deny to his words the meaning that he evidently meant them to have, we are handling the word of God deceitfully: and whether we do so in the icy speech of Hegelian philosophy after the style of Edward Caird in his Gifford Lectures, or in the fervid words of a vague and almost pietistic mysticism after the manner of Father Tyrrell in his "Christianity at the Crossroads" matters not. In either case we are reading into the New Testament what the writers of the New Testament never intended. There is then but one honest course to follow: either give up the Scriptures as no longer having authority, or take them at their face value and in their plain and obvious meaning.

But while I say that the theological position of Princeton Seminary has remained unchanged I am very free to admit that the issues of today are different from those of a former generation. The Calvinistic theology is a view of the world which takes account of the whole field of human conduct. All in fact that pertains to being, duty and destiny falls within its purview. Believing in the existence of a personal God we feel bound to interpret all events in the terms and under the great category of the divine purpose. If we believe in the incarnation we must believe that it was included in that purpose. If we believe that salvation is through faith, it is very hard to escape the conviction that both the salvation and the faith which is instrumental to it are to be included in that purpose.

All problems of ethics, all questions of duty, all phases of individual and social morality are therefore legitimately within the sphere of the Calvinistic theology. All the moral sciences and all the speculations of philosophers in regard to human conduct must come under the view of him who looks upon conduct as related to a supreme norm of Right and an ideal conception of the Good. In the nature of the case, therefore, we must occupy a great deal of territory in common with our brethren in other communions. With our friends in the Roman Catholic Church we protest against all forms of naturalistic and pantheistic philosophy; and we share with them the common heritage of the Christian world as it is embodied in the Nicene and Chalcedonian theology. With our brethren in the Lutheran, Anglican and Arminian communions we hold to the great principles of Protestantism and repudiate the corruptions of doctrine which have crept into the Church of Rome. And more than that, the things wherein we agree with our brethren of other Christian communions are more important than those in which we differ. We can therefore enter cordially into sympathetic relation with the irenic spirit which is so characteristic of our times, and that without ignoring or pushing into the background the distinguishing features of the Reformed Theology. Those distinguishing features I need not say concern the position of the Reformed Theology in regard to the divine purpose and the doctrines of grace in relation to that purpose. I know you will understand me when I say that the points which distinguish our theology are not necessarily those of greatest controversial importance at the present day. Intrinsically they are as important as they ever were, but relatively they are of less importance. In other words, there has been a subsidence of interest in regard to some questions due largely to the emergence of acute controversial interest in other and more fundamental issues. Men are not discussing the question regarding the subjects or the mode of baptism. The day of hot controversy between Calvinists and Arminians has passed. Men are not writing treatises on theories of inspiration. They are not discussing the question of the Adamic relationship or of this, that and the other view of the atonement. The reason is not that these questions are of no importance or of little importance—and I think there is far too much indifference to their significance—but that the thought of the theological world has been occupied in recent years and is still occupied with questions which bear more radically upon the truth and value of historic Christianity.

Into the discussion of these questions I do not propose to enter. But I am safe in saying that the emphasis of contemporary debate is placed upon questions that are in their nature philosophical and historical. If the Bible is a divine revelation there is practically no difficulty in ascertaining the dogmatic content of Christianity. But is it? That is the fundamental question with which Christian theologians are called to deal. That question involves a number of historical inquiries in regard to the origin of the books that constitute the Bible. These inquiries again are in many cases conditioned by the theory of the universe which constitutes the philosophical presupposition of those who enter upon historical investigation. I am far from saying that all who accept the results of negative criticism are advocates of a naturalistic or pantheistic view of the world. But it is quite certain that, for the man who holds an antisupernaturalistic philosophy, a supernaturalistic theology is impossible. Nor is it too much to say that antisupernaturalistic bias has been the determining influence in much of the historical criticism of the last century. It would be idle to say, as some perhaps may say, that we can afford to be indifferent to the questions mooted in philosophy and history, since our religion is one that is rooted in a personal relation to Jesus and makes no demand upon us for metaphysical subtlety or historical erudition: for the value that we attach to our personal relation to Jesus must depend upon the place which Jesus occupies in the scale of being, and that precisely is the question which is under discussion at the present day. We are being made familiar every day with the effect of a naturalistic construction of the phenomena of the world upon the attitude which men assume toward Jesus. There are, for example, those who think that Jesus was a normal man, pure-minded and the teacher of an exalted type of morality, who was cut off in the beginning of His days, but not before He became the founder of the Christian religion. They look upon the supernatural elements of His life as the additions of a later generation of His followers who fitted to Him the prophecies of the Old Testament and imputed to Him the supernatural elements regarding His birth and resurrection which we find in the Gospels. Some of those who take this view of Jesus are very much interested in what they call the creed of Jesus—that is, in what Jesus believed. I can understand that there may be some intellectual interest in discovering what Jesus believed, just as there is in finding out what Confucius or Plato believed. But I cannot attach much importance to it. If Jesus was a human being like the rest of us and His range of vision was limited to His times, I fail to see any great advantage in knowing what He believed. He did not know the Copernican theory of astronomy; He had no knowledge of the doctrine of evolution and therefore had not seen how that doctrine has affected the entire philosophy of conduct.

This human being, however, men are willing to accept as embodying their ethical ideal: and I am safe in saying that with some people Christianity consists in regarding Jesus as an ethical ideal. Let us give a moment's thought to this view of Christianity. It is quite clear that if Jesus is simply an ideal man we need no faith in God as the presupposition of our attachment to Jesus. An atheist may be a good father and a public-spirited citizen; he may admire the character of Jesus and be willing to join a society membership in which consists simply in a promise to live according to the teachings of Jesus: atheistic Christianity is therefore quite a possibility and if by and by we have an organization of atheistic Christians we need not evince any surprise. But that is not all; for if Jesus is simply an exponent of ideal morality, there would seem to be no need of the historic Jesus. It is not the man Jesus but the ideal embodied in Him that is of value; and all efforts to realize that ideal in our own lives will proceed upon the basis that it corresponds to the judgments of moral value of which we find ourselves in possession. No great harm would follow, therefore, if we lost the historic Jesus altogether; as lose Him we are very likely to do if we follow the naturalistic methods of historical criticism to their logical results.

It is very interesting to watch the efforts of critical thinkers to escape from the obvious supernaturalism imputed to Jesus in the Gospels. They fall into hopeless difficulties. Those, for example, who regard Jesus as an ideal teacher are confronted by the eschatologists who say that Jesus was primarily not a teacher at all, but that the motive of His ministry was to preach the near approach of the end of the present social order and the setting up of the Kingdom of God. They hold that He shared the eschatological opinions current in later Judaism, and that He believed Himself to be the Son of Man who, in a short time, was to come again in the clouds of heaven, in power and great glory. His ethics were no ideal scheme of human conduct but were of an interimistic character, intended to serve the purpose of the short interval between His first and His second appearing, their alleged defects making them inadequate as a permanent norm of conduct in the existing socio-political order, as obviously also in that condition of things when men neither marry nor are given in marriage but are as the angels in heaven.

If the Bible is to be interpreted on a naturalistic basis, and it is merely a human Jesus who is presented to us in the Gospels, there is great plausibility in this view. How the eschatological and the ethical conceptions of the life of Jesus are to be harmonized, it is hard to say. But we can hardly be expected to feel much interest in a Jewish visionary who succeeded in convincing a few followers that He was the Son of Man who was within the space of a single generation to bring about the end of the present order of things and set up the Kingdom of God. And whatever be the genetic relation of present Christianity to the eschatological teachings of Jesus, one can not help feeling that a great strain is put upon human belief when we are taught that the world-conquering religion of Christ had its origin in the deluded judgment of a Jewish enthusiast respecting the end of the world. If the view which we are considering is correct, we are left to wonder how Christianity survived the disappointments of the primitive believers and how the followers of Jesus maintained their faith in the second coming by successive postponements of the event. We wonder that a religion can still call itself by the name of Jesus after it has given up the idea to which He consecrated His life. Those who put a naturalistic interpretation upon the eschatological feature in the teaching of Jesus and who, at the same time, regard this as the leading feature of His ministry are fond of showing that it has undergone changes of interpretation until now, in the minds of some, it has vanished away. The parousia, looked for as imminent at first, has come to be regarded as indefinitely postponed; or it has been exchanged for the problem of *post mortem* destiny; and this, in turn, is giving way in some quarters to a doctrine of the Kingdom of God synonymous with social regeneration and the uplift of society. So the eschatological and the ethical conceptions of a merely human Jesus meet at last on common ground, and Christianity resolves itself into an effort for the spread of good-will among men. The success of Jesus, in other words, is the victory of a social programme against which the life of Jesus was, in a certain sense, a protest.

I can well understand that men will hesitate to think that the growth of Christianity has been adequately explained by such a view of Jesus. Men may be easily forgiven for finding Jesus too uninteresting to be the subject of much consideration in these later days. When, therefore, still in quest of an adequate cause for the great religious phenomenon which we call Christianity, some turn to Paul and find in his strong supernaturalism, his wide world-view, his faith in the resurrection of Jesus and the atonement, his belief in the doctrine of sin, and his philosophy of salvation, the real secret of victorious Christianity, I do not wonder. It is true that Paul's theology was supernatural through and through, but it was not the superficial supernaturalism of a visionary looking for the speedy end of the world. It was a supernaturalism that made its appeal to what Paul believed to be accredited facts and, at all events, it did not belie its claims by building them upon a confessed historical failure.

But the kaleidoscope of criticism is capable of still another twist. Liberal Christians who are satisfied to find in a human Jesus, possessed of unusual ethical insight, a sufficient explanation of Christianity must reckon now with a more radical school of thinkers. When it was the fashion to reject most of the Pauline writings and put the Gospels down into the second century, it was not difficult to suppose that the supernaturalism which envelopes the life of Jesus was a matter of comparatively slow growth. But with Paul's writings rehabilitated and the Synoptic Gospels, particularly the Gospel of Mark, forced back to a period in all probability prior to the capture of Jerusalem, it is not so easy to place a mythical interpretation upon the Gospels or to regard the miraculous features of the life of Jesus as the harmless exaggerations of admiring disciples or the idealized representations of a later generation of Christian believers. So deeply embedded is the supernaturalism of Jesus in the earliest records of Christianity that we must accept this supernaturalism as orthodox Christians have always accepted it, or we must construct a pre-Christian Jesus out of the eschatological and apocalyptic literature of the period covered by a century or more before the Christian era. In other words, according to the radical school of which I am now speaking the historical Jesus never existed. To the liberal Christians, they say, in effect, "Give up belief in the historical Jesus altogether, or else accept the supernaturalism with which the earliest Christian records invest Him."

I do not mind having these men fall out and quarrel among themselves; I like to read the biting sarcasm with which they attack one another, because I feel that when they fall out the old faith may come into its own. But the position which they have brought us to is this: you can not get the supernatural elements out of the earliest records of the life of Christ, and you are compelled either to seek the origin of the Gospel portraiture of Jesus in a pre-Christian myth or to stand by the simple, plain narrative of the supernatural as it lies on the face of the

Gospels themselves. Clearly, then, the issue is sharp between a natural human Jesus and the ever-living and incarnate Jesus, between a Christianity that is supernatural in its inception and a Christianity that can be explained by a system of natural causation.

When, however, you have explained Christianity on the basis of natural causation and eliminated the supernatural, it is a religion for this world and it has no reference to a world to come. You can make Jesus what you like, and say, if you please, that He is a prototype of the modern socialist; but whatever you say, this remains—He and His methods have nothing whatever to do with anything outside the boundaries of this earthly life. Abolish poverty if you can, but you can not abolish death. Give us pure food and better sanitation, equalize the luxuries of happiness in as large a measure as you can—it makes no difference: it is but a little time until the rich man will leave his plenty and the poor man will leave his want; death will come alike to both, and to neither has the gospel a word to say with respect to eternal life.

It must be remembered, however, that many who are unable to accept the full account of miraculous Christianity given us in the Gospels are yet far from denying that there are unescapable elements of supernaturalism in Jesus. Whatever doubts they may have in regard to the Virgin birth or the story of our Lord's resurrection, they are impressed with His unique personality; they feel that He is the fullest revelation of God; and that for the purposes of their religious nature He is to them as if He were God. Moreover, they make a great deal of the Messianic consciousness of Jesus. I can not help feeling, however, that the argument for the supernatural element in Jesus, based upon the reports of His subjective states given us by the evangelists, is but a poor substitute for the objective supernatural facts which are presented to us in the Gospels, and that when faith in these objective facts is weakened, men will be disposed to account for those subjective states which go by the name of the Messianic consciousness by regarding them as the offspring of an unbalanced mind. It is so easy apparently for some men to pay flattering compliments to Jesus after they have discredited the facts which justify them. The truth is that non-miraculous Christianity is not alluring. Men are slow to give up the traditional supernaturalism of the gospel story. We honour the faith and religious fervour which still retains a minimum of the traditional doctrine regarding the Divinity of Jesus, even though it be at the expense of a rigid logic, and though it do more credit to the religious feelings than to the intellect. But, nevertheless, we feel prompted to say, "You have discarded the great supernatural facts of the life of Jesus; you have stripped Him of the insignia of divine royalty; what boots it now that you pin upon His breast the gaudy decorations of a minimizing theology?" It seems impossible to compromise between the naturalistic and the supernaturalistic view of Jesus. If we give up the account of His divine mission as the evangelists present it, then we must conclude that no authoritative divine message has ever reached us and we are no better off than men were in the days of the Greek philosophy. We have had Platonists and Aristotelians, Stoics and Epicureans, idealists and materialists; we have had agnostics in abundance from Protagoras down to our own times. But they brought no message from the other world, and none since then has come to us. We are as ignorant as they were in regard to the great problem of destiny. The hypothesis of a merely human Jesus makes Christianity a moral philosophy and kills its claim to be a message from God. Think of what this means to us. How we have boasted of Christianity! How we have looked upon it as the only ark of safety! How we have urged men the world over to take refuge in it and have God shut them in! This proud ship of Christianity! we have freighted her with all our hopes and we have embarked in her the fortunes of our souls. She has plowed the ocean this well-nigh two thousand years; she has weathered the storms of persecution; she has sailed through the fogs of superstition; she has encountered the collisions of philosophy; she has been swept from stem to stern by great waves of scepticism; but in spite of it all, we have paced her decks with a sense of unwavering security; we have felt sure that no wind could harm her, no sea could swamp her, no obstacle arise to check her onward way, until, at last, in an unhappy moment she struck the iceberg of historical criticism, and down she went to a fathomless grave.

Are you ready to take that view of Christianity? Oh! you who think perhaps that a theological seminary is a place where men spin gossamer webs of metaphysical divinity, get heated in controversy over the dating of a few books, and discuss the relative merits of various theories of the atonement, I want you to understand what the real issue is; and when Mr. Lovejoy would have us break the entangling alliance of religion and history, I want to know whether you are ready to have that alliance broken. Do you realize the situation? Do you hear with calm complacency and unconcern the order that is given to leave the proud ship of Christianity, and lower the boats of philosophy? Are you ready to sit in your little dory of philosophy and, under an unlighted sky, look out over the waste of black water and hope that somehow, somewhere or somewhen you will drift to some shore of happy destiny? Is that your position? You have cut loose from history, but you can not cut loose from reason. What are your prospects? You are sure of your own selfhood. You have satisfied yourself that mechanism can not explain the world. Some will tell you of a pluralistic universe of separate souls bound together by no common tie. Some will tell you that our separate selfhoods are only momentary manifestations of an infinite self; and some again will tell you that there is a numerical distinction between God and the finite spirits which He has created. You will argue, and you will do well to do so, that the truths of reason point unmistakably to God. You will say that these judgments of worth and value need God to give them meaning. Men will tell you that the religions of the world—Christianity among them— are simply separate modes of God's manifestation of Himself. You have ideals that you say ought to be realized and which are index fingers pointing like prophecies to a world to come. You call this man good, and this man bad; this man, you say, is brave and that man a coward. What do you mean? You look forward to the fulfillment of your ideals; but look back, look down: where did you get these ideals? They are but nature's way in the broad process of change which has adjusted you to an environment and which makes it possible for you to live. You are the victims of a wholesale deception. A gigantic imposture has been practised upon mankind in order that nature might secure to herself the perpetuating of the life of humanity. What are you going to say? Are you going to say that you have no interest in philosophy and that these things do not concern you? You repeat, "I don't care what philosophers may say, I believe in historical Christianity." If you do, have you no interest in other people? Do you not desire to help them, to prevent them from making shipwreck of their own hopes? Have you no interest in showing them that the philosophy which robs the world of Christ and religion of God, which puts the world of ideals under the imperious sway of meaningless fact, which makes the word "is" the be all and end all of existence and has no place for ethical norms and moral obligation, is only one way of explaining the facts of the universe; and that there is another way, a better way, a safer way, a more logical way of construing the same facts, which will rehabilitate us in our old faith in God and in Jesus Christ whom He has sent; will save us from the disappointment that speaks in the bitterness of regret and says, "We hoped that it was he who should redeem Israel"; and from the depths of the despairing pessimism which says, "They have taken away my Lord and I know not where they have laid him"? Would you not like to help them? My friends, that is what this Seminary is for. Will you help us? Will you give us books, will you give us buildings, will you give us professors, will you give us men with special learning and peculiar aptitude to enlist in the greatest work the world can do? Will you do it? Will the great, rich Presbyterian Church say "No" to Princeton Seminary which is ready to do what needs to be done, and withhold from her the sinews of war? I put this upon the conscience of the great Church that I am privileged to serve. And, my colleagues, my friends, my brothers, what are we for? What can we do in the face of what some regard as an appalling disaster? I think we can do something. I think we can rally the crew and cheer them up; I think we can stop a panic among the passengers and let them know that the ship is safe. I think that there are some of us—and I speak the more confidently because I am not included in the number—there are some of us who have a right to speak in the expression of expert opinion and declare with the authority of ample knowledge that no harm has come to the ship, but that she will go prosperously on. I admit there are two ways of looking at theological study. There is a scientific way—and there is a large place for it—where we regard men of every shade of opinion as with us engaged in the same scientific pursuit, dispassionately seeking to get the truth, the whole truth and nothing but the truth. There is a place for philosophic calm and the placidities of scientific inquiry. But there is another view. These men who are arrayed against us are the King's enemies, and we who hold commissions as officers in his army owe it to that commission that we draw sword in defence of the King's dominions.

> "Soldiers of Christ, arise!
> And gird your armor on,
> Strong in the strength which God supplies
> Through His Eternal Son."

And you, my friends, who are about to go out after the period of training in this Theological Seminary, bear with me if I say a single word to you on the nature of your calling. If you go out with a feeling that you are simply representing the moral aspect of society, that your great work is to engage in the development of social morality, that your great object is to be considered as authorities on civic righteousness; if your rallying cry be the uplift of society, which means, in its last analysis, simply more luxury for the poor and more self-denial for the rich; then let me tell you that you have misunderstood the real meaning of your work. You are to bring a message of hope from another world to dying men. Your thought must move in a transcendental sphere of unseen realities. You are called to deal with a set of emigrants who are setting sail for another shore; your work is not so much to furnish them luxuries on the voyage as to put into their hands a passport that will be useful to them when they land. Men will deride your message; will challenge your credentials; will speak of your work in the patronizing tone of worldly disdain. You will sometimes be tempted to surrender to the current of anti-Christian sentiment. But be strong. Know well the strength of the cause which you have espoused and be unwavering in your loyalty to it. And remember that no small part of your duty is to see to it that you earnestly contend for the faith once delivered unto the saints.

PRINCETON THEOLOGICAL SEMINARY

A LITTLE BOOK OF LOVE AND LIFE

SERMON

BY THE REVEREND ETHELBERT DUDLEY WARFIELD, D.D., LL.D.
President of Lafayette College
President of the Board of Directors

"These are written, that ye may believe that Jesus is the Christ, the Son of God; and that believing ye may have life in his name." John xx: 31.

"THESE are written, that ye may believe." This book is a book with a purpose. No mere biography, no calm and colorless study of the life of a man. It is a great plea. A plea made at the judgment bar of every soul to which it comes. A plea for the hero to whom the heart of the writer was attached by the strongest ties of obligation, the tenderest bonds of affection, that He may receive the full meed of praise and honor to which He is entitled; but far more a plea for the reader that he may share the fealty of the writer and find for himself that life in which the author rejoices.

No mere dry-as-dust zeal has led the writer to seek out, after the manner of biographers, every minutest fragment of information in regard to the subject of his book, and record it with pedantic care. Out of the immense stores of a memory crowded with knowledge and overflowing with information he selects with thoughtful reserve the matter most significant and germane to his purpose and marshals it with the consummate skill, not of the literary artist, but of the convinced disciple.

The whole world might not contain all that could be

written of the life of his Lord. A few pages may suffice to prove Him to each sincere and sin-sick soul Christ and Lord. These are those pages. They belong to the literature of power, not of art, nor of criticism. They have proved their power in the experience of tens of thousands of devoted lives. They have been the warm sunshine winning back to loveliness and life frost-bound spirits held in the cold indifference of a living death. They have been as a rock in a storm, a safe foothold for many an imperilled heart. Upon them have critics flung themselves through ages upon ages, only to find themselves powerless to break the compelling power in the story which they tell. No figure can portray, no tongue can tell, all that these precious pages have meant to the Church of Christ. There they are a few leaves of a book, but here they are in the heart the living testimony of one who knew and loved Him who was for the writer and for us the resurrection and the life.

The unvarying tradition of the early church attributes this book to John the Apostle, and tells us that the elders of the church of Ephesus constantly besought their beloved bishop to write out for those who should come after him, and should not hear his living testimony, the story that he was accustomed to tell of the living and dying and rising again of his divine Master. At last yielding to their entreaties he wrote the book that bears his name.

The story is worthy of the book and the book of the story. It is clear that the date is late. John is already far on that long way which led him last of all the companions of the Lord to the grave. Mark and Matthew and Luke have written their Gospels. John and the church at large have these noble pictures of Jesus' life. He does not need to repeat the main features of a history already so familiar. He rather needs to enrich it with special features of Jesus' teaching, to show that from the first men were repelled as well as attracted by His words of loving appeal as much as by those of high authority, and to draw out with power and plainness the great meaning of it all—the Messiahship of Jesus, His Sonship, and His gift of life through belief in His name.

In a spirit characteristic of his Lord, John throws across the opening passage of his narrative the morning beam of divine revelation. Jesus seems never to have omitted an opportunity to bring the Old Testament teaching into His own. Paul had already in his second letter to the Corinthians flashed this same sunbeam into his message when he wrote: "God who commanded the light to shine out of darkness hath shined in our hearts to give the light of the knowledge of the glory of God in the face of Jesus Christ." John gives it a new and richer meaning as he develops in a few words his doctrine of the eternal Word.

Turning then to his story he brings the forerunner, whose disciple he was, upon the scene, and in a narrative all athrob with life details day by day the opening of Christ's ministry as he knew it. The short records of each day's incident are like the strong wing-beats of an eagle mounting up to its place of more than world-wide vision. Yet no simile can equal the simple facts of the narrative.

For John gives us here an old man's memory of a momentous day in his youth; of the day that he first met Jesus. The day on which we first met Jesus must be to each of us, however unfruitful our lives, a day of deep significance and precious memory. But to John with his capacity for love, his capacity for being loved, who was the beloved of Jesus, what must that day have been! Yet it came in no blinding splendor, no revelation of things unutterable. The simple story, as is generally true of the things that mean most to the soul, is a tale of every day in its outer features. John the Baptist is standing with his disciples and Jesus passes by. John points Him out, saying: "Behold the Lamb of God." Even the heart of John, the young and eager disciple, seems not to have kindled at the words. It is only when on the next day the Baptist again makes the same declaration that John and Andrew are aroused and follow Jesus. Already a seeker after God, John speedily comes to share with Andrew and Philip the belief that they had found Him of whom Moses in the law, and the prophets, did write, and that He was Messias.

Thus John makes us see that it is to the heart prepared that Jesus comes as the Christ. And even he was not at once ready for all that great truth imports. The seeker after God became the disciple of Jesus. He went and saw where he dwelt. He abode with Him. The old home was forsaken. The old life was left behind. The busy hands no longer drew the nets. Now it is that he takes the open road with Jesus and learns new lessons by the way. The old world takes on new meanings. The sower as he sows the seed, the digger after hid treasure, the thirsty wayfarer as he draws water from the well, even the familiar fishermen as they toil at their nets, have a new significance, and require fresh interpretations. The simplest things seem to have deeper meaning, but the greater mysteries of life grow more plain. The long sought clue to the deepest mystery of all is at last discovered. The love of God is manifest in the flesh. He beholds in Him who is the Christ the very Son of God.

Day by day the meaning of it all works itself out. Sometimes in His words, His wonderful words of life; sometimes in His silence, the silence of One whose spirit walks with God; sometimes in His deeds, His acts of help and healing; sometimes in His inaction, the submission of One who knew how both to bear and to forbear; always and forever, the Great Teacher led the responsive pupil up along the shining way of life. Now it is a day of sunlit glory as when He was transfigured on the mount, now of tremendous shadow turned to light as when Lazarus is raised up, but often it is half in sunshine, half in shade, and, ere the Lord of Glory was perfectly made known, a *via dolorosa,* through Gethsemane and on to Calvary.

While there is a great tenderness in John's picture of Him to whom he had listened as his master, and learned to acknowledge as his God in the throes of the awful agony of His night of humiliation, there is also a noble restraint. Over it all rests the assured calm of Him who knows the sequel. That the day dies but to return again in restored beauty. That the tragedy, awful as it is, is not of death unto death, but of death unto life. That the crucifixion of love is also love's coronation. And to John as he writes, the sorrow of his soul for the sufferings of the best beloved is assuaged by the consolation of that dear Lord who, though He died, still lives; though He suffered, reigns in glory.

And so the narrative moves with growing power and never wavering confidence to the confession of the restored faith of Thomas: "My Lord and my God"; and Jesus' benediction: "Thomas, because thou hast seen me thou hast believed: blessed are they that have not seen, and yet have believed." Here he pauses. Surely what has been written must suffice. Surely the object of his writing will be attained. And so he says: "Many other signs truly did Jesus in the presence of his disciples which are not written in this book; but these are written, that ye might believe that Jesus is the Christ, the Son of God; and that believing ye might have life through his name."

It is the fashion in the critical world to approach such a book as this through an introductory study of its date and authorship, its authenticity and its relation to contemporary thought. A mist is thereby often raised that obscures its clearness and dulls its brightness. It is its own best answer to such objections as have been raised in regard to it. As in a court of justice no questions may be raised as to the character and credibility of a witness until he has told his story, and as a story told with convincing directness, simplicity and evident familiarity with the subject testified to, possesses and controls the minds of judge and jury despite the assaults of any cross-examination, so this book justifies itself generation after generation to those who approach it with an open mind.

Whoever wrote it knew Jesus and knew Him as Christ and God. Who could have known Him so fully and so completely as the beloved disciple? Who could have written of Him with such a soaring spirit entering into the fulness of His love and His purpose to save men from sin for eternal life as he to whom has been assigned for symbol the eagle rising above the darkness of the storm and baring his eye to the full blaze of the flaming sun? But whoever wrote it, it has fulfilled its purpose and will continue to do so through the ages to come in giving to many their fullest vision of a divine Saviour and their surest grasp upon eternal life.

This beautiful book then is the story of a great friendship. How we delight to talk of such friendships, to call friendship the "master-passion," to praise those who have shown a great capacity for friendship, to applaud the self-sacrifice of the few who have effaced themselves for their friends as Jonathan did for David. Friendship indeed is marked by some of the finest of human virtues. Affection perhaps comes first, then generosity of heart; when testing times come, affection deepens into devotion, and generosity into capacity for sacrifice; faith and trust and constancy are found in the bright constellation. In all these things this book abounds, for Jesus was the friend of John and John of Jesus, and no ennobling trait of friendship is wanting in the story.

But who could ever be content to call this merely the annals of a great friendship? It defies limitation to merely human ties, to a life bounded by the cradle and the grave. Perhaps a higher mode is found in the rare and beautiful devotion of a disciple to a great teacher. Plato has dignified such an association and John surely glorifies it. Socrates, too, led Plato to look with longing out through the gates of death. Philosophy brings into such a relationship the exalting power of intellectual aspiration and moral purpose. John found in the fellowship of Jesus all that philosophy had to offer and more than philosophy had to give—the transforming power of a great faith. He not only looked out beyond the gates of death, he looked forth into the eternal years of God and brought heaven down to earth.

But John had more than this to tell. He had a philosophical ideal and a practical purpose. He had lived into an age when men were seeking to philosophize away the facts of his history as they had earlier denied their occurrence. He sets himself to testify to his facts, to establish their relation to history and prophecy, and vindicate for every soul who will accept it the vivifying power of faith. And this for no mere academic purpose. Philosophy was not self-sufficient for him. It was to make men understand the real meaning of life; of a life lived in love for love's own dear sake; of a love that was divine in source as well as in character; of a life that was eternal as well as divine. In short, John set himself to make men understand and embrace life and love in the assured faith in Him who was Himself Life and Love.

We are prone to think that our difficulties are peculiar to our own age and greater than those of any other time. But the very same features of Christ's gospel are emphasized by John as need emphasis to-day: first, the historical connection of Christianity and Judaism, the oneness of the revelation of God in the Old and New Testaments, that salvation is of the Jews, that Jesus is the Christ; second, that the Word was made flesh, that Jesus is the very Son of God; third, that the life which Jesus came to proclaim is natural and real, as Tertullian has beautifully said: "The soul is by nature Christian"; and, finally, that entrance into that life is through belief on the name of Jesus.

The position of John gives significance to the purpose of his Gospel. He is no longer the young disciple full of eager devotion, but of as yet unchastened heart. He has not only passed through the tragedy of Jesus' earthly career, with its rising hopes and declining fortunes, with its blinding lights and its unfathomable darknesses, with its poignant sorrows and heavenly joys; he has not only found the clew to its mystery, and the purpose of its plan; but a long life has made him understand the attitude of men to the gospel he had to preach. He knew how strong are its attractions, how great its repulsions. He knew what barriers sin could raise before it, what opposition it could arouse in hearts dominated by the power of Satan. The minister of the Word speaks in him. Nothing is more striking in the arrangement of his material than the way in which he shows how throughout Jesus' teaching He drew some and repelled others. And this is surely the accent that the aged man of long experience alone would have been sure to give. Despite the warmth and tenderness that singled John out as the beloved disciple, and has made all his writings peculiarly the reflection of the love of God in Christ, this characteristic has brought into his Gospel the hot note of him who so loved his Lord that his heart flamed out against those who despised and rejected Him. Were it not for this we should be somewhat at a loss to know why he should have been singled out by such a name as a Son of Thunder. As it is the Gospel is not only warm with a spirit of life sprung from the sources of divine love, but it is also palpitant with a sense of the condemnation which is due to all rejection of love and mercy, with warning to those who choose death rather than life.

We are apt to select from this book passages of rare and exquisite beauty; the great teachings of Christ as to the new-birth, as to Himself as the light of the world, His discourse at the Last Supper, and His wonderful prayer, that prayer in which John Knox tells us he cast his anchor; and neglect the full current of the book as a plea for the entering into eternal life through faith in Christ. To do so is to pay less than due regard to John and to his Lord. It is in its very power to persuade, to warn, to arouse, to convince, to send forth to serve, to create in the heart that peace which the world cannot know, that its perennial power resides. This is no doubt partly due to the fact that in revealing his Lord, John also writes his own spiritual biography. Certainly in so doing he does away with the possibility of much honest wavering as to the meaning of the life he records.

John grew up in the hope of Israel, he became the disciple of the Baptist whom he accepted as the promised forerunner of the Messiah, he was led by the Baptist's express indication to become the follower of Jesus, he learned from Jesus to reconcile His humiliation with His mission of redemption and to find in the salvation of sinners the coming of the Kingdom, he drew from the teaching of the Old Testament as well as from the bitter experience of his actual life the meaning of the blood-bought pardon, and he looked upon his risen Lord with his own eyes and believed. From these things there grew up within him a new life which he knew by the evidence of daily witnesses to be of the very Spirit of God. In the power of that life he lived and labored and wrote. But all of this is as it were but the shadow. It is to be read in the Gospel. But the substance of that Gospel is the other life, as real, as completely the outgrowth of the Old Testament, as entirely involved in the story of the redemption of men by the sacrifice of Calvary. Yet are the two inseparable. As the Word was made flesh and dwelt among men, so the Master lived again in the disciple.

No wonder that John cries: "Now are we the sons of God, and it doth not yet appear what we shall be. But we know that when he shall appear we shall be like him, for we shall see him as he is." Already the oneness of the life of the disciple and the teacher had been known and felt by him. The complete outworking of the power of a transforming faith alone remained. It is no wonder that he who wrote this book should have breathed on those for whose spiritual life he was so solicitous the benedictions of his letters; no wonder that to him was given the visions of the Apocalypse. The glorious beauty of the images in which the brightness of heaven is represented for us has never been surpassed by the mind and pen of man. Yet it is not in those visions, but in the discourses preceding the passion and in the portrayal of the suffering Saviour that John has reached most surely the ground and anchor of our hopes.

Let no rude hand rob us of the robust realities of those pictures. Through suffering He passed, so must we pass to gain the fulness of knowledge of the meaning of life and love; through death He passed that we in passing through the death of the body may enter into the fulness of life with Him; from death He returned in the triumph of Him who Himself is life. In His life is manifested for us light and life.

The world has never been content with itself. In the heart of man there has ever been a divine unrest. Not always felt, nor by every one. Most notable in the nobler few; in times of special need, it has become more general and more poignant. Always upon a quest, it has never found its goal. A few have assumed the rôle of great teachers, the many have been content to learn of them, or like the blind and insensate mob to drift, or drive madly on without an object and without a care. To all seekers after truth, truth which to him finds embodiment in a life, John offers this little book. He repeats the Master's words to those who rejected Him: "Ye search the scriptures because ye think that in them ye have eternal life; and these are they which bear witness of me; and ye will not come to me that ye may have life." He clearly understood the blindness of men. But he trusted to the Spirit testifying with his words to make men accept Jesus as the Christ and the very Son of God.

Not only have they proved for us the persuasive words of a living and abiding faith, but also words of inspiration and strength and of tender consolation. Let us often keep before our minds the words themselves and the glorious beauty of the Son of God which they portray, and, also, the benign figure of John, the aged, ministering to the church at Ephesus, telling over and over again of his fellowship with Jesus, drawing about him old and young with the sublime story that he tells, illustrating it by his own life of love, of heroic constancy, of undivided loyalty. When we study his book there is room in our hearts for one person—Jesus only. But we may sometimes withdraw our minds a little from that central sun, and thank God for the beauty and the power of the love of Christ made manifest in the disciple.

PRINCETON THEOLOGICAL SEMINARY

THE FUNCTION AND THE GLORY OF THE MINISTRY OF GRACE

ADDRESS

BY THE REVEREND JOHN FLEMING CARSON, D.D., LL.D.

Pastor of the Central Presbyterian Church, Brooklyn
Moderator of the General Assembly of the Presbyterian Church
in the United States of America

IT is a distinct privilege and honor to have a part in such a signal celebration as that of the One Hundredth Anniversary of Princeton Theological Seminary and it is hard to resist the temptation to pause and pay tribute to this great institution and to the distinguished men, living or departed, who have made it great. But justice to the subject assigned compels me to hasten to its consideration, waiting only long enough to greet and congratulate the young men who this day complete their seminary training and stand on the threshold of their ministerial careers.

Young gentlemen, you stand in a noble succession and in a succession which has always commanded the confidence, respect and appreciation of men. You are entering upon a life-work incomparably more important than any other service to which men give themselves; a work that is related to interests more awful and august than those with which any other work is related, and a work whose achievements and results are more enduring and more wonderful than any of the other results and achievements of the labors of mankind.

The subject assigned to me is: "The Function and the Glory of the Ministry of Grace." In the statement of this theme there is nothing that requires explanation, no hidden thought that waits to be released, no word that needs definition. There is one word in the phrasing of the theme that was more frequently upon the lips of the fathers than it is upon ours and this fact, as well as the vital place which the word occupies in the theme, justifies us in lingering for a little in the fellowship of that word. Grace is a word that the fathers understood, loved and accentuated. Grace is that faculty or force or element of being that comes unbidden and serves unrequested and unrequited. It is the love that pities the sinner, redeems from sin, and bends all its energies toward the complete and perfect recovery and restoration of man. It is absolutely free, a priceless gift that can neither be bought nor bartered nor sold. Let that radiant word come back in all its might and hold dominion in the soul, and then the church shall march with triumphant pæan to God's high goal and guerdon.

The use of this word "grace" in the subject defines the ministry in broad terms. The ministry of grace is a service that, however sustained, is unpurchased and unpurchasable by man and that does not stand in its successions and orders and institutions as a method of man's salvation, but as a medium through which the grace of God that bringeth salvation is revealed unto all men. Thus the term declares at once the independence and exaltation and the subserviency and lowliness of the ministry of grace.

1. This broad definition intimates that the ministry of grace is rooted in the very nature of God, and finds its object in the need of man. In this reach from the highest to the lowest, its supreme function is declared and its surpassing glory is enshrined. In the heart of God is

eternal love and in the heart of humanity is the undying need of that saving love. The function of the ministry of grace is to declare and to interpret the love of God to the heart of man. In fulfilling that distinct function the glory of the ministry of grace shines forth.

2. In the presence of such a service as this we are ready to accept the truth that the ministry of grace is an institution of God and that the ministers thereof are called of God. However men may debate and differ as to its vestments and ceremonials, as to the visible form in which it expresses itself, as to the outward ritual through which its inward spirit breaks upon the world, all will agree that in its essential spirit the ministry of grace has come down from heaven, and that it is here because God has sent it.

The evidences of the divine institution of the ministry of grace are manifold. The object for which it exists attests it. Its persistence through the ages—its refusal to be shelved by any studied neglect, or to be crowded out of place by any competing aspirants—confirms it. And the fact that the outworkings and issues of the ministry of grace are in God's keeping affirms its divine institution and sanction.

This is the vital fact that gives character and power and glory to the ministry of grace—the minister is the ambassador of God. His ministry is more than his message; his responsibility larger than his utterance. He is a God-called, a God-sent man. Conscious of his divine call and commission, his ministry rings with a note of authority that challenges the world. His voice is oracular. His message is a summons. He is bold, with a holy boldness, to declare the whole counsel of God, and confident, with a holy confidence, to speak God's truth. He works in the spirit of Seneca's pilot, who said to Neptune:

"You may sink me, or you may save me,
But I will hold my rudder true."

He meets any opposition in the spirit of Curran, in his defence of Bond, who, when he heard the clatter of the arms of his threatening antagonist in court, said: "You may assassinate me, but you cannot intimidate me."

This is the ministry our age needs—a ministry whose manhood stands out in bold and flaming relief, whose service is impelled by a mighty imperative and constrained by an irresistible necessity and whose message does not stammer in fearsome uncertainty, is not stifled in mincing ambiguity, or hidden in any conventional finesse.

It ought ever to be an adequate inspiration to the minister to know that the work is God's and that God has called him into the fellowship of His Son under whose institution it is carried forward. The work committed to the ministry of grace is the same work that summoned the Son of God to earth. It is the work in which Paul gloried and for which he counted himself unworthy. It is the work that challenged the fiery energy of Tertullian, that commanded the scholarship of Athanasius, that girded the sturdy will of Luther, that kindled the fine fervor of St. Francis, saint of purest renown, that inspired the sublime genius of Calvin, that nerved the fearless strength of Knox, that evoked the bewitching eloquence of Jeremy Taylor, that directed the apostolic zeal of Wesley, that buttressed the giant power of Edwards—the work of reconciling men to God that they may be saved from their sins, comforted in their sorrows and glorified in their death. This is the glory of the ministry of grace—it is a co-partnership with Christ and a fellowship of men of varying abilities through whose transparent souls the radiance of heaven has broken over earth.

3. This ministry of grace, ordained by God, is authenticated by God's people. While certain believers were assembled together, an unseen voice was heard saying: "Separate me Barnabas and Saul for the work whereunto I have called them." That was the divine call and the divine authorization. But not immediately did the men thus called go forth as fully and sufficiently authorized and empowered. There is in the incident another factor that may not be arbitrarily left out. After the unseen voice had spoken and after the assembled disciples had fasted and prayed "and laid their hands on them, they sent them away. So they, being sent forth by the Holy Ghost, departed." We may put too much emphasis on this laying on of the hands, or on it we may put too little; but the fact stands out that the inward call was ratified by the outward ordinance, the spiritual mission was confirmed by the tactual commission, the divine empowerment was certified by the human authentication. The gifts and powers of the Holy Ghost are not tied to the agencies ordained for their transmission. The Spirit worketh when and where and how He pleases. But still the fact remains that there is a way which is of God's appointment—a ministry which He first commissioned and which they whom He first commissioned passed on to others. Call this apostolic succession if you please, ridicule its pretensions and deride its efficiency, but you cannot dismiss from human history the fact that

the ministry of grace is not only an ordinance of divine appointment, but also of church authentication. Christ did not leave His fellowship and truth in the world unorganized and disembodied; He built His church and, through His church, He sends forth ambassadors. This distinguishes the ministry of grace from every other vocation—it has back of it the authority of the Church of Christ.

4. The ministry of grace, ordained by God and authenticated by the church, is in vital and permanent relation to the moral order of the world and to the unfolding history of humanity. The claim of its divine institution can be substantiated only by the eternal necessity and the essential rationality of the ministry of grace. In the counsels of God are woven the essential and eternal needs of human nature and of human history. It cannot be assumed that the divine seal rests upon any commission that does not convey a message that every man needs to hear, and that cannot grow obsolete with any conceivable civilization. The herald of God's counsels will be inspired with an unusual and sustained confidence when he speaks to his fellows under the profound conviction that what he has to say, the whole world, from prince to pauper, needs to hear and heed.

5. The ministry of grace, charged with a message to all men, is commissioned to the evangelization of the world and to the establishing of believers in the doctrines and practices of the Christian faith. For the fulfilment of this twofold function the ministry of grace has an evangelistic and a teaching mission. The preacher is a herald, the substance of his message is the proclamation of the free forgiveness of sins and the heritage of eternal life through the mediation of Jesus Christ. The passion

of the ministry of grace is to save men from their sins, and, by the sweet and holy, the winsome and wooing note of divine persuasion, to lead to Christ. The final reality of the religious life is a man's personal relation and allegiance to his God. After much talking about "the enthusiasm of humanity", "the service of man", "social ministry", and other freezing abstractions, we must come back to the Master's love of men. "Jesus loved Mary, and Martha and Lazarus". "Who loved me and gave himself for me". "That is the superlative wonder in the altogether wonderful evangel of grace—the divine love can concentrate on everybody, as though each one were everybody, and there was only one child in the Father's house." This marvel of grace is the substance of the evangel that is committed to the ministry of grace.

The ministry of grace has a teaching mission and its message not only voices the evangelistic appeal of the Gospels, but also moves in the deep, broad grooves of the Pauline Epistles. In fulfilling its teaching function the ministry of grace does not come into competition with any other teaching agency. Its wide, splendid province is the revealing and the interpretation of the eternal verities. It may be of service to art, literature and philanthropy, but its concern is with the message from the very heart of the eternal to the souls of sinful men. Its music is set, not to the keynote of moral philosophy, or material rewards, or esthetic beauty, but to the exceeding abundance of the grace of God, which has in store for the human soul a kingdom which eye hath not seen.

As a teacher the minister is a specialist. He deals with men, it is true, on every side of their nature—physical, intellectual, spiritual; and with every department of their living—domestic, social, commercial, civic—but always and everywhere he deals with them from the religious point of view. He is not a teacher of science or of philosophy; he is not an instructor in domestic science, or in political economy; he is not a leader in social functions or commercial enterprises—he is a teacher of religion. Therefore, his specialty is theology.

It is not uncommon to hear that theology is a declining science, that its majesty is waning like the splendor of some dying star, and that its voice of power is growing faint as the murmur of some distant sea. We are told that men are weary of theology and that the church is in revolt against it. There never was a more preposterous or perverse delusion. Theology is the abiding interest of men. It is the theologian who is listened to whether he speaks in the literature of history, imagination, poetry, science, or religion. So long as men believe in God, so long will they fashion for themselves a theology of some sort. The preacher announces himself as a teacher of God, and men demand of him, and have a right to demand, that his teaching concerning God and man's relation to God shall be definite, clear and exact. Men do not ask from the minister a final statement of truth, for they know that no statement of truth can be final, but they ask for something that shall be sufficiently near the eternal fact for which it stands to serve them. Men resent dogmatism. They welcome theology, a clear, scientific setting forth, not in technical phrase, but in orderly array and system of the great truths of revelation.

The ministry of grace is ordained to inspire men to noble aspirations, lofty living and consecrated service. Its aim is to relieve the fag and strain and stress of life;

to keep faith serene and strong; to hold before men the true values of life; to cause hope and courage to sing in every heart; to make men feel how near the heavens are to earth; to quicken the soul to divine endeavor and make the heart burn with a holy passion for the Lord Jesus—this is the high and holy and enviable purpose and privilege of the ministry of grace.

The ministry of grace has a prophetic function. It is successor not to the priestly order of the Old Testament, but to the prophetic office. The prophet was the most notable figure in ancient Israel. When he was in the ascendant, the nation rose to its best; but when he was ignored, silenced, or banished, the people deteriorated and the nation declined. The prophet was the man that saw and said. The chief characteristic of the prophet is that he sees God, sees Him in the light of all the ages, and sees Him in the life of his own day and declares and interprets His truth to his day. The function of the ministry of grace is to tell forth great truths, dominant principles, and so point out the broad highways along which all men and all their affairs move to their inevitable destiny.

All these several phases of the ministry of grace—its evangelistic, its teaching, its inspiring and its prophetic function—unite in realizing its supreme end, the setting forth of the tremendous realism of the priesthood of Jesus Christ, its profound spiritual and moral necessity, and its design as an historical fact to produce a definite historical and spiritual result—the redemption of mankind. Not simply the salvation of men, but a new-born humanity, and through that a reconstructed society, a redeemed race of mortal men and women on this earth. This is the Kingdom of God, which the prophets foretold and for which the apostles longed and labored. This Kingdom is the revelation, the keynote of all the dispensations. For its establishment the ministry of grace is to labor by preparing the way for the coming of the King and, in its establishment by the enthronement of the King, the ministry of grace will realize its eternal coronation.

6. The ministry of grace is equipped with the Word of God and endowed by the Spirit of God for the fulfilment of its divine mission. As an ambassador of God the minister does not make his message. He delivers the message that has been entrusted to him. He is not called to proclaim his own ideas or speculations, but to preach God's Word; not his own guesses at a thousand things, but God's revelation of truth and righteousness. The preacher has not a roving commission to wander up and down the universe of knowledge. As Christ's ambassador he must take the latitude from his Master; and Christ concerned Himself with the relations of the human soul to God, and all which is contained in that fellowship. The minister will never exhaust that revelation. He will never feel equal to the high and holy duty of declaring it, but he will declare it and he will declare it with the tone of confidence and certainty, for it is God's eternal truth. Criticism and investigation have not changed the truth of God. The intellectual play on the surface has not touched the deep verities. The truth is a fixed quantity, and is a firm path through the highway of the ages. The great guiding lines have not become confused by the march of time; they are as true and significant today as on the day when they were first penned and they have as clear and confident a message for today. Men tell us that the need of the hour is to

adjust truth to modern conditions. The need is that we adjust modern conditions to truth. I do not see how truth can be adjusted to conditions, but I do see how conditions can and should be adjusted to truth. You cannot adjust the polar star to the ship's compass, but you can set the ship's compass by the polar star.

In unfolding the Word of God the ministry of grace depends upon the guidance of the Holy Spirit, knowing full well that He alone can disclose and interpret what He has first inspired. Put emphasis upon the personality, upon the intellectual equipment, upon the all round ability of the preacher, but ever remember that the power that melts men's wills into God's will is not in human genius, but in God's grace. This divine grace is not necessarily independent of human genius. On the contrary it ordinarily uses that genius as the channel of its operation. Hence the insistent and imperious demand for a ministry that is equipped, efficient, enlightened and enlightening. No man with any power of vision can be blind to this demand, and no man with any integrity of mind can ignore it. The rock-bottom need of the pulpit is baptized intellect. This is the secret of the pulpit's mastery over men and the strength of its position in society. From Paul to Jonathan Edwards, from Jonathan Edwards to Archibald Alexander, from Archibald Alexander to Charles Hodge, from Charles Hodge to men whose presence on this occasion alone prohibits the mention of their names, the pathway to the throne of pulpit power is lined with the monuments of mountain-minded men. There was spiritual enduement, but along with it there was a natural endowment that would have given its possessor commanding influence anywhere among men. Behind the voices that have stirred the world, the messages that have thrilled and enkindled human hearts, were thinking, reasoning men, speaking out of the large and the rich manhood in themselves to the manhood of other men. But they were sanctified, set apart men, men baptized with the Holy Ghost. Those last words, "baptized with the Holy Ghost," let us into the presence of that unique distinction that forever differentiates the endowment of the ministers of Christ from any mere natural endowment. It is endued endowment. It is the permeation of all natural qualities and forces with a divine presence and their control by a divine power. That which gives the ministry of grace its authority and its power, either to evangelize or to teach, is not the native gifts of its ministers, however great they may be, but the enduement of the life with the majesty and glory and grace of the Holy Ghost.

PRINCETON THEOLOGICAL SEMINARY

THE MAKING OF A MINISTER

ADDRESS

BY THE REVEREND RUSSELL CECIL, D.D.

Pastor of the Second Presbyterian Church, Richmond, Va.
Moderator of the General Assembly of the Presbyterian Church
in the United States

THE word "minister" in the Scriptures has many uses, but for our purpose on this occasion, it means "the minister of the Word". He is the chief officer in the church of Christ, and his multifarious duties are indicated by such scriptural titles as ambassador, bishop, evangelist, minister, pastor, preacher, presbyter, teacher, and steward. Among these titles, priest does not appear, and indeed is made conspicuous by its absence. The sacerdotal function attaches to the whole body of believers, and not in any special or exclusive sense to ministers of the Word. It is the privilege of any disciple of Christ to offer spiritual sacrifice unto the Lord without the mediation of an ecclesiastical functionary. We are not, therefore, concerned with the question of the making of a priest.

The minister of the Word should be a man. It does not appear that women were called to this office in the early church. Women were engaged in many Christian activities, and their labors were highly blessed of God, but they were not designated as ministers of the Word, and it can not be shown from the New Testament that any woman occupied this office.

The kind of man needed must be learned from the Holy Scriptures. The office is many-sided, and the duties of it are grave and responsible. The minister must labor in the spiritual realm, in an atmosphere both strange and uncongenial to worldly minds, and into which no one should venture rashly without an adequate acquaintance with the character of the work required of him and some manifest fitness for it. God can without doubt use any kind of a man to work His will, and the history of the church shows that for the glory of His grace He has often "chosen the foolish", "the weak", "the base", and "the despised" "to confound the wise" and "the mighty" (1 Cor. 1:26–29), and He will presumably continue this course as long as His infinite wisdom directs; yet from our point of view, as enlightened by the teachings and example of the apostles and our own experience, we believe that the best material out of which to construct a minister of the Word is a manly man. Whatever the great Head of the Church may do, as it pleases Him, in the selection of material, He has not authorized those acting in His name to "lay hands suddenly" (1 Tim. 5:22) on any kind of a man who offers himself for the ministry. Some men are constitutionally unfitted for the office, and should be firmly rejected, as an honest builder rejects an unworthy piece of timber in the construction of a handsome edifice. We should encourage manly men, of noble minds and honest hearts, to undertake this work.

Of course the minister should be a godly man; that is, a God-like man; one whose knowledge of God is first hand; not a simulator, or an imitator, or even that sort of an investigator, who is "ever learning and never able to come to the knowledge of the truth" (2 Tim. 3:7); but a man of deep spiritual experience, who has heard the voice of the Spirit in his own soul and has obeyed it, and has become like God in his love of truth, of righteousness, and of men. It is impossible to make a true minister of the Word out of an unregenerate and ungodly man.

He must also be a God-called man. There is a difference here which some seem willing to obscure. A godly man and a God-called man are not necessarily identical. Not every godly man is called to preach. The minister should be able to say,

> "Sunset and evening star
> And one clear call for me!"

It is just as impossible to make a minister of Christ's evangel out of an uncalled man as it is out of an ungodly man. "No man taketh this honour to himself", not even the devout child of God. It is bestowed from above. God chooses those who are to preach the Word, and in some way makes clear to them His will. Various elements may enter into a call, the man's own convictions, the indications of providence, the judgment of the Church, the desire of his friends, but a call there must be.

So much in brief as to the material out of which the minister is to be constructed; now as to the method. With material of the right kind furnished, what of the process through which it should be put in order to make a minister? It should be said that entire harmony of view does not exist in different branches of the Christian church upon this subject, but this is not the time or the place to discuss divergencies of opinion. An effort will be made simply to suggest in outline certain things which are of value in this process; it would be rash to say "things which are essential". With the right kind of material in hand, who can point out definitely what things are essential to the making of a minister? Some things we know are of value to any minister, but when a man is evidently sent of God with a message to the people, it is hazardous for us to prescribe things which we believe to be essential to him for the proper delivery of it. It cannot be forgotten that some men who have fulfilled a fruitful ministry have entered upon their work with very little of what is usually regarded as helpful preparation. This is not an indication, however, that preparation is useless to the man of God. Any ablebodied man with an axe in his hand can go into the woods and build some sort of a house to shelter himself from the weather, but if he were a well trained carpenter with a chest of fine tools at his hand, he could build a better house. The fact that some men have preached the gospel with power without having received any special preparation for their work does not argue that they might not have done it more effectively had they enjoyed the advantages of theological education.

Early environment is an important factor in the making of a minister. Family life, youthful association, school and college experiences contribute not a little to the formation of his character and to his usefulness in the service. The apostle Paul owed much to the superior advantages for mental and moral culture which he enjoyed in the plastic period of youth. His life from the beginning was evidently projected upon an elevated plane by his parents, and he himself had always cherished high ideals of personal piety and duty; and to his early training no doubt much of his remarkable efficiency as a minister was due. He appreciated the same thing in Timothy, and took occasion to remind his son in the faith of the religious atmosphere of his mother's home and of his education from childhood in the Holy

Scriptures. Many of the great preachers have traced the elements of their power to these early sources. We can hardly overestimate their value in the make-up of the minister, and the church will find herself poor in ministers of the right kind unless the spirit of Christ dwells in our homes and schools and colleges.

But on this occasion we are chiefly interested in the work of the theological seminary. Many useful ministers have never seen the inside of a seminary, but schools of the prophets and institutions for the training of men in sacred learning have existed in the church throughout the most of her history, and the vast majority of those who have served in the sacred office have received their preparation in such institutions. As we are celebrating the one hundredth anniversary of the founding of a great theological seminary, the character of work done in such an institution demands our attention.

It may be said at the outset that it should not be mechanical. Students are not to be regarded as empty barrels to be filled with theology, headed up with a diploma, and thus made ready to be shipped to various parts of the world where they can be opened on the Sabbath day for the spiritual nourishment of the people. Nor are they thermos bottles to be charged with hot air, or only with "milk for babes"; but they are living men to be trained for a holy service to living men and women. The work done in the seminary therefore should be instinct with life and in close touch with human interests. Human needs and sorrows, human hopes and aspirations should lie upon the hearts of instructors, and no effort on their part should be spared to quicken the sympathies of their students with the suffering and struggling masses of mankind.

Let me mention as the first requisite of a theological

seminary a wholesome spiritual atmosphere. It may be thought by some that this goes without saying among those who have devoted themselves to the sacred calling, but that is not true. The student of theology is tempted to become spiritually morbid on the one hand, or spiritually apathetic on the other. One needs to be encouraged in healthy normal development, and another needs instruction in spiritual ideals and the toning up of his notions of the kinship of ministerial character and conduct. If the spiritual atmosphere of the seminary is either too fetid or too frigid, the best results in the making of ministers can not be secured. One extreme is perhaps as dangerous as the other. In the active work the course of the true minister lies between religious fanaticism on the one side and worldliness on the other, and unless therefore he comes from the seminary with a robust character, with clear conceptions of gospel truth, and with sound views as to the spirituality of the church both in its purpose and in its method, he is almost sure to be "corrupted from the simplicity that is in Christ."

This is not the time or the place to discuss with any fulness matters of curriculum. There are some things, however, which I wish to say. The course of study in a theological seminary should be comprehensive in its scope and scientific in its methods. It should embrace everything that can throw light upon the origin and history, the significance and worth of Christianity; it should honestly face all the difficulties of revelation and inspiration; and it should refuse to deal superficially with any of the great problems of supernatural religion. A theological school above all others should be thorough in its investigations of the foundations on which revealed truth rests, and should send its students out to their work well established in their faith in the Holy Scriptures. Men who do not believe the Bible, the source from which their message comes, certainly can not preach it to others. Preaching to be effective must be positive and dogmatic, not negative and apologetic, and what the character of it shall be must depend upon the kind of instruction the minister receives in his seminary. The teachers in our seminaries therefore should be scholars second to none in their own departments, but they should also be men of faith; otherwise, the students who sit at their feet will have no message worth delivering. Ministers should not be educated to disseminate unbelief, but, as Paul says, they should be so "established in the faith" (Col. 2:7) as to be guides and helpers of those who seek a firm footing in the divine truth. If our seminaries are to turn out men of feeble faith, they had far better cease to exist. Unbelievers are plentiful enough now without training men to add to their number.

But while the curriculum of the seminary should be broad and thorough, it should not be forgotten that all men who are called to preach the gospel are not called to become technical scholars. There are different departments of church work for which men should be specially prepared; and experience shows that, for the attainment of this end, the course of study in the seminary has not always been happily arranged. It has been too much of a procrustean bed upon which all classes of students, if they desire a degree, are compelled to lie. The law of adaptation of means to end has not been wisely applied. In recent years, this matter has been receiving more attention and it should continue to do so. In addition to a comprehensive and thorough-going required course, why should not the seminary add a large number of electives, adapted to fitting men for the growing needs of the church? The complicated religious activities of our day demand a variety of ministers, and many think that the theological seminary is a failure as a place for preparing men for meeting the demands of present conditions. It is charged that the men sent out are not fitted to grapple with the task before them, and that they are outstripped by others trained in the school of experience and in minor institutions, who are laboring in organizations of an undenominational character. There is enough truth in this charge to awaken the church to the importance of equipping her seminaries for dealing intelligently with every species of practical church life. We can not disguise the fact that many extra-ecclesiastical movements owe their origin to a wide-spread feeling that the church is not meeting in an adequate manner the demands of the age in furnishing men capable of dealing with present day practical problems. I do not appear as an apologist for movements of this kind, nor do I admit that the church is inadequately equipped for evangelizing people of all grades of society and for taking care of the needy, but I do believe that there is a weakness in her system of theological education which if corrected would render unnecessary most, if not all, of the extra-ecclesiastical movements of the day. I believe thoroughly in the doctrine that the church is the divinely ordained agency for the evangelization of the world. Our seminaries should cultivate more and more the missionary spirit, and instruct their students in the vast work of modern missions. Every student who leaves the halls of a theological school should be a missionary. Whether his life work be in a seminary, in a city church, in the slums, on the frontier, or in the foreign field is a matter of secondary importance compared with the interest he feels in the evangelization of the world and the earnestness with which he devotes himself to it. It is an open question in which position he can be of greatest use. The efficiency of every minister will depend upon his personal piety and equipment, but the pastor or the theological professor can be as truly missionary in his desire to obey the command of the Master as the man who labors among the heathen.

More attention also should be given to the study of expression. It is strange that men who have consecrated themselves to the gospel ministry should care so little to cultivate the art of public speaking; and yet, nothing is truer than that many a good sermon fails to be effective because of a poor delivery. Our seminaries should make more of this matter, and more emphasis should be laid upon the importance of correct composition and impressive delivery. The forms in which truth is clothed and the manner in which it is presented are matters of vital moment which many a minister learns, or far more frequently discovers that he has not learned, long after the day of his usefulness has passed. A man charged with a great message to the people should certainly study the best way to deliver it. Of what use would a magazine gun be on the field of battle in the hands of a man who did not know how to operate it? How can a pious and learned minister of the Word fulfil the functions of his office if he be unable to clothe the truth in living words and utter them with a voice and emphasis which will claim the attention of the people? I know this subject usually receives indifferent attention in the seminary, but after more than thirty years' experience in preaching the Word, I am convinced that the process of making ministers might be improved if more serious study were given to the arts of composition and delivery.

I close with the remark that Christian people everywhere feel that humanizing influences should be thrown around the young men in our seminaries; that they should not be cloistered scholastics, withdrawn from the stirring life of the day; but that they should be men of loving hearts, who, when they come forth to their work, are able to sympathize with the poor and needy, and know how to dispense the gospel of the grace of God to our perishing race.

PRINCETON THEOLOGICAL SEMINARY

PRINCETON IN THE WORK OF THE PASTORATE

ADDRESS
BY THE REVEREND WILLIAM LEONARD McEWAN, D.D.
Pastor of the Third Presbyterian Church, Pittsburgh

THE glory of a theological seminary consists in the number and character of the men it trains for the gospel ministry. However eminent may be the scholars produced, as distinguished from preachers, and however excellent their services to the church and the world in the defense of truth and the refutation of error, it must still be true that the chief work of a theological seminary is in the preparation of men for the service of preaching. Scholars are the by-products of such a school. They are vastly needed. They are greatly used. They are to be honored and appreciated. We take pride in, and give thanks for, the great scholars who have come from this institution. A theological seminary exists, primarily, for the purpose of training, for pastors and preachers to the common people, men who believe they have been called of God into the ministry of the gospel. That school of the prophets most fully meets its end which sends forth in largest numbers men who are qualified to "rightly divide the word of truth", who preach with holy confidence "the unsearchable riches of Christ", and who have also learned that, with full and accurate scholarship and persuasive eloquence, they cannot do their work without the presence and the power of the Holy Spirit of God. It is by this standard we measure to-day the work of Princeton Theological Seminary for these hundred years.

This school of the prophets was born in the fulness of time. In the early years of the nineteenth century the necessity for the establishment of a theological seminary by the Presbyterian Church was evident. Theological education was in a chaotic state. Colleges such as Yale, Harvard, Princeton, Hampden-Sidney, and others were preparing men for the ministry, and many individual pastors had classes of young men under their care. There was a growing and wide-spread conviction that the Presbyterian Church ought to establish a school for the one purpose of training ministers.

The Presbytery of Philadelphia, led by Dr. Ashbel Green, brought the matter to the attention of the General Assembly in 1805. In 1808 Dr. Archibald Alexander of Philadelphia, the retiring Moderator, emphasized the Church's duty and responsibility for the supply of ministers. The Committee of the General Assembly, appointed in 1810 to draft a plan for a Theological Seminary to be established at Princeton, presented resolutions which were adopted, one of which was,

"That, as filling the Church with a learned and able ministry without a corresponding portion of real piety, would be a curse to the world and an offense to God and His people, so the General Assembly think it their duty to state that in establishing a seminary for training up ministers, it is their earnest desire to guard, as far as possible, against so great an evil. And, they do hereby solemnly pledge themselves to the Churches under their care, that in forming and carrying into execution the plan of the proposed seminary it will be their endeavor to make it, under the blessing of God, a nursery of vital piety as well as of sound theological learning, and to train up persons for the ministry who shall be lovers as well as defenders of the truth as it is in Jesus, friends of revivals of religion, and a blessing to the Church of God".

The Board of Directors held their first meeting in Princeton on June 30th, 1812. On the 12th day of August the Seminary was formally opened by the inauguration of Dr. Alexander. Three students matriculated at the opening. The number increased to nine before the close of the first year.

The Assembly of 1813 elected Dr. Samuel Miller of New York City as a professor, and in 1820 Dr. Charles Hodge was added to the Faculty. These professors, by God's grace and under His guidance, laid the foundations of Princeton Seminary. They planted the seeds which through the years have grown, bearing the fruits upon which the Church has lived. They started those streams that have brought life whithersoever they have come, and which have deepened and widened with each succeeding generation.

Princeton Seminary has had illustrious names on the roll of its Faculty, and the great men who have been among its teachers have been known and honored among the lovers of evangelical truth throughout the world, but there have not been any who have not delighted to recognize and rejoice in the leadership of these three great heroic scholars and saints.

Never were men more unlike in temperament and talents, and never were men more united in the one supreme purpose of teaching and interpreting the Word of God. They supplemented each other until the impression made upon the students was not confused, but clear, definite, distinct and, perhaps, unique. This impression was the Princeton stamp upon its students. It was not so much the imparting of a particular system of theology, as leading men to a love for the truth, an unqualified acceptance of the Word of God as the infallible rule of faith and practice, and a great sense of responsibility upon every teacher of the Word. There was a full appreciation of high scholarship, with a devout and humble sense of dependence and a thorough evangelical spirit.

Dr. Alexander's distinguishing characteristic was a wonderfully clear and penetrating insight into Christian experience. He had himself been brought to a knowledge of Christ after much sense of sin and travail of soul. Under the trees in the mountains of Virginia he had spent hours and days in fasting and prayer and the study of the Bible. He had learned to observe closely his own mental states and exercises and to weigh carefully the experiences of his soul. He was peculiarly qualified to deal with young men preparing for the ministry. His great ability as a teacher and his broad scholarship were united with a child-like simplicity of heart, transparent sincerity, and a great loyal, personal love to the Lord Jesus Christ. He was also a man of plain common sense, and he knew how to deal with men of every class. It is not strange that his coming to Princeton, humanly speaking, was the means of a revival of religion in the College and in the town during the first year of his residence.

Dr. Miller had a comprehensive view of pastoral duty. He understood and loved the polity of the Church. He was a great authority in the department of history. When he was called to undertake the work of a professor, coming from the foremost pulpit in the land, he wrote in his diary,

"Resolved, that I will endeavor, by the grace of God,

to set such an example for the candidates for the ministry committed to my care as shall convince them that, though I esteem theological knowledge and all its auxiliary branches of science very highly, I esteem genuine and deep piety as a still more vital and important qualification.

Resolved, that, by the grace of God, I will not merge my office as a Minister of the Gospel in that of Professor. I am persuaded that no Minister of the Gospel, to whatever office he may be called, ought to give up preaching''.

Dr. Hodge's characteristic that marked him from others was the emphasis he put on objective faith in Christ. Those who heard him speak of the love of Jesus Christ for sinful men, the glory of His Person, the greatness of His redeeming grace, never forgot how his whole soul seemed to bow in adoring worship and his heart to overflow in grateful love as he preached and taught. His class-room was a place of worship. When he was considering the call given to him to become a teacher in the Seminary he wrote, "I believe that I would rather be homeless and penniless through life than in any way whatever enter such an office unsent of God". "It seems to me that the heart, more than the head, of an instructor in a religious seminary qualifies or unfits him for his station". The first sentence in his inaugural address was, "The moral qualities of an interpreter of the Scriptures may all be included in piety, which embraces humility, candor and those inward feelings which can only result from the operations of the Holy Spirit".

Dr. Alexander was here thirty-nine years, Dr. Miller twenty-six years and Dr. Hodge fifty-two years. Under these greatest scholars of their generation and most attractive Christian gentlemen there was formed a certain type of pastor and preacher. They accepted the Bible as the Word of God, and sought intelligently to explain it to the people. They understood and received the Reformed Theology as the system taught in the Bible. They believed in the form of government of the Presbyterian Church and the dignity and authority of its courts.

At the time the Seminary was opened this country was at war with Great Britain. The fourth President of the United States, James Madison—a graduate of Princeton College—was closing his first term of service. The population of the country was about seven million. A new national spirit was rapidly forming. The tide was moving west. New territories were being settled. New communities were being formed. The Church had need of more ministers. Into these fields the Seminary began to send its graduates. They worked a quiet but thorough revolution in the ideals and accomplishments of the pastorate. They exercised great influence wherever they went. The Church and the country felt the reinforcement of the army of the Lord in the coming of these strong, trained preachers and leaders. They set higher standards for the ministry. They led the Church to expect better service. They influenced whole communities by their superior attainments and ability as leaders. They became the evangelists under whose preaching great revivals swept over the country.

In the first ten classes graduated there were two hundred and fifty-six students. From these graduates there were six moderators of the General Assembly; two bishops of the Protestant Episcopal Church; fifteen college presidents, presiding over such colleges as Princeton, Yale, Jefferson, Dickinson, Hanover, Centre, Western

University of Pennsylvania and others. From these classes there went forth missionaries and pioneers to every part of the land. Throughout the South, from which many of the students came, over the wide, opening West to the far Pacific slope, their influence was felt.

It would not be possible in the limits of this address even to mention the names of the Princeton men who have done their work for the Church and for God in this land, for, with the graduating class of this year, there are five thousand nine hundred and forty-seven Alumni.

It would be interesting to take up one class after another, and make mention of the services of its members.

In the first class of the Seminary was William Anderson McDowell. Graduating from Princeton College in 1809, he had already been pursuing a theological course under the president, Dr. Samuel Stanhope Smith. Upon his graduation he settled at Bound Brook, N. J., and afterwards in the First Church of Morristown. Threatened with pulmonary trouble he spent the winter of 1823 in Charleston, S. C., and was pastor of the church there for ten years. He was elected moderator of the General Assembly in 1832, and, by the Assembly of 1833, was appointed Secretary of Domestic Missions. In this office he served until his death in 1851, doing an unsurpassed work. Of him it was said, "Being dead he yet speaks, and will for generations continue to speak, in the Churches planted by his instrumentality, the missionaries encouraged by his sympathy, and the souls brought under the enlightening influence of the Gospel by his unwearied exertions".

From that same first class was graduated Benjamin Franklin Stanton. Remarkable revivals accompanied his preaching during his nine years' pastorate at Hudson,

N. Y. He was pastor of the church at Hanover, Va., from 1829 to 1842. After the death of Dr. John H. Rice, he was lecturer on theology in the Union Theological Seminary of Virginia. He died of consumption in 1843. Dr. Weed said of him, "For twenty years he was dying of consumption, and knew he was dying of consumption, still he never ceased to preach while he had strength to stand in his pulpit"; and the Honorable Ben Butler testified, "In his theological views Mr. Stanton conformed, *ex animo,* to the standards of the Presbyterian Church as expounded at Princeton".

From the second class there went forth sixteen men. John Finley Crowe was pastor in Hanover, Ind., and in 1824 began the school which grew into Hanover College, with which he was connected until his death in 1860.

From this second class John Todd Edgar went forth to labor in Kentucky and Tennessee. He was moderator of the General Assembly in 1842.

Eliphalet Wheeler Gilbert, from the second graduating class, labored in Wilmington, Del. twenty years, where there is a memorial church bearing his name. He was president of Dickinson College, pastor in Philadelphia, and director of this Seminary for six years.

Elisha Pope Swift was a member of this class. He labored in Pittsburgh and Allegheny for forty-one years. He was a professor in the Western University of Pennsylvania and instructor in the Western Theological Seminary. He exerted as wide an influence, left as deep an impression and did as much constructive work as any of the great men who have labored in that part of the country. He founded the missionary society which afterwards became the present Board of Foreign Missions.

In the third class there were seventeen men. Among

these was Jeremiah Chamberlain. He founded three colleges, one of which was Centre College, Kentucky.

George Washington Gale, a member of this class, led a colony from New York state and settled in Illinois, where his name was given to the town of Galesburg. He was the founder of Knox College.

Thomas Charlton Henry, of this class, died in 1827, thirty-eight years of age, but not until he had received the degree of D.D. from Yale, and had been associated with the movement that resulted in the founding of Columbia Theological Seminary of South Carolina.

Sylvester Larned went directly from the Seminary on a mission to the Indians of the Southwest, and to investigate the religious conditions of the city of New Orleans. He is described as the most finished orator and the most effective preacher in America in his day. Wherever it was known that he was to preach crowds thronged the churches. People of all classes were attracted by his preaching in New Orleans and a splendid church building was erected by popular subscription, and he was called to be the pastor. He died of yellow fever in New Orleans on his twenty-fifth birthday. It would be hard to find any other man of whom such estimates of power and promise were made.

Samuel Lyle Graham, of the class of 1818, was a missionary and pastor for seventeen years. Extensive revivals are recorded in the churches in which he preached. He was elected to the chair of Ecclesiastical History in the Union Seminary of Virginia in 1838. During his professorship he continued to preach regularly. When he was sick with his last illness in 1851, Dr. Rice came into his room and said, "Dr. Alexander has got home before you", thus bringing to him the news of the death of his dearly beloved teacher. The dying man raised himself in bed and cried out, "Oh, is it possible? Is it so? I had almost shouted 'glory'. Heaven has seldom received from earth such an inhabitant. His society in heaven will be invaluable".

There is not time to pronounce the names of all the eminent graduates of this Seminary, who have been known throughout the Church. There have been forty-two moderators of our Church, and fourteen moderators of other branches of the Presbyterian Church, making fifty-six in all. Of the seventy-eight professors in theological seminaries connected with the General Assembly of our Church at this time, exactly one-third, or twenty-six, are graduates of Princeton. There have been one hundred and twenty-four chaplains in the Army and Navy. There have gone out four hundred and twenty-five foreign missionaries who have labored in all the lands where the Church has thrown its battle lines. There have been one hundred and three secretaries of the Boards of our Church and of agencies connected with it. There have been one hundred and sixty-one presidents of colleges and universities. There have also been six hundred and eighty professors and teachers, and sixty-six editors.

By general consent, perhaps the most eminent preacher ever sent out from this school was Dr. James W. Alexander of New York, of the class of 1824.

Albert Barnes, of the class of 1823, was for forty years the pastor of the First Church of Philadelphia. When his name was known throughout the English-speaking world, and his books were printed in tens of thousands, he died while making a pastoral call on a sick parishioner.

PRINCETON THEOLOGICAL SEMINARY

Henry A. Boardman, of the class of 1833, had but one charge. He was pastor of the Tenth Presbyterian Church of Philadelphia for forty-seven years. He was moderator of the General Assembly in 1854, and elected to the chair of Pastoral Theology in Princeton Seminary in 1853. During his pastorate three thousand four hundred and fifty persons united with his church, fifteen hundred of them on confession of their faith.

No history of Kentucky could be written without recognizing the influence and the work of the sons of Princeton. Woven into the civil and ecclesiastical history of that state are the names of Robert J. Breckinridge and John Breckinridge, John C. Young and William C. Matthews, Nathan L. Rice, Stuart Robinson, Thomas Cleland, L. W. Green and many others.

Nor would the history of Western Pennsylvania be complete without the names of Elisha P. Swift, Wm. S. Plumer, Wm. M. Paxton, M. W. Jacobus and George T. Purves.

Indeed if there were time to revive the memories of those who are familiar with the great movements that are written in our history, the reading of the names of the men whose influence has been great in the time of crisis or through long years of service would be sufficient— James W. Alexander, John C. Backus, for forty-eight years in Baltimore; J. Trumbull Backus, for forty-one years in Schenectady, N. Y.; George D. Baker, for a score of years in Philadelphia; Albert Barnes, forty years in Philadelphia; Charles C. Beatty, for sixty years in Steubenville, Ohio; William Blackburn; Henry A. Boardman, for forty-seven years in Philadelphia; Rob't J. Breckinridge of Kentucky; James H. Brookes of St. Louis; T. W. Chambers, nearly half a century in New

York City; William C. Cattell, Joseph Christmas, founder of the American Church in Montreal; Bishop T. M. Clark; Richard F. Cleveland (father of a president of the United States); Theodore L. Cuyler, for thirty years in Brooklyn; Doak of Tennessee; J. T. Duryea, Philemon H. Fowler, Sam'l W. Fisher, P. D. Gurley of Washington, D. C.; Leroy J. Halsey, A. A. Hodge, C. W. Hodge, E. B. Hodge, F. B. Hodge, William H. Hornblower, William Henry Green, Charles K. Imbrie, pastor, secretary and editor; Sheldon Jackson, Bishop John Johns, M. W. Jacobus, S. H. Kellogg, John M. Krebs, of New York; John C. Lowrie, Willis Lord, Bishop A. N. Littlejohn, J. M. Ludlow, Erskine Mason, Bishop C. B. McIlvaine, David Magie, George W. Musgrave, Thomas Murphy, N. G. Parke, R. M. Patterson, W. S. Plumer, S. I. Prime, William M. Paxton, George T. Purves, Nathan L. Rice, Rendall of Lincoln, David H. Riddle, Stuart Robinson, Charles S. Robinson, W. D. Snodgrass, William A. Scott, W. B. Sprague, J. G. Symmes, E. P. Swift, H. J. Van Dyke, C. Van Rensselaer, Charles Wadsworth.

It was, of course, my purpose to refrain from speaking of the living men, some of whom have not fallen short in reputation and service of the greatest of those who have finished their work. They stand today in places of importance and usefulness all over the land. I beg to make two exceptions to the rule adopted.

In "The Presbyterian" of this week is the following letter from James Park of the class of 1846, the oldest living graduate of this Seminary:

"I matriculated in the Seminary in September, 1843, and took the full course, graduating in 1846; and, by the grace of God, through Jesus Christ, have been permitted to serve him in the active ministry of the Gospel for three score years; and for the past six years to hold the position of Pastor-emeritus in the congregation in which I was born, and to which, by its call, I gave the last forty years of my active ministry.

Now, on the verge of the ninetieth year of my life, the infirmity of old age denies me the pleasure of being present at Princeton's celebration in May. But as long as life and memory last, my heart and soul shall rise in praise and gratitude to God for the founding of Princeton Theological Seminary, and, for me, the favor of sitting at the feet of such men as Dr. Archibald Alexander, Dr. Samuel Miller, Dr. Charles Hodge, and Dr. Joseph Addison Alexander.

May the good hand of God always, henceforth as hitherto, be upon thee, 'O Princeton, loved of God and men' ".

The other exception is that of a graduate of this Seminary who for twenty-six consecutive years has been serving four country churches in Pennsylvania. His father preceded him in a pastorate of thirty years in the same field. The people are poor. The churches are small. The community is primitive. In these twenty-six years he has gathered three hundred souls, mostly on confession of their faith. This is not a large number, to be sure, but they have been gathered from a scant population. In these years these churches have contributed out of their small resources fifteen thousand eight hundred and sixty-two dollars for their congregational expenses, less than six hundred and fifty dollars per year. In the same time they have contributed eight thousand two hundred and twenty-six dollars through the Boards of the Church, of which sum forty-three per cent. has gone to the cause of foreign missions. But out of that man's ministry the Church received another contribution. One son from that charge is a missionary in the home field, and one son and two daughters are in the foreign field, and two daughters are now in preparation for the foreign field. Strong elders also, serving in prominent churches and doing active work, were trained under this man's ministry. Neither earthly honors nor pecuniary rewards have come to this pastor. He is a representative of a great number of faithful men who do their work as unto the Lord.

In all these hundred years Princeton Seminary has been true to the ideals and standards of its first great organizers, and it has been loyal to the Word of God. No student has, by reason of any teaching from any professor, had his reverence for or belief in the Word of God, as the only infallible rule of faith and practice, weakened or destroyed. No student has here learned to question the essential deity of the Lord Jesus Christ, or has lost any of the passionate loyalty of his heart for Him as Saviour and Lord. No student passes through these halls without having it impressed upon his heart and mind and conscience that the only salvation for a lost world of sinful men is that gospel which is the power of God unto salvation to all them that believe. Men who have the spirit of this Seminary go forth to their solemn calling as preachers of the gospel, caring for the vital and essential truths of revelation, and putting these things above the temporal and the accidental.

From this Seminary have been graduated about six thousand men, the greater part of whom (a little over half) remain until this present day. From more than two thousand pulpits every Sabbath day they preach the

Gospel of Jesus Christ to multitudes of men and women. Year after year they stand in their places, the broken ranks being re-filled, proclaiming the everlasting righteousness and the infinite love of God. Who can estimate their influence upon the thought and life of this nation?

Standing this day between the living and the dead, representing the army of the sons of Princeton, we know that the thoughts and prayers and sympathy of men from the East and the West and the North and the South are turned toward this place and these services. Yea, may we not also believe that we are surrounded by a great cloud of witnesses who have finished their labors on earth, and that they feel there what we say here, "I thank Christ Jesus our Lord, who hath enabled me, for that he counted me faithful, putting me into the ministry"? And we who are here may humbly, reverently and sincerely add, "and I thank Him that in His good Providence it was given to me to study the mysteries of His grace and the deep things of His Holy Word in this School of His Prophets at Princeton".

CENTENNIAL CELEBRATION OF

PRINCETON ON THE MISSION FIELD

ADDRESS

BY ROBERT ELLIOTT SPEER, D.D.

A Corresponding Secretary of the Board of Foreign Missions of the
Presbyterian Church in the United States of America

THE first name in the biographical catalogue of Princeton Seminary is just what it ought to be, the name of a home missionary, John Covert, who entered the institution at its beginning, pursued the full course, was graduated with the first class, of 1815, and then spent the three years of his brief life in the ministry as a home missionary in South Carolina and Georgia. In that first class of sixteen students, six names are entered as names of home missionaries. One of these men, in love for the unfortunate, gave the last years of his life as chaplain in our most famous prison. A second, as city missionary, worked on our most famous city thoroughfare of human need. The four others were flung in a long line from Georgia to Wisconsin. And that same class, as we have already been reminded, gave Dr. William A. McDowell for seventeen years' service as secretary to the Assembly's Board of Home Missions.

There were sixteen men in the second class as well, and of these sixteen, six also entered home missionary service, and one out of this class had laid upon him the work of foreign missions, was ordained in the old Park Street Church in Boston for that service under the American Board, but was turned aside from this purpose, for work first as an agent of the American Board in the Middle States and then as pastor in Delaware and Pennsylvania. He was the man of faith and of will, as we shall see, who laid the foundations of the foreign missionary organization of our Church.

In the first five classes that went out from the Seminary, the first name found on the roll in the biographical catalogue in each case is the name of a home missionary. The first foreign missionary who went out from the Seminary went from the class of 1818, Henry Woodward, to work for fourteen years under the American Board as a missionary in Ceylon, and from that year, down to the present, there have been only three classes in all the long history of the Seminary which have not made their contributions to the foreign field. And those three classes, 1820, the class of Bishop McIlvaine, 1823, the class of Albert Barnes, and 1842, gave one-third of their entire membership to the varied forms of home missionary activity.

We look back today reverently over the long record of the years. Through these sacred walls there have passed between five and six thousand men, one-half again as many as have gone out from any other theological seminary in the land; and one out of every thirteen of these men has gone into the foreign field. We may not say how many have gone into the home mission field, for not one of all the long list who have wrought here in America but has woven his life into the character and destiny, into the very making of our nation. But more than four hundred and ten men, not counting foreign students or those who have spent their lives among the American Indian tribes, have gone to the distinctively foreign fields of the Church; more than half again as many as have gone from any other institution in the land. Oberlin, I believe, leads our theological seminaries in the percentage of foreign missionaries, one hundred and forty-nine out of seven hundred and seventy-three, or one out of every five and a half of its students, have gone to the foreign field. As far as I have gathered information, Princeton Seminary comes next, with Newton, one out of every thirteen of the students of these two institutions having gone abroad. In the first quarter of the century of its history Princeton sent forth fifty men; in the second quarter of the century it sent seventy-five; in the third quarter of the century it sent one hundred; and in the last quarter of the century it sent two hundred. Up to 1875 it sent one out of every eighteen of its students abroad; since 1875 it has sent one out of nine. Those who talk of Christianity as a spent force, of the decline of the missionary conviction, are men who speak in ignorance of the simple facts of this institution's life.

It is impossible here to do much in the way of singling out the great missionary classes in the Seminary's history. The class of 1902 heads the list with the largest percentage of its matriculated students going out to the foreign field, thirteen out of fifty-nine,—one out of four and a half. The two classes that come next, having sent one out of every five, were the class of 1870 and the class of 1906. The two classes that come next, having sent one out of every six, were the classes of 1869 and 1907.

To man after man here today his own class will come back. The memory of faces "loved long since and lost awhile" mingles with the recollection of great lives that are still being lived. I can only suggest three or four of these great classes which stand out in the list of the Seminary's achieving men. There was the class of 1853, with Frank F. Ellinwood, pioneer in the field of comparative religion, a scholar who was also a statesman, a leader and a little child, and John Livingston Nevius, founder of churches, trainer of native leaders, the constructive critic of mission policy and beloved philanthropist, and Charles F. Preston, the man of the magic tongue in Southern China, and here at home to ensure for us a missionary construction of Christianity, Caspar Wistar Hodge.

There was the class of 1856, which sent out Henry Martyn Baird for eleven years of useful service as Secretary of the American and Foreign Christian Union; Samuel R. Gayley to lead a brief and notable life in northern China; Charles R. Mills, to lead a life notable and long, thirty-eight years, in the Province of Shantung, and two saints of God, if any such ever breathed, Daniel McGilvary and Jonathan Wilson, who lived for fifty-three years in Siam and among the Lao people. In the city of Bangkok there came recently to the German Club a German naturalist who had been studying trees. "Gentlemen", said he, "you think me to be a skeptic, a rationalist, but I have read the Bible enough to know about the person of Jesus Christ, and I want to tell you that the good old missionary with whom I lodged in Chieng Mai is more like Jesus Christ than any other man that I have seen on earth." He was speaking of Jonathan Wilson, who with his classmate and beloved brother, Daniel McGilvary, had founded a mission, created a literature and made a people. Sweet and pleasant were they in their lives and in their death they were not divided.

The class of 1867 rises before our minds. Out of its seventy matriculates it gave Baldwin to Turkey, Butler to China, Dennis to Syria, Douglas (afterwards Member of Parliament and Senator in Canada) and Heyl and Wherry to India, Thomson to Mexico and Chamberlain to Brazil. It gave Richard C. Morse also to be the leader of the Young Men's Christian Associations of North America, Dean Griffin to Johns Hopkins University, Bloomburgh to Lafayette College, Sparhawk Jones and Henry Stebbins to the home ministry and not less than eight men to home missionary service.

I think also of the class of 1870, which sent three-fifths of its membership into the home and foreign field, two-fifths to be home missionaries and one-fifth foreign. Nine of its men were scattered over Asia and South America, five of whom are now on the fields to which in the first place they went out; nine men who have spent over two and one-half centuries in foreign mission work, with an average of nearly thirty years. Let me repeat the honorable roll,—MacKay of Formosa, Chambers and Hubbard of Turkey, Howell of Brazil, Imbrie, Miller and Green of Japan, and Lucas and Seeley of India. And this class gave us also the present President of our Board of Foreign Missions, George Alexander, whose reserve prevents our expressing to his face our personal affection and for whom accordingly here today to the Seminary's praise we dare to speak of the Church's gratitude and regard.

And it is not only the classes that have sent out these great groups of strong and influential men to mould the nations at home and abroad of which I would speak. I recall also the classes which are signalized by the gift of only some one or two men,—1863, with Hunter Corbett, patriarch and apostle, as its only and sufficient foreign missionary contribution; the class of 1860, with Charles

M. Hyde, a foundation layer in the Sandwich Islands; the class of 1845, with its contribution of John B. French to China and David Trumbull to Chile, who buried their lives at the foundation of new nations.

I stood a few years ago with bared head before the monument in the English cemetery in the city of Valparaiso, and read upon it the inscription to David Trumbull's memory and career. It was a tribute to the man who stamped for generations with his high character the mercantile community of a great city; who gave his life with great affection to the service of an alien people; who brought them the great truths of the gospel and two institutes of human liberty, and who, making the greatest of all political sacrifices for his adopted country, transferred to it his citizenship, and passed away in its grateful confidence and love.

And what David Trumbull and John B. French did is only typical. Of the twenty-four foreign missions of the Presbyterian Church, nearly two-thirds had their foundations laid by men who went out from this Seminary. In Africa the founders were John B. Pinney, of the class of 1832, who began the work in Liberia, and Mackey, of the class of 1849, and our honored friend, Dr. Nassau, whose presence we recognize here today, of the class of 1859, who were the pioneer builders of the mission work further south in what is now the German Kamerun.

In India, John C. Lowrie, of the class of 1833; Morrison, of the class of 1837, "the Lion of the Punjab"; Charles W. Forman, of the class of 1847, and Owen and Wilson and Janvier and Orbison and Loewenthal, the linguistic genius, were the founders. Truer men than these never were in these halls, nor wrought for God anywhere in the world. Far above the names of statesmen, the names of these men are written. Many of them will be remembered forever in the annals of the land that they served. And this is no partial judgment uttered in the warmth of this anniversary; it is the judgment of a great Indian Governor, W. Mackworth Young, uttered when he came home from his service as Lieutenant Governor of the Punjab. He called attention to the great names which the Punjab bore on its roll of honor, such statesmen as John and Henry Lawrence, Herbert Edwardes, Donald McLeod, who "honored God by their lives and endeared themselves to the people by their faithful work," but he added, "I venture to say that if they could speak to us from the great unseen there is not one of them who would not proclaim that the work done by men like Clark and French, Newton and Forman, who went in and out among the people for a whole generation and who preached by their lives the nobility of self-sacrifice and the lesson of love to God and man is a higher and nobler work and more far reaching in its consequences".

I think of the long list of men who went out from Princeton to China from the very beginning, Mitchell, '30, Orr, '36, Lowrie, '41, French, '45, and Loomis and M. S. Culbertson, of the class of 1844. The latter laid down his commission in the United States Army, and his professorship in West Point Academy, that in answer to his mother's prayer and the call of God, he might come here to fit himself for missionary service. He was one of the great foundation layers in the port cities at the mouth of the Yangtse and it was he who did much to protect Shanghai in the face of the Taiping Rebels. When the American minister said to him, during the

Civil War, "Culbertson, you might be a Major-General if you were at home now," Culbertson replied, "Doubtless I might; men whom I taught are in that position," and he named Newton, Rosecrans, Thomas and Sherman, and Tower and Van Vliet, and he might have added Lyon and Reynolds and Grant. "But," he added, "I would not change places with one of them; I consider that there is no post of influence on earth equal to that of a man who is permitted to preach the Gospel to four hundred millions of his fellow-men".

We recall Stephen Mattoon, of the class of 1846, and Stephen Bush, of the class of 1848, who laid the foundations of missionary work in Siam, and who began the political relations of Siam with the western nations. The United States Government's treaty with Siam was negotiated in 1856, and Dr. Wood of the embassy wrote that "the unselfish kindness of the American missionaries, their patience, sincerity and faithfulness, have won the confidence and esteem of the natives and, in some degree, transferred those sentiments to the nation represented by the missionary and prepared the way for the free and national intercourse now commencing. It was very evident that much of the apprehension they felt in taking upon themselves the responsibilities of a treaty with us would be diminished if they could have the Rev. Mr. Mattoon as the first United States Consul to set the treaty in motion." In 1871, the Regent of Siam frankly told Mr. Seward, the United States Consul-General at Shanghai, "Siam has not been disciplined by English and French guns, as China has, but the country has been opened by missionaries."

The motion to open our Church's mission in Japan was made by James W. Alexander, in the Board Meeting on

January 8th, 1859, and not less than ten graduates of the Seminary have labored in this mission.

We think of the seven men, who, in Mexico and Colombia and Chile, and the Argentine and Brazil, laid the foundations of our modern missionary activities, Parvin, '21, in Buenos Ayres; Trumbull, '45, in Chile; Fletcher, '50, and Simonton, '58, in Brazil; Pratt, '55, in Colombia; and Pitkin, '66, and Thomson, '67, in Mexico. And I might go on and on, but the roll is too long in glory and honor for us to do more than simply glance at its lustre today.

And it is not only on fields far away that the great creative work has been done. We have been already reminded of the men, who, at home, in the pastorate and home mission service, stirred the great moral forces which have dominated the life of the nation, and have lifted up and taken down again from their pinnacles the little statesmen of a day. But we must think also of the great mass of men, back of these, whose names are not written visibly on the roll, who in quietness and obscurity, did the great work of God in the dark, and laid the foundations for the walls of the nation's temple. But here and there stands out the name of some unique character among them; Sheldon Jackson, for example, of the class of 1858, who, two generations ago, was agent of the American Systematic Beneficence Committee, and in three months canvassed the land from New York to Leavenworth. On one Saturday, he visited ten pastors, and the next day preached to four denominations. We think systematic beneficence a discovery of our own time, but there are few ideas stirring the church in its organized life today which the fathers did not know two or three generations since. Jackson came to the Seminary

PRINCETON THEOLOGICAL SEMINARY

when there was whispering through all these halls the summons of our martyred dead in the Indian mutiny. His large heart heard the whispering voice and obeyed. There was a real student volunteer band here then, which Jackson at once joined. He offered himself to the Foreign Board for Syria, Siam or Bogota, but was sent to the Choctaws, to pass on from them to the Christian Commission in the Civil War, then to work in the western states, then to the great northwest, then to Alaska. On the frontiers of the nation's life, he wrought his creative and enduring work, far away, as Frances Willard wrote to him, "on the distant edge of things, where God's most friendless children turn towards you their eyes of pathos and of hope".

One after another, we remember men like him today, who, taught by their old Mother here that duty is a long loyalty, and that there are no short terms in the service of the Kingdom of God, have laid out ample lives in the age-long work of building the church on earth. I think of fourteen men who went out to the mission field, whose terms of missionary service aggregate seven hundred years. Some of these are living now: J. M. W. Farnham, of the class of 1859, the oldest foreign missionary graduate of the Seminary, still working after 53 years, in Shanghai; John Wherry, of the class of 1861, a pioneer of the North China Mission; Andrew Watson, of the same class, a father and guide of the remarkable mission of the United Presbyterian Church in Egypt. The list would include P. J. Gulick, of 1828, for 52 years a missionary in Hawaii and Japan, G. W. Wood, of 1837, for 48 years a missionary in Turkey, W. W. Scudder, of 1846, for 48 years a missionary in India, and C. C. Baldwin, of 1847, for 47 years a missionary in China. I have not been curious to make the calculation, but I suppose we should find it to be literally true that the years of foreign missionary life given by the sons of this institution would be equivalent to the time of two men preaching the gospel from the hour of our Lord's birth down to this present day.

And I can count six home missionary men whose terms of service aggregate over three hundred years; Porter, '31, founder of the church at Fort Dearborn, now the First Church of Chicago, for 50 years a home missionary worker; Lewis Thompson, '40, of Oregon and California, who gave 57 years of service; Allen H. Brown, '43, of New Jersey, with 67 years; Thomas Fraser, '45, of the Synod of Pacific, with 48 years; David C. Lyon, '45, Synodical Missionary in Wisconsin, Minnesota and Dakota, with 48 years; and H. M. Robertson, '48, of Wisconsin, with 41 years. The Seminary has been wont to send out from these walls men who believed that the work into which they went was not work that called for part of life for a little time, but who knew that God asked for all that He had given or might give.

And beyond these men are the many who have had no joy of half-century service! How many of them will come back to our memories here today! I can think, looking down on your faces, of name after name, of year after year, coming back to you now. How the dear memories glow, of the younger men to whom came no such privilege as the joy of the long, long work of which we have been thinking; Gerald Dale of Syria, who burned his short life out in fourteen years, "the model scholar, the model Christian, the model gentleman of Princeton Seminary", as Dr. Charles Hodge described him; Albert Whiting who laid down his life in China and at whose grave the Chinese knelt down to worship; and Edson Lowe, of the class of '85, whose memory is cherished worshipfully still in the capital of Chile, and one I will dare to mention, just one, who is living still, quietly, simply, doing his work far off in a distant field, John N. Forman of India, but for whom some of us would not be here today but would be doing our work in other places, and fulfilling our duty in other callings. It is worth while remembering what one life or two can do, when we note in the history of this Seminary that prior to the work which that little company of men in the modern student missionary crusade accomplished, only one out of eighteen of our students went to the foreign field, while since the year 1886, one out of every nine has gone.

There are more sacred memories even than these that throng upon us. I stopped in on my way here to stand again before the tablet in Stuart Hall that commemorates the half dozen sons of this Seminary who met with tragic death: Freeman, '38, and McMullin, '54, who laid down their lives on the parade grounds at Cawnpore; Walter Lowrie, '41, and John Rogers Peale, '05, the first and the last, in China; Janvier, '40, and Loewenthal, '54, who died in northwestern India; McChesney, '69, whose name is not on the tablet, who died for Christ on the waters of southern China. After this, you remember, the tablet says, "Of these the world was not worthy." And as I stood reading the names once more with the brief and simple record, there came flashing through my mind what Dr. Mackay will remember, the monument that stands in front of the Parliament Buildings in the city of Ottawa, the great brown granite boulder, and the exquisite figure of Sir Galahad standing upon it, and underneath, the bronze tablet that describes the heroic death of Henry Harper, as he tried to save another's life in the waters of the Ottawa in the winter time. Galahad is standing with his head thrown back, as though he looked far beyond the black swirling waters of the Ottawa, to the fair hills of Paradise, and the life laid up there for those who here their lives laid down for men. And below the lovely figure and the lovely face is the simple inscription, "And Galahad said, 'If I lose my life, I save my life.'" The old Mother taught many of her sons that great fidelity.

And we turn from the service that the Seminary has given in the missionary activities of our own Church for just a moment to mark what she has done for other Christian bodies. I suppose not less than one quarter of the students of the Seminary who have gone out to the foreign field, have gone in connection with other Christian organizations. Prior to the year 1837, Princeton gave thirty-nine men to the American Board; twelve of them to the Sandwich Islands alone, among them Richard Armstrong, the father of Samuel Chapman Armstrong, surely one of the most notable characters of the last generation in our land; not less than twenty or thirty to our sister Church of the South; MacKay of Formosa to the Church of Canada; Wood to the Dutch Reformed Church of South Africa; Watson and McClenahan to the United Presbyterian Church; Scudder and Miller and Van Ess and others to the Dutch Reformed Church of the United States; Stevenson to the Irish Presbyterian Church, and other men to the New Hebrides and Manchuria. The Seminary has not been narrow-minded in her ministry to the Church of God throughout all the world.

There is time only to allude to those general gifts which

the Seminary has made through her sons to the literature of missions. It would not be easy to repeat the long list of men who have made these contributions and the great books which they have given to the Church. I must be content with singling out only five. William M. Thompson, '32, author of "The Land and the Book", still perhaps the most charming and authoritative book on the Holy Land; R. H. Nassau, '59, author of the unique and authoritative book on "Fetichism in West Africa"; James S. Dennis, '67, who wrote a standard apologetic treatise, showing what Christianity is and alone can do, demonstrating its divine origin by its actual social effects throughout the world; Samuel H. Kellogg, '64, as bright a genius as ever went out from these walls, a student of comparative religion and author of what is to this day the best statement of our Christian faith as contrasted with Buddhism in "The Light of Asia and the Light of the World;" and John Livingston Nevius, '53, whose book on "China and the Chinese" was the best book of the time on China, and who wrote a little book on missionary methods which has made a deeper impression than any other book on missionary policy and principle throughout the mission field. And if one were to turn from all this to the educational foundations laid for the good of the whole Christian Church by the men who have gone out from this Seminary, he would only pile up the debt which the Church of Christ in all the world owes to those who have taught in these walls.

I must speak before closing of what the Seminary has given to the work of missionary administration. Seven secretaries for the Board of Home Missions have gone out from this institution. With two brief intervals, I believe that for eighty years the administration of our home missionary work has been in the hands of graduates of this institution. And the Congregational Church has drawn two of its home missionary administrators from our Alumni roll, and the Baptist Publication Society one, while many agents have been provided for other missionary activities at home. If we turn to our own Foreign Missionary Board, every President and Chairman of our Executive Committee from the foundation down to this day, has been either a graduate or a director or a teacher in this institution; Samuel Miller was the first President of the Board, and William Phillips the first Chairman of the Executive Committee and these have been followed by James Lenox, William Adams, William M. Paxton, John D. Wells and George Alexander. Of the ten secretaries of our Board of Foreign Missions, five have been students of this institution, and two of the other five sent their sons here. There has never been a day since our foreign missionary work began when a son of this institution has not been carrying responsibilities for our missionary policies. And what the Seminary has done for us in these regards, she has done also for other Churches as well. She has given two foreign mission secretaries to the American Board and five to the American and Foreign Christian Union, one to the Irish Presbyterian Church, one to the United Presbyterian Church, one to the Southern Presbyterian Church, and twenty-three assistant secretaries and agents. And last of all, the Seminary gave from its second class that one life to which Dr. McEwan referred at the beginning, one of the best gifts God ever made to our Church, the life of Elisha P. Swift. Swift was born in 1792 in Williamstown. He was a lad of fifteen at the time of the "Haystack Prayer-meeting".

He came here to Princeton, and took his theological course, and was then ordained as a foreign missionary by the American Board, but was turned away from that ambition to serve the Board as an agent at home, and then to settle first in the church in Dover, Delaware, where Samuel Miller was born, and later in the Second Presbyterian Church in the city of Pittsburgh. From that pulpit, he blew the trumpet that rallied around him and the Synod of Pittsburgh the forces which were to bring into being the organized foreign missionary life of our Church.

And what Swift did may suggest best the few things I have to say, in closing, of the general convictions, the great missionary conceptions for which the Seminary has stood. From the beginning she adopted and made her own Elisha Swift's principle that the missionary enterprise was not an optional thing to be carried on by volunteer organizations in which the individual Christian man had his choice of participating or not, but that the missionary enterprise at home and abroad was the Church's first and organic obligation. We have a statement of Swift's view and a specimen of his logic in a paper of his in which he pours scorn on the idea that the church courts are for routine business and for litigation, but not for the corporate prosecution of the Church's chief business which is missions. "On what appointment," says the writer, "do pastors and elders sit in the house of God and hold the keys of the Kingdom of Heaven, but that which commissions them to go and disciple all nations? If, at the bar of such courts, by the very fact of their lawful existence, the perishing heathen have no right to sue out the payment of a Redeemer's mercy, then the most material object of their sitting is cancelled; and that neglected, starving portion of mankind, who enter with a specific claim, are turned out to find relief by an appeal to the sympathy of particular disciples. Will 'the Head of all principality and power' stay in judicatories where the laws of His kingdom are so expounded? Until something more is done for the conversion of the nations, what article on the docket of business can be relevant at any meeting, if this is not? Shall a worthless, unsound delinquent be told that, according to the Word of God, and the constitution of the Church, he has a right to come and consume hours of time in trifling litigation; and shall a world of benighted men, who have received as yet no hearing, and no mercy, and no information that Jesus has left a deposit for them also, be turned over to the slow and uncertain compassion of individuals?"

Dr. Lowrie has told us that Samuel Miller was one of the first to make a contribution for the new Western Foreign Missionary Society, which embodied Swift's principle. And beginning with the year 1837, the whole stream of the Seminary's foreign missionaries was turned toward the church activity of our own body. The theological issue between the Old and the New School entered in, I know, but also I know that the Seminary believed in Swift's conception. And we owe to these men, and most of all to Swift, what is our most priceless possession to-day, the recognition of the missionary obligation as the inalienable duty of the entire Church, the conception of the whole Church as a missionary society, of which every member of the Church is a member by virtue of his relationship to the Church herself.

We owe to these men and to the old institution not only this clear perception of the church theory of missions, but also a large and courageous faith. Younger men are wont to think that the great visions are theirs, but our fathers were young men in their day, and what is more, they were men of God and seers in the Spirit, and they had their great visions too. I have been reading in the earliest records of our Board (for this is its seventy-fifth anniversary) the purposes cherished in the establishment of its first missions. Swift planned for stations across Africa when the interior of the continent was unknown. The missionaries went to Calcutta under instructions that they were not to stay there; they were to go northwest as far as they could go. It was hoped that they could plant their stations in the Vale of Kashmir, cross the roof of the world and press on to the far shores of Lake Baikal; they were not to be content till there should be opened a Christian mission station where none has been opened to this day, in Kabul of Afghanistan. We owe it to the fathers who went before us to stand afraid before no opportunity and flinch at no call.

From the very beginning, they taught us also the glory of a great and unswerving fidelity. For twelve years, Stephen Mattoon and Stephen Bush labored in Siam, before they had their first convert. At the end of six years, the missionaries numbered sixteen in Ningpo, and they had six Chinese converts. The men who have gone out from these halls have always known the duty of staying by duty until the sun went down. They were taught that God was patient, and that His servants need not be anxious or afraid.

And I dare even to say also, that these men learned somewhere (maybe the old Mother did not know that she was giving it to them, but in the pure milk of the gospel which they drew from her breasts, it must have come to them) that what we hold which is peculiar is less important than what we hold in common with all Christian men. From the beginning the sons of the Seminary have striven faithfully for what a few minutes ago we were praying,—the unity of Christ's Church on earth. Men were taught here that there is no chasm between the different forms of missionary service, that the whole Church must some day and everywhere be made one mighty army, and they went out to Mexico and Brazil, to Japan and China and India, cherishing the dream from far across the hills of the day that is waiting, when the desire of the Saviour's heart shall be fulfilled, when, united to Him, the sin of our schisms shall be over and we shall all be gathered together in one, as He and His Father are one.

And lastly, the Seminary has always sought to breed in her sons a dauntless and unfearing supernaturalism. The missionary enterprise is too vast for a mere human will to sustain. Its difficulties, its necessities, its problems, its ideals, call for God. Its sufficiency is in Him alone. Here men learned that God was "in the beginning" and that God stands back of the end. With God and by God and for God such men have dared all things, and have not fainted or grown weary.

With all this in our past, my friends, what may there not be in our future, if we, to whom this past has been given, do not lie down to sleep upon our great tradition, but answering its summons and its call, rise up to greet the new day which is entreating us, in the spirit in which James Alexander and Elisha Swift would greet it —this new day with its unprecedented world situation which confronts us, which is God's gift to us, and not God's gift only, but God's test of our worthiness to be the heirs and executors of such a past?

PRINCETON THEOLOGICAL SEMINARY

PRINCETON IN THEOLOGICAL EDUCATION AND RELIGIOUS THOUGHT

ADDRESS

BY THE REVEREND WILLIAM HALLOCK JOHNSON, Ph.D.
Professor of Greek and New Testament Literature and Exegesis
Lincoln University, Pennsylvania

Mr. President, Fellow Alumni, Ladies and Gentlemen:

ONE thought is in every mind today, one sentiment in every heart, one word upon every tongue: Princeton the mother of us all!

The history of Princeton Seminary for the past one hundred years constitutes an important chapter in the history of the Christian Church. That chapter, if fully written, would contain many sacred passages from individual biographies. It would tell of the aspirations and vows of Christian parents as they dedicated a beloved son to the work of the ministry; it would tell of the development in the growing boy of a holy purpose to serve God in the gospel of His Son; it would tell of the deepening of thought and experience and the strengthening of purpose and conviction in the three years of the Princetonian Arabia; it would tell of the fruitful years of service and sacrifice for church and country in the pulpit at home, and in laying the foundations of Christian civilization abroad, in that work of spiritual imperialism which Mr. Winston Churchill of England has spoken of as the glory of the Anglo-Saxon race, and which is the glory of any race or any institution privileged to have a large share in it.

Our hearts have been stirred as we have listened to the eloquent story of what Princeton men have accomplished in the home pulpit and on the mission field. The thought has come to me, how abundantly have the wisdom of the founders of this Seminary, the devoted labors of its Faculty and governing boards, and the generosity of its benevolent friends been justified by the result. They builded better than they knew. Where, from a business standpoint, could one find a better investment of money? Where, for every dollar invested, has there been a richer return in lasting and far-reaching influence for good?

The theme assigned to me this afternoon will, I fear, seem rather scholastic after addresses which have carried us up upon the heights; but I beg you to remember, when thinking of the achievements of Princeton Alumni, the good Presbyterian doctrine, "What have I that I have not received?" The fond mother feels that she is responsible for the successes of her children, and Princeton may well rejoice today in the service of her sons, and may even sympathize a little with the feelings of Nebuchadnezzar, when he said, "Is this not great Babylon that I have builded?", without being guilty of the deadly sin of pride. You may say that Princeton men were originally endowed with those qualities which would ensure ministerial success, even if they had gone to some other seminary. This is no doubt true, but Princeton is responsible for two things: she has attracted to herself men of large mental and spiritual calibre, and she has given them a training upon which success has in multitudes of cases, as we have heard, been built. I believe that there is a causal connection between the Princeton training and the ministerial success, whether causation be construed in terms of uniform sequence with the Humeian philosophy, or in terms of power or efficiency with Dr. McCosh, and with Professor Ormond, who has trained generations of theological students in the principles of a sound philosophy.

How shall we estimate the value of Princeton's contribution to theological education? Adopting the quantitative method, we might speak of Princeton's age, of the number of her graduates and of the number of these engaged in theological education. As the oldest seminary of the Presbyterian Church, Princeton has naturally exerted a profound influence over theological education. In the South, the Union Seminary of Richmond was founded soon after Princeton by men from the Log College, and the founders of Columbia Seminary set before them the goal of making that institution "the Princeton of the South"; while in the North, such institutions as McCormick, Western, Lane, Danville, Lincoln and San Francisco were founded by Princeton men or had Princeton men among their earliest instructors. Princeton, it has been said, cannot be jealous of the prosperity of these younger institutions, because they are in a large measure her own offspring. As the pioneer among the seminaries of the Presbyterian Church she has blazed the path which others have followed.

Princeton is not only the oldest Presbyterian theological school; she is, in the number of her graduates and former students, the largest school for theological education, of any name,[1] in America. Some five thousand eight hundred men have studied within her walls, her nearest competitor being the Southern Baptist Seminary of Louisville, Ky., with a total of about four thousand and

---

[1] "The total number of students up to 1910 was 5,742, of whom 3,076 were living" (J. H. Dulles in *New Schaff-Herzog Encyc.*, Vol. XI., p. 374).

fifty matriculates.[1] Some one hundred and eight of her graduates have been teachers in the Presbyterian schools of theology in this country, while others have taught in other divinity schools, here and abroad, among them Dr. McCurdy, of Toronto, Dr. Jacobus, of Hartford, and one who for many years was the only native American to occupy a full professorship in a German university— Dr. Caspar René Gregory, of Leipsic, soon to give to the world the fruit of a lifetime of study in a great critical edition of the Greek New Testament. Of the theological teachers in our Presbyterian seminaries, almost one-third are Princeton graduates. Of these, there are two in Auburn, one in Western, one in Kentucky, five in McCormick, one in San Francisco, three in Lincoln, one in Newark, and four in Omaha. The distinguished presidents of McCormick and Omaha Seminaries, as well as of Princeton Seminary, are Princeton graduates.

Dr. Patton, I believe, has recently expressed the desire that he might be at the head of a school for the training of college presidents, but if he would study the statistics, he would find that his ambition is already gratified. We cannot think of Washington and Jefferson, for example, without thinking of Dr. Moffat, nor of Wooster University without thinking of Dr. Holden, whose energy has raised it from its ashes. And what would Lincoln University be without the forty-six years of splendid service and sacrifice of Dr. Isaac N. Rendall? Some of the honored guests from abroad may have been accustomed to think of Princeton as merely a center of theological learning. Now, certainly, they realize that the term Princeton has a wider extension; and those of us who are

---

[1] This is the estimate of President E. Y. Mullins. Andover reported a total of 3,538 students up to 1908.

PRINCETON THEOLOGICAL SEMINARY

Princeton men in a double sense rejoice in the fact that a graduate of Princeton Seminary, Dr. John Grier Hibben, is, in a few days, to be formally installed as the head of the great University whose hospitality we enjoy today.

Beside theological and college teachers, Princeton has contributed to the Presbyterian Church fifty-six moderators of General Assemblies, and five bishops to the Protestant Episcopal Church, Bishops McIlvaine, Johns, T. M. Clark, A. N. Littlejohn and J. H. Darlington. She has not, as yet, produced a Pope, but has trained three stated clerks of the General Assembly.

The specific quality of Princeton's influence in theological education is traceable to two causes: the personality of Princeton's teachers and the high standard of her theological course.

History, it has been said, is the biography of the world's great men. The history of Princeton is the record of her great teachers, of the patriarchs and prophets who laid the foundations of the Seminary, and of those who so skilfully and so devotedly have built upon these foundations. The secret of long life and prosperity is said to be found in the choice of a sound ancestry, and no institution has been more fortunate in its spiritual progenitors.

An estimate of the four great men who have left the impress of their personality not only upon this Seminary, but directly or indirectly upon so many in the Presbyterian ministry, was given me recently by the graduate of the Seminary who is oldest in years, Dr. David Tully, of Media, Pa., of the class of 1850.[1] Dr. A.

[1] Rev. James Park, of Knoxville, Tenn., of the class of 1846, is the oldest in date of graduation.

Alexander had "the keenness of a Kentucky rifle-man in his insight into spiritual experience"; Dr. Addison Alexander was "a whirlwind as a teacher and preacher"; Dr. Samuel Miller was "a prince in church history and the Chesterfield of the Presbyterian Church"; and Dr. Charles Hodge was "the greatest analytical mind that this country has produced, certainly since the days of Jonathan Edwards." The same authority says that he never knew any group of men who could "state truth so clearly and defend it so ably."

The gifts of God to the theological seminary are first teachers, then scholars, then preachers. Often in Princeton's history these three offices have been happily united in the same man, but always she has included within her Faculty some of the greatest preachers, the most gifted teachers and the profoundest scholars of the Christian Church in America. Her Faculty has often been recruited from men prominent in the pastorate and pulpit. Two, for example, both famous as models of pulpit eloquence, were taken from the pastorate of the First Presbyterian Church, New York. One of these was Dr. William M. Paxton, to me a beloved pastor as well as teacher; and in his pulpit in boyhood days I have heard the thoughtful and spiritual sermons of Drs. A. A. and C. W. Hodge. The other was Dr. Samuel Miller, of whom history records that he preached occasionally before the Tammany Society, once on the Fourth of July, upon the theme, "Christianity, the Grand Source and the Surest Basis of Political Liberty." Two Princeton professors have been called to the pulpit of the Fifth Avenue Church, Dr. J. W. Alexander and Dr. Purves. In student days, we regarded Dr. Purves' Sunday night sermons as a regular part, and not the least important part, of our theological course, while a sermon by Dr. Patton was in student days (and was yesterday) more than a sermon—an event in our intellectual and spiritual history.

The two great pillars in the temple of Princeton were Drs. Archibald Alexander and Samuel Miller. Princeton's history is but the lengthening shadow of these two great teachers, leaders of the church and devoted servants of God. Even to enumerate the distinguished teachers who have followed them would be impossible in this address. Dr. Addison Alexander, teacher, linguist, commentator, preacher, signally gifted in all these rôles, was an intellectual and spiritual giant, of whom it has been said that "to have possessed any one faculty in the measure in which he possessed all, would have been enough to constitute a man of mark." How shall we do justice to the memory of Dr. Charles Hodge in the presence of many who have sat under his instruction and revere his memory? Even among his colleagues in Princeton, Dr. Hodge stands out, like Agamemnon, preeminent among many and foremost among heroes. Measured by the number of students that he taught (some three thousand) or by the years of his service, or by the depth and permanence of his influence in molding conviction and shaping character, or by the affection and veneration felt for him by successive classes of students, or by the persistence of his influence in the generation since his death through the use of his published works as text-books in most of the seminaries of the Presbyterian faith, Dr. Hodge stands out as easily the foremost theological teacher in the Christian churches of America.

We cannot speak in detail of those contributions to theological scholarship which have caused the name of

Princeton to be known and respected in all parts of the learned world. The richest contribution which the scholar can make to the world of sacred learning is perhaps a learned and devout commentary upon some great book of the Bible. To unfold the rich treasures of Scripture through exegesis is its best defence. Drs. Addison Alexander and Charles Hodge did not anticipate all the discoveries and discussions of later years, but their commentaries are still widely studied, and may be studied with profit as examples of thorough scholarship, sound judgment in exegesis, and spiritual insight. Exposition of the Scriptures has in Princeton ever led to theological construction: theology without exegesis, to adapt Kant's well-known phrase, is empty; exegesis without theology is blind. Upon the writings of Princeton men in systematic theology a large part of her reputation may be said to rest. In other departments, such as philology and archaeology, Biblical introduction, apologetics, church history, church polity, Biblical theology, ethics and philosophy of religion, Princeton has kept abreast of, and helped to advance, the scholarship of her day. The founders of the Seminary and their descendants by ordinary generation and spiritual inheritance have exerted a steady stream of influence through books, pamphlets, addresses, articles in periodicals and Bible dictionaries. "The Princeton Review," inseparably associated, under its several titles, with the names of Alexander, Hodge, Dr. Green and Dr. Warfield, has been recognized for three generations as the foremost organ of the Reformed faith; it has been an engine of power in the church and the country, "spreading the fame of Princeton among the nations." To the contributions of her own scholars must be added those of her occasional lecturers upon the "Stone" and other foundations. The list includes such names as those of Drs. Storrs, Mark Hopkins and Henry J. Van Dyke, of America; of Drs. Flint and Orr, and Sir William M. Ramsay, of Scotland; and Drs. Kuyper and Bavinck, of Holland; together with many names notable in the world of missionary literature.

The influence of Princeton's teachers has been felt wherever the gospel has been preached by Princeton men. The secret of her influence in theological education has been the succession of apostolic men who have occupied her professorial chairs. These have been men who have magnified their office, not content merely to give formal instruction in the truths and doctrines of the Word, but ambitious to inspire as well as to instruct, to animate with zeal for the work of the Kingdom, and to set before their students a strong and attractive example of Christian and ministerial manhood.

Another reason for the prestige and influence of Princeton as a school of the prophets has been her high standard of ministerial training. We have been passing through a period of educational transition and perhaps of confusion. The wonderful development and ever-extending boundaries of the sciences, the obvious utility of scientific study as a preparation for many vocations in life, the relative depreciation of the classics, the demands of a not infallible, but very human student body, seeking the line of least resistance, the development of elective courses, the application of candidates for the ministry without classical training, the marked popular interest in sociological questions growing out of our industrial organization and the progress of democracy, all of these causes have had their effect upon the theory and the actual arrangement of our theological curricula. Coupled with these changes in general educational policy, have been changes within the theological field itself, affecting the traditional views of the Bible and of its doctrines, and so of the gospel which ought to be preached. We are met with the question: Why not dispense with the dead languages and the dry bones of scholastic theology, and study the living problems of the day? Why not take this sorry theological scheme of things— this curriculum—entire, and shatter it to bits, and then remold it nearer to the heart's desire?

I know that we are here on controversial ground, and that every seminary has its own problems, and must decide for itself how it may best serve the church and the cause of ministerial education. I congratulate Princeton Seminary, however, upon reaching her one hundredth anniversary without finding it necessary to make her theological course any easier, or to change the principle upon which that course is organized. In the midst of changing conditions and theories, Princeton has stood her ground requiring a high standard of admission, requiring for graduation a knowledge of Hebrew and of Greek, and requiring exegesis in the original tongues.

Those hours of Hebrew in the junior year are indeed for the average student a hill of difficulty, but it is good to bear the yoke and to endure a little intellectual hardship. The mental discipline itself is not to be despised, and may help the preacher in later years as he grapples with a difficult text, and says, "I will not let thee go, except thou bless me." The short cut into the ministry, it is well to remember, may lead to the short cut out of the ministry, and the road may be made so smooth and easy as to lead readily into the by-paths of a real estate and insurance agency.

In these days of specialized Biblical criticism, it would be certainly a misfortune if the decision of Biblical questions should be taken out of the hands of the ministry, and relegated to a learned and cloistered caste. Critical discussions about the Pentateuch or the Psalms, or Isaiah or the Synoptic problem can only be appreciated by those who have some knowledge of the ancient languages. It is not necessary that the preacher should be a specialist in philology, but it is desirable that the ministry, to whom are committed the oracles of God, should have in their hands the instruments of scholarship, and be able for themselves to "search the scriptures whether these things are so."

In a scientific age, it will be a serious handicap to the preacher not to be able to refer to the fundamental documents of his faith. The necessity of the ancient languages in a theological course stands or falls, indeed, in my opinion, with the importance of exegesis, and our estimate of the importance of exegesis is bound up with our views of the authority and inspiration of the Scriptures. If there is no water of life, there is no need to draw from the fountain of the original text. If the preacher is not to preach the Word, his time will be wasted in studying the languages in which it was written. But the preacher, who believes that only in the Bible can he find his message for the salvation of men and the good of society, will wish to know all he can about the Bible. He will shrink from no labor which may make him a "workman that needeth not to be ashamed." Whatever the changes of the future, I hope, that in these days of higher standards of professional preparation, Princeton will not let down the bars in deference to the clamor for an easier course.

Our hope and dream for Princeton is that with expanding resources, she should offer, in some way, as extra-curriculum or elective, or fourth year or graduate courses, all the subjects which might be taught by the theological university. Let her offer courses in all the religions, and in all the languages, in all the philosophies, in all the Biblical books, in all the doctrines, in all the periods of church history, in the philosophy and psychology of religion, in ethics and economics and sociology. Let her send out Oberlins into the country churches who shall improve the roads and the schools and the methods of agriculture. Let her send out sociological experts, men with the modern outlook upon social problems, and able to apply the most exact and scientific methods to their study and to their solution. Let there be courses that will give to the foreign missionary a specialized training for his work. Let elocution be emphasized so that the preacher, on fire with his message, may deliver it in a manner commensurate with his theme. Let the circumference of the course be as wide as possible, but let the center, about which and upon which all else shall be built, be the study of the Bible. Thus will the Seminary give to the preacher a message large enough to fill his heart and mind, and great and important enough to carry to the ends of the earth.

Courses in psychology of religion, in religious education and in ethics will be attractive and useful to the preacher, and other studies, in history, literature, science and philosophy, will be broadening and helpful. But in the name of efficiency, let us put the most important things first. Let us not crowd in the squash courts and Turkish baths and palm gardens, if we have to crowd out the life-boats.

I have seen efficient ministers without scholastic training—Paul had more training in the schools than Peter; but I never saw an efficient minister without the Bible in his hand and in his heart. When we speak of efficiency and social service, let us not forget our church history. Let us look at Luther and Calvin, and what they accomplished, and how they accomplished it. Luther and Calvin might have studied history and psychology and political and social science till they were as old as Methusaleh, and they would not have produced one tithe of the political and social results that they did achieve by studying the Bible, by translating the Bible, by expounding the Bible, and by building, as they believed, upon the Bible great systems of doctrine and of duty.

Turning, for the few moments which remain, to the second part of our topic, we may say that Princeton's influence upon religious thought has been constructive, conservative and comprehensive, and that it has flowed notably in two channels, those of Biblical criticism and doctrinal theology.

Princeton's influence has been constructive. She has not been content with a repetition of the old formulas. Out of the Scriptures, as she believes, she has reared an imposing and positive system of truth, not novel in its essential features, but built up in full view of opposing systems, and with constant reference to the science and philosophy and criticism of the time. The articles of Princeton's creed have not been prefaced with a "perhaps" or an "I don't know", yet at times her words spoken in moderation and wisdom (for example, upon the principles of subscription to the Confession, or upon the atonement as adapted to all, sufficient for all, open to all and honestly offered to all) have brought assurance and relief to the whole Presbyterian world.

Her influence has been conservative. She has not believed with Ibsen that "the life of a normally constituted truth is twenty years at the outside". Her appeal has been from the fashion of the age ofttimes to the mature verdict of the ages. Her faith has been liberal in the sense indicated by Bishop Brooks, who said the term should be used not of a faith which believes little, but of one which believes much. Whether with approval or not, we must recognize the notable consistency of her position. She has exemplified her favorite doctrine of the perseverance of the saints. For one hundred years, she has stood like a Gibraltar amid the shifting tides and currents of human opinion.

Princeton's influence has been comprehensive. She has expounded and defended both the Old and the New Testaments, which the history of criticism has shown to be joined together as closely as ever, for better, for worse; for richer, for poorer. She has taught the great central doctrines of the Christian faith, human sin, a Divine Redeemer, and redemption through the blood of His Cross; and she has defended the outposts of the Reformed theology. She has expounded the doctrines of revealed religion, and has defended those fundamental truths of natural religion which lie at the basis of all religion and all ethics.

In analyzing Princeton's influence upon religious thought, we find that two principal streams may be distinguished; her influence in the spheres of Biblical criticism and of doctrinal theology. In considering questions of Biblical criticism, her attitude has been reverent rather than patronizing. She has not sat in the seat of the scorner. Her attitude again has been scientific in that, whether her conclusions have been correct or not, she has, at least, considered the available evidence from tradition, from philology, from archaeology, from comparative religion, not omitting the testimony of the Holy Spirit, bearing witness by and with the Word in our hearts. Her attitude has been courteous, toward criticism and toward the critics. Dr. William Henry Green stands as Princeton's leading exponent of the higher criticism. He has been called "the most influential Hebrew teacher of his time among English-speaking men"; he was the chairman of the American Old Testament Revision Committee; but he will be longest remembered as "the leading defender in this country, if not in the world, of the authenticity and integrity of the Mosaic books." It was his work in this field which led Dr. Willis J. Beecher to say that he had "caused American scholarship to be recognized throughout the Western, the Eastern and the Australian continents." Dr. Green, as a scholar, a Christian and a gentleman, was a model to all those who would enter the field of theological discussion.

While there is a contest between faith and unbelief, while men approach historical evidence from different philosophical standpoints and hold their philosophy dear, the Bible with its revelation of a Divine Christ will be the great storm-center, the great battle ground of controversy. Progress may be made by research, by reflection, by calm discussion and the weighing of arguments, by proving all things and holding fast that which is good; but perhaps no final agreement will be reached until we come to know even as we are known, or until we reach a condition of moral and spiritual indifference, and, like Gallio, care for none of these things.

I am not a prophet to forecast the probable course or duration or outcome of the controversy over the authorship and the trustworthiness of the books of the Bible; but I may venture to predict that an institution whose delight is in the law of the Lord will continue to enjoy the promise of continuous vigor and seasonable fruitfulness. And I may express the conviction that that institution which in the coming years of the century does most to train men to preach the Bible, and to induce men to study the Bible, to believe in and to obey the Bible, as the revelation of God's will and God's love for the salvation of men and society, that institution will not be at the end of the procession, but will be marching right in front in the vanguard of the world's advance.

Princeton Seminary has been for a century the consistent champion of that system of doctrine which has been variously called Augustinian, Calvinistic, Reformed, Westminster, or simply Princetonian. Princeton has produced the greatest textbook, the great monumental treatise, of this type of theology in the English language, its best popular exposition (in Dr. A. A. Hodge's "Popular Lectures"), its most genial and persuasive teachers, its keenest polemical defenders. Not all of us, as students, were able to bear all that we were taught by our theological professors; but I believe I speak for the great body of the Alumni when I say that we have absorbed a surprisingly large amount of Calvinism, and in our deepest convictions, as these have been deepened by experience, are true to that system of doctrine which places God's will above man's will, God's power above human weakness, God's grace above human merit, and makes God's glory the supreme end of man's existence.

We live in a time when there is a general desire for a fuller outward expression of the essential unity of the Christian church. The branches of the church, engaged in a common work, animated by a common purpose, are longing for some fuller expression of their essential unity in Christ, the great Head of the church. The middle walls of division, which have stood for centuries without a breach under the heavy guns of theological controversy, may at last be melted by the fires of Christian love. But whatever the movements and readjustments of the future, under the guidance of God's providence and of His Spirit, we believe that the essential truths which Princeton has taught with such conviction, for which she has contended so earnestly, and which she has made men see so clearly, whether they accepted her teaching or not, that these truths in the church of the future, coming down through Augustine and Calvin and the Westminster and the Princeton divines, will be a possession for all time, and that they will be incorporated as a valuable and integral part into the great stream of catholic Christianity and catholic Christian thought.

To these "five points" of Calvinism, may Princeton continue to be true. First, a lofty ideal of Christian and ministerial character, an ideal which has produced in history such men as Coligny, William of Nassau, John Knox, Dr. Alexander "the great", and Charles Hodge "the gracious". Second, an intelligent faith and a high standard of training for the ministry. Third, the authority of the Bible, given in the lovingkindness of our God, as the rule of faith and life. Fourth, the sovereignty of God in His grace and in His providence. Fifth, the doing of the will of God upon the earth; for the Reformed faith is in its very essence a reforming faith.

As we review the record of one hundred years of the Seminary's life, we cannot repress a feeling of profound gratitude for the streams of influence which have gone out from the Princeton fountain into the pulpits of our land, into the mission field and into the deepest thoughts and convictions and experiences of men.

As she faces the new problems of the newer age may Princeton go on her way, forgetting the things that are behind. May she go forward to a larger usefulness in the service of the church and of humanity. May she go forward with new hope and courage, with wise leadership, with holy ambitions, to great constructive achievements, and may all of us, her sons, set our faces in hope and expectancy to the coming of the better day, when the glory of all human achievements and of all human institutions and the glory of the ministry and the crown of a redeemed humanity shall add lustre only to the Saviour's brow, and all shall join in the song, "Not unto us, not unto us, O Lord, but unto thy name give glory".

PRINCETON THEOLOGICAL SEMINARY

PRINCETON IN ITS EARLY ENVIRONMENT AND WORK[1]

ADDRESS
BY CHARLES BEATTY ALEXANDER, LL.D.
New York City

HENRI ROCHEFORT has said that after men become fit for nothing else they write reminiscences. When the invitation came to me to deliver one of the addresses on this memorable occasion, I, with the sensitiveness natural to men of my years, was tempted to think, from the subject assigned to me, that the committee perhaps imagined me a contemporary of the fathers of this institution, and hence able to speak from personal knowledge of its early days. The committee would not have been far wrong, if this had been their impression. It so happens that I spent a portion of every year from 1850 to 1859, in the kindly hospitality of the old Alexander house, and like most early impressions, the recollections of that time are most vivid.

Dr. Archibald Alexander died in October, 1851, and I do not recall him.

I well remember being taken as a little boy to see Dr. Hodge in the house across the campus, and being told not to forget that I was to meet one of the great scholars of the age.

At the period I have mentioned, the only buildings on the campus were what is now called Alexander Hall, the Miller Chapel, and the old Library. It was a great

[1] Owing to the limitations of time, portions of this address were omitted.

[455]

source of interest to me to visit a little museum, on the first floor of the Seminary. It contained a few shells from the South Seas, and copper coins. There were also some beads, which I understood were the costume of dusky converts before they adopted the traditional garb of civilization. There were, moreover, certain idols in the cases, which in my early innocence, I supposed might occasionally, in moments of backsliding, be worshipped by the students, but later learned that they had been sent home by missionaries, after being discarded by their disciples, very much as the Indian braves of the day sent home to their lodges the scalps of the conquered.

Above all, I remember the current of life which flowed through the house. The family then consisted of Joseph Addison Alexander, and his two brothers, William and Archibald, and their sister, Janetta. Hardly a day passed without a visit from some returning graduate or eminent personage from abroad, and there were frequent calls from the other members of the Faculty. I remember the intense interest shown in the work of every graduate, and the eagerness with which all news of the Alumni was sought. The early professors always kept their hands on their former students, wherever they might be, the hands of sympathy, of imagination, of Christian love. I have since thought, that this interest bound the graduates very closely to their *alma mater*.

Of course, I recall Dr. Addison Alexander and all his well known peculiarities. In a few lessons he sought to make me a great Oriental scholar, but I clearly proved that the mantle of Elijah had not fallen on Elisha.

Before leaving these personal reminiscences, let me say that I have had great pleasure in sending to the Seminary Library the English Bible which Dr. Archibald

Alexander used daily for over thirty years. It contains, in his own handwriting, the entry of the births and baptisms of his children. In the cover, Dr. Alexander pasted several verses, which form the best possible clue to his character. They are as follows: "To love him with all the heart and with all the soul and with all the strength is more than all whole burnt offerings and sacrifices." "I dwell with him that is of a contrite and humble spirit." "But to do good and to communicate forget not." "The Lord is nigh unto them which are of a broken heart and saveth such as be of a contrite spirit." Well may it have been said of him by his biographer that at the time of his call to Princeton "no man of eminence could think more humbly of himself." From the worn appearance of portions of the book, it would seem that the Psalms and the Major Prophets were the most frequently read. I have also sent to the Library an ancient Hebrew Old Testament, used daily by Dr. James Waddel Alexander, and another read by Joseph Addison Alexander from 1828 until his death.

Let me now turn to the subject assigned to me. Let us consider for a moment the condition of the country at the time of the foundation of the Seminary. In 1811, the people were preparing for the expected war with England. The things common to a new country characterized American life. Traveling facilities were poor. There was not a steamboat west of New York City. Transportation between Princeton and Philadelphia was by coach. In these days of the railway, bicycle, motor, telegraph, telephone, photograph, and electricity in all its forms, one can hardly imagine the primitive character of our national life.

The educational advantages in the country were far

from what they are today. Harvard, Yale, Princeton, and some lesser colleges set the standard, but the school facilities were limited, and the teaching inferior. The morality of the people was characterized by the laxness of a new land, and strange sects sprang up, "Halcyon," "New Light," and the like, due in a large degree to a lack of religious training.

Sharing in the general educational and moral depression, theological education was at a low ebb. Ministers were being prepared either by private instructors, or by what they could pick up in their college courses. This condition is indicated in "The Brief Account of the Rise, etc. of the Seminary," published in 1822. It states that the founders deeply lamented the want of such an institution, and saw with much pain the extreme disadvantage under which their candidates for the ministry labored, in pursuing their theological studies. They saw young men with very small previous acquirements in literature and science, after devoting only twelve or eighteen months, and in some instances much less, to the study of theology, and even for that short time almost wholly without suitable help, taking on themselves the most weighty and responsible of all offices.

But in spite of the gloomy outlook, intellectual, moral, and spiritual life was beginning to revive.

Something vital happens before the green blade appears. Although at the beginning of the last century there seemed little hope of improvement, the first decade of the nineteenth century showed a marvelous renaissance, of which the foundation of the Seminary forms a part.

There was a reaction proceeding in Europe from eighteenth century infidelity. W. G. Ward in his recently published "Life of Newman" says that this reaction was heralded in 1802 by Chateaubriand's "Génie du Christianisme."

The great idea of Christian foreign missions was born at the Haystack meeting in 1806. The temperance movement began in Moreau, New York, in 1808, when a society was formed pledging its members to drink rum only on special occasions. The first missionary society was founded in 1806. Twenty-four benevolent societies, the first growth of the immense charities of our own day, were incorporated in the first decade. The New Jersey Bible Society was founded in 1815, and shortly afterwards the American Bible Society.

The life manifested in these agencies, so new and so startling, is also to be remarked in the Government. The appearance of Clay, Calhoun, Webster, Cheves and Lowndes, at Washington, revealed a determination to end the humiliating trade difficulties with France and England by an aggressive war.

With this new spirit so manifest in the political and social life of the country, the Church awakened to its responsibilities and opportunities as it had not done before. The leadership in thought as well as in action fell upon men unprepared by education to bear it. As a response to the call of the time, loud and insistent, Princeton Seminary was born. The men who promoted it appreciated that on the one hand an ignorant ministry is a national misfortune, and that on the other, a cultivated, educated ministry is a national blessing. Therefore, the organization of this Seminary was not only a religious, but a patriotic service.

It is remarkable that the founders of the Seminary made it independent of any college already in existence.

It would have been easy to graft it upon Nassau Hall. Indeed, in 1805, the College of New Jersey showed considerable uneasiness at the project of a separate seminary, for the trustees sent a communication to the Assembly setting forth, that the college was founded with a particular view to furnishing men for the ministry, that the trustees were devoted to this object, and that an opportunity was afforded by the college for the study of divinity. This exhibits the change which has taken place in public sentiment, when the object of so many universities and colleges now is to secularize learning.

The plan for the Seminary adopted by the Assembly of 1811 described the kind of men it was desirous of supplying to the Church in words which might well have been written by John Calvin. The author was Ashbel Green. "It is to form men for the Gospel Ministry, who shall truly believe and cordially love, and therefore endeavor to propagate and defend that system of religious belief and practice which is set forth in the Confession of Faith, and thus to extend the influence of true evangelical piety and gospel order."

This Seminary has been called "the home of Calvinism." Today no thinking man should be ashamed of the title. Any institution might be proud to furnish to the Church men whose ideas of liberty and justice, whose zeal and love for men, whose scholarship and power are characteristic of the school of Calvin.

Calvin had died two hundred years before this Seminary was founded, but just as his theology had persisted, so did his views of an educated Protestant clergy continue to influence the Presbyterians of the world. He had a fine jealousy as to the character and competence of his professors. He was himself professor of theology.

His theological graduates were described by a French bishop as "modest, grave, with the name of Jesus Christ on their lips." He made Bossuet and Massillon possible. On his return from Geneva, John Knox copied Calvin's methods of education, and these ideas were brought here by our Scotch and Scotch-Irish and Puritan ancestors.

Michelet said of Calvin's disciples, "If in any part of Europe blood and torture were required, a man to be burnt or broken on the wheel, that man was at Geneva ready to depart, giving thanks to God and singing Psalms to him." If it be thought that this is an excessive estimate of the character and heroism of the present day Presbyterian minister, let me quote from the report of the famine and cholera of 1900 in Gujarat made by Sir Frederic Lely, one of India's greatest administrators. He says: "There was Milligan, Presbyterian missionary, who, when he heard that the district was in sore need of strong men, volunteered to help and was put in charge of a thousand persons on whom cholera had already taken hold on a relief work. There was Mawhinney, also a Presbyterian missionary, who also took a similar trust in the adjoining native state of Sunth. Each of them took up his abode among the people in a hut like their own; he restored order and cleanliness; he instilled some of his own courage; and then each within a month of the other was stricken with the disease from which he had saved others, and died the death of a Christian." Such men have always been among the graduates of this Seminary.

The early professors here seem to have been imbued with Calvin's ideals and with his spirit, in that he is described as a man of invincible calm, of balanced speech, gentle toward weakness, severe toward vice, severest of all toward himself. Beza in his dedication of Calvin's "Petits Traictés" to the Duchess of Ferrara declares that Calvin was of such integrity of conscience, that he fled from all vain subtle sophistries, and all ambitious ostentation, and never sought anything but the pure and simple truth.

It is evident from the writings of the first professors that they had Calvin's character and work in mind, as they attempted their important task. Dr. Miller in his inaugural address pointed out that witnesses for the truth in the dark ages were all friends of sound learning, and he closed by saying: "Wickliffe, Luther and Calvin are all gone, but the Kingdom of Christ did not die with them. It still lives and it will live forever." Dr. Alexander wrote shortly after to a friend, "We go on here upon our old moderate plan, teaching the doctrines of Calvinism, but not disposed to consider every man a heretic who differs in some few points from us." Earlier, in the stirring circular issued by the General Assembly in 1816 in aid of the Seminary, reference is made to Calvin, as one of those who have done more for the illustration and defence of the common salvation, than hosts of unlettered, though pious, ministers. Truly, to use Comte's aphorism, "The living are dominated by the dead."

Let me now briefly allude to the intellectual life of the Seminary during this early period. It is difficult in this age of specialization to realize all that the first professors did. By them the plan of the theological curriculum was developed into substantially what it is today. They themselves taught every branch of the theological encyclopedia. In the revival of 1815, the professors threw themselves into the work with all their heart.

They preached frequently in Princeton and in the neighboring towns. Their sermons might serve as examples to those whose ideas of evangelistic preaching do not include the fundamental principles of Calvinistic theology. Dr. Alexander was not content to teach simply a system of doctrine. He aimed to send out warriors of the Cross. To this end, he studied the religions of heathenism, and the erroneous faiths of every age, and he knew what should be said to refute their doctrines. A fresh examination of the literature relating to Dr. Alexander, and of the books which he wrote convinces me that too much stress has been laid on his sweetness of character, great piety and spiritual common sense, and too little on his profound and varied learning, marvelous for the place and time.

It is hardly fitting for me to say too much about my grandfather and his sons, but too much cannot be said of Dr. Samuel Miller, who united patience, learning and eloquence with all the social and courtly graces and the most fervent piety. He came to Princeton the year after Dr. Archibald Alexander, and found the curriculum created and the means for maintaining the religious life of the students perfected. He was of inestimable use in forming the manners and bearing of future ministers. Perhaps his example and precepts extend to the present day. I often re-read his book on "Public Prayer", full of good sense and of a quiet and appropriate humor. It was fortunate for the infant institution that its two heads should be so different in type: Dr. Miller, with his long training of city life as pastor of the First Presbyterian Church in New York, brought to the Seminary the experience of the metropolitan pulpit, and Dr. Alexander, whose great characteristic was a tender regard for the feelings of others, a ripe scholarship and the simplicity which is characteristic of most profound thinkers.

Thomas Chalmers said: "The Heraldry of an Institution of Learning is its Alumni." And perhaps Dr. Alexander's and Dr. Miller's greatest contribution to the Seminary was an early appreciation of Charles Hodge. As a student, he developed into a man of massive learning, sound exegesis and great skill as a teacher. I am glad to allude to the intimate personal friends of my father, his sons, Archibald Alexander Hodge, who by the flame of his genius made even the darkest theology glow with an almost supernatural light, and Caspar Wistar Hodge, who with the modesty and reserve of a great scholar, made the New Testament new in another sense to successive classes of faithful and admiring students.

Just as a faculty may be judged by the students, the product of their training, so the trend of thought in the Seminary's life may be judged by the contributions of its faculty to the current literature of the day. "The Biblical Repertory," begun in 1828, gives a good idea of Princeton's thought, as developed during the sixteen preceding years, for it is fair to assume that it contained the ripe result of the professors' various studies during that period. I call your attention to a few subjects on which they wrote in the earlier numbers. Dr. Miller wrote a review of Cooke, "On the Invalidity of Presbyterian Ordination", and on certain extremes in pursuing the temperance cause, which recalls the fact, that in one of his first letters after arriving in Princeton, he offered to send Mrs. Green, through President Ashbel Green, some very good claret. Another subject was "Use of Liturgies," another "Thoughts on Evangelizing the World," and in 1821 he published his "Letters on Unitarianism." The following were contributed by Dr. Alexander: "The Bible a Key to the Phenomena of the Natural World," "Priesthood of Christ," "Pelagianism," "Inability of Sinners," "Christian Baptism," "Organization of the Presbyterian Church," "Character of the Genuine Theologian," "Articles of the Synod of Dort," "The Foundation of Opinions and the Pursuit of Truth," "Melanchthon on Sin," "Catechism of the Council of Trent," "English Dissenters," "Evidences of a New Heart," "The Scottish Seceders," "Woods on Depravity," "Symington on the Atonement," "Practical View of Regeneration." His books on the Canon, Moral Science and Religious Experience, will not be forgotten. It is not necessary in the presence of such an audience to comment on the breadth and depth of these topics.

If there were time here today, we might leave the beaten tracks of those days and hear the voices of the early professors speaking through their students in quiet villages and lonely hamlets, on frontiers and in the wilderness, in foreign lands and at home. The memory of these men is not preserved on any stone or monument. Nor is it best kept alive even in the Seminary so beloved by them, but in the truth which they implanted in ministers' lives and handed on by them to homes widely scattered; to burdened, toiling, sinning men and women, to whom it meant pardon, peace and eternal hope; to children whose plastic lives were moulded; to the heathen world, to whom it came as the shining of the Star of Bethlehem. In these things are indelibly written the testimony of the Church and of the world to the founders of this Seminary.

No one who has studied the history of this great school can fail to be impressed by the sincere fidelity to the principles of its founders, which has been manifested in those who succeeded them. There are many who do not agree with these principles, but they must be constrained to admire this tenacity and constancy, considering the atmosphere of unstable equilibrium in which the theological world lives and moves.

In visiting the graveyard here, I sometimes think that even if all other records were to be destroyed, a history of Princeton and its institutions, might almost be reconstructed from the inscriptions on those venerable tombs—the tombs of presidents, professors and other benefactors who did loyal service to the Seminary and to the University.

There is one group of graves which I cannot look upon without personal emotion and unspeakable sorrow at the loss of those, all of whom loved Princeton, and of some who had for this institution a paternal as well as a filial affection. It is a comfort and encouragement to turn to this Seminary—a living monument in which I trust my family may claim a share.

One does not have to be a professional theologian to be aware that the kind of thought for which Princeton Seminary has always stood most firmly is now attacked persistently from many quarters. Voices come to us from across the sea and are raised here at home telling us that the sun is fast setting upon the old faith, and that the doctrines taught here will pass away like those of the Athenian and Roman schools. It may be said that in our own country the Seminary stands in a somewhat isolated position. Isolation has been the portion of the exponents of truth in all ages. Although not an expert in these things, I venture to predict that if the sort of theology which is taught here should die, and if its enemies should grant it decent burial, like the Lord of Life Himself, it will have a triumphant resurrection.

Yet even if these sinister prophecies of the foes of Princeton theology should be fulfilled to the uttermost, if this Seminary should perish amid the ruins of its great traditions, I should wish that its remains might be marked and made memorable by a Cross. For it is the Cross which has been the inspiration of its founders and their successors, even as it is the hope and the glory of this passing world. For the gospel which it teaches is an unconquerable force. The Cross which it uplifts is the world's greatest power. And by the gospel of the Cross, this Seminary will stand in spite of attack, in spite of any storm of criticism or unbelief until its work is done, and God comes to take the talent given to our fathers, from whom we have received it with its increase, to the praise of His eternal glory.

CENTENNIAL CELEBRATION OF

ON SOME CHURCH PROBLEMS

ADDRESS
BY THE RIGHT REVEREND ALEXANDER STEWART, M.A., D.D.
Principal of St. Mary's College and
Primarius Professor of Divinity in the University of St. Andrews
Moderator of the General Assembly of the Church of Scotland

Professors and Members of Princeton Theological Seminary:

MANY honours and privileges have fallen to my lot since I was called to occupy the chair of the General Assembly of the Church of Scotland in May of last year, but few indeed rank as highly in my estimation as the honour and privilege you have so graciously conferred upon me in inviting me to be present at your One-hundredth Anniversary Celebration and to represent one of the great divisions of our Scottish Christianity on this occasion. I beg to offer you most sincere congratulations both on my own behalf, on behalf of the Faculty of Divinity of St. Andrews, Scotland's most ancient University, and of the Church of Scotland.

A hundred years does not seem a long time in the life of an institution but there is ample room in the course of it for the emergence of great spiritual forces, the attainment of wide influence and the achievement of much practical good. I am sure you feel that you can look back upon it with pride and satisfaction and with deep thankfulness to God who has guided you so far on your way. I do not need to assure you that the name of Princeton is well-known and highly honoured far beyond the bounds of this country and wherever Protestant

Christianity is understood and valued. In Britain and especially in Scotland the theological teaching of Princeton is regarded as one of the noblest examples of adherence to a clear and definite expression of the Christian faith. It is not necessary to agree with all its tenets or even to occupy the same fundamental position in order to appreciate its value. To those of us who hold that truth has many sides and that the full-orbed truth can only be attained by a combination of these different aspects, it is most instructive and helpful to have any of these clearly set forth, and embodied in suitable forms. It is refreshing amidst the jar and conflict of modern thought to find one school and succession of teachers who have maintained with practically entire consistency a testimony to one system of thought worked out with logical completeness and forming the inspiration of a very noble type of piety.

From the time when it was founded by the General Assembly of the Presbyterian Church in 1812, Princeton has stood for a close adherence to the Westminster Confession of Faith. All its great names have been associated with this fundamental position. From its first head, Dr. Archibald Alexander, conspicuously in the teaching of Dr. Charles Hodge, and down to the present day, its teachers have been faithful to the task originally committed to them. This task as I have said, even in the view of those who cannot altogether accept the conclusions to which the teaching of these eminent theologians points, is yet extremely valuable as representing one side at least of that all-inclusive truth which all theology worthy of the name desires. In many ways we in the East may have departed somewhat from the strictest form of Calvinism, but we all honour John Calvin, of keen intellect, logical precision and dauntless courage, and while declining to follow them in every jot and tittle, we all honour the Westminster Standards as one of the most remarkable intellectual structures based upon Scripture and making a generous use of reason and philosophy that the modern world has seen. It has to be remembered that the Westminster Standards had to present a solution of many questions for which it may be the material was not yet available. Such solution was demanded of them by their age and unless they attempted to supply it, they would have been regarded as altogether defective. It did not follow therefore, that the solution supplied to such questions was absolutely the best—it was only the best possible at that time. We need not be surprised that much material has since accumulated which the Westminster Divines could not anticipate, and indeed that many questions have emerged which then lay wholly below their horizon. That is our justification for saying that while we hold the Westminster Standards in the highest respect, we can not admit that they are the last word in theology, and that theological science has no new treasures as well as old to bring forth to the world.

I trust I may not be misunderstood in making these remarks. I am quite sure that you would not wish me to pay a compliment to Princeton at the expense of the honesty of my own convictions. Fortunately, I do not need to sacrifice the one to the other as I very sincerely respect the Seminary, its founders and representatives and believe in the very great value of its teaching although unable to rank myself among its closest disciples. I should like in this connection to make special reference to Dr. Charles Hodge whose life-work was an example to all earnest workers in the theological field; his untiring industry, his vast learning and penetrating intellect made him indeed one of the prophets of this school and his work has influenced many who again have not accepted all his conclusions. His stupendous work on Systematic Theology with its admirable arrangement, its careful array of argument on this side and the other and its clear-cut and unambiguous style must be at once the admiration and the envy of all who are engaged in the same field. His beautiful life at Princeton both in public and private and the influence he wielded over so many young minds and through them over the thought and culture of this whole country are no less deserving of attentive and reverential respect. I never knew him except through his works, but I had the pleasure on my last visit to this country of meeting with his nephew who was then a professor at Lincoln University. On the same occasion I had the pleasure of meeting here Dr. W. H. Green, as also your President and another who is still spared to be one of the great ornaments of your Seminary, Dr. Benjamin B. Warfield whose work upon the Westminster Symbols cannot be sufficiently valued and admired.

I have thought that instead of expatiating upon matters which are familiar to you all, with which indeed you must be better acquainted than I can possibly be, it would be of more interest to you were I to touch upon one or two of the prominent phases of our Church life at home particularly those which are attracting attention at the present time.

In the forefront of these must undoubtedly be placed the question of the union of the Church of Scotland and the United Free Church. For many years the desire for union has been in the air, and since the accomplishment of that between the Free Church of Scotland and the United Presbyterian Church the desire has been deepened and accentuated. On the one hand there has been a profound sense of the disadvantage which separation entails, the waste of resources, the overlapping of agencies, often the display of a spirit of emulation and rivalry unworthy of great Christian communities,—on the other hand the advantages of a strong National Church, carefully organized, giving its witness with definiteness and firmness, able to make its voice heard in all matters of social interest and importance, and to exercise a powerful influence in the National Councils has moved as an ideal before the minds of many. For two years strong Committees of the two Churches have been considering together the causes which prevent union, and have done a most valuable work in formulating the position of each Church in regard to those questions in which conciliation and compromise are necessary before any project of union can be entered into. Since arriving in this country I have observed from the newspapers that communications have been taking place between the two Committees embodying a plan by which these questions may be dealt with and possibly disposed of. So far as I am aware the scheme thus propounded leaves many unsettled questions for subsequent discussion and adjustment. But that such approaches have been made and have been most cordially hailed on both sides as a step in the right direction is of happy augury for the future of the movement. The desire for union is a most natural and proper one and in harmony with the whole spirit of our religion. Religion is life, and the essense of the religious, of the Christian life is love,—

and love draws together, makes one. Then a powerful motive in the same direction is the need for combination for practical work. There is much for the church to do and it can best be done by common effort. Union is strength, division wastes strength. No wonder that, apart from what has been construed as the intention and desire of the Saviour himself, the vision of unity has been cherished by all good men. It might be questioned indeed whether in a condition short of the millennium, complete unity of organization would be a good thing for the church as a whole. Whether it would not as in the past be a temptation rather than an advantage to her and lead to countless abuses, to tyrannies, and to the re-establishment of such a politico-religious machine as we see exemplified in the Church of Rome, where the organization is stronger than the men who work it and moves on by an inertia of its own, impervious to the suggestion of reform and pursuing ends which have been found in the past inimical to the liberties and the social advancement of men. But we may be quite certain that a true union, one beneficial in all respects can only be the outcome of a feeling of unity, a sense of oneness in feeling, in aim, in conviction. Therefore it has always seemed to me that the first step should be co-operation in all possible directions. We should certainly have for example, common action in regard to home and foreign missions. This might lead to federation and then when the members of the different Churches felt themselves so far at one, they might fairly say, Why should we remain apart, why should we keep up separate organizations? Let us unite and let our outward union be the symbol and the consequence of our felt unity of spirit. Whether this will be the course actually pursued on the present occasion or not, it seems difficult to see how by any other method a healthy union can be brought about, —one, that is, which shall be a union of hearts.

There are obviously one or two dangers to which such a movement is exposed and which must be carefully guarded against. All human motives are not the highest and most human action proceeds from motives in which the higher mingle with lower elements. One motive which may enter in here is the desire for power—power it may be of the individual, it may be of a party or school of thought. A united Church can do things on a bigger scale, it affords a wider sphere for the energies and ambitions of its ministers and members, an impulse set agoing within it affects a wider area, the men who lead it bulk more largely in the view of the general community, and it may be that the zeal of men more or less consciously influenced by such dreams will urge the movement on perhaps faster than it should go.

Another ground on which union receives support from many is probably indifference to the distinctive principles which the Churches represent. It was the zeal of our forefathers often manifested no doubt in regard to minor points of belief and practice, often expressed far too dogmatically and enforced with bitterness that created the lines which divide us: it is an indifference perhaps equally excessive and unwise that would altogether give them up. The violence of controversy in the older days seems often to us in inverse proportion to the importance of the views and opinions in regard to which it concerned itself. We are tempted to go to the opposite extreme. There may seem to us nothing worth fighting about, wherefore since union would be pleasanter and bring with it many contingent advantages, let us all be one, let us sink our differences which have no longer any real meaning for us.

These seem to me to be the dangers to which the movement towards union is exposed—that its ends may be missed and its benefits forfeited when it is sought on any other ground than love and confidence and general agreement.

But while I point out these dangers I would not forget the great company of those who untouched by indifference, or by ambition, desire union for the good of the Churches and the advancement of the Kingdom of God among men. They find it quite compatible with a sincere attachment to religion to recognise the distinction between the non-essential and the essential and to postpone the former to the latter, the secondary to the primary elements of the faith, that which they hold in common with others being in their view more important than the things which divide brethren in Christ. We feel that it is the maintenance of this attitude which really makes for the ultimate union of the Churches, and as I understand that questions of union or reunion are not unknown among those whom I am addressing I trust that this brief indication of the position in Scotland may not be without interest or profit to you.

One of the most important developments in the life of the Churches in Scotland and especially, I think I may say, in that Church which I specially represent, is the increasing interest in what is known as social work. It has indeed in recent years engaged the attention of many of the most thoughtful and devoted members of all the Churches. It is an earnest and not altogether unsuccessful attempt to cope with the problems of poverty and vice which are so rife in our midst. It was a most happy utterance of one of the most able Scottish preachers of the last generation when he said that to the Church militant there should be added the Church beneficent, and long may it be true of the Church of Christ that its people look not only on their own things but on the things of others and continue to provoke one another to love and to good works. That such efforts after the amelioration of our social system should proceed from the bosom of the Churches and be stimulated by the faith and love there engendered is only what was to be looked for. It must be a question however whether such work can be carried out to its full extent by means of the organization which the Churches can supply. However successful the philanthropic efforts which have already been set on foot may have been, I mean our "labour homes" and other similar institutions, it is admitted that they only touch the fringe of a great difficulty. They have given an impulse, they have shown the way, they may serve as models for further effort. But it is a question whether when the problem comes to be attacked on a commanding scale the methods at present in use will prove adequate to the strain, whether in fact the church organization is the suitable one to undertake it. Two difficulties seem to me to emerge here. In the first place while there may be found in the Church men of ability, of organizing power, of personal devotion, willing to give gratuitous service in order to set on foot institutions of the kind here and there throughout the country, the work is too great for sporadic effort and the peculiarly church organizations are not adapted to carry it on. It may be under the auspices of a Presbytery and blessed by a General Assembly but it is by a Committee generally consisting of laymen and generally self-constituted that the actual work is done. It may be said to be the work of the Church in so far as the workers are church members and are willing to place that work as it were to the Church's credit.

In the second place similar work may be undertaken by different Churches and carried on by them independently of one another. That it should be so is a distinct loss. It is a loss to its systematic prosecution and to its effectiveness. The divisions of our Churches are here a distinct hindrance to good work. It is better that all such work of the same kind should be carried on by the same organization except in so far as it can be locally distributed. The tendency will be for those engaged in it to draw nearer to one another notwithstanding the separative influence of ecclesiastical connection. One remedy is no doubt the union of the Churches, another which will probably come first, is the separation of this work and its management from official connection with any special Church. If we look at the history of the church in the past we see how all inclusive the church once was. Philosophy, art and such rudimentary science as then existed, found in it not only a patron but a home. One by one they gradually emancipated themselves from her dominance and assumed first semi-independence, then altogether independent positions. As with the intellectual, so it may be with the practical departments of human activity. These also may emancipate themselves from the control of the Church, though they have been nurtured and grown so far to maturity under her care. The great questions of temperance, of peace and of social well-being will probably give rise in the future to organizations of an extent and complexity not yet experienced and so as to be beyond the power of the

Churches themselves to manage, while when separated from the Churches they may be neither altogether forgetful of their origin, nor ungrateful for the help which when most needed was so willingly given. It is indeed an instance of that division of labour, of that specialisation, which is the note of the best work in these days.

What we seem in these respects to be moving towards is a Church engaged first and foremost in its purely religious work of prayer and exhortation, of caring for the souls of men and by its witness to God and salvation bringing an ideal element into their lives. So that while "knowledge grows from more to more," there may "more of reverence in us dwell." The arrangements of the Church must have these ends primarily in view. Its message should be one of love to man as well as love to God, and this would remain the case even though it should find it desirable and even necessary to delegate to appropriate organizations the carrying out of that practical work of which it would remain the preacher and the inspirer even as it had been in earlier times the pioneer. Its members would join one or other of these organizations according as their special sympathies led them. In reality, as inspiring and helping on all movements towards good ends, the Church would make these but branches of its own activity and thus would regain in effect its ancient ideal of supremacy over all manifestations of human thought and action. But its rule would be no longer political or administrative but moral, and occupying such a position, ceasing to entangle itself with controversies whether on doctrinal or practical points, it might readily and safely become one in outward order. Within it might be intellectual differences but also an assured liberty. It would live for the highest welfare of man, it would seek to consecrate all man's activities to the glory of God.

With regard to the important question of doctrine, I do not know that there is anything very new, as there is certainly nothing very startling to report. It is quite possible that the whole situation would appear to you somewhat chaotic. The centre of gravity has on the whole somewhat shifted from the intellectual cultivation of Christianity to the endeavour to realise, on the one side, its spiritual life, and on the other, its practical requirements. I speak mainly for my own Church, but I think that my words are applicable to the entire position of religious life in Scotland. We have had of late no heresy hunts; the various doctrinal tendencies at work among us have had free scope for their development. We have what we may call High Churchmen laying stress upon the continuity of the Church's history and upon the Sacraments as the nourishment of the Church's life. We have Broad Churchmen representing a more ethical form of Christianity but still recognising as the inspiration of Christian life the spirit and example of the Master. We have the Evangelical with his more or less spiritual forms of preaching and worship bearing his witness to some of the central truths of traditional orthodoxy. The Church of Scotland two or three years ago altered its formula of subscription to the Confession of Faith making it much simpler and especially doing away with the somewhat provocative sentence of the older formula which required a man to acknowledge the Confession as the Confession of "my faith." It is still doubtful what the result of this movement may be. At first sight it would seem to encourage a freer attitude towards, and perhaps a more hostile criticism of, the Confession of

Faith. But on the other hand, the slackening of the chain may result in greater steadiness of progress since there is always an impulse to proceed in the opposite direction when it is felt that too great pressure is being used to maintain a certain course. It may be that under the relaxed formula orthodoxy may regain some of its lost influence and attractiveness. It is questionable if the legal situation is really changed. The Church under the new formula is bound to the Confession of Faith as the Confession of its faith and is no doubt morally as well as legally required to maintain discipline in this respect among its ministers and teachers. Its doctrine must remain fairly within the lines of the Confession of Faith liberally interpreted and it may be said that any other course might not only raise legal difficulties but would be at variance with what may be regarded as the general standard of opinion and feeling within the Church itself. The conviction has no doubt been firmly impressed upon many of the most thoughtful among us, that as there are many men, many minds, there can never be even with the greatest unity of organization complete uniformity in thinking. There will always be divergent views and opinions, and these will be held with more or less tenacity. We would frankly recognise that different Churches, different Church systems, different forms of worship, are adapted to different peoples and to those of varying temperament among the same people. We can only approach the gate of God by the pathway which leads from our own special nature to Him. We do not start from the same point as others, we do not pursue the same road, though we may in the end reach the same goal. These considerations raise a problem of which it may be suggested that the solution will be found not only in the growth of a spirit of toleration so that I will fully and frankly recognise that you have as full a right to your opinion as I have to mine, that each of us may hold firmly to his own view and neither interfere with the other, but in an increase of mutual understanding, of intellectual sympathy, which will enable me to bear with opinions which are at variance with my own because I see how they have been arrived at and on what grounds it is possible to hold them without their being condemned as arbitrary or irrational. Christian knowledge and belief is like a tree which has mighty limbs, many branches and innumerable twigs and stems. Now if the extremity of such a twig or stem represents the doctrinal position of one man or section of men the other extremities will represent the positions of other men or schools of thought. It is then possible by tracing the lines of development backward as it were to see clearly the points at which divergences which are so apparent first took place and how they came to be what they are. First, you have the great lines of cleavage, then the adoption of the more important principles in the guidance of thought, then the preference accorded to the principles of less weight and degree of certainty until you come down to the individual position. To understand the genealogy of beliefs in this way not only enables us to hold our own position more definitely and intelligently, but to understand and allow for the positions of others as we see how these have been arrived at. When controversy occurs it will also be more intelligent for it is useless to contend about minor points when the attitudes of the combatants are fundamentally opposed. We must first see where the root-opposition lies and we may then argue the question out more successfully. But in proportion as the distinction is recognised between the primary and secondary in doctrine, the more men feel themselves in sympathy on the great principles of Christianity, the more will they be able to bear with one another however sincerely they may hold to the points on which nevertheless they cannot help but differ.

But it is time to draw these somewhat discursive observations to a close. In what I have said I must be understood as speaking mainly for myself. I would not have my Church understood as committed to any of my statements as such, though I have endeavoured to interpret what I understand to be her attitude as nearly and clearly as I can. Every Church has its difficulties and problems and it is well when we are able to learn something from each other's experience. Though separated by the ocean I have no doubt that you and we have much of that experience in common. In endeavouring to solve our own problem we are indirectly at least helping to solve those of others. Each of us represents a side of truth, each of us has to deal with certain aspects of practical life, we each put our trust in the same God who rules and guides the world and the hearts of men. We each glory in the Christian name, and profess our loyalty to the same Lord and Master, we each hold fast the same hope of eternal life having our anchor in that which is within the veil. The more therefore we can feel our oneness in thought and life the better for us all. We need not look forward with misgiving, our faith is the substance of things hoped for, the proving of things not seen. That our aspirations even the highest of them will be fulfilled we cannot doubt; the end will be attained though as yet we can but guess at the way in which it may be brought about. It may often seem as if the foundations were shaking so that we dread to part with the old and fail to bid a welcome to the new, when it is only an opening of fresh channels for the same eternal spirit. Let us not be wanting in faith and insight. *Sursum corda.* The future is in the hands of One whose ways are higher than our ways and His thoughts than our thoughts. To Him be glory in the Churches through Christ.

CENTENNIAL CELEBRATION OF

A SCOTTISH ESTIMATE OF PRINCETON THEOLOGY

ADDRESS

BY THE RIGHT REVEREND JAMES WELLS, M.A., D.D.

Minister of the Pollokshields West Church, Glasgow
Moderator of the General Assembly of the
United Free Church of Scotland

President Patton, Fathers and Brethren:

ON this great day in the history of Princeton I have the peculiar honour and happiness of bringing to you the warm greetings and congratulations of the United Free Church of Scotland.

During the last hundred years Princeton has been in fraternal alliance with the Scottish Presbyterians. Your Church and ours are equally free, but you were free born, while our fathers, from the days of John Knox, had to purchase freedom at a great price. In 1843 the founders of the Free Church of Scotland, in their devotion to spiritual independence under the headship of Christ, severed their connection with the State. Your fathers were then among the most generous allies of the Free Church, and the memory of their brotherly kindness is still gratefully cherished among us. Princeton, too, though always sparing of such honours, gave the degree of D.D. to twenty-one of the leaders of the Free Church when the Universities of their native land withheld such honours from them. Princeton also conferred the same honour on several of the ministers who, in 1847, formed the United Presbyterian Church of Scotland. No other Church in the world can have better reasons than ours for rejoicing with you today and praying for your prosperity. In blood, in tongue, in creed, in aspiration and experience we are brothers. It is only the intervening ocean which hinders this kinship from becoming identity.

PRESBYTERIANISM AND LIBERTY

Presbyterian Princeton is the oldest representative in this land of some of the chief forces which have created and nourished the greatest republic the world has known. Your ninety-two millions are, beyond all comparison, the largest community of English-speaking people on the face of the earth. Great is one's surprise in discovering the perfect unanimity of many famous thinkers regarding the origin of your republican polity. It seems that you owe this boon to Calvinism.

Bancroft tells us that "the first voice in favour of independence came from the Presbyterians". He adds that "the revolution of 1776, so far as it was affected by religion, was a Presbyterian measure". You will not grudge us our satisfaction in knowing on the authority of Chief Justice Tilgham that the form of your republic is "borrowed from the constitution of the Church of Scotland", of which your Church is a genuine daughter. Bancroft and d'Aubigné unite in crowning Calvin as the father of America. Ranke calls Calvin "the virtual founder of America." Taine declares that Calvinism has guaranteed constitutional liberty to mankind, and of Calvinists he says, "These men founded the United States". Thorold Rogers asserts that "Calvinism was the pioneer of religious liberty". Lord Morley assures us that, "To omit Calvinism from the forces of western evolution is to read history with one eye shut". Green the historian writes, "It was Calvinism that first revealed to the modern world the dignity and worth of man". Mark Pattison says that Calvinism saved Europe. It is thus no wonder that your Declaration of Independence was called in England "the Presbyterian Rebellion" and that Horace Walpole then intimated in the British Parliament that "Cousin America had run off with a Presbyterian Parson".

These impressive testimonials prove that religious and civil liberty are twins, and that religious liberty is the first born, and the maker of heroic men.

Your Seminary has always taught that the church of the New Testament is a complete spiritual republic, the freest society under heaven, the parent and guardian of liberty and order. Presbyterianism is republicanism applied to the Church and republicanism is Presbyterianism applied to the State. George Buchanan, the first moderator of the Church of Scotland, and Samuel Rutherford in his "Lex Rex" expounded, almost three hundred years ago, the very principles which lie at the foundation of our government and yours. These principles teach us "to honour all men", and to foster that love of liberty and resistance to oppression which are native to all noble hearts. They have given its deathblow to mediaeval feudalism.

Within the last four months one-fourth of mankind has avowedly adopted your government as their model. This is surely one of the most momentous events of modern history. By and by the Chinese may discover how much they owe to Princeton and Scotland.

PRINCETON THEOLOGICAL SEMINARY

THE EVOLUTION OF GOVERNMENT

Surely the most astounding marvel in the evolution of government is the fact that in the heart of the cruellest military despotism, the apostles planted a commonwealth of souls, a perfect republic, which the ingenuity of nineteen centuries has not improved. This was done on behalf of a society which embraced many slaves, and when the greatest sages taught that slaves had neither souls nor civic rights. Moreover this new society created, even in slaves, the sense of manhood and freedom and the virtues without which no republic can truly prosper. Here, at least, the church is not behind the age. In this region the future can never excel the past.

These facts are a most impressive illustration of the widespread civil and social benefits which accompany and flow from a living Christian faith.

THE SCOTCH AND THE SCOTO-IRISH

I feel tempted to quote the recent testimony of your ambassador to our country, the Honourable Whitelaw Reid, in praise of the Scot and the Ulster Scot. He said in Edinburgh, "It was the perfervid Scot that sent the flame for independence through every colony on the continent, never from that hour to die out." Of the fifty-six men who framed the Declaration of Independence eleven were of Scottish descent. When they hesitated, Dr. Witherspoon, a genuine Scot, persuaded them to sign it. Of the college-bred men in the Convention one-half were Scots or Scoto-Irish. Alexander Hamilton, your Alexander the Great, the framer of your constitution, was the son of a Scot. The Scottish race supplied three of the four members of Washington's first Cabinet, two-thirds of his governors of States, and also eleven of your first twenty-five presidents. Their influence was out of all proportion to their numbers. These facts justify Dorner, the German theologian, in saying that Presbyterianism has been very successful in training men in patriotism, citizenship and the duties of public life.

Moreover the church-doctrine of your Princeton school is in complete harmony with the teaching of Jesus Christ and His apostles. We are thus the real Catholics. We do not need Christ's vicar as Christ Himself is with us. The apostolic church had no room for any official caste of so-called priests. Our orders are for order only. We are persuaded that as there is only one God, so there is only one Mediator between God and men. We rejoice in the inspiring truth that all the faithful are priests unto God. This divine democracy secures the noblest of all aristocracies, the aristocracy of Christian character and service, and it teaches us not to overvalue the aristocracy of birth, of wealth, or of intellect. It reminds us that the king and the beggar are made of the same clay and that, when under the power of God's grace, they equally bear the same divine stamp and superscription, and are all united in a sacred brotherhood.

We may thus congratulate ourselves that our Presbyterianism is in thorough accord with the aspirations after liberty and unity in all parts of the world, and that it can live and thrive amid the most diverse national conditions. A colonial statesman said lately that it stands well the test of pioneering. The secretary of the Pan-Presbyterian Alliance reports that Presbyterianism has about one hundred millions of adherents, and that they speak in one hundred and eighty languages.

CALVINISM

Princeton has always been one of the chief strongholds of Calvinism. As we call no man master, we may justly regret the habitual use of Calvin's name in this connection, but it now seems unavoidable. Reformation divinity is often called Calvinism, but injuriously, for it claims to be simply the divinity of the New Testament. It professes to explain God's plan so far as He has revealed it to us. Revelation, however, leaves us with a large margin of mystery. It was Calvin's sole aim fairly to interpret at once the Bible and Christian experience. He offers us, not a philosophy, but the creed of one who looks at all things under the aspect of eternity, who has been overmastered quite by Christ as his Teacher, Redeemer and Lord, and who cherishes a noble fear lest he should ever think meanly of God. His theology is broad-based upon the Scriptures, and its keynote is in these words, "Man's chief end is to glorify God and to enjoy Him forever". It thus does justice to the nobility of man as made by God and for God, and as capable of being re-made by the Spirit of God.

Utterly dependent on God for every breath we draw and every morsel of bread we eat, are we to believe that we are less dependent on Him for the life of the soul? The sovereignty of God is the sovereignty of a Father, not the capriciousness of an eastern despot. It is the love that will not let go. Moreover, grace is also sovereign because of its exceeding and unsearchable riches. With God, the past, present and future are contemporaneous:

they are as an ever present now. He "will have all men to be saved", and we may be perfectly sure that His eternal decrees are not at strife with that will.

OUR INTELLECTUAL DIFFICULTIES

The greatest of all problems is to explain how the divine and human wills can combine and co-operate. But this problem does not confront us only or chiefly in the domain of theology. Sir William Hamilton, the famous professor of Logic in Edinburgh, often told us that no difficulty of this sort emerges in theology which had not previously emerged in philosophy, and that we could apprehend with certainty many things which we could not comprehend. Historians of modern thought are telling us that idealists, materialists, moral philosophers and metaphysicians are now more disposed than formerly to confess their failure to reconcile natural necessity and moral freedom, though they know both to be real. They have here what they call an irreconcilable antinomy. A great thinker says, "All theory is against the freedom of the will, and all experience is for it". Freewill itself is an inexplicable miracle. Freewill and predestination form an arc the top of which lies beyond our ken. We believe that the two sides meet somewhere, and we may also believe that they are wisest who are as little anxious to reconcile them as Paul was. Theology has neither created nor increased these unescapable difficulties. They all lead up to the problem of the permission of evil in God's world, and its enticing power—a stubborn fact over which men have brooded since thinking began, and brooded in vain.

PRINCETON THEOLOGICAL SEMINARY

DR. CHARLES HODGE

I mention Dr. Charles Hodge, as in my student days he was the best known in Scotland of your professors. Forty-five years ago, in company with Dr. Patrick Fairbairn and Dr. John Hall, then of Dublin, I visited Princeton and spent a whole day with Dr. Charles Hodge. I may almost claim to be an alumnus of Princeton, for in my youth I read and margin-marked the three encyclopaedic volumes of his pellucid "Systematic Theology". He has done much to remove objections against our creed, and to propitiate the objectors. He loved pacific more than polemic divinity. The salvation of all children dying in infancy was one of his "oft recurring fervours". Believing that, in the theology of the heart and in their devotions, all sincere Christians are one, it was a joy to him to minimise, so far as he could, the differences and to maximise the agreements among them. He gladly admits that the evangelical Calvinist and the evangelical Arminian are usually one when they pray and praise and preach, and two only when they dispute. His son, Dr. A. A. Hodge, at the close of his "Evangelical Theology", maintains that Calvin alone does full justice to the godward and the manward sides of the truth, but he adds, "The difference between the best of Calvinists and Arminians is one of emphasis rather than of essential principle. Each is the complement of the other. They together give origin to the blended strain from which issues the perfect music which utters the perfect truth". Your Whittier happily describes such a situation when he says,

"To differ is not crime;
The varying bells make up the perfect chime."

The theological pendulum keeps swinging between God's sovereignty and man's responsibility. He who begins with God will incline to Calvinism, and he who begins with man will incline to Arminianism. Arminians would say that man is saved by the human will and the divine: we would say that he is saved by the divine will and the human. But we cannot hope to explain exactly where and how the spirit of God and man's spirit meet. John Newton used to say, "I am considered an Arminian among high Calvinists, and a Calvinist among strenuous Arminians". He concluded that he must therefore be near the centre of revealed truth.

THE DECLARATORY ACTS

Your Church and ours have recently made earnest efforts to remove regrettable impressions concerning the implications or supposed implications of our creed, and to bring it into greater and more obvious harmony with the proportions of truth in the Bible. We both believe that no mere human confession can be accepted as final and permanent. To your Confession of Faith you have accordingly added two chapters and a declaratory statement. Our Declaratory Acts are in substantial agreement with yours. They set forth the love of God—Father, Son and Holy Spirit—to all mankind, God's gift of His Son to be the propitiation for the sins of the whole world, and a salvation sufficient for all, adapted to all, and freely offered to all. These explanations exclude every view that would hamper any one in urging the general offer of the gospel. We rejoice together in the revealed things which belong to us and to our children for ever, while we pause in reverential silence before the secret things which belong to the Lord our God. Assured that the veil over the future has been woven by the hand of love and leaving all these deep mysteries to the justice and mercy of God, we are thankful to have light enough to guide our feet, while there is darkness enough to exercise our faith. We frankly recognise that we must often be content with saying, "I do not know; shall not the judge of all the earth do right?" These Declaratory Acts have added to the many evergrowing streams of tendency which are now making for the union of all the evangelical Churches.

If, in some minds, the idea still lingers that our Calvinistic creed fosters gloom and fetters the evangel, let us appeal to the facts. At the close of the eighth chapter of his Epistle to the Romans, Paul recites his creed. He emphasises God's foreknowledge, predestination, effectual calling, election, and the final perseverance of the saints, and he closes with his most triumphant "Hallelujah Chorus." The explanation is that these high doctrines are our Zion's palaces and bulwarks, that God is known in them for a refuge, that they are ever a palisade around the fold and never a barricade in front of the door, and that, by making grace greater and surer, they help to evangelise the heart and life. There must be some strange mistake when these themes terrify.

Need I enumerate the names of some of the evangelists who have accepted this side of revealed truth as frankly as John Calvin did? Among them are John Bunyan, your President Davies, President Jonathan Edwards, Brainerd, Elliot, Nettleton, Whitefield, Chalmers, McCheyne, William Burns, Spurgeon and D. L. Moody. Did their theology impoverish their evangelism? Has not John Owen said, "God doth not take it well to be limited in anything, least of all in His grace"? Has not an old evangelist of this school written, "There is mercy enough in God, merit enough in Christ, power enough in the Spirit, scope enough in the promises, and room enough in heaven for thee"?

We are often told that ours is a transition period of feeble convictions, many concessions, and manifold self-indulgences. Writers of many schools of thought—Froude, for example—tell us that Calvinism, beyond every other creed, has been the mother and nurse of heroic men and women. Do we not need to-day a large infusion of it to put iron into our blood and to fortify ourselves against the subtle influences which threaten to rob us of many of the noblest fruits of the Christian faith?

THE STORY OF YOUR SEMINARY

It has been a veritable benediction to me to read the lives of Archibald Alexander, Samuel Miller, and Charles Hodge, your three mighties, who were all cast in the amplest moulds of nature and grace. Might not one of the products of this centenary be a brief popular biography of these three Greathearts? It would surely enrich the lives of your students to have their souls and imaginations amply furnished with such beautiful and inspiring models. My acquaintance with their careers lessened my surprise when I read that upwards of one half of those whose names are in the American "Who's Who?" have been reared in clerical homes. With peculiar satisfaction I note that several of your leaders have been the founders of large Levitical families. Some say that their creed was too stern, but it was a life as well as a creed, and it blossomed and brought forth fruits.

PRINCETON THEOLOGICAL SEMINARY

The doctrines of grace created in them the graces of our holy religion. The nobleness of their lives has had a supreme reward, for it gained the loyalty of their children, their grand-children, and their great-grand-children. The beauty of the Lord our God was upon them; and your programmes, this audience, this palatial Hall and the many academic buildings around declare how God has established the work of their hands.

As we were impressively reminded yesterday, Princeton has also been a nursery of great missionaries. Many of your students have had a large share in home mission enterprises. Two of them were the founders of the "World's Student Christian Federation", while over four hundred have devoted themselves to the work of Christ in non-Christian lands, and God has granted exceptional success to many of them. The genius of this place has always fostered missionary and evangelistic zeal.

THE CHIEF NEEDS OF OUR AGE

We seem to have greater discouragements and greater encouragements than ever before. Modern life is growing more intense in good and evil. But it is best to go over the ridge at once and pitch our tent in the sunshine. May we not regard the World Missionary Conference held in Edinburgh in June 1910 as at once a most impressive exhibition of the triumphs of the gospel beyond any or all of the Oecumenical councils of the early church, and also as an inspiring summons to the mighty work of evangelising the whole world? Great enthusiasm has been evoked by the Tercentenary of the authorised English Bible, and its amazing and evergrowing circulation. Then, practical sympathy with the struggling millions is one of the most commanding features of the twentieth century. May we not hail this as the birth time of a marvellous era in which the people of America and Great Britain shall for ever renounce war as a means of settling disputes, and set the whole world a crowning example of peace on earth and goodwill to men? This sacred cause will be greatly promoted by the arrangements already made for celebrating, on Christmas Eve 1914, the Anglo-American Peace Centenary. No war can be a foreign war to us as all men are our brothers. For all these hopeful signs of the times, let us thank God and take courage. Ours is a storm-tossed age, but the ever-living Master is with His disciples in the ship. What we should dread most is not an agitated church, but a becalmed church. Some are advising us to throw over a part of the cargo, but that would not help us to weather the storm.

Surely, too, the competition for souls is keener than ever, keener even than the competition for gold. Our age demands from the preacher an unhesitating and authoritative message, intense reality, thorough earnestness and a ceaseless desire to reveal the supreme claims of Christ and the manifold winsomeness and gladness of Christian service. While, in a largely secular age, so many themes are clamouring for recognition in the pulpit, it is not always easy for the preacher to put first things first, and rigidly to exclude those alien subjects which drain his energies into side channels and weaken the sense of what is vital. We must remember that Christianity requires perpetual propagation to attest its divine origin. Unless it conquers the world anew in every age, the church must be the affair of one generation only. Hence the preacher must be ever doing the work of an evangelist and fostering the passion for souls. Let us be fully assured that deliverance will never come to us by putting social gospels and social services in place of the evangel of Jesus Christ. Nothing can mend the world but what mends the spirits of men. In my youth, I spent unforgettable days among the worst of our outcasts. I soon discovered that those who expected, attempted and achieved great things among them were saturated with the apostolic faith, and cherished the sacred mission hunger, rescuing zeal and creative spiritual power. Some of them had a real genius for winning souls, and refused to despair of any. I believe that, under heaven, there are no more beautiful and satisfying spectacles than those of men, women and children once sunk in vice, but now uplifted by the grace of God, clothed and in their right mind, and surrounded with all the fruits of prosperous industry. These modern miracles add a new charm to life, for by them the greatest Christians are made out of what seems the poorest human stuff. They assure us that the gospel has lost none of its ancient power and that the Acts of the Apostles has not yet been rounded with its final Amen. All social reformers should study these words of our Lord, "Seek ye first the kingdom of God and his righteousness, and all these things shall be added unto you"—given into the bargain as surprising industrial, civil and social by-products, given as a generous bonus of earthly goods. Not otherwise can the fallen find a place in the sun.

Many in Scotland deeply feel the need of a great revival of religion. They are conferring about it in the hope of discovering the hindrances and having them removed. They are recalling several fruitful revivals in our land, and specially the revival which visited many parts of your country about fifty years ago, and kindled sacred fires in Ireland and Scotland. Many among us are brooding over the promises concerning the Holy Ghost whom God hath given to them that obey Him. God grant a fresh baptism of power to your Church and to ours.

I have attended all the gatherings of this great Festival except the first. I was privileged to address the students of the University while you were seated at the Lord's table. I have been deeply moved by the words spoken here, by the sacred songs sung, by the prayers offered, by the audiences, and by the spiritual atmosphere. Such experiences should help to make our service more devoted and more fruitful in the coming days.

Reverend Fathers and Brethren, with all my heart I thank you for your generous kindness to me as the representative of the United Free Church of Scotland. It will give me joy to report the inspiring tokens of manifold success amid which your venerable Seminary is closing its first century of Christian service. It is our heart's desire and prayer that your School of the Prophets may be the generous mother of a growing band of consecrated and gifted men who, by the grace of God, shall do exploits in establishing and extending the Kingdom of our Lord and Saviour Jesus Christ.

Peace, the very peace of God, be within your walls and prosperity within your palaces. For my brethren and companions' sakes, I will now say, Peace be within you.

IRISH AND AMERICAN PRESBYTERIANISM

ADDRESS

BY THE RIGHT REVEREND JOHN MACMILLAN, B.A., D.D.
Minister of the Cooke Centenary Church, Belfast
Moderator of the General Assembly of the Presbyterian Church
in Ireland

Mr. President:

THREE centuries ago, the confiscated lands of Ulster presented an opportunity for the peaceable settlement of that province and opened a door of refuge for the people of Scotland who were suffering under the intolerance of James I, the chief article of whose new creed was, "No Bishop, no King," and whose unkinglike declaration was set forth in the solemn vow, "I will make them conform or I will harry them out of the land."

The settlers brought with them their industry, their thrift and their faith; and they were followed by scholarly and godly ministers like Edward Brice, Robert Blair, Robert Cunningham, James Glendinning, John Livingston, James Hamilton, John Howe, Josias Welsh, George Dunbar, and Andrew Stewart, whose apostolic patience and heroism have never been surpassed in the history of the Church of Christ.

Among the settlers were adventurers of various degrees of moral declension, and fugitives from justice as well as law; until it came to be a proverb applied to the most graceless and hopeless in the Lowlands, "Ireland will be his hinder end." That "end" would have been disastrous indeed, had the colonists been left to the mercy of the "careless men" who desired only their own gain, and the conservation of their own power; but the Lord visited them in His "admirable mercy" by giving them ministers of their own, "eminent for birth, education and parts," whose labours resulted in revival, transformed lives and fruit unto holiness. These ministers have won for themselves the honour of being the founders of the Irish Presbyterian Church; and their line has gone through all the earth, and their word unto the end of the world.

In the course of one century, there were organised in Ulster eleven Presbyteries and one hundred and forty-one congregations. The waste places were reclaimed, the primeval forests disappeared, the last wolf was put out of the way, lint was in the bell, the bleach-greens were covered with fair linen clean and white, the whirr of the spinning-wheel and the click of the loom sounded in almost every dwelling; and the desert rejoiced and blossomed as the rose.

Ballymena, the modern Bangor, Coleraine, Comber, the modern Londonderry, Newtownards, Portaferry, and many other centres of industry were created; and Belfast, which in 1649 was denounced by Milton as "a barbarous nook in Ireland", had started on its way to becoming Ireland's commercial capital, with a population now approaching half-a-million souls.

To these men the Bible was statute book and library. The Psalter, with the Paraphrases, was their song-book at work and worship; and they found expressed in its strong and rugged verse all the growing enrichment of their spiritual experience. It was stored in the memory against the cloudy and dark day, the lonely vigil, and the last scene of all. I could take you to places on their farms where they were accustomed to sing and pray, as they herded their cattle or sought momentary relief from their toil. The strains of Martyrdom, and Elgin, and Coleshill, and Devizes, linger still among their valleys and hills.

The Lord's Day was the great day of the week. On it "they went out", according to their own phrase, to meet their neighbours and the public; and, above all, to meet Him whom their souls loved, and who had given the promise of His presence to the two or three gathered together in His name—and at times it was long before the after-glow on their faces melted into the light of common day.

The Sacrament of the Lord's Supper was the central ordinance of their faith, and its observance the chief event of the year. It was preceded by two days of fasting and prayer, and succeeded by a solemn thanksgiving and consecration; whilst the service of the day itself began in the early morning, and, with a brief intermission, closed at nightfall. There were occasions when scenes occurred like those which took place at the Kirk of Shotts under the preaching of their own John Livingston in 1630, when five hundred were lifted into a new or a higher life; or like those enacted in the Covenanting times, when, on the far-off moor or in some amphitheatre among the lonely hills, outed ministers broke the bread of life and thousands of communicants lifted to their lips the consecrated elements and returned to their home or to their hiding, not fearing the wrath of man because they had seen the face of God.

The school, which was regarded as being scarcely less important than the church, consisted of four walls, sometimes of mud and sometimes of masonry, a thatched roof, small windows as often as not unglazed, an earthen floor, logs in the rough from the neighbouring bog to serve for seats, and a fire which burned or smoked in the centre of the room, the smoke escaping through an opening in the roof, or else lingering to create a semi-opaque atmosphere, not uncongenial to those boys who were bent on idleness or full of fun. The master was often arrayed in a long black coat, tow-wig, horn-spectacles, and armed with a hazel rod.

> "Full well they laughed with counterfeited glee
> At all his jokes, for many a joke had he;
> Full well the busy whisper circling round
> Conveyed the dismal tidings when he frowned."

And yet he taught the boys to read and write and cast accounts; and introduced the more ambitious among them to Cicero and Caesar, to Horace and Homer, and prepared them for the university. Where the schoolmistress reigned, she patiently taught the A B C, promoted her pupils to the Book of Proverbs, the Gospels, and the Shorter Catechism; and, when the girls had finished their samplers, their scholastic education was completed.

The home was humble, consisting of "but and ben" and added accommodation to suit growing domestic need. The inmates aimed at making it a "little church" and a "seminary of piety," instinctively acting on the principle that the domestic hearth-stone was the corner-stone of the State.

Of course, there were other homes of much larger dimensions, equipped with all the comforts procurable at that period; but they were occupied by those persons to whom special grants of lands had been made at a merely nominal figure, and who "undertook" responsibility for the settlement of the surrounding areas. These landowners, however, professed the same faith as did the people whom they subsequently designated their "tenants", and ordered their daily lives according to the same religious principles.

Candidates for the ministry were obliged to pursue a regular academic and subsequently a regular theological course, when such a requirement implied long and perilous journeys to Glasgow and Edinburgh or Amsterdam; for Trinity College, Dublin, in contravention of the purpose of its founder, was closed against them. Students were exhorted to remain at the university for "laureation" and some were advised to betake themselves to "a way of living" other than the ministry on account of lack of learning and of natural capacity—and laggards profited from such salutary advice. When it became impracticable for all candidates to study abroad, a "School of Philosophy" was established at home; and two pastors were appointed to give instruction, one in Hebrew and the other in Greek, each to receive the modest remuneration of £10 per annum. All ministers were exhorted by the Synod to spare no pains in preparing for their pulpit prayers and sermons; in acquiring a working knowledge of Hebrew and Greek, of the chief controversies of Divinity, of the English Bible—so that its language might freely flow from their lips; and of the English tongue so that they might speak in a plain unaffected style and "accommodate their addresses to the understanding of the people." The Rev. Matthew Clark of Kilrea, who acted a soldier's part during the siege of Londonderry, and who afterwards became minister of the town of that name on this side of the Atlantic, preaching from the words of the Apostle—"I can do all things", thus began—"Aye, can you, Paul? I'll bet a dollar on that!", as he placed a Spanish dollar upon the Bible. Then with a look of surprise he continued, "Stop, let us see what else Paul says—'I can do all things through Christ who strengtheneth me'. Aye, so can I, Paul; I withdraw my bet": and he carefully replaced the money in his pocket, after he had succeeded in arresting the attention of his audience.

During my year of office, I have conducted services in a church in memory of a dear friend in the ministry whose rural parish had been lacking in educational advantages, and from whose study there went forth, without prescribed fee or reward, fifteen young men to the university and to professional life. One of my friend's predecessors was Dr. Samuel Edgar, who founded the "Academy", in which James Thomson, the father of Lord Kelvin, was a pupil and afterwards a teacher, and from which forty youths proceeded to college and to ordination. I have done duty in a church in the city of Armagh, the son of whose first minister was Francis Hutcheson. As probationer, Francis was persuaded to relieve his father on a Sabbath during the temporary indisposition of the latter; but he broke down so completely in the devotional service that the worshippers were dismissed a couple of hours in advance of the accustomed time. He, however, was appointed Professor of Moral Philosophy in the University of Glasgow, had the courage to adjudge the English language an adequate vehicle for instruction—the first preceptor in that institution to do so—and he became the founder of the Scottish School of Philosophy, in which Dr. Thomas Reid, Sir William Hamilton, and Dr. McCosh were subsequently successive master-builders. I do not mean to infer that it is always more easy to become a philosopher than to be an edifying preacher!

The intercourse between Ulster and the mother-country was close and constant. Our people claimed kindred with Patrick Hamilton, and George Wishart, and John Knox, and Alexander Henderson, and Samuel Rutherford, and Margaret Wilson, and Andrew Melville, and Janet Geddes. Melville once said to the king, "Your Majesty, there are two kings and two kingdoms in Scotland: there is king James, the head of the commonwealth, and there is Christ Jesus, the King of the Church, whose subject James is, and of whose kingdom he is not a king, nor a lord, nor a head, but a member." Janet Geddes flung her stool at the head of the minister who, at the bidding of Laud, proceeded to read from an enforced liturgy, with these indignant words, "Fause loon, do you say Mass at my lug?" In the county of Down, a strong-minded woman was brought before the Downpatrick Court of Assize for what was considered a most heinous offence—interfering with the official robes of the new minister sent by the Bishop to take the place of her own, now silenced and forbidden to exercise his ministry. She admitted the accuracy of the charge, and suiting the action to the word, made confession, "These two hands pulled the white shirt over his head." Carlyle declares that the war precipitated by Janet Geddes was far more glorious than that precipitated by Helen of Troy. Macaulay traces English liberty to Janet's action. Henry Grattan describes "the Presbyterian religion as the mother of the free constitution of England." John Richard Green affirms that "it saved Scotland from a civil and religious despotism and in saving Scotland, it saved English liberty as well." It certainly saved Ulster, and in saving Ulster, it saved more than Ulster—as we shall see.

It may be asked in what way, and to what degree is the Ulster Scot superior to the mere Scot? The late President McKinley declared that the coming of the Scot to Ulster marked an epoch in the world's civilization. Last November, Lord Rosebery, on the occasion of his presiding at a lecture delivered in Edinburgh by His Excellency, the Ambassador of the United States, said that he loved Highlanders and he loved Lowlanders, but when he came to that branch of the Scottish race which had been grafted on to the Ulster stem, he took off his hat in veneration and awe!

When we came to Ulster, we were returning to our own, to the Scotia Major of the ancient world; to the land of Cormac, and Patrick, and Columcille, and Columbanus, and Gallus, and Killian, and John Scotus Erigena, and Pelagius, and Richard Fitzralph; we began to think with pride of the great schools of Bangor, and Clonard, and Clonmacnoise, and Durrow, and Kildare, and Derry, and Movilla, and of the achievements of their alumni at Iona, Lindisfarne, Burgundy, Bobbio and St. Gall, and of all the traditions which clustered round the *insula sanctorum et doctorum Europae* of the early Christian centuries. We were brought into contact with a quick-witted, warm-hearted people, possessed of the *perfervidum ingenium Scotorum,* which could appreciate a joke without the necessity of the proverbial surgical operation.

We had a very long and a very severe struggle for toleration—even for existence. A most determined effort was put forth to break our fathers' spirit, and to quench our fathers' faith. If Scotland had Claverhouse, and Laud, and Charles, and James, we had Laud and Claverhouse in imagination; and we had Charles, and James, and Tyrconnell, and Wentworth, and Phelim O'Neill, and Lord Donegal, and the Anglican prelates of that time. We became uncompromisingly Protestant and as uncompromisingly Presbyterian, which—with its franchise and freedom of the Kingdom of God enjoyed by women as well as men—is the strongest and most democratic form of Protestantism; and we became whole-hearted Evangelicals, which are the highest type of Presbyterians, and supply the *raison d'être* of Protestantism. Driven back upon the sublime truth that behind all things we see, changeless amid things which change, evolving slowly His own vast designs, making all things—the prosperous and the adverse—to work together for good to them that love Him, is a living God, with all the attributes of a divine personality—a quick eye, a warm heart, and a long arm, our people became intensely Calvinistic, and strengthened themselves by saying or singing such words as these:—

"Art thou afraid His power shall fail
   When comes thine evil day?
Or can an all-creating arm
   Grow weary or decay?
Supreme in wisdom as in power
   The Rock of Ages stands;
Though Him thou canst not see nor trace
   The working of His hands."

There were three periods of persecution to which our people were subjected and which culminated respectively in the Black Oath under Charles I, the Act of Uniformity under Charles II, and the Sacramental Test Act under Queen Anne.

Every person over sixteen years of age was commanded to take the Black Oath, by which he renounced the Covenants and swore a *carte blanche* allegiance to the king, no matter what the king might enjoin for the future in Church or State. Multitudes of Presbyterians, against whom the Oath was chiefly or entirely directed, refused to comply, and the most cruel sufferings were inflicted upon them. As an instance, we take the case of Henry Stewart, who—with his wife, his two daughters and his man-servant—was arrested, conveyed to Dublin, tried in the Court of Star Chamber, in which the form and spirit of justice were alike ignored, fined in the sum of £16,000, and cast into prison until the uttermost farthing would be paid—because he had the courage to honour his conscience as his king.

At first, the Church, as by law established, was comprehensive enough to admit the ministers from Scotland to her pulpits and in the case of an ordination, the Bishop joined with the other presbyters present in prayer, and the laying on of hands: but after the Act of Uniformity came into force, all ministers in Ulster were required to submit to Episcopal ordination or to abandon their position in the Church. Of all the ministers in the Synod, only seven submitted to such conditions. In a single day, Jeremy Taylor, who wrote on the "Liberty of Prophesying", silenced thirty-six of the best ministers of Down, whose ministry had been accompanied by revivals and other unmistakable signs that the Lord had been working with them, confirming the word by signs following. In a single year, sixty-four ministers went forth, not knowing whither they went.

In 1704, after the siege of Londonderry, defended by Presbyterians, who were at the lowest calculation fifteen to one of all other Protestants within the walls of the city, which was fortified and inspired by Presbyterian ministers at a time when Bishops denounced the impiety of taking up arms against the "Lord's Anointed", and changed their public prayers every week and almost every day as the omens seemed to indicate the final issue of the struggle; after the battle of the Boyne, at which —according to Hallam—the British constitution was saved, and which was rendered possible by the previous stand made at Londonderry; the Sacramental Test Act came into operation, according to which it was made necessary for every person holding office to receive the Sacrament of the Lord's Supper in the Episcopal Church or else demit his dignity. Our people had too high an estimate of the spiritual significance and aim of the Sacrament to pervert its meaning and to degrade its divine institution; and they were too brave to deny their fathers' faith. Of the twelve aldermen in Londonderry, ten were Presbyterian, and of the thirteen burgesses in Belfast, nine adhered to the same faith; and every one of these resigned his office rather than be false to his convictions. Adam Murray, the hero of the siege, was compelled to part company with the horse which had been his faithful servant and fellow-soldier during that period of agony. Presbyterian churches were closed. Jonathan Swift had the bad eminence of nailing up some of them with his own hand. Ministers were outlawed and imprisoned, prohibited from meeting in Presbytery or conducting a service, or performing a marriage ceremony, and were fined £100 for administering the Sacrament of the Lord's Supper; bequests were alienated; the Eighth Commandment was set at nought, the Regium Donum—a Grant made by William III in recognition of services rendered to his cause by Presbyterian ministers and their people—was for the time discontinued; and in the event of a place of worship being allowed to exist, it was situated remote from town or village or in some position so obscure and so inaccessible as but too literally to represent the "Church invisible."

We have an illustration of as pathetic a scene as is unfolded in the pages of civic or national history—"There was a little city and few men within it; and there came a great king against it, and besieged it, and built bulwarks against it. Now there was found in it a poor wise man and he by his wisdom delivered the city. Yet no man remembered that same poor man. Then said I, Wisdom is better than strength". For though Wisdom is despised, her day will come if the God of Wisdom reigns.

Almost two centuries ago, a movement was inaugurated as remarkable as any in the history of the human race, as divinely directed as the exodus of the children of Israel from the house of bondage to a good land and a large, where they prepared a faith for mankind and a Saviour for the world. In 1636, a small craft, called the "Eagle Wing" in anticipation of a swift passage, sailed from Groomsport near Belfast with one hundred and fifty passengers—the flower of Ulster's enterprise and faith. After proceeding twelve hundred miles in the direction of New England, she was driven back to Carrickfergus Bay; the distressed sufferers, who, for two months had been exposed to most trying and perilous experiences, assuredly gathering that the way out of Ireland had not yet been made manifest. Ireland still needed them, and there they learned to suffer and be strong. When the young eagles are ready to fly, the nest will be so stirred up that they shall be thrust out of it, and compelled to essay the larger world of sun and sky by the use of wings, of whose existence they have not dreamed as yet.

In 1718 five ships left Belfast carrying one thousand persons. Sometimes an entire congregation emigrated, sometimes as many as seven congregations with their ministers. During a lengthened period of the eighteenth century an average of twelve thousand a year left the land of their fathers for the land of the free. Men sold their household goods to realize their passage money, and those who had no money mortgaged their freedom and their earnings for four years in advance. They braved the winds and the waves, carrying with them the blood, and brains, and youth, and strength, and skill of Ulster to help to make your land what it is today. Their church they valued above all earthly things and after their church, in point of worth, came their disjunction-certificates, which they valued as a traveller values his passport or a student his parchment. Last month, I conducted the service in a church, the senior minister of which had given sixty years of service to one parish. He informed me that at the beginning of his ministry seventeen families left in one day; but not until the Communion season had come round and they had pledged themselves anew to their Lord and to one another, and had sung the Paraphrase:—

> "I know that safe with Him remains,
>   Protected by His power,
> What I've committed to His trust,
>   Till the decisive hour.

Then will He own His servant's name
Before His Father's face,
And in the new Jerusalem
Appoint my soul a place."

After the benediction, the disjunction-certificates were tendered to the brethren and sisters, who had worshipped for the last time in the sanctuary which to them had been the dearest spot on earth; and on the following day, they were convoyed to the sea by their neighbours and their pastor, who commended them to the care of Heaven. When men like these went forth, then or in earlier days, to New Jersey, Pennsylvania, Maryland, Virginia, Ohio, or the Carolinas, territories unshadowed by the ecclesiastical rule which had embittered their lives on the other side of the ocean, they proceeded to build their log-dwellings and their log-sanctuaries, and to sing the Lord's song in a strange land; and as they sang it, the land ceased to be strange, for they recognised it as the Lord's land, which they proceeded to claim for Him.

In 1776, one-third of the population of Pennsylvania was Ulster-Scot, and one-third of the people of the Colonies was of kindred origin. At the Revolution considerably more than half a million of our people had made their home here; their descendants in this country are probably ten times more numerous than all the Presbyterians in Ireland at the present day, and the tide of emigration is still flowing.

In 1683, Francis Makemie, a native of the County of Donegal, who at the age of fifteen had been the subject of a work of grace, who was a graduate of the University of Glasgow and a licentiate of the Old Laggan Presbytery, responded in his twenty-fifth year to a call for help addressed to that Presbytery by Judge William Stevens of Rehoboth on the banks of the Pocomoke in Maryland. Makemie strengthened the scattered community by his definite Westminster teaching, organised them into the Presbytery of Philadelphia in 1706, prepared for the formation of the first Synod ten years later, and in 1789 for that of the General Assembly, of which John Rodgers, his compatriot, was Moderator. Makemie died at the age of fifty, exhausted by labours prosecuted with the zeal of an apostle and the widened outlook of a statesman; for with patriotic eye he surveyed this land from Barbadoes to Boston, declared that it was "a country capable of superlative improvement", spent his strength to accomplish that end, with the result that he has made every subsequent Presbyterian and American his debtor. He was not only exhausted on account of his unremitting labours, his health suffered not a little from persecution and imprisonment. The then Governor of New York betrayed his spirit of hostility towards this heroic pioneer, who had dared to proclaim the Evangel within his jurisdiction, by describing him to his official correspondents in London as "a jack-of-all-trades, a preacher, a doctor-of-physic, a merchant, a counsellor-at-law, and which is worst of all, a disturber of governments." He died in 1708; and, a century after, a statue of heroic size was erected over his last resting place in Virginia by the grateful Church which claims him as her earthly founder. It is interesting to observe that his daughter was spared to see the establishment of that civil and religious liberty, for which he suffered and strove.

When Makemie arrived at Rehoboth—which is, being interpreted, "There is room"—he was surprised and delighted to discover William Trail, who had formerly been the clerk of the Laggan Presbytery, who was pursuing quiet pastoral work in the peninsula between

Chesapeake and Delaware Bays, and who subsequently became his successor in the ministry of the mother church of the United States. As soon as the first Presbytery was constituted, Makemie ordained John Boyd, whose period of earthly service came to a close in the same year as his own, and whose weather-beaten monument, with its striking inscription, stands over against the replica of his own statue in the Witherspoon Building, Philadelphia. He also brought from the Old Country, on one of his visits thereto, George McNish and John Hampton to recruit the slowly growing band of the heralds of the Cross on this side of the ocean.

In 1716, William Tennent, a native of the county of Antrim, a graduate of the University of Edinburgh, a minister of the Episcopal Church, and son-in-law of the Rev. Gilbert Kennedy, one of our own most distinguished ministers, applied to the Presbytery of Philadelphia for admission as a member, pleading that Arminian doctrine and ceremonial worship and the government of the Church in which he had been ordained had "affected his conscience so that he could no longer abide therein". On being received by the Presbytery, he made grateful reply in a speech in the Latin tongue, elegantly composed and earnestly spoken. Like his Master, Tennent drew young men unto him; blessed the Church of his adoption with his gifts and his devotion; founded "Log College" at Neshaminy, which Whitefield declared more closely resembled an ancient "School of the Prophets" than anything he had ever seen, and which constituted its founder "the Father of Presbyterian Colleges and Theological Seminaries in America."

Webster, in his "History of the Presbyterian Church

in America, from its origin till the year 1760," gives the biographies of fifty-five ministers of Ulster birth or origin, more than one-fourth of the entire number serving the Church during that period. It is admitted that these men exercised a profound influence, both doctrinal and constitutional, on the growth and development of the infant Church. The Adopting Act of 1729, by which the Westminster Confession of Faith and the Catechisms were accepted as a confession of the Synod's faith, brought the American Church into line with the Synod of Ulster and with the mother Church of Scotland. Webster, writing in the middle of the last century, declares that Ulster has continued for one hundred and fifty years to be "the great nursery" of the American Presbyterian Church. When I think of John Glendy, who was the minister of the church of my boyhood, who fled from Ireland in the tragic days of 1798, who became successively chaplain of the United States Congress and of the United States Senate, and a minister of great eloquence and power; of the incomparable John Hall, who came to New York in 1867 and exercised a unique influence over the American Continent, of which every Irish Presbyterian was so justly proud; and of the men who in Princeton have greeted me as a fellow-countryman and who are rendering such splendid service in this vast and high field, I am convinced that the ministerial succession is still being well maintained.

The people of Ireland did not lose interest in their kinsmen across the sea, nor did their kinsmen forget their friends in the old home. In 1754, the Rev. Gilbert Tennent, son of the founder of "Log College," presented to the Synod of Ulster a petition from the Synod of New York and the Trustees of the College of New Jersey, appealing for financial help for that recently established seat of learning. The Synod of Ulster was unanimous in granting a collection, which resulted in £500. In 1760, an address from the Corporation of Philadelphia and that of New York was presented to the Synod of Ulster, making an appeal on behalf of distressed ministers and their families, and on behalf of members of the Church, held captive by their enemies; and the sum of £412 was contributed.

The Governor of Pennsylvania was recently walking along the banks of the Schuylkill in company with a distinguished British visitor, who remarked that, according to tradition, George Washington was able to throw half-a-crown across the river at its widest point, and who referred the question to the gentleman supposed to be possessed of the local knowledge. The Governor replied that he was not aware of the particular fact, but that he was convinced of the truth of the general principle that half-a-crown would go farther in George Washington's day than in his! So these two sums, a little less than five thousand dollars, would go farther in the middle of the eighteenth century than in the first quarter of the twentieth. America has returned the kindness an hundred fold; for ever since, there has been flowing towards our shores a veritable river of gold, which has gilded and sweetened the intervening waters, and gladdened many an Irish heart and home, north and south and east and west.

We gave one president to the College of New Jersey in the person of Dr. Samuel Finley, an alumnus of "Log College," under whose presidency half the students of Princeton became subjects of a genuine revival. Dr. McCosh was accustomed to say that the human body be-

PRINCETON THEOLOGICAL SEMINARY

came completely changed in the course of every seven years, and, at the end of his first week of years in this land, he declared himself a genuine American. That being so, and as he laboured with conspicuous success in Belfast for seventeen years, I am more than doubly justified in affirming that in him Ulster gave another, and one of her most distinguished presidents, to Princeton. The late President McKinley believed that it would be difficult to find a single faculty, academic or theological, in the United States, which did not include one or more Ulster members. I do not know how many members of the Princeton Faculty can trace their birth or descent to Erin, but I know that for a very long time one Irishman has been a valued member of the Faculty, Dr. George Macloskie, beloved by his many friends in Ireland as he is beloved by you.

To Princeton Theological Seminary, we gave the men who sat at her cradle and nursed her to strength—the Alexanders and the Hodges, whose names are still borne by the living and legible in the places of the dead, and whose form and features are traceable in those who still survive among us; and if there is one name, which more than any other is dear to our ministers and theological professors, it is the name of Princeton. If there is one Church of the Presbyterian order which more than any other loves Princeton theology, it is the Irish Presbyterian Church, called to maintain an immovable position between ritualism and Romanism on the one hand, and rationalism on the other, to uphold the supremacy of Scriptural revelation, and to be loyal to the doctrines of Grace—the *decus et tutamen* of the Church of the living God—without which we should not feel that we had a place in the land or a message for the age.

I find that upwards of one hundred graduates of Irish universities have, for a longer or shorter period, studied theology in Princeton; some of them remaining with you and some returning to us. I am acquainted with a dozen of our ministers and missionaries, whose memories of Princeton are of the most filial and grateful kind, and who look upon her as being to them the birthplace of a larger and more consecrated life. In 1851, John Byers, a son of our Church, graduated from the Seminary, after pursuing his full theological course. He sailed as a missionary to the Far East accompanied by his wife, a daughter of Erin, then in her nineteenth year. After less than a twelvemonth's service, a breakdown in health suggested his return to America, which he was destined never to reach. The extreme kindness received by his young widow from the members of the Church in the United States was to her an abiding inspiration. She returned to her native land with her infant son, now a man of title and distinction in the academic and medical world, to found Victoria College and to achieve a work for the education of women and for the cause of temperance and philanthropy, the far-reaching results of which we can only inadequately and but partially estimate. Our most distinguished exponent of Princeton theology was Dr. Robert Watts, a graduate of the Seminary, who filled the chair of Systematic Theology in the Assembly's College, Belfast, and who revered his preceptors as Saul of Tarsus revered Gamaliel or as his own students revered himself.

For myself, I can never speak of Princeton but with reverence and affection. When a young man leaves the university, filled with a sense of the wonders of ancient literature and civilisation, of the discoveries of modern science and the daring speculations of philosophy, he may fancy there is no additional knowledge to be acquired, may become jealous of the suggestion that there is a faculty as trustworthy as any of those he has been sedulously cultivating, and that there are realities in the Kingdom which cannot be shaken, more enduring and more precious than any of those he has been so anxious to contemplate and appraise. The atmosphere of the Princeton of my day was a revelation to such a student and presented to him theology as the true and undisputed "Queen of the Sciences."

There was Dr. Charles Hodge—*clarum et venerabile nomen*—with his look and his life, the transparency and humility of his nature, his consecrated genius, his wide and deep learning, his unfailing reverence for the Scriptures as the Word of God, his prayers which were the constant communing of his soul with the Eternal, made articulate for the moment and audible in our ears, his talks in the Old Oratory, his chivalrous devotion to the Saviour, and the marvellous manner in which he brought His love and life down into our lives, making us at times hold our breath and enabling us always to realize the truth of the poet's words:—

"And warm, sweet, tender, even yet,
A present help is He;
And faith hath still its Olivet,
And love its Galilee."

There was Dr. W. H. Green, with his profound scholarship, his keen appreciation of the issues at stake, his stern sense of duty and responsibility, his urgency as to the use of opportunities which never would return, his power as a preacher in exposing the sinfulness of sin and discovering the grace which saved from its guilt and power, and the place freely accorded him by scholars of every school of thought, east and west.

There was the beloved Dr. C. W. Hodge, whose lectures hushed his class and frequently made it resemble more a company of boys gathered round a Communion Table than aught else. In addition to these, were the gifted and subtle Dr. A. A. Hodge; the faithful and conscientious Dr. James C. Moffat; that clear thinker and most helpful and practical guide, Dr. A. T. McGill; and the gentle and cultured Dr. Charles A. Aiken. These honoured preceptors made upon my classmates and myself an impression which will not be effaced till the last syllable of recorded time. I feel certain that I ought to submit the tone of high moral and spiritual earnestness on the part of my fellow-students—with their devotion to study, their brotherly kindness, their regularity at morning and evening prayer, their uniform courtesy to the members of the Faculty and to one another, and the harmony which characterized the life of our community—as being among the most formative and beneficent influences of the period, the memory of which is to us all as perfume in the garments.

The prophet in his vision saw a stream issue forth from under the threshold of the house of God, situated on the mountain top. The stream, flowing with deepening and widening volume, became a river dispensing health and plenty along its course; trees growing on its banks, whose fruit was for food and whose leaves were for medicine. It flowed into the Salt Sea, transforming the source of death into a place of life, revealing a second heaven in its depths, and crowding its shores with unwonted scenes of happy human activity. There was life whithersoever the river came. So from this place, there has gone forth a river of Truth, which has blessed three and thirty generations of students, who in turn have been the means of sweetening and sanctifying and comforting the lives of succeeding multitudes of the children of men in almost every nation under the sun.

I should like, before I close, to indicate another service which our people rendered to this Republic. George Canning, one of the most brilliant of British foreign secretaries, clasped hands with Thomas Jefferson across the Atlantic in the bonds of international peace, convinced that Britain and America could stand against the possible coalitions of the world, and declaring as premier, "I called a new world into existence to redress the balance of the old". George Canning only recognised the existence of the new world and induced George IV to do likewise in the King's Speech of 1825; but the Ulster Presbyterians did their part in calling that new world into existence. The National League of Scotland and Ulster prepared the way for the Declaration of Independence. A century after the adoption of the Solemn League and Covenant by Scotland and Ireland, the Rev. Thomas Craighead led in its renewal by his people, who, with uplifted hands, declared their separation from the Crown which had violated the Covenant. The Mecklenburg Convention, which was the outgrowth and embodiment of Craighead's spirit, and which consisted of Ulster men, announced in 1775 the principles of the Declaration of Independence before Jefferson stamped its words with the impress of his genius, or Charles Thompson of Belfast committed it to the handwriting in which it is preserved; before another Ulster man read it to the people, or a third gave to it the wings of the press. In that period of a nation's birthpangs, the Ulster Presbyterians were American; and in their stand they had the sympathy and the powerful moral support of that illustrious Irish statesman, Edmund Burke.

The Declaration of Independence gave hope to those who struggled for justice in Ireland, and the struggle at length was crowned with victory. We have now religious equality. Our Church is protected by the law of the land. Our General Assembly has been visited by the Lord Lieutenant, a ruling elder of the Church of Scotland, and by the Countess of Aberdeen. A goodly number of our ministers have been appointed to act in turn the part of Chaplain to His Excellency. Our Moderator has equal precedence with the Archbishops of the other Churches, and a place is assigned him at State ceremonies. The "barns" in which our fathers worshipped have given way to sanctuaries comely and commodious, and in many instances, to ecclesiastical edifices which are an ornament to the parish and a feature of the landscape. The use of hymns and instrumental aid in public worship is now permitted and is fast becoming the custom, largely through your example. Our Church House, which comprises the various offices of the Church and the Assembly Hall, was opened a few years ago by the Duke of Argyll at a cost of £80,000; and it is the finest building of its kind in Ireland, and among the finest of its kind in the world.

We have a mission field at our door, and we endeavour to approach our fellow-countrymen, not along the lines of controversy, but along those on which we agree, emphasizing the love of God, the Saviour's finished work, the priesthood of believers, and the supremacy of Scripture; and we have reason to believe that such seed thus sown yields fruit—especially when it has the opportunity of germinating and fructifying in the freer atmosphere of this land.

We follow our kindred to the British Dominions beyond the seas by means of our Colonial Mission; we help the Reformed Churches on the Continent of Europe; we maintain a successful Jewish Mission at Hamburg and Damascus, whilst our foreign missionary operations in Kathiawar and Gujarat and especially in Manchuria have been crowned with remarkable success. Our temperance crusade has received unmeasured stimulus from the record of your achievements in this momentous reform. Our Theological Seminaries, or "Colleges" as we designate them, were never better manned. From one of these—that at Belfast, of which Dr. Leitch, one of the greatest masters of New Testament Greek in the United Kingdom, is the president—I bear hearty felicitations; and it is only in a technical sense that I am unable to render a similar service on behalf of Magee College, Londonderry.

We have an Orphan Society which provides for the Church's fatherless or orphan children, an Old Age Fund for the aged, which is available ten years before the Government Pension may be obtained, and every retired minister is secure for life of his manse and at least £100 a year.

It will be easily understood that we have suffered during centuries of persecution through persons and families—unable to brave social ostracism, ambitious to obtain office or emolument, and not unwilling to sweep from their pathway any consideration, however sacred, which blocked their material progress—falling away from their ancestral faith and practically confessing the quixotic nature of their fathers' resistance unto blood by conforming to the State-endowed type of belief and worship, under which their fathers' lives were made bitter. The names of such persons bear witness to the contrast between their fathers' nobler fortitude and their own.

Although year by year, we suffer from emigration, by which we are deprived of the enthusiasm and enterprise of our youngest and strongest, we do not grudge our youth to our Colonies nor to this Republic, which our people regard as almost a second home. Notwithstanding the constant tribute paid by us to the newer countries of the world, the income of our Church from all sources for the year 1910–1911 was double that of forty years ago, and was the largest total ever recorded—amounting to one million five hundred and twenty-three thousand eight hundred dollars. We have been enriched by gifts from our kindred, by bequests for public purposes, by memorials of utility in memory of departed friends, and by the enlarged sympathies and most salutary example of those who return to visit the old land.

Mr. President, there has, of course, been no meeting of our General Assembly since your kind invitation to take part in this Centennial Celebration was extended to me; had there been such a meeting, I should have been commissioned to offer you the most fraternal, or, shall I say, the most maternal congratulations of our Supreme Court. If the Lord spare me to return to the opening of the General Assembly on the third day of June, I shall have nothing to say which will give me greater pleasure in the saying of it than that I witnessed this celebration, met the members of your Faculty, saw five hundred

Alumni assembled to do honour to their *alma mater,* and looked upon the faces of, and exchanged salutations with, as many members of the class of '78 as have found it possible to be present. I congratulate you, Sir, whose name with that of Professor Warfield, is a household word among us, and whom we regard as one of the greatest and most brilliant living defenders of "the faith once delivered to the saints". I not only congratulate you on what you have done, but I pray also that the desire of your heart may be abundantly fulfilled as you look toward the future; that this day, with all its grateful emotions and with all its sanguine hopes, may be but the fair beginning of a time.

I have not said what I had hoped to say, and I had not even hoped to say all I felt, for—

> "Words are weak, and most to seek
>   When wanted fifty-fold;
> And then if silence will not speak,
> And trembling lip and changing cheek—
>   There's nothing told."

CENTENNIAL CELEBRATION OF

CONGRATULATORY ADDRESSES

FROM THE PRESBYTERIAN CHURCH IN THE UNITED STATES OF AMERICA

BY THE REVEREND WILLIAM HENRY ROBERTS, D.D., LL.D.
Stated Clerk of the General Assembly
American Secretary of the World Presbyterian Alliance

IN the name of the General Assembly of the Presbyterian Church in the United States of America, and speaking for the Committee appointed by the Assembly, I present congratulations to the oldest and the foremost of the American Presbyterian theological seminaries. There was a day of small beginnings, both for the Church and the institution, but in the kindly providence of God, both have been prospered, so that today they are in the vanguard of the hosts of religious progress.

It is to be understood that in congratulating Princeton, the Assembly is not to be regarded as singling the institution out in any specific manner for special laudation, but as paying to it a merited tribute of praise and high regard as the first in a long line of sister seminaries.

The General Assembly, also in congratulating Princeton upon one hundred years of successful service, recognizes that it speaks to the whole body of officers, teachers and Alumni, for whom the word "Princeton" stands, and for whom it has a vital and inspiring significance. Princeton is not only a faculty, and not only a collection of buildings, but further an idea controlling thought and act, and set forth not only in documents but also in the lives of many persons.

PRINCETON THEOLOGICAL SEMINARY

The relation of the General Assembly to the Seminary is expressed in the Plan of the institution by the statement: "As this institution derives its origin from the General Assembly, that body is to be considered as its patron and the fountain of its power."

The cause of the founding of the Seminary by the Assembly was the fact that there was "a demand upon the collected wisdom, zeal and piety of the Church to furnish a large supply of able and faithful ministers." At the beginning of the nineteenth century there was no sufficient provision for an educated ministry. The Assembly, therefore, acting within its constitutional authority, determined to establish "a new institution, consecrated solely to the education of men for the Gospel ministry." The General Assembly of 1811 adopted the plan for the theological seminary, and distinctly stated in it the design and purposes in the following terms: "And to the intent that the true design of the founders of this institution may be known to the public, both now and in the time to come, and especially that this design may at all times be distinctly viewed and sacredly regarded, both by the teachers and the pupils of the seminary, it is judged proper to make a summary and explicit statement of it.

"It is to form men for the Gospel ministry who shall truly believe and cordially love, and therefore endeavor to propagate and defend, in its genuineness, simplicity and fullness, that system of religious belief and practice which is set forth in the Confession of Faith, Catechisms, and Plan of Government and Discipline of the Presbyterian Church, and thus to perpetuate and extend the influence of true evangelical piety and Gospel order.

"It is to provide for the Church men who shall be able

to defend her faith against infidels and her doctrines against heretics.

"It is to preserve the unity of our Church by educating her ministers in an enlightened attachment not only to the same doctrines but to the same plan of government."

The location of the institution, which was named in the Plan, "The Theological Seminary of the Presbyterian Church in the U. S. A.", at Princeton, New Jersey, gave to it the name by which today it is known throughout the world.

The congratulations of the Church are tendered in view of accomplishment in four lines, the first of which is the production of "an educated ministry." It is the glory of the Presbyterian Churches in all lands that they have always insisted upon an educated ministry. Obedient to the command to teach all nations, believing in an open Bible, and in the use of the reason which God has given man, these Churches have been intolerant chiefly of ignorance, have erected schools and colleges rather than cathedrals, and have made the centres of their worship not altars but pulpits, and exalted their ministers not as priests but as teachers. Filled with this spirit the Church founded this institution, and rejoices in the manner in which the trust reposed in the Seminary has been fulfilled.

Carrying out the trust imposed by the Church, through the Assembly, it is recognized that the educational progress made by the institution has been for the most part due to its able and scholarly faculties, whose abilities and wisdom under God have been largely instrumental in the production of ministers, competent both by abilities, learning and training, for the high and holy office of ambassadors for Jesus Christ. Beginning with men such as Archibald Alexander, Samuel Miller and Charles Hodge, this line of efficient teachers has been distinguished in every generation for unstinted and eminent service both to students and to the Church.

The Assembly recognizes also the faithfulness in service of the men who by its appointment have assiduously labored as directors and trustees of the seminary, performing carefully the several duties imposed upon them by the Church. The results approve them as workmen not needing to be ashamed.

Another point of congratulation deals with and has to do with the system of religious belief named in the Plan of the Seminary and set forth in the Westminster Confession of Faith, whose first and most emphasized doctrine is the inspiration and authority of the Bible. The Confession declares that the Holy Scripture is "the Word of God written," and all "given by inspiration of God to be the rule of faith and life." Loyalty to the Bible as the Word of God, the only infallible rule of faith and life, has been a chief characteristic of the teaching of this Seminary and of the lives of its Alumni. Princeton men have not treated the Bible as some others do, dealing with it as if it were a mere human book; and the reason therefor is to be found in their recognition of its *a priori* claims to reverence and obedience, and the valid criticism of the attitude of their antagonists is to be found in the belittling by the latter of the controlling supernatural element in the Book, an attitude which is of the very essence of a proud unbelief.

Accepting the Bible as the Word of God, Princeton holds to the Calvinistic System as a whole. Princeton men are not Calvinists because their fathers were, but because they have thought out and fought out for themselves the way to the greatest of the facts of the universe, a sovereign God, an almighty Saviour, and an infallible Bible. These three facts are the only sufficient solutions of the mental, moral and spiritual problems which confront and trouble mankind. Believing in the universe as a product of mind, Calvinists realize first of all that, when the Master of the Universe has points to carry in His government, He impresses His will in the structure of minds. And Calvinists believing thus in divine foreordination, require answers, not only as to what they must believe, but also as to what they ought to do. Once having come intelligently to the conception of the sovereignty of God in His universe, they accept all the system of doctrine in Holy Scripture connected with that sovereignty, and there remains for them only the duty of obedience to God. Calvinists are men of action as well as men of faith. And, therefore, Princeton has prospered.

The Plan of the Seminary also requires the Seminary to provide for the Church men who shall be able to defend her faith both against infidels and heretics. Defenders of the faith, not a few in number, have been trained in this institution for the service of the Church. No statement of the Seminary's history can be complete without the acknowledgment of what has been done by it in the way of the education of the scholar, not only for the professor's chair, but for the aggressive dissemination of the Calvinistic and Biblical system of truth. The Seminary has sometimes been criticised for endeavoring to educate "defenders of the faith," but in so doing it has been simply faithful to its trust. And far more could have been done, if the Church had provided adequately for the accomplishment of this duty of the institution.

The plan of the Seminary also brings out the idea that it is to preserve the unity of the Church through educating ministers in an enlightened attachment to the plan of government of the Church. To representative ecclesiastical republicanism, of which the American Presbyterian Church is an example, this institution is devoted. It has shown this devotion repeatedly in many ways. The greatest danger in recent years to the Church as to the State in this land has been found in an excess of individuality, but of late there has been a tendency to go to the other extreme, in an excess of corporate organization. The government of the Presbyterian Church is a reasonable compromise between the two extremes just indicated. We do recognize individuality, but we also accept and use those coöperative forces of human society, that in this generation are the greatest source of profitable service to mankind in general. There is an individuality in which self-will is the supreme force, and there is also an individuality which, overcoming the limitations of self, finds in the use of great coöperative forces its principal source of power, its chief influence, and the highest reward of profitable service. The individuality of self accomplishes but little of far-reaching and enduring value. The individuality which is altruistic makes for world-wide good. It has given birth to the nation in things political, it is the strength of the Church in all its work. The value of this coöperative tendency has been made clear in this Church for over two hundred years, and the oldest republic on the American continent congratulates this institution which today celebrates its centennial, upon its loyalty to Presbyterian government, and in particular to that form of government as it finds the greatest expression of its beneficent authority and influence in the General Assembly. That authority and influence, for instance, has planted and carries on foreign missions in fifteen different countries, and has broadcasted the national territory with missions and congregations. And this institution has ever been loyal to the supreme governing body of the Church, and so has been influential in that general administrative system which finds, as does the Seminary, the fountain of its power in the Assembly. This Seminary's loyalty to the Assembly is loyalty to the Church.

The General Assembly congratulates itself that forty-three of its moderators have received training within the walls of this institution, that fully one-half of the leaders in the missionary and benevolent work of the Church have sat at the feet of its professors, that out from the institution have gone hundreds of home and foreign missionaries, who have carried the gospel to every portion of our own country and throughout the world, and above all that here have been trained a great number of the pastors of the Church through four generations, men who have built up, energetically and successfully, the foundations of the Kingdom of Christ in this and in other lands. No one can estimate the good that has been accomplished through the ministers educated within these walls, who serving faithfully in their respective spheres of labor, have built up Christ-likeness in many human lives, and have laid the foundations of churches and organizations which have become powers in the Church universal.

The Assembly acknowledges gratefully the loyalty of a wide constituency which, from the origin of the institution, has furnished the resources which have enabled it to maintain with some degree of adequacy the principal objects for which it was established. It would be invidious to name the great ones among these benefactors, for many are they who have contributed, from the Female Cent Societies of 1815 up to the bequest of nearly two millions of dollars by one individual. Back of both the cent and the millions is to be found the spirit of loyalty to Jesus Christ and His truth.

The Presbyterian Church has never conceived of the Church of Christ as limited within the bounds of any one denomination or confined to any one branch of the Church. Its standards have always maintained that all who profess the true religion together with their children constitute the Church universal. Thus believing it has acted upon the great motto, "In essentials, unity; in nonessentials, liberty; in all things, charity". The doors of the institution, therefore, have always been open to students of all the evangelical Churches, and the influence of the Church through the Seminary has gone out by many such through the length and breadth of this and other lands. The Seminary is to be congratulated upon its catholicity of spirit and conduct.

The Assembly congratulates Princeton and its constituency upon the hopeful future. We need not fear as to what the character of that future will be. At times, it is true, doubts enter into some minds, and pessimistic views are taken of the outlook. Time and again, however, the providence of God has vindicated the fidelity of this institution to the truth in the past, and loyalty to its convictions of truth has brought it prosperity where adversity was dreaded. What is needed is to stand by the truth with patient courage and aggressive faith, at no time controlled by either fears within or fightings without. It has been said for instance that the principal use of a conservative was to act as a brakeman. That is not the fact, and it has not been the fact in the history of the Presbyterian Churches, except as those who are conservatives have failed "to lift up the hands that hang down and the feeble knees." The place of the conservative is that of the conductor, not of the brakeman. The brake may need to be applied to a train, but only at the order of the conductor. The conservative well grounded in doctrine can lead in all progress along practical lines. Unhampered by doubts as to what he is to believe, he is free to do the things for which God's providence opens the way. And within the Presbyterian Church the leadership belongs to those who are loyal to Presbyterian principles. Strength of conviction means loyalty, and it also means respect from men of differing views. Presbyterians have always recognized the right of other Christians to hold strong convictions, and claimed a similar right on their own part. While with strength of conviction must always be found that catholicity which is true Christian charity, it is also true that Christians must be true to themselves. The primacy which Princeton has, not only by heredity but also as an actuality, can be made, therefore, more sure and more manifest as the years roll on, by its firm adherence to the fundamentals of the Presbyterian system of doctrine.

The Princeton of the future we believe, has a greater prospect of usefulness before it than has ever been known in the past. Relying upon Him who is the almighty Father, trusting to the care of Him who is the divine Saviour, guided by the infallible Word, it will

PRINCETON THEOLOGICAL SEMINARY

increase in true service from year to year to that Church of Jesus Christ which is the only enduring thing upon this earth. Men come and men go, but the Church endures. Heaven and earth shall pass away but the Church shall not pass away. It is deathless with the life of the eternal God. Serving the Church with fidelity to Christ, and acting in accordance with the divine law, the devotion of the past and the present will be the inspiration of the future, and Princeton will earnestly and effectively do its part in the upbuilding of that temple of living stones, in the completion of which, the love of God for the world shall one day find the consummation of its power, its grace, and its glory.

FROM THE OTHER PRESBYTERIAN
AND REFORMED CHURCHES

BY THE REVEREND JOHN CRAWFORD SCOULLER, D.D.
Pastor of the Fourth United Presbyterian Church, Philadelphia
Moderator of the General Assembly of the United
Presbyterian Church of North America

President Patton and friends of Princeton:

IT would seem on such an occasion as this, and in such a presence, one ought to begin with a quotation from the Scriptures, yet to do this, in your presence, I am free to acknowledge, I hesitate. There is a vast difference between what we say the Scriptures say, and what they really do say. We may differ in opinion as to what certain of the Scriptures mean, but theological professors ought to know at least what they say.

There is a portion of Scripture which comes to me from my boyhood that illustrates what I mean. I was taught to reverence old age, because "gray hairs are honorable." But in later life, I found that there was a distinction as I met from time to time some who were wearing the crown of glory, yet about whom there was nothing that was worthy of honor; and I was glad to learn that the quotation was wrong, that the Scriptures did not take any such position as that, but that the quotation was, "The hoary head is a crown of glory, if it be found in the way of righteousness." We are not called upon to honor a thing because it is old, but we are called upon to honor this institution because it has always been in the way of righteousness. We do honor to ourselves in honoring it here this afternoon, because behind these old institutions lies the whole secret, the forceful and faithful teaching of the science of God.

I have been greatly impressed while walking around among the University buildings here, and our hearts are with your new president in the work he has before him. But when I think of the Theological Seminary with its special work, the teaching of the science of God, I am profoundly impressed.

I bring congratulations from our Church, because this institution, during all this number of years, has stood for the faithful teaching of this science of God, and it has, I believe, sought to bring into that teaching all of the resources of philosophy, metaphysics and kindred sciences on the ground that a man's faith in the Word of God is not shaken on account of this higher learning, but that it makes him a better witness and better able to testify to that Word; and he goes forth better equipped and better prepared for this work.

PRINCETON THEOLOGICAL SEMINARY

We rejoice that this Seminary has stood all these years for the deity of Christ, for the revealed Word of God, for the indwelling Spirit, and stood faithful to them all; and I bring the congratulations of a Church which, as you know, believes with you in the higher learning, and thinks that it has done the very best it could with the material that has been furnished during all these years.

In the early history of our branch of the Church, we built the log-cabin school alongside of the log-cabin church, and afterwards we built the log-cabin seminary.

We bring the congratulations of a Church which has thoroughly endorsed the work of this Seminary, a Church which receives with gratitude everything and everybody who bears the Princeton hall-mark. We differ from your branch of the Church not so much in character as in behavior, and as we read the early history of the Church in common with your own, for we were one, we see there were troublous times; there were circumstances which called for very wise action on the part of the leaders of the Church. While your ancestry did not always agree entirely with my ancestry, it is no puzzle to those who know these said ancestors.

Mrs. McFadden had invited some friends to her home one afternoon to enjoy the refreshing shade of her front lawn. As they were seated together, they heard the music of a band, and a troop of soldiers marched by. Mrs. McFadden said, "That is Company L. My boy John belongs to that company." As the soldiers came along, she pointed him out, the fourth man in the third column, and said, "Isn't he noble and manly?" After he had gone by, there were a great many complimentary things said, perforce, about the soldierly appearance of the men. Mrs. McFadden said, "I noticed one thing you may have failed to notice; in all that marching company of men, my son was the only man who had the step". Now, I presume that my ancestry, while they were very few, rejoiced in the fact that they had the step.

One of the branches of our Church has been called the "Seceder Church," and as I came to read the history through, I thought the name was somewhat appropriate. From time to time, there were a few people who seceded —dissented and seceded. I think it might fairly be called the "Church of the Apostolic Secession."

But while we have been such, we were also a Church of union, as our name bears witness. It is true that after uniting two branches, it nearly always left three Churches, each one of which thought it had the step; but let us hope they were all in the way of righteousness. Whatever we have been as a Church, whatever we are as a Church, we owe much to Princeton Theological Seminary, not because she has trained so many of our ministry—though she has trained some, of all of whom we are proud—but because she has had much to do with the shaping of the course of training in our seminaries. One of our seminaries—I don't know whether you know it or not, Dr. Patton—is a few years older than yours; it was founded in 1794. But it was not founded with all wisdom: the influence of the theological teaching of this Seminary has had much to do with the shaping of the curriculum in our own Seminary, and we can trace the trend in its life to this.

We rejoice in this, and we are glad to bring you its congratulations this afternoon. May the influence of Princeton abide and be wide-spread.

PRINCETON THEOLOGICAL SEMINARY

FROM OTHER CHURCHES

BY THE RIGHT REVEREND DAVID HUMMELL GREER, D.D., S.T.D., LL.D.
Bishop of the Protestant Episcopal Church in the
Diocese of New York

Mr. Chairman; Gentlemen:

I AM surprised and pleased to find in this Presbyterian assemblage how much at home I am here. You all seem just like Episcopalians. Whether it is because I am so much like you or you so much like me I am not prepared to say. Perhaps because of this somewhat ambiguous identity on my part I was called up a few days ago by an enterprising journalist who said that important news had just come into that office; the cannibals, it had just been learned, had eaten two Presbyterian missionaries, and he wanted to know what I was going to do about it. There seemed to be nothing to be done, though I might have said, "Let the good work go on."

Dr. Patton said to me a moment ago that if ever the Episcopalian Church wanted an archbishop, and he thought the signs were pointing in that direction, he would nominate for the office our friend Dr. Roberts. I promised him—in fact, I made a sort of contract with him on the spot—that if Dr. Roberts would become an Episcopalian we would make him an archbishop. We don't want an archbishop in the Episcopal Church, but I thought I was safe in making the promise.

Mr. Chairman and gentlemen: I am glad of the opportunity this occasion gives me to acknowledge my personal indebtedness to the Presbyterian Church, if not for my theological training, at least for some measure of my intellectual training. In the college at which I was a student (not Princeton, but elsewhere), the Exposition of the Westminster Confession was a prescribed part, at that time, of the established curriculum, and I had to take a course in it once every week. Whether my present soundness in the faith is due to that fact I do not know, but I do know that it was at the time good mental training for me. The intellectual discipline which it gave me, while it did not have the effect to make me in any sense a great metaphysical critic (which I am not), "profoundly skilled in analytic," able like Hudibras "to sever and divide a hair twixt sou' and sou'west side"; it did I am sure sharpen somewhat my limited mental faculties and give them a finer edge. It taught me how to think. Professor Tyndall says in speaking of his indebtedness to Hegel, Fichte and others, that while these eminent teachers called on him to act he reserved to himself the privilege of taking his own line of action and of becoming not a philosopher but a scientific student. So, while that study of the Westminster Confession did teach me to think, I did not as the result think myself into the Presbyterian Church, but reserved to myself the privilege of thinking myself more fully into the Church in which I was born and of which I am still a member.

But I am not here to speak personal words or to give a personal greeting, but as the topic or toast implies, to give you greeting in behalf of my own "and all the other Churches." I appreciate the compliment with its implication of a recognition that there is a little marginal fringe in Christendom beyond the line and border of the Presbyterian Church. And what shall I say for those other Churches? Is there a common bond that binds them all together and unites them all with you? Most assuredly there is. It is the dominion, the personal dominion, not of the dead and absent but of the living Christ, which in spite of all the changes so many and so great which have taken place in the past has not been disturbed, but has strengthened and increased and widened more and more with the "process of the suns." Whatever their differences may be, it is that personal dominion of the living Christ which binds them all together. It is also that personal dominion of the living Christ which constitutes the distinctive feature of the Christian religion and that differentiates it from all other religions. Those other religions survived as religious codes or systems, but their founders, except as more or less influential names, have not survived with them. But the Founder of the Christian religion does indeed survive, not merely in His teaching, not merely in His influence, like that "of the sceptred sovereigns who still rule us from their urns," but as a living Person, living in His Church, as the power of His Church; its power in the past, its power in the present, and the power by which it will not only do its work in the world but will do the world's work, and which like nothing else will help to solve the world's pressing and present problems, social and economic, national and international, or whatever they may be.

While therefore in one sense it would be arrogant and presumptuous for me to venture to speak in behalf of the Churches of Christendom other than my own, I am confident that I may do so in the name of that living Christ whom they all acknowledge, and to whom, in spite of all their differences, they give their allegiance and their faith. Those differences do indeed exist. We are not blind to them. Even Dr. Roberts intimates that there are some differences in the Presbyterian Church; and it cannot be disputed I think that such differences do exist, if not in your theology, at least in your theological emphasis from that of a hundred years ago when your Seminary was founded. But I am one of those who believe that these diversities or differences will in time be healed, and that these discords will at last melt and merge somehow into a deeper and richer harmony. I certainly do not wish to repudiate, nor do you, the theology of the past. We are born of that theology; it is our inheritance. We could not repudiate it even if we would. And so with the living Christ we shall meet the duties of today and the issue of tomorrow, facing the future, yet planted firmly on the past; and so like Dante's pilgrim we shall journey on and up the rough and rugged mountain side towards the distant mountain top, with the hinder foot still firmer.

FROM THE SEMINARIES OF THE PRESBYTERIAN CHURCH IN THE UNITED STATES OF AMERICA

BY THE REVEREND JAMES GORE KING McCLURE, D.D., LL.D.

President of McCormick Theological Seminary
Chicago, Illinois

IT is a great privilege before this remarkable audience on an occasion of so much significance to attempt to express the congratulations and good wishes of the theological seminaries of the Presbyterian Church in the United States of America.

There is a sense in which, like Jerusalem which is from above, Princeton is the mother of us all. We have

PRINCETON THEOLOGICAL SEMINARY

all come to our birth since she entered upon her beginning. We have all been influenced by her methods, her spirit, her teaching and her successes. In a thousand ways she has been to us the guide of our youth, the director of our manhood and the companion of our maturity.

Her existence is the justification of our own existence. A new system of training Presbyterian ministers in the United States came to its initiation in her. That system in due time secured the approval of the Church. Because of that approval of the system which Princeton represented, we had our birth.

All these seminaries come, therefore, today to bring their greetings to their mother, to lay at her feet their tribute of gratitude, to express to her their appreciation of all that she has been to them, and to assure her of their present and of their abiding affection. Never did children gather about a beloved parent in the hour of that parent's honor with more genuine and more profound esteem than do the children of Princeton gather about their mother at this glad time.

If it is a great privilege to speak as the representative of the theological seminaries in the Presbyterian Church in the United States of America, it is likewise a great responsibility to attempt in any wise to forthtell the sentiments of their hearts. These seminaries are twelve in number. Their locations are widely scattered. They virtually extend from the Atlantic to the Pacific coast, covering the intermediate portions of this good land. One by one, according as the Church has felt that there was a need, each has arisen to occupy a definite portion of our territory and attempt the work that seemed to be needed. We minister both to those whose faces are white and those whose faces are black, both to those who are conversant with the English tongue and to those who are conversant with the German, Bohemian and other tongues. The influence of these seminaries extends far beyond the general locality in which they are placed. That influence has gone into every portion of the world, for there is not a nation upon the earth today without representatives from one or more of these seminaries who in their places are trying to bring the highest possible blessings to those about them.

Then, too, this should be noted, that Princeton has been the one who to so large a degree has contributed her graduates to the working faculties of these scattered and useful seminaries. When the full record of this Centennial Celebration shall have been gathered up, it will be seen that man after man of those who in the later years of their lives became so thoroughly associated with the seminaries in which their work was done that men ordinarily think of them only in connection with such seminaries, received their training and were prepared for their usefulness in Princeton.

That there are so many seminaries of such diversified types, with such fields of influence and with such a product of helpfulness, is suggestive of the growth that has taken place in our country since the action of our General Assembly whereby Princeton Seminary, one hundred years ago, became a possibility, and suggestive, too, of the growth of our denomination, which has spread far and wide until it covers the land; and suggestive, also, of the growth of the system of education itself which first came to its expression in the founding of this institution. Theological seminaries are today a fixed part of our religious life. Toward them the thought and prayer of the Church turn with confident expectation that they will furnish the material whereby the work of saving the world shall be advanced.

It is noticeable, too, in this connection how few of all the thousands upon thousands who have been connected with our seminaries as students have failed to lead helpful lives. They have gone to small and large place alike. They have met every kind of difficulty, and even every kind of privation. Each one of these seminaries has its roll of Christian martyrs. Each of them can tell of numberless instances in which its graduates have opened blind eyes, comforted lonely hearts, and led darkened souls into the light and life of God. There is no such beautiful product anywhere to be found upon the earth as the product of theological seminaries. And our hearts grow warm and our tones tender as we think of this wonderful privilege, granted to our seminaries, in having part in the refreshing and saving of humanity.

But beside the privilege and the responsibility of this hour, there is the humor of it. To think that one individual like myself should attempt to speak as the representative of all our seminaries when there is such a variety of individuality in these seminaries, in the type of men constituting their faculties and in the proportions and emphases of truth which they express!

It is sometimes said of our Presbyterian Church that one of its great tendencies is to develop individuality. We liken our Church to a splendid piece of solid hickory. Hickory is strong, but it splits easily. Our Church, in its emphasis upon the fact that each one of us finally stands alone before God in his individuality, creates an atmosphere in which there is danger of great diversity of sentiment. Besides, we do attempt to explain much of the workings of the Divine mind. We do not hesitate to go back even into eternity itself and deal with what we call the Eternal Decrees, and that is a long way to go. There is ever a possibility that one and another may not follow exactly the same track in getting to the original sources. And then this, too, is true; that we attempt to define very closely. We hold to the general proposition that it is only through definition that there can be close and accurate reasoning. But just so soon as we define, we separate; and separation is bound to produce varieties of interpretation.

Now for me upon this occasion to stand here and attempt to be the mouthpiece of all these seminaries, in all their varieties of expression, in all their different types of temperament, in all their definitions, would be a most hazardous undertaking. I am afraid that Bedlam would be quietness itself compared to the scene which would ensue, if I, on my own responsibility, should have the audacity to make a brief statement of the faith of all these seminaries and of the individual members of their faculties and lay it before this audience at this time!

And still these varieties of expression are evidences of our fidelity to convictions. There could be nothing so serious to the welfare of the world as to have all our seminaries cut exactly upon the same pattern. Men cannot be true to themselves, to their times, to the needs of their localities and put into formulated statement with the same degree of emphasis and proportion their religious beliefs. Ours is a very comprehensive Bible. James and Paul are in it, though at first glance to some minds they might seem quite apart the one from the other. Ours is a comprehensive Confession of Faith. The long debates that led up to its acceptance did not and could not cause all minds to acquiesce in the *ipsis-*

sima verba of one another's views. Ours is a comprehensive Church, and men of different births, of different spiritual experiences, of different attitudes toward methods of evangelization are bound to arise, and our glory is that these seminaries aim to meet all needs and to send out men prepared to carry their own special messages to the needy hearts of mankind.

So there is to my own mind great felicity in this opportunity. Variety expresses itself here and now in harmony. We are one in our purpose. There is not a single divergence from fidelity to our testimony to the greatness, the goodness, the lovableness of God. Princeton has always made God large. So each of us and all of us in our special lines intend to lift God before the world in such a way that all shall see His matchless majesty and goodness, and shall be drawn to adore and serve Him. When Dr. Charles Hodge was here, his opening prayer in the classroom was again and again offered with a tremulous tone, while the tears flowed down his cheeks. As he drew near to the God whom he reverenced and loved, his heart was submerged with tenderness and devotion. Such a God, sovereign indeed of heaven and earth, creator and ruler of all He has made, than whom there can be no other, making Himself known in the fulness of His benignity in Jesus Christ, is the God that each seminary exalts.

We are one, too, in the fact that we never overlook in any wise, the nature, the place, the power and the guilt of sin, nor do we ever overlook or in any wise minimize the redemptive work of Jesus Christ, God's Son, our Lord and Saviour, who came into this world to bear the sins of God's people, and to bring us into harmony with the Father. Nor do we ever overlook or minimize in any wise the convicting, regenerating and sanctifying grace of the Holy Spirit. Every one of us holds to the unique place of the Bible. It is our authority. Every problem of philosophy, every problem of life, is tested by the Holy Scriptures. Nor does any one of us fail in loyalty to the Presbyterian Church, whose children and servants we are.

As we are one in our purpose, we are all one in our gratitude. We thank God that Princeton has always had convictions which she has never hesitated to avow. We thank God for the scholarly methods which have always characterized her teaching. We thank Him too for the scholarly requirements which she has demanded of those who have been prepared by her for the gospel ministry. The mere mention of these causes of gratitude is suggestive of what uncertain results would have followed to the Presbyterian Church and to the Church of God throughout the world if Princeton had not been distinguished in these lines.

Where shall we stop in speaking of our gratitude? Who can be so appreciative of the men who have served in Princeton's Faculty as ourselves who in our own faculties recognize the temptations and the difficulties of theological education? We bless God with overflowing hearts for the generations of instructors who have succeeded one another through these one hundred years, and who have left an indelible stamp of goodness and greatness upon our Church and upon the world. Nor can I omit to express gratitude for those who in the position of directors and of trustees have nourished this institution, have strengthened its life and have given it increasing development for good. And once again my heart glows with thankfulness as I think of the multitudes of

PRINCETON THEOLOGICAL SEMINARY

students who having been made ready in this institution have gone like rays of sunlight wherever the darkness of sin is, to chase away the shades of night, and bring the world into the light of God's eternal day.

As we are one in our common purpose and in our common gratitude, we are also one in our common wish. That wish is that God may look with constant and abounding favor on this institution as it enters into the new century; that Princeton's graduates who are here today, and those who are elsewhere throughout the world, may always have the seal of God's blessing on their hearts, homes and work; that this institution, with each new year of its life, may see more clearly and more deeply into the eternal verities, and may be used by God increasingly to the bringing in of that time when every knee shall bow in the name of Jesus Christ, and the kingdoms of this world shall become the Kingdom of our God and of His Christ.

And to His name shall be all the praise.

FROM THE SEMINARIES OF OTHER CHURCHES

I

BY THE REVEREND WILLISTON WALKER, Ph.D., D.D., L.H.D.

Titus Street Professor of Ecclesiastical History
Yale University Divinity School
New Haven, Connecticut

WERE this an occasion commemorative of Princeton University, instead of the Centennial of Princeton Theological Seminary, I should be tempted to make large assertions of Yale ownership, if not in present successes, at least in educational origins. I should not merely claim its first three presidents, Jonathan Dickinson, Aaron Burr and Jonathan Edwards as sons of Yale, but I should look upon some portion at least of its material structure as belonging to Connecticut as I recall that, in 1753, when the legislature of New Jersey proved an unsympathetic step-mother, that of Connecticut granted aid to the then struggling college by a lottery "for the encouragement of religion and learning" as the act ran.

Yet even in Princeton Theological Seminary, I would claim for Connecticut a certain share, for it was in a General Assembly in which the Congregational churches of Connecticut were then regularly represented that your foundations were laid. I remember, also, as a representative of Yale, that President Theodore Dwight Woolsey, whose name is venerated among us, had his theological training in Princeton Seminary. As a Congregationalist, moreover, I rejoice to recall that it was the example of a Congregational Theological Seminary —that of Andover—that in some measure stimulated the endeavors, the fruition of which a century ago we now commemorate. We have not always looked at Christian truth from the same angle of vision. Yale and Princeton have had their dissimilarities theologically as in other respects. But deeper than any differences of interpretation has been, I believe, a profound similarity in desire to know the truth and to advance the Kingdom of God by loyal service to our common Master, the ever-living Christ.

It is not only as an official representative of Yale and of its department of theology, but in an unofficial sense as a messenger of Congregationalism, and of theological training far wider than the Congregational field, that I would bring you heartiest congratulations. What a wealth of hallowed memories a hundred years involves. What consecrated service by good men living and dead. What hopes and labors and prayers. What a host of servants of God have here had their preparation for their work and their stimulus to consecrated endeavor. Well may you rejoice that the providence of God has led you thus onward in ever increasing usefulness these hundred years.

Our thoughts on such an anniversary turn naturally to the past. It is with the achievements of the century just closed that we have chiefly to do. But we should be unworthy sons of those who laid the foundations in their poverty, rich only in faith in God, if we in our time failed to have something of their breadth of vision and willingness to meet enlarging needs. In a real sense they were Christian pioneers. They saw that the churches needed a better trained ministry. They felt that the provisions of the past were inadequate to the demands of the present. They began their work with courage and with determination to equip the servants of the churches more perfectly for their tasks. The century that has gone has witnessed a constant enlargement in the opportunities of Christian service. Once it was sufficient to train for the pulpit only. Then came the demand for missionary preparation. Now religious education and social betterment in the name of Christ are knocking at our doors. The conception of the ministry is widening as the Church becomes increasingly conscious of the multiformity of its mission. It must have its pastors and missionaries. It needs its teachers and its social workers in town and country no less.

CENTENNIAL CELEBRATION OF

If we would have men a hundred years hence look back upon us with something of the honor with which we now reverence the founders of American theological education, we must have something of their largeness of outlook. We must see the needs of our times as clearly as they saw the necessities of theirs. We must plan with equal courage to meet the demands which are upon us. As they enlarged the opportunities for ministerial training beyond what had satisfied the age before them, so must we go forward. A training for wider service, in many differentiated forms, must be our ideal. Theological education cannot rest where it now stands, if we are to have the spirit which led them to plan their mighty advances. The task before us is to make our schools more adequate to meet the needs of the century in which we live.

But on this festal day our chief thoughts are of rejoicing and of congratulation. As members of a sisterhood of schools for ministerial training we bring our heartiest greetings to the Theological Seminary of the Presbyterian Church in the United States of America. The good hand of God has led you through a hundred years of service. Loyal devotion and grateful recollection look to you this day from all over this land and from countries beyond the seas, and joy with you. May He who inspired the founders, and has so prospered their work, grant you in increasing measure His favor in the years to come. May Princeton Theological Seminary have an ever larger share in bringing on the glad time when the Redeemer's Kingdom "shall have dominion from sea to sea, and from the river unto the ends of the earth".

PRINCETON THEOLOGICAL SEMINARY

FROM THE SEMINARIES OF OTHER CHURCHES

II

BY THE REVEREND EDGAR YOUNG MULLINS, D.D., LL.D.
President of the Southern Baptist Theological Seminary
Louisville, Kentucky

Mr. Chairman, Ladies and Gentlemen:

I WISH to acknowledge the great honor conferred upon me in being asked to represent the theological seminaries of the Baptist denominations on this most interesting and notable occasion, and I rejoice to bring to Princeton the congratulations of the ten or twelve Baptist seminaries in the country.

I must, in a very few minutes, catch a train for an engagement very much like this in another theological seminary, and really I feel that what I have to say might be eliminated from this programme. I feel very much like the minister who got a note one Sunday as he was about to begin his sermon. His wife had reached the church, and had seated herself in a crowded pew, when she remembered she had left the roast beef on the gas stove, and knew that unless the meat was taken off that there would be no roast beef for dinner. But, with the usual resourcefulness of the pastor's wife, she wrote a note and handed it to her brother, who was an usher, and he, with the usual instinct of an usher, took it to the pastor, supposing it was a pulpit notice. And just as the good man was all athrob with the magnificent message that he was to deliver, he opened and read this note, "Go home and turn off the gas."

I am not quite sure but that the reverse of that would be in order at this time, turn off the gas and go home. I have allowed me ten minutes. It is a serious problem how I should utilize it. I feel, from the Baptist's point of view, I might try to stimulate the Presbyterian conscience as to the greatness of the achievements of Presbyterianism during the last one hundred years, but from the addresses I have heard, I do not think you need any stimulus of that kind. I did think of speaking, however, on another line which has been greatly neglected during these two days, viz., Calvinism; but that is too large a theme for a man to undertake to discuss in ten minutes in the absence of previous discussion on the programme. By the way, that is no reflection on Calvinism.

I learned Calvinism in Princeton Theological Seminary—I didn't come here as a student, but my teacher of theology did. James P. Boyce, founder of the Southern Baptist Theological Seminary, was an alumnus of Princeton; he taught me theology. He was one of the greatest leaders the South ever had. Basil Manly, a professor of the institution of which I have the honor to be president, was an alumnus of Princeton Theological Seminary. So Princeton is a household word in the circle of the institution with which I am connected. It is a special joy, therefore, for me to bring you greetings from our Faculty, and representatives of the Baptist institutions of the country. I will not attempt, in these few minutes, to indicate what we, of the Baptist seminaries, feel by way of appreciation of the work done by Princeton. However, if I were to attempt to do this, I would sum it up in this: three perils which Princeton has avoided, and three conditions which she has fulfilled for a triumphant Christianity.

PRINCETON THEOLOGICAL SEMINARY

In the first place, and briefly, the three perils Princeton has avoided. First, the peril of reducing Christianity to the vanishing point in the form of an essence. You have taken the thing itself and not the mere essence of it. With you, Christianity has been a voice, and not a scientific echo of a voice; nor a humanitarian echo of an echo of a voice. John the Baptist crying in the wilderness was a voice. What we want is a voice and what the world must have is a voice if it is to have a feeling of the power of God in its heart.

Another peril Princeton has avoided, as we interpret it: it has not eliminated the positive note from Christianity. We believe, and you believe in the open mind and the freedom of investigation, but you have appreciated the fact that no preaching that has power can be without the positive note. You will not do much with sinners preaching a gospel to them which says: "Except ye repent"—as it were—"and believe the gospel"—so to speak—"you will be damned"—in a measure. That sort of a message does not carry and will not win. Again you have avoided the peril of defining Christianity as esthetical instead of moral and spiritual. Inclination and taste do not determine what the world is. With you, religion has been a form of the real, an order of fact; it has been based upon the eternal God and upon the God in the human soul. I cannot elaborate this.

The three conditions which we think this institution has fulfilled and which are the essence of this triumphant Christianity are these:

First, with you, Christianity has been a message rather than an inquiry. I do not say it may not be both, and certainly I am the last man to say inquiry is not in order in any sphere, but Christianity, to be a power, must be a message. Your Dr. van Dyke said the coat-of-arms of the present age is three bishops prone and above them an interrogation point rampant. Princeton has not adopted that coat-of-arms. Christianity to be a power must be a message. In order to have a fact, there must be definiteness. The soul cannot feed on abstractions. Just as a bird cannot fly in a vacuum, nor a tree root itself in a fog bank, nor a vine climb a moonbeam, so the soul cannot subsist upon a mere abstraction about God and about religion.

Christianity and religion are a form of the real, and, in a scientific age, the man who says you cannot know, the man who puts an interrogation point before the great realities of religion, is predestined and foreordained from the foundation of the world to be defeated in his effort to defend religion at all.

For an age that has been nurtured at the breast of physical science has been taught to love the living and the true, and unless religion is brought inside the category of reality and truth, religion is doomed. And we and you believe religion belongs to an order of fact, co-ordinate in worth as order of fact, as real, as autonomous, as authoritative as physical science in its own sphere, or any other department of human investigation. You have fulfilled that condition. Christianity with you is, first, a message; second, it is an experience. A message without an experience behind it is powerless. It is only the experience that can give momentum to the message. It is utterly impossible for theology to accomplish anything unless behind it is a life; so I say, as we understand you, you have stood for that.

Imitation Christianity has lost its power; mere creedal Christianity has lost its power—a gold piece is worth more than a brass piece, but an imitation gold piece isn't worth any more; Beethoven's compositions have more music than ragtime, but the mere notes of the two have no difference so far as they are printed on the page; a fire has more heat than an iceberg, but the picture of a fire has no more heat than the picture of an iceberg. I say reality is the key-note, and without it our creeds come to naught.

Princeton has also stood for the conviction that there must be messengers who embody the message and the experience. I cannot elaborate; that I leave with you. These are the three fundamentals of triumphant Christianity which we believe you have fulfilled. The traveller in the Alps, around the valley of Chamonix especially, is struck by the fertility of all the region. He does not understand the source of all this fertility until he discovers the many streams which flow down Mt. Blanc, which lifts its head fifteen thousand feet in the air, snow-crowned eternally. As Mt. Blanc enriches the valleys so Princeton Seminary has stood like Mt. Blanc among the seminaries of this country. In a thousand ways, you have not known, she has sent down her largess of blessing into the valleys, and we rejoice in what she has done. And the reason Mt. Blanc can thus bless the valleys is because she lifts her head to the very skies where, from the inexhaustible heavens themselves, she draws her supply, and so Princeton has drawn her supplies from the eternal sources.

So we join you today, O Princeton, in doing honor to Him whose name is above every name to us, for He is the centre of all experience for us. He is the problem that is at the core of philosophic thought; He it is with whom men must reckon.

CENTENNIAL CELEBRATION OF

"Majestic sweetness sits enthroned
  Upon the Saviour's brow;
  His head with radiant glories crowned,
  His lips with grace o'erflow."

I join with you in saying—

"No mortal can with Him compare,
  Among the sons of men;
  Fairer is He than all the fair
  That fill the heavenly train."

FROM PRINCETON UNIVERSITY

BY THE REVEREND JOHN GRIER HIBBEN, Ph.D., LL.D.

President of Princeton University

Mr. Chairman, President Patton, men of Princeton, both of the University and of the Seminary:

I AM speaking this afternoon not only for the present, but also for the past. Many voices come to us today, long since stilled, it is true, but eloquent in our memory; I speak not only for Princeton University, but by virtue of our historical continuity, also for the College of New Jersey, and back of the College of New Jersey, the Log College, and back of the Log College, the school house on the hills of Scotland and of Ulster in Ireland.

I am aware of the fact, and, indeed, it is one of our most cherished possessions, that the men who founded the College of New Jersey were men of the same spirit and of the same faith who founded the Princeton

PRINCETON THEOLOGICAL SEMINARY

Theological Seminary one hundred years ago, and the names that are conspicuous in the history of this last century, intimately associated with the Theological Seminary, are names to be found on the roll of the College of New Jersey and Princeton University; the Greens, the Alexanders, the Millers, the Hodges and all the long roll of honor, which I have not time to repeat name by name. There has been a close connection of friendly affiliation between our two institutions, but at the basis of it all is the foundation of a common faith and a common hope.

With that as our present day inheritance, upon this occasion, we, who are here representing the present Princeton University, pledge you that we will endeavor, so far as lies within us, to preserve the faith and hope of our fathers and to remain true to the gospel which they professed.

As president of Princeton University, I am not only representing today the various branches of the Presbyterian Church, but I represent all the denominations, I think, which are also represented in your gathering here, all the Churches that have come to bring their greetings to Princeton Theological Seminary. We, in a broad spirit of tolerance, uphold the ideals of the Christian faith in Princeton University, not in the name of any one denomination, but with a catholicity that extends a welcome to all the sects of Christendom. There has been a note sounded throughout this celebration of Christian unity, and we can, I believe, in Princeton University, furnish a contribution towards this end; because there we are able to bring together these various faiths of Christendom.

The point of contact between the University and the

Theological Seminary today is that of the department of philosophy. It is in the department of philosophy that most of the Seminary students come to us as graduate scholars; it is in the department of philosophy that the questions emerge which are the great central questions, not merely of the theology taught by Princeton, but the great central questions of life. And I wish to state to you who are here today, that as regards the teachings of Princeton University, we stand for a spiritualistic philosophy in an age of materialistic and utilitarian creeds. By spiritual philosophy I mean that we would interpret the great central humanizing power of the universe not merely in terms of Force or of Power—spelling these words, if you please, with capital letters—but in the name of a person, a person like ourselves.

I am not afraid, gentlemen, of the charge of anthropomorphism that is so often made. It is urged upon us that we should abstractly interpret God, and that we should assign to Him only negative attributes. When we take the sum total of negative attributes, however many there may be, the sum always amounts to zero. In the place of that interpretation we would put that of the personal significance of God, a spirit whom we can worship in spirit and truth. I am not afraid of interpreting God according to the highest and best and noblest that we find in human nature; man who was made in the image of God must be, in the last analysis, the standard for the interpretation of God. And that is not humanizing the Divine. It is because we recognize in our consciousness the divine spark, and where we find it aflame in the highest and noblest quality of man, we may take that as an indication—an intimation, if you please—an intimation, if not a definition, of the nature of God. I refer particularly to man as a purposeful being, man as you find him today, dominating the whole face of the earth. God as a person is a God likewise purposeful in the universe. Man is not like the plants and animals, incapable of adapting his environment to himself and compelling his surroundings. I am not speaking of his physical surroundings, but of the moral and mental and spiritual surroundings of his life. Is it not the great glory of these men who have gone out from this Seminary, as they were praised yesterday afternoon, that they have not accepted the environment of the world, but have gone to the very ends of the earth with the one purpose of creating the moral, mental and spiritual environment in which the light of reason might shine forth and the goodness and glory of God be manifest?

The great strife today in philosophy is in reference to the doctrine of personality; it is not merely whether there is a personal God in the universe, but whether in the heart of the human being there is a person or only a state of consciousness.

We stand, in Princeton University, for the central doctrine of personality, that the man is a soul, that he is a person in a universe of persons. And the one doctrine today that grows out of this, which we must insist upon, is that the persons of the world are bound together in one great family, that we are all one organization. We cannot say to man, "Go out into the world and follow the law of the animal and plant evolution; go into the world with one creed, one idea, of the survival of the fittest; do what you please, do your own work, push forward, and let the devil take the hindmost." We insist that this is not the doctrine of life. It is not the survival of the fittest; it is that other doctrine which has come down to us from the beginning of the Christian centuries, that man is in this world, like his Master, "Not to be ministered unto, but to minister." These are some of the fundamental doctrines that our philosophy has emphasized, and we believe finally, that all philosophical thought culminates in some great system of ethics, the philosophy of conduct, and that we cannot have a philosophy of conduct, as a great German philosopher once insisted, without presupposing the fundamental postulates of God, of freedom and of immortality.

PRINCETON THEOLOGICAL SEMINARY

RESPONSE TO CONGRATULATORY ADDRESSES

BY THE REVEREND FRANCIS LANDEY PATTON, D.D., LL.D.
President of the Seminary

MY dear friends, it is the duty of a well instructed host to "speed the parting guest", and so I am not intending to inflict upon you anything in the way of a long speech, but it is my privilege to say a word or two before we separate.

There has been going through my mind, during the delivery of these excellent speeches to which we have been listening, a verse of the old Scottish version of the 133rd Psalm:

"Behold, how good a thing it is,
And how becoming well;
Together such as brethren are,
In unity to dwell."

And amid all the theological diversities and the ecclesiastical differences that have been manifested here, it has been delightful to think of the pervasive spirit of unity that has characterized our celebration. Not that I, for a moment, feel that it is in any sense derogatory to one's position or that it interferes at all with the larger charity we should have, to feel an interest in a particular form of belief, to have theological preferences, or even to participate, for that matter, in theological controversy; for

I remember reading, a great many years ago, a very interesting book by the Earl of Crawford, the spirit of which is very well indicated by its title, "Progress by Antagonism". I think the world owes a great deal to theological controversy. Creed-statements, it is true, have been monuments built upon the battlefields of faith. They commemorate victories: but they also serve to promote peace; for they indicate the points in which Christians agree as well as the matters in which they differ.

I think I represent—I am speaking personally now, I don't pretend to be official about it—but I think that I am the very embodiment of broad church theology in the best sense of that phrase when I say that I haven't any kind of prejudice against any kind of belief that in any kind of way conserves anything that is of intrinsic interest and permanent value to mankind; and it is one of the interesting things connected with this celebration that so many men of so many phases of Christian belief have come here to join us on this Centennial occasion. There are times when it is important for us to emphasize points of difference between those who profess and call themselves Christians; times, that is to say, when we feel specially called upon, whatever be the denomination to which we belong, to protest against what we conceive to be error. This, however, is an occasion when it is fitting that we should recognize our points of agreement and rejoice that we hold so much theological territory in common. We have been very much gratified by letters of congratulation we have received from our friends in this country and our friends across the sea, in fact from all parts of the world. Not the least gratifying by any means are those that have come to us from Roman Catholic institutions, regretting that they could not be with us, expressing the fact that, of course, they differed with us and we with them, but at the same time recognizing the service that Princeton has done in the world in certain phases of scientific theology. I wish that representatives from some of these institutions had been with us today—and there is one such representative—for if they had been, I would have said, "Now, my friends, you know I differ with you a great deal, but I want to tell you that as between the present Pope of Rome and the Modernists, I would vote for the Pope of Rome every time." I will go farther and say, that should there ever come a day when men use the sacred name of Jesus to disguise sentimental atheism, we shall have reason to reckon among the important forces in the religious world those organizations which lay special emphasis upon the first article of the Apostles' Creed, "I believe in God the Father Almighty, Maker of heaven and earth". I want to say that so far as the theology of Princeton Seminary is concerned—and I admit that its peculiarities have not been brought into the foreground during this celebration—I think you will go away with the conviction that at all events, it is not yet actually dead. I do not think that it is even moribund, but I wish to say that, if it should die and be buried, and in the centuries to come, the theological palaeontologist should dig it up and pay attention to it, he will be constrained to say that it at least belonged to the order of vertebrates.

Oh, gentlemen, you who have come to us over long distances by land and sea, you who have come to us from other Churches with varying theological convictions, you who have come back to sit under the old roof-tree once more and to get fresh inspiration from the old Mother, we thank you for coming; you have made us glad that you have been here, and now, as you go away, God speed you on your journey and God bless you in your work.

www.ingramcontent.com/pod-product-compliance
Lightning Source LLC
Chambersburg PA
CBHW052042290426
44111CB00011B/1594